Politics in Nᴜᴡ

Politics in New Zealand

3rd edition

Richard Mulgan
updated by Peter Aimer

AUCKLAND UNIVERSITY PRESS

For Aurelia

First published 1994
Second edition 1997, reprinted 1998
Third edition 2004, reprinted 2007

Auckland University Press
University of Auckland
Private Bag 92019
Auckland, New Zealand

© Richard Mulgan 1994, 1997, 2004

ISBN 1 86940 318 5

Printed by Printlink Ltd, Wellington

Contents

List of Tables

Preface

This book is intended primarily as an introductory text for under-graduate students of New Zealand politics. Readers with a general interest in New Zealand's rapidly changing political scene may also find it useful. However, while every effort has been made to keep the writing as simple and jargon-free as possible, no apology is given for treating politics as the subject of professional academic analysis.

While the general structure and approach of the first edition have been retained, the text and references have been extensively revised to accommodate political developments since 1993, particularly the change in the electoral system which is having far-reaching effects on New Zealand politics. The major rewriting has been in Chapters Five (Parliament), Six (The public sector and the public service) and Ten (Political parties) but new sections have also been added to Chapters Three (The constitution) and Thirteen (Pluralist democracy under strain). Thanks are again due to Michael Crawshaw, for research assistance, and to friends and colleagues for information and advice: Peter Aimer, Jonathan Boston, Gary Hawke, John Martin, Elizabeth McLeay and Nigel Roberts. Dedication is offered to my wife, Aurelia, in loving thanks for her support throughout the preparation of both this edition and its predecessor.

RGM
Canberra, December 1996

In this 2004 edition, the factual content, further readings and bibliography have been updated to take account of political developments and sources published since 1997. The author's theoretical perspective and interpretations are unchanged unless obviously overtaken by events.

EPA
Auckland, December 2003

1

A Pluralist Theory of the State

Concepts and theories

Political science, the academic study of politics, aims at a systematic and critical understanding of the major state institutions and the activities associated with them. Like any other academic discipline, it seeks generalised, theoretical knowledge of its subject matter rather than the simple recording of factual information. This, in turn, requires careful definition of key concepts and of the theoretical assumptions implicit in them. The need for conceptual precision may be obscured because political scientists commonly use the language of everyday politics and do not have as well developed a technical language as many other disciplines. The academic study of politics may therefore seem to be simply a matter of political experience and common sense, essentially the same as expert journalism (a role in which political science academics are most visible to the public).

This is a mistake. While political science does use the same language as those whose behaviour it observes and explains, some important terms in this language need to be more carefully defined and analysed than they are in normal political discourse. Moreover, while the unnecessary use of jargon is rightly to be deplored, there are areas of political science which are conceptually sophisticated and where technical language is unavoidable and appropriate. These areas often draw on terminology developed in other related disciplines, such as sociology, economics and philosophy.

An introduction to the academic study of New Zealand politics should therefore logically begin with a discussion of key terms and major theoretical approaches to politics. While the material covered in this chapter is handled as simply and straightforwardly as possible, it does involve an inevitable degree of abstraction which some readers may find uncongenial. They may therefore prefer to begin with later chapters, for instance Chapter 2, which provides an overview of New Zealand society, or Chapter 3, which introduces the main elements of the constitution, and to return to this chapter when they have more experience of social and political analysis.

The state

The main focus of this study is the institution or set of institutions known as the New Zealand 'state'. All societies or groups of people living together involve some mechanism of social organisation and control. But not all societies have had 'states'. The state, as we understand it, is a product of European history. It arose during the transition from the medieval to the modern world when Europe became politically divided into a number of competing territorial units. Each of these countries or states was controlled by a sovereign power which claimed a monopoly of legal authority within its boundaries and total allegiance from its citizens. During the nineteenth and twentieth centuries, as a result of European colonialism and the spread of European institutions and assumptions, the state became universally accepted worldwide as the basic unit of political organisation. The international political world, as viewed for instance from the United Nations, has become a system of territorially based, sovereign nation-states. Each state claims the right of national self-determination within its own boundaries while recognising the governments of other states as similarly legitimate authorities in their respective territories.

The state can be understood as both the country as a whole or as a particular set of institutions within a country. An individual nation-state such as New Zealand, especially when viewed from outside, may be taken to mean the political community of New Zealand citizens and residents, the total society of all who live within the boundaries of the country. But what gives New Zealand identity as a separate independent political unit or state is one aspect of that society, the set of distinctive governmental institutions whose authority is recognised as legally binding within the territory. These institutions are the New Zealand state in a narrower, more exclusive sense, seen as distinct from the rest of the society. A modern state thus implies the existence of a complex and differentiated society in which one can distinguish between state and non-state aspects of society – between, in other words, a public and a private sector. It is in this narrower sense that the New

Zealand state forms the subject matter of this book and of political analysis generally.

Concentration on a single state, within the framework of a worldwide system of sovereign states, should not obscure the fact that this system is evolving rapidly and that individual states are increasingly subject to international pressures. The need to trade in international markets and the demands exerted by an international financial system place considerable limits on the economic independence of individual states. Growing acceptance of international ethical standards, such as those promulgated by the United Nations, challenges the right of individual state governments to act without external interference. No state, particularly one as relatively small and economically vulnerable as New Zealand, can be treated in isolation. Though the focus may be national and local, the context must be global and international.

The central characteristics of the state are territorial and legal. In maintaining control within a given territory the state claims a monopoly of legal power, the right to enact laws and enforce them through the courts. It also claims the right to extract the material resources necessary to support its activities by way of taxes levied on its citizens or on others who wish to do business within its borders. The purposes followed by states are not fixed or universal. Most states seek to provide a minimum of 'law and order', that is, the personal security of individual citizens and their property and the collective security of the nation as a whole. But the broader values and goals which states should pursue and the principles which they are required to uphold vary greatly and are the perennial subject of political argument and conflict.

State institutions include government departments and the publicly funded bureaucracy, Parliament, the courts, the police, and the armed forces. In terms of constitutional law, these institutions have often been divided into three groups, depending on their relation to what is seen as the central function of the state, the function of law-making: those institutions which make the law – the legislature (in New Zealand, Parliament); those which carry out or execute the law – the executive (in New Zealand, ministers and the public service); and those which interpret and enforce the law – the judicial branch (in New Zealand, the courts supported by the police and the prison service). These distinctions are by no means hard and fast. In New Zealand's system of parliamentary government, as will be seen, Cabinet is the supreme decision-making body and, effectively, has both legislative and executive functions. The police may be seen as having an executive as well as a judicial function. Indeed, to describe the institutions of government in terms of the three-fold distinction between legislature, executive and judiciary may be not just to describe them but also to suggest a view of how they ought to operate. It may suggest, for instance, the doctrine of the separation of powers: that the executive power of ministers should be kept distinct and separate from the legislature, as it is, for instance, in the United States (Chapter 3: 56). Thus any attempt to analyse and describe the institutions of the state may lead one to adopt a particular perspective of appraisal and critical judgement. A certain type of classification or explanation will usually suggest a particular line of improvement or reform. There can be no entirely value-free political analysis.

The boundaries which mark the state off from the rest of society are imprecise. Some institutions, for instance government departments such as the Inland Revenue Department or the Ministry of Defence, are without question elements of the state. They are established under legal, statutory authority to fulfil a clear public function and are publicly financed through taxation. On the other hand, some social groups or organisations are just as clearly outside the state, for instance individual families or privately owned businesses. But some institutions are partly public and partly private. State schools or hospitals, for instance, may be publicly owned and subject to regulation. But they may be free of direct responsibility to ministers and Parliament and therefore free of immediate government control. While some of their income may be derived from taxation, some may come directly from individual members of the public through fees or other forms of personal contribution. That the distinction between state and non-state aspects of society is blurred is typical of social analysis. Distinctions must often be imposed on a mass of social behaviour which is highly interrelated and not neatly divisible into wholly self-contained segments.

'State' and 'government'

Is the 'state' the same as the 'government'? Sometimes 'government' is a term of narrower application than the 'state', focusing on the government of the day, on those who happen to hold certain key positions within the state at a particular time. New Zealanders talk, for instance of 'the Bolger National Government' or 'the Fourth Labour Government'. In this sense, the government means primarily the elected politicians in power, that is, the ministers in the Cabinet and perhaps also the other members of their parliamentary team, the government back bench. These people may be a key element in the state but they are only one part of the much larger state apparatus. In this sense, governments may come and go but the state itself continues.

On other occasions, however, the two terms may be used interchangeably. The institutions of government may be understood as coextensive with the institutions of the state. 'State control' and 'government control' mean the same thing. Public ownership or public provision of services may be referred to by either term, as with 'state housing' or 'government superannuation'. Most New Zealanders would therefore normally see little difference in meaning between these two terms.

Among academics writing about states and politics, the choice of terms may reflect different traditions of analysis and different theoretical assumptions. Mainstream political science in the English-speaking, Anglo-American world has traditionally preferred the term 'government', while continental Europeans have tended to use the term 'state'. This reflects a difference in legal and constitutional history. The legal systems of England and the United States are based on a distinctive legal tradition, grounded in the English 'common law', a system of law derived from the accumulated precedents of individual judges' decisions. Anglo-American legal theory, its 'jurisprudence', did not employ the word 'state' as a central term of constitutional law, preferring 'legislature' and 'executive' or 'government'. As the academic study of political institutions grew out of the study of legal structures, English-speaking political scientists naturally adopted the institutional terminology of their constitutional law and referred to 'governments' rather than 'states'. Indeed, when separate university departments of politics began to be established, some of them (for instance, at Harvard, Sydney and the London School of Economics) were named departments of 'Government'.

In continental Europe, on the other hand, the legal systems of the various European countries were based on the so-called 'civil law', a system of law derived from Roman law, in which the concept of the state (*état* in French, *Staat* in German) developed as a central organising concept for the institutions of legal control. It was therefore correspondingly natural for continental theorists of politics to adopt the 'state' as their focus for analysis. Contemporary theories of government which have their intellectual roots in continental European rather than Anglo-American theory are thus more likely to use the term 'state'. This is particularly true of the academic discipline of sociology, where theoretical discussion of government is largely derived from the contrasting theories of two German social theorists, Karl Marx and Max Weber, both of whom used the concept of the state (*Staat*). Arguments about whether 'government' or 'state' is the proper term for analysis may therefore be arguments about whether to adopt a particular perspective – the broader and potentially more critical perspective of sociology or the narrower and less radical approach of traditional political science.

Politics and the political system

Apart from 'government' and 'state', another key term is 'politics'. 'Politics' refers not so much to particular institutions as to a particular type of activity or process associated with institutions. Politics may be defined as the activity or set of activities involved in the making of collective decisions, decisions which will be binding on the members of a collectivity or group. It involves, for instance, processes of discussion, argument, bargaining, pressure, manipulation and compromise. All these processes assume that there are differences of values and interests among members of the group in question and that these differences will be resolved peacefully, without resort to force. As a process of collective decision-making, politics may occur in any type of group, in families on decisions about family matters, in workplaces over issues which affect those working in a particular business, and so on. It thus makes sense to talk of 'the politics of the family' or 'the politics of the workplace'. Political science, however, focuses on the central or core type of politics which concerns decision-making in the institutions of the state.

The analysis of the politics of government decision-making involves more than just the behaviour of those working in the state institutions themselves. The political process includes the activities of privately owned and funded organisations which aim to influence government decisions. For instance, crucial political roles are played by political parties which sponsor candidates for elections (Chapter 10) and by interest groups which seek to influence government decisions in their direction (Chapter 9). Political behaviour is also influenced by general social factors, such as economic trends or ethnic differences (Chapter 2). There are few, if any, aspects of society which may not at some time in some respect be politically relevant.

Political scientists commonly refer to all the politically relevant aspects of society as the 'political system', a useful term which serves to separate out those aspects of society which impinge on the state and politics. The notion of a 'system' indicates that the various parts of the process are closely related and interact with one another. A study of the New Zealand political system thus suggests a study which will not confine itself to the state and government institutions but will look at any aspect of society which will be relevant to understanding political decision-making and the workings of state institutions. The state remains the focus; this is what distinguishes political science from other social sciences such as economics or sociology. But in exploring this subject matter, political science will clearly need to build on the findings of these other subjects.

Rival theories of the state

The state and the political system can be viewed from a number of different perspectives. Some of these perspectives have been developed into complex and self-contained theories of the state. Such theories involve assumptions about the nature of society and the main divisions within it. They contain a view of how the state functions in society and how political power is exercised. They also, implicitly or explicitly, incorporate a set of moral and political values against which the performance of the state can be judged and changes recommended.

The theoretical perspective being adopted in this study belongs to the branch of state theory known as 'pluralism'. Though it has many varieties, pluralism is particularly associated with the theories of post-war US political scientists, such as David Truman (1951) and Robert Dahl (1961). Pluralism may perhaps best be understood in contrast to other, rival theories of the state. One set of these consists of theories of social or structural dominance which analyse societies in terms of a basic division between those who exploit and those who are exploited. The state is seen as an instrument of exploitation which helps to maintain the dominance of the ruling group. The longest-established and most influential of such theories is marxism, based on the theories of the nineteenth-century political economist and social theorist, Karl Marx. Marx viewed societies in historical terms, as passing through a series of stages or epochs, including feudalism, capitalism, and eventually communism. In each era, before the conflict-free, classless society of communism is reached, the fundamental factor in social behaviour is the conflict between economic classes, particularly between those who own and control the means of economic production and those who are forced to work for them and are exploited by them. Modern societies, such as New Zealand, are living through the era of capitalism in which power is in the hands of the capitalist class, the owners of financial and other forms of capital.

In exercising their power over the exploited working class, the ruling capitalist class uses a number of mechanisms of control. One is the state, including the legal system and the law enforcement agencies, which are run in the interests of capitalists and the owners of private property. Another mechanism is ideology, the system of ruling ('hegemonic') ideas and values which encourage people to pursue the interests of capitalists without overt coercion. For instance, many workers value hard work and individual self-reliance but these values are of benefit to capitalists only, not to the workers themselves. They are instances of 'false consciousness', whereby people subscribe to mistaken beliefs which misrepresent their true needs and interests. Another instance is the view that the modern state can be neutral between the classes or provide a trustworthy vehicle for the genuine political aspirations of the exploited workers.

Other theories of structural dominance have adopted some of the concepts and assumptions of marxist analysis, but identify a different division within society as fundamental and interpret the state and ideology accordingly. Feminism sees the conflict between male and female as the basic conflict in society. For feminists, the state is an instrument by which men have oppressed women. The dominant male-centred ideology encourages false consciousness about the respective roles and capacities of men and women, preventing women from achieving true equality. Another theory of particular importance in New Zealand is that associated with the opposition to colonialism. Anti-colonialists, such as some Maori nationalists, see the basic social division as an ethnic division between the original, indigenous people and the invading colonisers. For them the modern state is an agent of colonial conquest by which one people has been subjugated and continues to be oppressed by another. The ideology supporting this oppression emphasises the supposed superiority of the invaders' western culture and encourages the indigenous people to abandon their own culture and their own structures of authority.

Contrasting with theories of structural dominance, all of which analyse the state in terms of a social division between groups of oppressors and oppressed, is the market liberal theory of the state which is grounded in public choice theory. Public choice theory, also sometimes described as rational choice theory, takes its assumptions from economics, looking on society as essentially a collection of individuals, rather than groups. Each individual person has his or her own wants and preferences and is assumed to act rationally in a way which will maximise the benefit to himself or herself. The state, like other social institutions, is therefore a focus of self-interested interaction between individuals. Citizens, as voters or members of pressure groups, seek to gain benefits, in terms of policies favourable to their interests, while resisting costs such as increased taxation. Those who derive their livelihood from the state, such as politicians, bureaucrats and teachers in state schools, similarly try to control the system to their own advantage, enhancing their power and privileges, often in opposition to the interests of the taxpayer.

These summaries of rival theories of the state, it should be noted, are highly abbreviated and simplified, indeed over-simplified. The purpose has been to mark out some opposing poles of contrast against which the pluralist theory of the state can be defined. But the reader should be aware that these summaries do not do justice to the power and subtlety of these alternative theories, all of which have important contributions to make to our understanding of New Zealand politics.

The main features of pluralism and how it is distinguished from these other theories can be listed under a number of headings.

A plural society

Pluralism assumes that in societies such as New Zealand's, people live their lives as part of a large number of different groups with differing interests and values. Individuals belong, for instance, to different economic classes, status groups, families, ethnic groups, localities, churches and so on. People's social behaviour is largely to be understood in terms of these groups and interests (though some room may be left for purely personal or accidental factors). Political analysis therefore must also take account of group behaviour. Description and explanation of particular areas of government policy-making will usually require the identification of different sectional interests, both outside and inside government, each pressing for policies and decisions which will best suit them and their members.

The pluralist view of society thus has a different starting point from public choice theory, which begins with individuals rather than groups. A totally individualist view of society, such as that adopted by public choice theory and economics generally, tends to overlook the extent to which people are creatures of their social environment. Individuals behave in ways that cannot be adequately explained without reference to the various social groups to which they belong. Public choice theorists have raised interesting questions about group behaviour (Chapter 9: 212) but their analysis is seriously incomplete.

At the same time, pluralism also rejects the view of marxists and other theorists of structural dominance that there is one fundamental and overriding social division which provides the key to understanding social and political behaviour. Pluralists certainly recognise the importance of factors such as class, gender and ethnicity in influencing social behaviour and the distribution of political power. But they are unwilling to accept any one division as fundamental or to see other divisions as either offshoots of this one overriding division or as largely irrelevant. For instance, a thorough-going feminist might look on all males as exploiters and all women as exploited; the supposed conflict between different types of men, e.g. between male bosses and male workers, would be treated as relatively insignificant. Conversely, a thoroughgoing marxist would look on conflict between men and women of the same occupational class, between men and women lawyers or teachers, for instance, as largely irrelevant in comparison with the conflict between the classes of capitalists and workers. A pluralist, on the other hand, will keep an open mind about which particular division or conflict is relevant until evidence is forthcoming to confirm a particular analysis of a particular incident or instance. In this respect, pluralism is an open-ended or 'eclectic' theoretical approach, picking the specific theory or theories which best help to explain particular aspects of political life without being wedded to any one approach.

Pluralism has sometimes been characterised, particularly by hostile critics, as assuming that there are no major inequalities in society, that all groups and interests compete on equal terms for political influence and that the political system responds equally to their political pressures. However, such a rosy-eyed view of modern western societies is not a necessary part of pluralism. Most pluralists, particularly those who style themselves as 'neo-pluralists', would now recognise that, in capitalist democracies, certain groups and interests, particularly dominant economic interests, but also certain gender and ethnic groups, have definite in-built advantages and, conversely, that there are other groups who are systematically disadvantaged. The essential difference between pluralists and others is not that pluralists reject the existence of social and political inequality but rather that they reject the assumption that one type of inequality overrides all others. Power may not be equally dispersed among all social groups but neither is it concentrated in one particular group or interest. In practice, however, the difference between pluralists and theorists of structural dominance may often be merely one of emphasis. Many of those who espouse the marxist or a feminist perspective, for instance, would agree that there are some social conflicts which cannot be adequately explained by either class analysis or gender analysis alone.

One respect, however, in which pluralism does part company with theories of structural dominance is in its unwillingness to accept explanations in terms of 'false consciousness'. Structural dominance theories all assume that social and political power is exercised, in part, through ideological manipulation. Members of the exploited groups, whether workers (and unemployed), women or Maori, are socialised into adopting certain opinions and values which are in the interests of the dominant group but contrary to their own real interests. Workers think it is praiseworthy to work long hours for little pay; women see value in spending their lives waiting on men; Maori reject their own culture as being backward or out of date. In this way, the dominant groups are able to harness the exploited groups' energies and efforts without open coercion. Until the consciousness of exploited people has been 'raised' by critical reflection, they do not clearly see what is good for them or where their true interests lie.

Pluralists, on the other hand, are less likely to accept that people can be fundamentally mistaken about their own interests. They assume that people's interests derive from their long-term and relatively stable wants and subjective preferences. At base, that is, the best judges of people's own interests are people themselves, whether as individuals or as members of particular groups, rather than any particular social critic with a single view of how people ought best to live their lives. Certainly, people can be mistaken about what is in their interests on particular occasions. For instance, those who want to increase their economic prosperity may favour policies or decisions which in fact diminish their prosperity or they may oppose policies and decisions which would actually advance their economic interests. It is also true that people's conscious wants and subjective preferences may themselves be affected and influenced by particular groups in society. The power of the media may be used to make us want certain material goods which we might otherwise happily do without. Powerful commercial interests seek to manipulate our political preferences through encouraging certain activities and values which suit their own commercial interests but not ours.

None the less, pluralists assume that there are limits to the effects of such manipulation. People's values and wants may be largely the product of their social environment but that environment itself is not decisively manipulated by certain groups in their own interests and against the interests of others. When people say that they want certain things out of life, whether it is a steady interesting job or a life of ease without work, a wild social life or a settled family and a mortgage, it is assumed that these are their genuine wants. Indeed, these wants are a considerable part of our personalities, what make us individual people with independent value. Critical reflection may indeed lead individuals to revise their views of what they want out of life. But this is a question of replacing one set of genuine wants with another, rather than replacing false consciousness with true consciousness. Though, as individual citizens, we may wish to condemn some values as wrong or mistaken, we do not have the right to do so as social analysts. The pluralist accepts that there are many different types of people with different and equally genuine wants and values. The differences between them can not be explained away or reduced to one overriding difference or conflict. The plural society, a society in which people belong to many different, often overlapping groups with different interests, is not to be treated as an illusion but is to be accepted at its face value.

People's wants for themselves and their own social groups are not the only part of their values which is politically relevant. Also important are their views about the public interest or the public good, about what is good for the community as a whole. Most people, particularly those who are politically active, have attitudes and opinions about what type of society New Zealand should be and what the government should do, or not do, to bring this about. Indeed, some political philosophers consider opinion and debate about the nature of the public good to be the central essence of political activity. Pluralists have been criticised for advocating a narrow, group-centred view of politics which concentrates on sectional interests and rules out what is in fact the noblest type of social activity, concern for the common good. It is true that some pluralists have denied the importance of concepts of the common good and have looked on politics as simply the interaction of self-interested groups. However, this is not essential to pluralism. The version of pluralism which is being used in this analysis is one which allows that there is a concept of the public good or public interest, of wants and values which we all share as members of a political community. This form of pluralism, sometimes known as 'public pluralism', finds room for community values and the public good. Indeed, much of politics is taken up with conflict and debate between differing conceptions of the common good or public interest. At the same time, it does not accept that these common concerns are all-important or that politics and government are simply confined to dealing with matters of common interest. As well as belonging to one New Zealand public, New Zealanders, as members of a complex plural society, also belong to other sectional groups and interests which are of equal, sometimes more, value to them and which they may look to their governments to protect and enhance.

The active plural state

Theories of the state have differed over whether the state is itself an independent force in society with its own interests or whether it simply acts as an agent of other social forces. Theories of structural dominance, for instance, have tended to see the state as the coercive instrument of the dominant social group. In the more simplistic versions of marxism, the state, and politics generally, are treated as wholly determined by external social forces, namely the economic conflict between capital and labour. According to some pluralists, the main impulse for government decision-making comes from interest groups outside government, each pressing for policies which would suit them best. The role of politicians and government is limited to providing a forum for group competition and to brokering between the various competing interests and groups. The state is seen as a 'weather-vane' state, blown in the direction determined by the sum of the forces from the interest groups which put pressure on it.

However, few political theorists would today accept that the state is merely the offshoot or cipher of other forces in society. Theorists of almost every ideological bent now agree that the state is a powerful institution, or collection of institutions, with its own interests and objectives which it exerts against those of the rest of society. Most present day marxists allow that the state will have at least some autonomy or independence from the rest of society, though they differ over how much autonomy is compatible with their fundamental assumption that the economic structure determines the structure of politics. Public choice theorists have given considerable attention to the analysis of bureaucratic and political behaviour. Bureaucrats and elected politicians are seen as important political actors with their own independent objectives which they often pursue at the expense of the interests of the public.

Pluralists, too, have identified groups within the state which can pursue their own interests in competition with those of groups outside the state. This is a natural extension of the pluralist view that politics is based on the interaction of competing interests and values. The analytical framework is simply enlarged to include the institutions of the state and the groups who work within these institutions as part of the potential subject matter. Moreover, from the pluralist perspective, there is no need to see the state as a monolithic institution with a single political interest or single objective, an oversimplification to which other theories have been prone. The state can readily be dissected into a collection of different institutions and groups, many of them with different, competing interests. The most obvious conflict may be between politicians of opposing parties, between government and opposition. But there are also frequent differences between elected politicians and permanent public servants. Within the bureaucracy itself, there are divisions between different government departments with their own policy preferences, for instance between Treasury, which aims to constrain government expenditure, and other departments, such as Defence or Education, which wish to increase it. Thus, to the plural society must be added the plural state as an object of analysis.

Multi-faceted political power

The concept of power is central to the analysis of the state and the political system. The main reason why we wish to study these institutions is to see who controls what, who influences whom, and so on. 'Control' and 'influence' are aspects of power, the process by which one person or group gets some other person or group to do actions they would not do otherwise. But what counts as power and how it is to be identified are matters of debate among social and political scientists.

The simplest and least controversial form of power is where one person clearly intends someone else to do something they would not otherwise do and has the means to force that person to act against their will. Some instances of such power are open and clearly observable. For instance, a minister may issue written instructions to public servants under statutory authority backed by legal sanctions forcing compliance; a public lobby group may exert pressure on a minister through a media campaign, threatening loss of electoral support if the group's demands are ignored.

Some political scientists attempted to limit evidence for political power to behaviour which was clearly observable and, where possible, measurable. In this way they sought to copy the objectivity and precision of the natural sciences. This attempt is now generally discredited. There is much political power which cannot be observed simply from looking at people's overt behaviour. For instance, there is the important type of power known as the power of 'anticipated reactions'. Someone with the formal authority to make a decision chooses one option rather than another for fear of an adverse reaction if the other option is chosen. For instance, a public servant acts in a certain way to avoid a minister's displeasure or a minister delays taking action in order to avoid an adverse reaction from a powerful lobby. A whole range of issues may be kept off the political agenda because governments fear political damage if they are broached. These are all important examples of political power which cannot be observed from the actual behaviour of decision-makers, who behave in just the same way as if their decisions were not influenced by others. This type of power can only be discovered by investigating the decision-makers' motives for action, by trying to find out precisely why they took the action they did.

There are, in addition, important instances of what is sometimes known as 'structural power'. This is where certain groups or interests prevail, not necessarily through any intentional behaviour of the people involved, but through the influence of social or political institutions, through the way in which they are organised, the values which permeate them. For instance, the nature of the electoral system may be biased against small political parties and may prevent certain groups from gaining parliamentary representation; the economic importance of certain sectors such as farming may mean that governments have to give particular weight to the interests of farmers; the dominant position of Treasury in the bureaucratic structure may mean that particular attention is given to the policies supported by Treasury officials.

Such impersonal structural factors are obviously critical to understanding the working of the political system. The precise nature of structural power, however, has been a matter of controversy among social theorists. Some marxists, for instance, have argued that all political power is the product of socio-economic forces such as class conflict and therefore that all power is structural. The actual motives and intentions of individual decision-makers are irrelevant, particularly if they are the result of false consciousness on the part of decision-makers. At the other extreme, structural power has been said to be impossible. The concept of power, it is claimed, necessarily involves an agent to exercise that power, a power-holder. The impersonal nature of structural factors means that their influence cannot be identified with the exercise of power by any person or group. In this case, the concept of structural power becomes self-contradictory.

In part, the issue may be one of semantics, of how we choose to define our terms. Few would deny that the economic and political structures of modern capitalist democracies benefit the interests of financiers and capitalists ahead of others. Whether these effects are seen as actual power exercised by capitalists or simply as institutional factors which happen to benefit capitalists may be a relatively unimportant question. On balance, it may be best to accept that the concept of power does suggest some notion of deliberate agency or intention to control or be controlled. There must be some person or group planning to control institutions or behaviour towards their own preferences or there must be people consciously avoiding the potentially hostile reactions from the holders of power. The idea of power, and related concepts such as 'control' and 'influence' should therefore be reserved for those instances where clear evidence of deliberate action and intention can be discovered. Where no such intentions are evident, where people's behaviour is influenced by the impersonal structures in which they find themselves, it may be more sensible to talk of structural 'constraints' or structural 'factors' rather than structural 'power'.

These controversies over the possibility of structural power need not be pursued further in this study. Under the open-ended, pluralist approach being adopted here, different types of power and influence and different types of explanation will be encountered in the analysis of the New Zealand state and political system. The reader should be aware, however, that power and related concepts are by no means straightforward and are the subject of important academic controversy.

A pluralist's values: liberal democracy

Politics is an arena in which different values and interests compete and no observer can genuinely claim to be wholly objective or dispassionate. The very theoretical perspective which is adopted, the factors considered particularly relevant for analysis, imply that some aspects of political behaviour, some types of political action, are more important than others. This does not absolve us from a duty to be as careful as possible with the evidence that we do select nor does it give us licence to be openly prejudiced in our judgements. Conventions of academic objectivity and rationality are not to be discarded simply because there is no one incontrovertible position from which to argue. At the same time, it is important to recognise that any perspective involves a particular orientation to the subject matter and a particular set of assumptions about what is politically valuable and desirable.

A number of different assumptions have so far been identified as part of a pluralist perspective on New Zealand politics – a plural society, a plural state and a multi-faceted approach to power. What political values are implicit in these assumptions? One fundamental value is that people have interests and that these interests should be met through the political system. Another assumption is that people are by and large the best judges of their long-term interests and wants. These assumptions support the principles usually associated with what is known as 'liberal democracy', the type of government found in western-style capitalist democracies such as New Zealand. The basic liberal principle is that individual people should be free to live their own lives as they wish, subject always to respecting the similar rights of others. The basic democratic principle is that individual people should count equally and have an equal say in making decisions which affect them. These are the values implicitly underlying pluralist analysis. Attention will naturally focus on whether people, either individually or as members of groups, are exercising equal or unequal political power or whether their wants and interests are receiving equal or unequal attention from the political system.

The assumption that people count equally and that their interests should be met is common to most, if not all, theories of the state. However, not all theories agree that the institutions of liberal democracy offer the best means of achieving these goals. In the first place, theories of structural dominance would not necessarily accept the liberal principle that people's wants should be taken at their face value. If people's wants are the product of oppressive ideological and social forces, then there is little point in supporting a system which aims to meet these wants. Instead, political effort should go towards a radical transformation of society which will overthrow the structure of oppression and allow people to come to understand, and meet, their true needs. Thus marxists look to a future in which capitalism is replaced by an economic system in which property is held in common and there is no more class conflict or exploitation. For radical feminists, the existing social structure, particularly the existing family structure, requires fundamental change before women can be truly liberated. Similarly, anti-colonialists and Maori nationalists have seen the reassertion of Maori self-determination as lying in a radical overthrow of the colonising state, its institutions and its values.

In support, critical theorists can point to the failure of liberal democracies to live up to their principles of freedom and equality even on their own terms. In New Zealand, everyone is not equally free to pursue their own wants; nor does everyone have an equal political say in trying to satisfy their wants. The political system, instead of allowing each section of society to pursue its interests equally and fairly, as pluralism seems to promise, is systematically biased in favour of some interests and against others. Indeed, it can be argued, pluralism operates as part of the ideology of oppression by pretending falsely that liberal democracy offers its citizens equality and freedom when it does not.

Similar criticisms have been taken up by 'market liberals' or 'neo-liberals', theorists who adopt a public choice perspective and seek to limit the role of the state. As public choice theorists, the market liberals take people's preferences as given and, unlike the structural dominance theorists, do not aim for a radical transformation of people's conscious interests and values. However, they join the structural dominance theorists in pointing out systematic inequalities in existing liberal democratic states. Using public choice analyses, they identify certain structural factors in democratic institutions which prevent people's preferences from being satisfied. Bureaucracies pursue their own expansion at the taxpayers' expense; powerful vested sectional interests deflect governments from the public interest; elections encourage parties to outbid each other for short-term gain. Wherever possible people should be allowed to pursue their own interests directly through voluntary exchanges in a free market. The role of the state should be restricted to maintaining the conditions necessary for the effective operation of a free market, such as the protection of personal security and the legal enforcement of contracts. This market liberal theory of the state has been highly influential in New Zealand and other westernised democracies over the last decade, providing the main impetus for the radical restructuring of the public sector (Chapter 6). The proponents of the theory are sometimes known as the 'new right'.

However, the term 'new right' is more accurately reserved for those who combine the market liberal preference for limited economic intervention with conservative social values, such as support for patriotism, censorship or traditional family structures.

That there are systematic structural inequalities in modern liberal democracies is beyond question. Pluralists have not always recognised this unpalatable truth. Some of the earlier pluralists, particularly in the United States, complacently assumed that all groups in society had equality of political opportunity in modern democracies and that the interplay of interest group politics would tend to a fair result. However, most present-day pluralists, particularly those who are known as 'neo-pluralists', accept the criticism that modern capitalist societies in which liberal democratic institutions operate are inevitably biased in favour of certain dominant interests. At the same time, in contrast to market liberals, they hold that democratic processes and institutions, while inevitably uneven in their effect, tend to moderate the even greater inequalities which would result from unconstrained market exchanges. Thus, what distinguishes the pluralist perspective is not a belief that liberal democracy offers perfect freedom and equality so much as a conviction that no other form of regime offers anything better.

Further reading

Theories of the state
Dunleavy & O'Leary (1987); Held (1989)
Neo-pluralism
Lindblom (1977); Jordan (1990); Smith (1990)
Theory of New Zealand state in general
McLeay (1992); Roper & Rudd (1993); Goldfinch (2003)
New Zealand pluralism
Mulgan (1989), Chapter 2; Mulgan (1993); Moloney (1997)
New Zealand marxism
Bedggood (1980); Kelsey (1993); Dixon (1997)
New Zealand feminism
Bunkle & others (1992); James & Saville-Smith (1989); Du Plessis & Higgins (1997)
New Zealand anti-colonialism
Awatere (1984); Walker (1987); Walker (1990)
Neo-liberalism
Morrow (2003); Moloney (2003); Roper (2003)

2

The Plural Society

The comparative perspective

The New Zealand state and political system operate within the wider context of society as a whole. The pluralist theory of the state places particular emphasis on the complexity of society, on the variety of different groups to which people belong. From this perspective, most political activity is generated by the interaction of these different groups with overlapping and cross-cutting interests. Analysis of the political system must therefore begin with an account of New Zealand's plural society and the main social divisions within it.

Any account of a society implies comparison with other societies. For instance, one of the familiar beliefs that New Zealanders have about themselves is that they live in a 'small' country of 'only' three million people or thereabouts (the latest population total in the 2001 census is 3.73 million, but is estimated to have passed 4 million during 2003). Yet if one lists the nations recognised by the United Nations in order of population, New Zealand is only about half way down the list. From this perspective New Zealand is more of a 'middle-sized' country. The perception that it is small makes sense only if the view is restricted to larger countries. Indeed, the most common comparison New Zealanders make of themselves is with other so-called 'developed' or 'western' societies. These are societies with relatively high standards of living in the sense of high levels of mat-erial consumption. Most are relatively industrialised and urbanised, predominantly European in ethnic origin, and liberal-democratic in their political institutions.

One commonly used reference group is the twenty-seven countries of the OECD, the Europe-based Organisation for Economic Cooperation and Development. Among this elite group New Zealand is indeed small, only three countries (Ireland, Luxembourg and Iceland) being smaller (see Table 2.1).

TABLE 2.1

OECD nations ranked by size of population

OECD nation	Population in millions
United States	285.5
Japan	127.3
Mexico	100.1
Germany	81.4
Turkey	68.6
United Kingdom	59.8
France	57.9
Italy	57.3
Korea	47.3
Spain	40.3
Poland	38.6
Canada	31.1
Australia	19.5
Netherlands	16.0
Greece	10.5
Czech Republic	10.3
Portugal	10.3
Hungary	10.2
Belgium	10.2
Sweden	8.9
Austria	8.1
Switzerland	7.2
Slovak Republic	5.4
Denmark	5.4
Finland	5.2
Norway	4.5
New Zealand	**3.9**
Ireland	3.8
Luxembourg	0.4
Iceland	0.3

Source: *OECD in Figures, 2003* (www.sourceoecd.org/content/html/index)

However, if one takes another perspective, New Zealand may appear very large. To someone arriving for the first time in New Zealand from one of the neighbouring South Pacific countries, such as Tonga or the Cook Islands, New Zealand may seem overwhelmingly large in population (see Table 2.2). Similarly, though New Zealand often represents itself as a relatively agricultural country which it may be from an OECD perspective, this is not how it appears to Pacific Islanders. New Zealand is much more industrialised and urbanised than the island societies of the Pacific. Indeed, in the South Pacific region, New Zealand, together with its larger neighbour Australia, plays the role of a major metropolitan power, looming as large in the political and economic lives of the island states as the US, Germany or Japan do in the OECD.

TABLE 2.2

Populations of selected Pacific nations

Country	Population in thousands
Australia	19,485
Papua New Guinea (PNG)	5617
New Zealand	**3730**
Fiji	832
Solomon Islands	450
Vanuatu	204
Western Samoa	179
Federated States of Micronesia (FSM)	112
Tonga	102
Kiribati	88
Marshall Islands	54
Cook Islands	18
Nauru	12
Tuvalu	10
Niue	2

Sources: South Pacific Commission, (www.spc.int/AC/members.htm) (Populations are mid-year 2003 estimates.) Australia: *OECD in Figures, 2003* (see Table 2.1); New Zealand: Statistics New Zealand, *2001 Census of Populations and Dwellings - Total Population.*

Thus the view that New Zealand is a small agricultural country is a statement about the international peer group to which it wants to belong. It is an implicit rejection of the view that New Zealand is a Pacific nation, in the sense of sharing the values and aspirations of its island neighbours. New Zealanders may see their economic and strategic interests as closely bound up with the Pacific and Asian region. But they do not identify with them in terms of the type of society they want to be or the level of economic development to which they aspire. In the various groupings of nations used by the United Nations –

Asia, Africa, Latin America, Oceania etc., New Zealand, with Australia, is often classed with the 'Western European and other' group. If New Zealand belongs to any family of nations – and perhaps it belongs to no one family unequivocally – it is primarily to the European family. This comparative perspective is largely an expression of the values of the dominant Pakeha culture, the culture that is derived from the European settlers. It may well be rejected by Maori or Pacific Island New Zealanders who prefer to assert the primacy of non-western values. They may wish to reserve judgement on whether New Zealand is small, large or middle-sized. But some implied point of comparison cannot be avoided in any generalised description of how a society and its government operate. The point of comparison may vary, just as cultural traditions may vary. But there will always be one.

In the present analysis of the New Zealand state and its politics, the implied point of comparison, the implied peer group, for the most part, will be the other members of the developed world. These include the societies which are closest to most New Zealanders in values and aspirations and from which New Zealand's political and constitutional traditions are largely derived. This is not to dismiss the value of other cultural traditions which have a proper and legitimate place in New Zealand society. It is simply to recognise the reality that European or Pakeha ways of behaving predominate.

Ethnic composition

Considerations of comparative perspective immediately raise the issue of cultural difference and ethnic diversity. The New Zealand population is made up of a number of different ethnic groups, that is, groups who share a common ancestry and culture. Views have differed over the significance of the ancestral, inherited element in ethnicity. Some people have thought that ancestry was the sole criterion for ethnic difference or, as they would more probably say, 'racial' difference. The racial composition of a community was to be discovered simply by asking people about the identity of their ancestry. Most social theorists would now reject such a strict genetic approach to ethnic difference (Spoonley, 1993: Chapter 2). In part, this is a reaction against racism. Theories of genetic difference have been used to support disreputable theories of racial supremacy which claim that some races are inherently superior to others. Rejection of genetic criteria also reflects a growing realisation among social theorists that the distinctive social behaviour of different peoples is learned rather than inherited. Cultural difference is passed on from one generation to another through complex processes of social interaction. Thus, ethnicity is not purely or even mainly a matter of genetic descent or having certain innate racial characteristics. Being a Maori or a Croatian is primarily a question of cultural identity, of possessing certain values, observing certain traditions and practices, perhaps knowing the language of the particular group. But some inherited element is probably still necessary, even if it is not the most important factor. Though personal identification with a culture and its traditions is the key factor, ethnic identity usually implies having at least one ancestor who belonged to that group and with whose traditions one may identify. Ethnicity cannot be solely a matter of personal choice and commitment. Differences in physical appearance, such as skin colour, are often important factors in people's perception of ethnic identity, their own as well as other people's. 'Where are the brown faces?' is a common way in which Maori and Pacific Islanders voice complaints about the Pakeha domination of particular institutions.

The changes in attitudes to ethnicity can be seen in the various changes in the five-yearly New Zealand census questions on ethnicity. Up till 1981, people were asked to define their 'ethnic origin' in terms of proportion of descent, one quarter Maori, one quarter Cook Island Maori, one half European, for example. They were then allocated to a particular group according to these proportions: three quarters Maori and one quarter European was defined as Maori. By 1991 people were being asked 'which ethnic group [they] belong to' and were allowed to select more than one group. That is, the emphasis on origins had gone, as had the requirement that a person could belong to only one group. Ethnicity is publicly treated now as primarily a matter of personal self identification.

The Maori

The ethnic group with the longest history in New Zealand is the Maori, the people whose ancestors settled in the previously unoccupied land in a series of migrations from eastern Polynesia beginning about a thousand years ago. Their main social unit was the hapu (village), a group of whanau (extended families) living and working together. The main economic activities were agriculture, together with hunting and fishing. Ties of kinship and common ancestry were very important within both the hapu and the individual whanau. They also provided the links which joined numbers of hapu into larger iwi or tribes who traced themselves back to a common ancestor or to those who had arrived in a particular canoe. Rivalry between different iwi was often fierce and could lead to warfare. However, Maori society at all levels had well-developed methods of conciliation by which outright conflict could be mitigated or avoided altogether.

Political leadership lay with rangatira (chiefs) and kaumatua (elders) whose authority derived from descent. But their authority also depended on the support and consent of their respective groups who were consulted on all major decisions. Ineffective leaders could be replaced or sidelined and people of more lowly ancestry or outsiders could be given leadership roles (Metge, 1976: Chapter 14). In most cases formal power was restricted to males but women, particularly kuia, senior women of the leading families, were often extremely influential.

Before European colonisation there was no national Maori organisation or indeed any overall sense of Maori identity. That was to develop as a result of perceiving the contrast with the alien Pakeha and recognising how much all Maori (the term simply meant 'ordinary') had in common with each other in comparison. As contact increased, so the conception of the 'Maori people' developed, in part as a means of defending shared Maori institutions against the settlers and their governments. Even then, however, tribal sentiments and rivalries still ran deep and it was, and still is, a common misconception among Pakeha that all Maori have the same interests and preoccupations.

European colonisation radically transformed the Maori and their way of life. To begin with, the visitors were often welcome and welcomed. They brought new tools and skills and provided opportunities for trade and possible advantages over rival iwi. However, the rapid influx of settlers and their demand for land made deep inroads into Maori territory. When the tribes sought to resist, they were defeated by force of arms. In the later part of the nineteenth century, the Maori people faced severe reduction in numbers, even the possibility of eventual extinction, largely as a result of newly imported diseases. However, in the twentieth century, their numbers have steadily increased. At the same time, they have become more integrated into the dominant Pakeha society, a trend precipitated by the large-scale migration of Maori from tribal rural areas into the cities as the growth of manufacturing in the post-war period provided improved employment opportunities in urban areas, particularly Auckland and Wellington.

The contemporary position of the Maori people is therefore greatly changed from that of their ancestors two centuries ago, when they had the country to themselves. The Maori population is still, as it was at the time of the original colonial settlement, largely concentrated in the north of the country. A quarter of all Maori live in the Auckland metropolitan region and another third in the northern regions of Northland, Waikato and Bay of Plenty. Only about one eighth of Maori live in the South Island.

Four out of five Maori live in a city. But the strongest centres of Maori cultural life still lie outside the main centres, often in remote rural areas, where Maori make up a significant proportion of the local population, and their community life centres on Maori institutions such as Maori churches and local marae (meeting places). The urban migration has meant that most Maori do not live on their traditional tribal land. They are manuhiri (visitors) in the territory of the tangata whenua (local people) in the land where the cities have developed. Much of the effort by Maori leaders in recent times has been directed at revitalising iwi organisations and resources as a means of restoring lost mana (authority) and cultural self-esteem. This has paralleled a desire in government circles to divest itself of direct responsibility for Maori welfare. Many of the larger iwi or groups of iwi, such as Ngati Whatua in Auckland, Tainui in the Waikato, Te Arawa in the Bay of Plenty, and Ngai Tahu in the South Island are very effectively organised and control significant resources through tribal trust boards and other institutions. However, other smaller iwi may have greater difficulty in taking on the responsibilities now being pressed upon them. The major problem facing the continuing flourishing of Maori culture and identity remains the need to restore the links between the iwi leadership and the large number of their uprooted and disaffected members living in the cities. Of those who identified themselves as Maori in the 2001 census, 25 per cent did not claim affiliation to any iwi. Not all Maori activity is iwi-centred. Some Maori cultural life in the cities is based on organisations which are open to members of more than one iwi, such as churches, sports clubs, the Maori Women's Welfare League or the Maori district councils. There have also been some successful inter-iwi or pan-tribal marae developed in cities, catering for Maori of any iwi living there. At the same time, however, belonging through one's ancestors to a particular iwi remains essential for Maori identity.

In terms of many indicators of material achievement recognised as desirable by most New Zealanders, Maori are on average worse-off than the Pakeha majority. Maori are much more likely to be in lower paid occupations or to be unemployed than Pakeha. For instance, in mid-2003 the unemployment rate for Maori at 10 per cent was more than twice that for the total population (Statistics New Zealand, 2003). Maori comprise about half the prison population (53 per cent in 2001) (Department of Corrections, 2003). Maori are also much less likely to leave school with formal qualifications or to proceed to major established tertiary institutions. They also, on average, have a higher risk of dying as infants and a lower life expectancy. In recent decades Maori achievement has improved in some respects – for instance, in both income per capita and basic health statistics of infant mortality and life expectancy, they are both better off absolutely and closer to the non-Maori population than forty years ago. However, even if the gap has narrowed, Maori still do less well on average than non-Maori in terms of the standard of living which most New Zealanders value

The reasons for the Maori's relative lack of achievement are complex and disputed. The main explanation must lie in their history of being a colonised and conquered people. The dominant culture, in which their lack of achievement is partly defined, is one from which they at first kept themselves distinct, becoming marginalised, and which they then entered on inferior terms, restricting themselves by and large to unskilled occupations. These occupations were to prove particularly vulnerable to contraction as the domestic manufacturing sector was exposed to greater competition from imports.

This history supports an analysis in terms of one of the theories of structural dominance, either anti-colonial or marxist or a mixture of both. The anti-colonial analysis sees the dominant force behind these trends as part of the determination of the invading colonising people to subjugate the indigenous people and deprive them of their land and power. In the process, Maori people have become victims of institutionalised racism in the sense that most or all major institutions, both in the private and the public sector, are systematically biased in favour of the dominant culture and against Maori. Racist attitudes which either openly condemn or simply ignore Maori values and interests work to reinforce Maori social disadvantage.

The marxist analysis sees the cause as primarily economic. The seizure and exploitation of Maori land and then the influx of Maori (and Pacific Islanders) into the cities are all caused by the imperatives of capitalist accumulation. In the post-war period of expansion there was a need for additional labour. The migration of Maori and Pacific Islanders was part of a worldwide phenomenon in advanced capitalist countries. Capitalist economies needed more unskilled and semi-skilled manual workers. The local populations were insufficient to provide the necessary additional labour and so workers had to be imported from abroad.

Traditional marxists ignored ethnic differences and treated all members of the working class in a particular country as essentially similar, whether they were drawn from the dominant ethnic group or from an ethnic minority. But some theorists using an essentially marxist perspective have also incorporated an ethnic perspective into their analyses (Spoonley, 1994). When unskilled migrant workers are of a different ethnic group from the dominant home culture, they can more easily be treated as dispensable. They can become the victims of racial prejudice, which lends popular support to their treatment as second-class citizens deprived of full rights. Ethnically different migrants thus serve the interests of capitalists in being a group of unskilled workers prepared to work for very low wages and relatively powerless to demand improvements in their conditions. This analysis applies most obviously to migrant workers, such as non-Europeans in Europe and Pacific Islanders in New Zealand. But the Maori can also be seen as victims of the same process, being treated as migrants in their own country (as, for instance, in the very phrase 'urban migration'). If not formally deprived of citizen rights they have at least been socially marginalised and deprived of effective political influence.

Such an analysis linking economic forces and ethnic distinctions clearly has considerable force. However, like many such explanations, it does not tell the whole story. For instance, it should be remembered that relative Maori disadvantage applies to the position of average Maori and does not apply to all Maori. Thus there are many Maori who are well-educated and prosperous members of the professional class, just as there are non-Maori who are unskilled, uneducated and out of work. Indeed, some social theorists would argue that economic class is the only important factor in establishing people's social position and that ethnic distinctions are relatively insignificant. However, this too is implausible. The fact that Maori on average are relatively disadvantaged can hardly be an accident. It needs to be explained in terms which take into account their ethnicity as a factor.

When analysing the extent to which Maori interests are represented politically, it will be important to remember that there is no single tribes

Maori interest to be represented. Maori are divided into different iwi, with different histories and traditions as well as different economic resources and therefore making different demands on government. Moreover, cutting across the iwi lines are important class differences between those who are members of the Maori educated elite and those who live relatively impoverished lives, whether in the cities or in the country. Finally, there are differences of tactics about the best way to improve the position of Maori, whether it is by reasserting traditional Maori customs and values or by concentrating on advancement within the dominant culture and its institutions. These differences turn in part on which analysis of the present plight of the Maori is given prominence. Debate and conflict among Maori on these issues is to be expected. The task of the political system should be to make sure that the debate is politically articulated and that all sides have a fair chance of influencing the state in their favour.

Pakeha

The largest ethnic group in New Zealand is those of European origin, who comprise over 80 per cent of the population. It is these people whose values and institutions control the social and political life of New Zealand and a study of the New Zealand political system will inevitably concentrate very heavily on their behaviour. Yet, because of this very dominance, there are difficulties in precisely defining and even naming their ethnicity. Most such New Zealanders would simply describe themselves as 'New Zealanders' or 'Kiwis', thus identifying themselves with their nationality as fellow citizens. Being the predominant group, they see no need to distinguish themselves from the nation as a whole.

This is a familiar problem with ethnic groups which form a majority within a particular political community (Pearson, 1989). It is the ethnic minorities who feel the need to define themselves and to press for the recognition of their special ethnic interests against those of the majority which threaten to overwhelm them. The majority, on the other hand, can safely leave themselves undifferentiated in the secure conviction that what will be good for all or most citizens will be good for themselves. Moreover, they will often treat attempts by minorities to differentiate themselves as hostile and politically divisive behaviour. Such attempts will meet the response that everyone is equally a citizen, e.g. 'we're all New Zealanders'. This may signify a well-intentioned determination not to subject any citizens to discrimination on the grounds of ethnic or any other differences. But it can also be used as a cover for identifying the interest of the majority with that of the whole and therefore denying the legitimate interests of minorities.

Because of this resistance on the part of the majority to see themselves as a distinct ethnic group, there is also a lack of agreement about what they are to be called or how they are to be defined. Some terms, e.g. non-Maori or Tauiwi (foreigners), simply differentiate the population into those who are Maori and those who are not. This is unsatisfactory because, by lumping together all who are not Maori, it overlooks the existence of other ethnic minorities besides Maori, such as Pacific Islanders or Chinese. Other terms must be sought to identify those New Zealanders who are of specifically European origin. The term used officially in the census and other government documents is 'New Zealand European'. More common, though as yet rarely used officially, is 'Pakeha New Zealander' or simply 'Pakeha'. Neither is free of difficulty. Some New Zealanders who have European ancestors are unwilling to be described as 'Europeans' because this suggests that their home is really in Europe rather than in New Zealand. As for 'Pakeha', some reject it on the ground that it is supposedly offensive in origin, others because they do not like to be named in a language other than their own (Sharp, 1990: 64–69). But among those wanting to talk in terms of a 'bicultural' society, or of a partnership based on the Treaty of Waitangi, 'Pakeha' has increasingly become the favoured term for defining the dominant cultural group of European origin. As such, it has narrowed its original Maori meaning, which includes as Pakeha all people of European descent anywhere in the world. It is now confined to New Zealanders who are of primarily European descent. There are still blurrings of definition. For instance, are Europeans who emigrate to New Zealand Pakeha from the moment they arrive or should this name be withheld until they, or their children, consider themselves clearly at home in New Zealand?

Ethnicity implies a sense of shared identity and a shared culture. Much time and effort has gone into deciding what, if anything, Pakeha identity amounts to (Pearson, 1990a: Chapter 7; Spoonley, 1991; 1993: 57–61). Again, part of the difficulty is due to an unwillingness to see any New Zealand practices as distinctively Pakeha and therefore as foreign to other New Zealand minorities, particularly Maori. There is no doubt that Pakeha who travel overseas and come into contact with foreigners recognise that New Zealand is their home and that their values and practices vary, if only slightly, from those found in other countries. But the common origin shared with other former British settler colonies, such as Australia, Canada and the United States, as well as with Britain itself, means that the differences, though significant to fellow citizens of the same country, may often appear relatively minor in comparison with the basic similarities. However, Pakeha culture need not be confined to what is distinctive to New Zealand. It also includes the cultural roots in its British and European past which it shares with other countries. If some of its culture and values are shared with others, this need not affect their importance or genuineness for the people concerned. In just the same way, Maori have a past and cultural traditions which they share with other Polynesian peoples such as Cook Islanders and Tongans, a factor which need not diminish the importance of these common elements for the Maori.

The nature and even existence of Pakeha identity and culture are thus a matter of debate and disagreement. The Pakeha are the majority and it is usually not necessary to articulate a separate Pakeha interest or point of view. In political contexts, therefore, it is unlikely that Pakeha interests will need to be separately represented as such. For instance, Pakeha needs in health will not need a separate Pakeha health lobby in the way that specifically Maori needs might need a specifically Maori lobby. They can usually rely on the mainstream, on ethnically undifferentiated groups and organisations, to address their concerns. In this respect Pakeha influence tends to be unseen because it is so all pervading. But in social and political analysis it will always be important to look behind the facade of ethnic neutrality to examine the actual extent to which the specific interests of Pakeha and those of other interest groups are being advanced.

Other ethnic minorities

The Pakeha section of the population is descended overwhelmingly from settlers from the British Isles. Those who are not English in origin but Scots, Irish or Welsh have sometimes maintained a sense of that identity. This was particularly true of Irish Roman Catholics, whose religion and political allegiance was different from the rest. There are also descendants of settlers from other European countries who have to a greater or lesser extent preserved some of the original customs and identity. Prominent among them are those from Croatia, formerly known as Dalmatians and then (before the break-up of

Yugoslavia) as Yugoslavs. Other European groups include Jews, Dutch, Greeks and Italians. Some members of these groups have concentrated in particular areas and occupations but otherwise their separate identity is mainly limited to such activities as membership of churches or cultural clubs and informal family ties.

There are other ethnic groups besides Maori and those of European origin. In the nineteenth century, there was relatively free international movement of labour which brought Chinese and Indians to New Zealand in search of work. Some stayed permanently, founding small but not insignificant Chinese and Indian communities. Opposition to Asian migration, based on anti-Asian racial prejudice, subsequently reduced any further increase in their numbers until quite recently, when immigration policy has changed to allow the entry of people with skills and capital regardless of racial origin. Numbers of Chinese have increased from around 10,000 in 1966 to 36,700 in 1991. In the same period the Indian population has increased from 6700 to 25,700. Politically, New Zealand Asians have tended to keep out of the public eye, partly as a prudent means of avoiding stirring up Pakeha resentment. They have preferred to make use of the normal economic and educational opportunities available to them, out-performing all other ethnic groups, including Pakeha, in the proportion gaining high educational qualifications. In the 1990s, however, as the number of Asian residents has continued to increase and as their comparative wealth and success has grown ever more visible, particularly in Auckland, the issue of Asian immigration has become politically contentious and Asians themselves have been forced into a more prominent political role.

The most significant other minority in New Zealand are Pacific Islanders who make up nearly 4 per cent of the population. Though often classed as a single group they are really a collection of different groups, defined by the different islands from which they or their families have come. The largest group is from Western Samoa, a former New Zealand dependency which gained independence in 1962. The next largest Pacific Island group is from the Cook Islands, followed by Tongans and Niueans.

Some of the Pacific Islanders are New Zealand citizens by right. For instance, the Cook Islands and Niue are self-governing communities in free association with New Zealand, with their citizens having full right of access to New Zealand. Indeed, more of them live in New Zealand than in their home islands. Other Islanders, such as Samoans and Tongans, require permits to enter and work in New Zealand, though many of them have the status of permanent residents with full rights of citizenship, including voting rights.

TABLE 2.3
Ethnic groups in New Zealand

One ethnic group	Total	Per cent
European	2,610,408	70.3
Maori	294,726	7.9
Samoan	114,432	3.1
Chinese	100,203	2.7
Indian	59,823	1.6
Cook Island	51,141	1.4
Tongan	40,713	1.1
Niuean	20,148	0.5
Other	19,533	0.5
Total	**3,304,305**	**88.6**
Two ethnic groups		
European/Maori	193,503	5.2
European/Pacific Island	29,751	0.8
Maori/Pacific Island	17,661	0.5
Other	22,194	0.6
Total	**263,109**	**7.1**
Total: Three ethnic groups	**19,311**	**0.4**
Not specified	**143,598**	**3.8**
Total	**3,730,332**	**100.0**

Source: Statistics New Zealand, *2001 Census: Ethnic Groups*, Table 2b.

Pacific Island migrants were brought to New Zealand in considerable numbers by the same demand for manual labour that brought so many Maori to the cities in the post-war period. In many respects, the Islanders have the same experience as the Maori, living mainly in cities away from their original tribal homelands, the difference being that their homelands are in another country. Islanders suffer from many of the same socio-economic disadvantages as the Maori and for similar reasons. But the difference in their political status, the fact that they are migrants to New Zealand rather than indigenous to New Zealand, entails some differences in their situation. Like ethnic migrants elsewhere in the developed world, they can become the subjects of racial harassment, particularly if they are perceived to be taking jobs from local workers. Those whose residence is not permanent can become the targets of racial campaigns against migrant labour. On the other hand, they do not suffer the cultural deprivation felt by the Maori as an indigenous minority conquered in their own country. Pacific Islanders still have their own home under their own political control to return to. Even if they were not born in New Zealand they are still, in some sense, members of New Zealand society as a result of their own, or their family's, choice and can more easily adopt a positive attitude towards its values while still retaining their own identity and some of their traditional customs.

A bicultural or multicultural society?

New Zealand is thus an ethnically complex society. Like almost all nation states it contains people of different ethnic backgrounds living together under one law and one set of political institutions. For many years, this diversity was suppressed or dismissed. It was common to describe New Zealand as a 'homogeneous' society, that is, one where everyone was very similar in social values and background. Certainly, in comparison with other settler societies such as the United States, Canada or even Australia, the settler population, being overwhelmingly British, was relatively homogeneous in composition. But even so the claim of homogeneity only made sense if the Maori were either ignored or assumed to be gradually assimilating themselves into the dominant culture. Indeed, assimilation was for many years official government policy, a policy based on the assumption that European culture or 'civilisation' was superior to all others and that the Maori had the natural capacity to adapt to its ways and values, an adaptation that would obviously be in their own interests (Belich, 1986).

These assumptions, though still held by many Pakeha, have become publicly discredited as arrogant and racist. Official government policy has turned away from assimilation and monoculturalism. Public policy in New Zealand now aims at a bicultural or multicultural society. Biculturalism gives particular prominence to two cultures and traditions, the dominant English-speaking Pakeha culture and Maori culture. It stresses the unique position of the Maori as the country's first inhabitants and signatories to the Treaty of Waitangi. Multiculturalism on the other hand is the view that there are more than just two cultures and ethnic groups in the community, all of which have the right to flourish provided that they do not infringe the basic rights of citizens (Pearson, 1991).

These two theories are sometimes in conflict (Mulgan, 1993b; Sharp, 1995). In particular, multiculturalism is often used as a means of discrediting the attempt, implicit in biculturalism, to give special recognition to Maori ahead of other minorities. If the Maori and their culture are singled out for special rights or protection, it is argued, why should not the same privileges be given to Islanders, Chinese and so on? Conversely, some Maori have seen the acceptance of Asian migrants as a threat to their own attempts to seek justice from the Pakeha majority. Certainly, most migrants from non-British backgrounds have little cultural affinity with the enterprise of attempting to right the wrongs of colonialism or with the renewed emphasis on the Treaty of Waitangi which are at the heart of biculturalism.

There can be no doubt that, as a matter of actual fact, New Zealand is a multicultural society. There certainly are several, not just two, ethnic groups and cultural traditions coexisting in the community. More-over, in a democratic society all citizens should have the right to flourish free of ethnic prejudice and discrimination. However, this does not mean that special recognition should not be given to Maori within a democratic framework. All countries which practice equality of rights for all citizens, nonetheless have certain cultural traditions which predominate in their public institutions – British traditions in Britain, French in France, Japanese in Japan and so on. No one suggests that all democracies should recognise all languages as official languages or should not entrench the language and customs of their predominant people and traditions. Political communities cannot survive without historical traditions and their institutions should therefore be expected to reflect and reinforce these traditions. It therefore seems justifiable that the public practices of a community can be conducted in the culture or cultures which have, as it were, historical pride of place in that community. In New Zealand this means that both Maori and Pakeha cultures can be given particular emphasis in the public institutions and cultural life of the nation, Maori because of their historical priority and Pakeha because of their predominance. This is what the policy of biculturalism amounts to (Mulgan, 1989a: Chapter 1). Other cultures besides Maori and Pakeha can be guaranteed the right of survival and protection without necessarily being given the right of full public incorporation.

Economic structure

The aspect of the plural society which has the most profound influence on the political system is the economic structure, those institutions and interrelationships which are concerned with the production and exchange of goods and services. Economic imperatives, the need to earn a living or to subsist on earnings derived from others, are major concerns in most people's lives and governments are held responsible for much of the country's economic performance.

The function of economic production in New Zealand is shared among a number of different types of economic activity, or 'industries'. Their nature and number are a matter of conventional and somewhat arbitrary definition. For instance, the National Accounts, published by Statistics New Zealand, define thirteen different industries – agriculture, fishing, forestry, mining and quarrying, manufacturing and so on – which are then grouped into three broad categories or 'sectors' – 'primary industries', 'goods-producing industries' and 'service industries' (Statistics New Zealand, 2002: 390-1). Of these industries a group from within the 'service' sector and consisting of 'finance, insurance, real estate and business services' made the largest contribution (25 per cent) to the national wealth (Gross Domestic Product) in 2000. The next largest contributions come from 'manufacturing' (16 per cent) and more groups within the service sector – 'wholesale trading, retailing, hotels and restaurants' (15 per cent), 'personal and community services' (12 per cent), and 'transport and communications' (9 per cent) – followed by agriculture (6 per cent). (Agriculture, it should be noted, does not include all the contributions derived from agricultural products – manufactured processing of farm products are listed separately (Carter, 1994: 57).)

These figures illustrate a feature of most modern economies, namely the very high contribution to the economy made by the provision of services and the relatively modest contribution in percentage terms made by the provision of actual material goods, such as agricultural or manufactured products. Production of material goods remains essential to almost any economy but in modern economies it is not the major source of wealth. For New Zealand, however, the relative importance of material production changes when contribution to exports, rather than overall contribution to the domestic economy, is considered. Here the harvesting, growing and processing of products derived from New Zealand's natural resources loom much larger. Particular importance for exports has always lain with the various industries based on agriculture, that is, the breeding of stock, especially cattle and sheep, the growing of fruit and other horticultural products and the further processing of these into manufactured products. Together these make up over 40 per cent of exports. If to this is added the export contribution from forestry and related manufactured products, fishing and mining, the contribution of natural resources to New Zealand's export trade is over half (Statistics New Zealand, 2002: 533). But again it is important not to exaggerate this dependence. Important contributions are made by such industries as transport and trading, restaurants and hotels.

Those engaged in a particular sector have certain interests which they share with each other and which form the basis of much political policy-making. The sectional interests of those engaged in particular productive sectors are not, however, the only economically significant interests. Economic production in the various economic sectors directly involves only those who are in the paid workforce and they are less than half the total population. Not part of the workforce are those unable to work, such as children, many of the elderly and people suffering from chronic sickness or disability. In addition a significant fraction of the population consists of the unemployed, who are counted as part of the labour force because they are able and willing to work, but who are unable to find jobs. There are others who choose not to undertake paid employment, for instance parents, usually mothers, looking after young children, or the retired. All these people have economic interests in the sense that they have material needs which have to be provided for. Some, such as elderly living on savings and investments, may be reliant on their own resources. Others, particularly children, are more immediately dependent on relations. Others, again, such as the unemployed and some chronically disabled, may be largely dependent on state-provided benefits.

Each individual person is not simply a member of one economic sector group with one economic interest. Owners of companies across different sectors may all benefit from low interest rates and low rates of inflation. People in employment as well as pensioners may derive income from investments and therefore share an interest as investors. People employed in different sectors but in similar occupations may share a common interest, for instance secretaries in government departments and in legal offices, or managers of dairy factories and of supermarket chains. Indeed, in many cases, these shared occupational interests may have much more importance for the individuals than the actual sector of the economy in which they work. Moreover, people also have non-occupational economic interests as consumers, for instance as buyers of food and clothing, as houseowners or renters of housing, as owners and users of cars and so on. In each of these respects people share a similar interest with those whose consumption is similar.

Conflict among different economic interests is constant and inevitable. For instance, there will be conflicts of interest between different productive sectors which reveal themselves in disagreements over the proper emphasis in government policy. Exporters benefit from a low exchange rate which helps their products compete internationally. But a lower value for the New Zealand dollar hurts importers and adds to the national debt, which is counted in overseas currencies. Low interest rates advantage those borrowing to invest but not those whose income is derived from the interest gained by lending funds. Reduced taxation may be of some advantage to everyone who pays taxes but it will not help those on the public payroll who lose their jobs or who have their benefits cut as a result. Such conflicts of interest are a major source of political conflict over the direction to be taken by government policy.

Class and status

Most theories of the state agree that economic interests and the clashes among them are one of the main driving forces of politics. But different theories have different views about which economic interests and which economic conflicts are most important. Pluralist theories, as in the account of the previous section, tend to emphasise the diversity of interests among different economic sectors with the suggestion that economic power and sources of political influence are similarly diversified and dispersed. On the other hand, analysts writing in the marxist tradition tend to identify certain economic interests as fundamental across all sectors. They divide society into two antagonistic classes based on whether people own and control the means of economic production, regardless of sector.

Many New Zealanders are uncomfortable with the language of class because of the pervasive myth that New Zealand, like other ex-colonial societies, is a classless society. Class distinctions and snobbery were associated with the aristocratic values of Britain and Europe, values which most of the settlers were determined to leave behind. Yet the existence of class divisions and class distinctions in New Zealand can hardly be denied. Most New Zealanders would recognise the existence of a 'middle class' and a class below the middle class, though for the latter group they would usually prefer a social euphemism, such as 'lower socio-economic groups' or 'under-privileged', rather than the blunter 'lower class' or 'working class'. Such class differences are associated with differences in occupation, education, income and general lifestyle. In the cities, with socially stratified suburbs, class is associated with where people live as well as with what they do for a living. In the country, class distinctions depend mostly on whether or not someone owns a farm and if so, how large and valuable a farm it is.

Class differences are clearly connected with economic occupation but in what way is a matter of controversy among sociologists. Traditional marxism distinguishes just two main classes in capitalist societies. One is the capitalist class, or bourgeoisie, who are the owners of capital and the material means of production and therefore control the whole process of production. The other is the working class, or proletariat, those who are forced to work for the capitalists in order to survive. The workers are the true producers of wealth but most of it is taken from them by the capitalists who live off their exploited labour. Marx himself recognised that there were different segments within these classes and some intermediate groups who had a foot in each camp. But the clash between capital and labour was the dominant one and, as capitalism developed, would become increasingly significant as the classes became more polarised. Some marxists continue to apply such a class analysis to present-day societies including New Zealand (Bedggood, 1980). Others have adapted the model to account for what appears to be a major development in twentieth-century capitalism, one largely unforeseen by Marx – the growth in the number of people in the 'intermediate' or 'middle' class between capital and labour, for instance salaried managers and bureaucrats. To help account for this phenomenon within marxist theory, a distinction can be drawn between owning the means of production and controlling or having power over others. True capitalists both own and control. But there are some, e.g. self-employed tradespeople, who own their means of production but do not control others. And there are some, e.g. managers, who control others without themselves owning the organisations for which they work. This gives a fourfold class structure of owners, managerial middle class, self-employed, workers. This is closer to the structure of modern societies while still remaining true to the marxist emphasis on exploitation and control (Wilkes, 1994).

Other definitions of class place less emphasis on ownership and control and focus more on the distinction between different types of work, particularly the distinction between manual and non-manual labour. This distinction, for many people, seems to constitute the major difference between the middle and working class and is the class distinction found to be most politically relevant, for instance in explaining voting behaviour (Chapter 11). Within these two broad divisions, occupations are further ranked in terms of income, skill and general prestige. This yields a set of class categories in descending order, for instance professionals and higher managers, intermediate managerial, skilled non-manual, skilled manual, semi-skilled manual, unskilled manual (Gold, 1992: 5). This is similar to the categorisations of occupational classes used by marketing and advertising experts when trying to sell products to different sectors of the community. For instance, the market research company AGB McNair has identified a number of target groups such as 'liberal sophisticated', 'young hopefuls', 'settled seniors', 'affluent acquirers', and 'lonely and dissatisfied' (Drinnan, 1991). In such schemes, highly paid professionals, such as medical doctors and lawyers are placed high in the class hierarchy, even though from a strict marxist point of view their degree of economic power and ownership may be relatively slight. Some sociologists would call this a hierarchy based on 'status' rather than 'class', reserving 'class' for the analysis based on marxist categories. But that is, perhaps, too narrow a view. The status-based hierarchy fits closely with most people's understanding of what social class is about and there seems no point in denying it the name of 'class'.

Whatever basis is used for determining occupational class, the analysis of class structure must take account of those with no fixed occupation in the normal sense, for instance, the long-term unemployed, those, often illegal immigrants, who subsist on welfare benefits or unreported illicit earnings. Such people, who form a growing section of New Zealand society and of other similar societies, are often described as the 'under-class', a term which reflects the marxist view that, among the worse-off in society, only those who produce wealth, the working class or proletariat, can be rightly called a class. This is a somewhat narrow view. The so-called 'under-class' is as much a class as any other group whose position is defined in terms of occupation, ownership and economic control. Indeed, through its alienation from the political system and its effect on other classes and their aspirations, the underclass is one of the most politically significant classes in contemporary capitalist democracies.

Is the view that New Zealand is a classless or egalitarian society a total myth? Not entirely. Certainly, New Zealand society has always had the inequalities of wealth and economic power and the disparities of occupational status which are typical of all modern capitalist societies and, in recent years, as elsewhere, these inequalities appear to have been increasing. But the myth is not totally without foundation or political effect. Historically, many of the colonial settlers of New Zealand were inspired by an ideal of the independent settler living a life of economic freedom and self-sufficiency, typically as a farmer. They would belong to a society where every man (it was usually a male-centred ideal) achieved equal social respect and need recognise no one as a social superior (Vowles, 1987: 221). That most settlers did not end up as independent farmers and that most New Zealanders lived as wage and salary earners in towns and cities does not altogether undermine the potency of the myth. It is revealed, for instance, in the expectation of home ownership and in the favoured position often given to the self-employed in taxation policy. The unease at talk of class distinctions may, indeed, have helped to blunt the widespread development of class consciousness and may have therefore prevented the growth of militant trade unionism beyond a few relatively politicised occupations such as mining, transport and meat refrigeration. In this respect, the idea of egalitarianism, though not firmly based in social and economic fact (Pearson & Thorns, 1983), may nonetheless have been politically influential.

Gender

Another major social division is that between male and female. To the extent to which men and women have different social roles, they also share different interests. Women have traditionally taken the major part in child-rearing and domestic duties. For this reason, political issues concerning childbirth and child-care, such as issues of abortion, adoption or day-care, are still seen specifically as women's issues. When it was the norm for women to withdraw from the paid workforce on marriage, they engaged in a range of social activities, both informal and formal, centring on domestic life. Many organisations, such as churches and sports clubs, had separate divisions especially for women, usually meeting during the working week. These organisations formed a focus, not only for women's social life, but also for the articulation and promotion of women's interests in public policy.

However, the stereotypical 'normal' family of father in paid employment and mother looking after the children and doing the housework now applies to only a minority of families. Of those households containing children, approximately one quarter have only one resident parent, i.e. a 'solo' parent. Changing attitudes to women's family role, as well as economic necessity, have meant that many more mothers are now part of the workforce than previously. In more than half of two parent families, both parents are in paid employment. Half of solo parents (most of them women) are also in employment (Swain, 1994: 21). The pattern of women's organisations has changed with the increasing numbers of women entering the workforce and under the general influence of the 'women's movement' which began in the 1970s. For instance, women's groups are now found within many occupations, looking after the specific interests of working women.

The relation between gender and class is a contested issue among social theorists. Most traditional class analyses tended to associate women with the class of their husbands or fathers. As class was seen as being determined by occupational position in the workforce, it was the 'head of household', typically a man, who determined the class of all other members of the family, including all women members. At the same time, in a socially egalitarian colonial society, women had an important social role in maintaining the class position of their families. The institutions principally associated with promulgating and reinforcing ideas of social equality were largely restricted to males – hotel public bars, team sports (preeminently rugby), the armed forces in wartime (and the Returned Services Association in peacetime). All these were dedicated to 'mateship', the peculiarly colonial ideal of male solidarity and friendship (Phillips, 1987). Class divisions, especially the subtle distinctions of social status, were primarily the concern of women, particularly married women (James & Saville-Smith, 1990: 31–46).

As part of their rejection of women's subservient social role, feminists have objected to the identification of women's class position with that of male heads of households. In contemporary New Zealand society, with the number of female solo parents and the number of women in the workforce generally, it is no longer appropriate, if it ever was, to identify heads of households as male. Moreover, the whole concept of a household 'headed' by a wage earner ignores the importance of unpaid domestic work. Indeed, much economic analysis generally, and not just class analysis, can be criticised for leaving out the domestic sphere. This sphere includes a very significant component of national production, in terms of such necessary functions as care of children and the sick, cooking, house-cleaning, home maintenance, and so on. The fact that women have traditionally contributed much more than men to this domestic production means that women's economic contribution has been regularly overlooked (Waring, 1988).

According to feminist perspectives, women have not only contributed most to domestic production, they have also done so under duress as part of a process of subordination and exploitation. Women's exclusion from the public sphere and preoccupation with domestic matters have been reinforced by ideology and false consciousness. Women, and men, have been encouraged to believe that traditional male and female roles are naturally, even divinely, ordained.

Feminist analyses differ on whether the occupational distinctions of class, which have been largely, though not exclusively, differences between groups of men, have any significance in comparison with the division between male and female. Some radical feminists would see the exploitation of women by men as the only significant division within society. Thus all women who stay at home to look after their husbands and their husband's children are equally victimised, regardless of their husband's income or the life-style they can afford. Similarly, all women who go to work are also equally exploited, regardless of income or occupation. Most feminists, however, particularly those who would describe themselves as socialist feminists or marxist feminists, consider economic factors, such as the ownership of capital, to have independent significance, in addition to factors of gender. In this case, a gender-based analysis of women's exploitation by men is a necessary supplement to an account of class exploitation, rather than an alternative to it (James & Saville-Smith, 1990). Pluralist analysis will be open to evidence of interests specific to women and to their political expression through various women's organisations. Pluralists, however, are more cautious about analyses of women's interests based on theories of false consciousness and of what women ought to want as distinct from what they consciously want.

Leisure and recreation

As well as working, people also spend time at leisure. Surveys of leisure activities indicate that most leisure is centred on the household – watching television, reading, listening to music, visiting and entertaining friends, gardening (Gidlow *et al.*, 1994: 260; Wilson *et al.*, 1990: Chapter 11). Outside the home, people engage in a wide variety of leisure and recreational activities, such as walking, swimming, watching and playing sport, going to films and other entertainments, drinking in pubs, eating out in restaurants. A survey of New Zealanders' leisure found that one in two New Zealanders were members of recreation or sports clubs. One in three worked as volunteers for voluntary organisations such as sports clubs, educational groups and welfare organisations (Wilson *et al.*, 1990: Chapters 17, 18; see also Henderson & Bellamy, 2002: 100).

Political activity, in the sense of active participation in political organisations such as political parties or protest groups, may also be classed as a leisure activity. Most people avoid political organisations and confine their formal political participation to voting at elections and signing petitions (Perry & Webster, 1999: 89). In a broader sense, however, taking an active and critical interest in the news or discussing politics with family and friends may be counted as important political activities which are engaged in by a substantial number of citizens.

The social role of leisure is a matter of academic dispute. Certainly, consumption of leisure pursuits is an important indicator of people's class location in society. Sociologists of leisure with a marxist or feminist perspective also emphasise the wider economic and social functions of leisure activity, the degree to which people's tastes are influenced by advertising and the extent to which the provision of leisure commodities is in the interests more of the capitalist providers than those of the consumers. Media-inspired concentration on sports, entertainments and fashions may be seen as a means of diverting people's attention from the inequalities of society, and in the case of women, reinforcing their position of subservience to men.

There is undoubtedly some truth in this analysis. However, from the pluralist perspective, the preferences and aspirations which people reveal in their choice of leisure pursuits and life-style are not to be analysed away as false consciousness. As in market liberal theories, these preferences indicate people's own interests and values, which it is the function of the political system to take into account. Pluralist analysis will pay particular attention to interaction between the state and various leisure interests, as revealed, for instance, in the lobbying activities of leisure-related interest groups such as sports bodies or groups seeking to protect the environment for recreational purposes.

Religion

There are other sectional divisions within New Zealand society which may on occasion be politically relevant. One is religious affiliation, a factor which in some other countries, such as Ireland and India, is a source of intense conflict and the single most important determinant of political allegiance. Most New Zealanders (about 61 per cent) claim adherence to one of the Christian churches, including the Maori Ratana and Ringatu churches. Among the Christian churches the major denominations are Anglicans (28 per cent), Roman Catholics (23 per cent) and Presbyterians (20 per cent) (Statistics New Zealand, 2002:

44

118). Actual churchgoing, however, is confined to a relatively small minority of the population. Among adults surveyed at the time of the 2002 election, 57 per cent said they 'never' went to church while 20 per cent went at least once a month (NZES, 2002). The impact of church activity is greater among Maori and Pacific Islanders, where churches often provide a focus for ethnic activities

Like other countries with people of British origin, New Zealand has had a history of hostility between a Roman Catholic minority and other, Protestant branches of the Christian church. Roman Catholics, of predominantly Irish and Croatian origin, have not always shared the allegiance to British traditions and institutions of other Pakeha New Zealanders, many of whom had imported anti-Catholic prejudices from Britain. By establishing their own school system and other distinctively Catholic institutions such as sports clubs and hospitals, Catholics maintained a separate identity. However, sectarian conflict has greatly diminished in New Zealand and on most political issues the so-called 'mainline' churches, that is, the Roman Catholics and the other long-standing Christian denominations, such as Anglicans, Presbyterians and Methodists, are usually united on their attitude to social and political issues. (The main exceptions are the issues of abortion and contraception which are both opposed on doctrinal grounds by only one mainline church, the Roman Catholics.) These churches played a prominent role in the anti-apartheid movement and in the opposition to sporting contacts with South Africa, culminating in the Springbok Tour of 1981. More recently, their leaders have spoken out against what they see as an erosion of social compassion evident in attacks on the welfare state inspired by market liberal principles.

In addition to the mainline churches, there are also a number of newer Christian denominations, such as the Assembly of God, many with origins in the United States and marked by a 'fundamentalist' approach to religious doctrine. In contrast with the generally more liberal approach of the mainline churches, the fundamentalists are usually conservative on social and political issues, particularly in defence of traditional family structures and gender roles. Though the number of adherents are relatively few, they are often extremely committed and enthusiastic and have had some political impact.

Locality

Another type of potentially significant division is that of locality or region. People share common interests as fellow members of a particular district, town, suburb, city or province. The importance of local loyalties and local identity is not as strong as it was earlier in the century, when communications and travel were more difficult (Pearson, 1990). In such conditions, particularly in rural areas, people were isolated and more likely to develop close relationships with neighbours and others from the same locality. For Maori, because iwi identity is closely bound up with tribal lands, local roots have been, and continue to be, very significant, particularly to those still living on their ancestral lands. However, for the Pakeha, city living, the motor car and television have made people much less dependent on their immediate neighbours and have weakened the sense of local identity. Relations of kinship, class, ethnicity or shared leisure interests are likely to loom larger in people's lives.

Shared local interests, however, do exist, based on local institutions such as schools and sports teams. So-called 'service clubs', such as Lions and Rotary, have an important local focus, providing local amenities and contributing to local causes. Local chambers of commerce work to increase the level of economic activity in their areas. Local interests are also defined and sustained by institutions of local government (Chapter 8). The public apathy which usually surrounds the actions of local government underlines the relative lack of prominence that local interests have for most people most of the time. However, on occasion, communities may respond with quite energetic and determined action when threatened by unwelcome change, such as a disruptive building development or the closure of a publicly provided service. This indicates, perhaps, that local interests are dormant and usually taken for granted rather than totally unimportant in people's lives.

The plural society and the state

This completes the brief survey of New Zealand society intended to provide a context for a pluralist study of the political system. From this perspective, New Zealand society is made up of a large number of cross-cutting and overlapping groups, sectors, classes and so on, each with its own differing interests and values. Though we may sometimes wish to generalise about interests that all members of any group or section have in common, there will be variation and conflict among different members or among different sub-groups or sub-sections about what their interests or purposes ought to be. The pluralist picture of society thus repeats itself at each level of analysis – there will always be variation and disagreement right down to the level of the individual person.

This does not rule out the possibility of generalising but it does indicate that generalisations about human behaviour are never watertight or precisely accurate but always contain some element of approximation.

As will become clearer in later chapters, each of the different sections and interests intersects with the state in a variety of different ways. State-provided public services enter into our lives at every point We drive on the roads, use schools and hospitals, enter into legally enforceable contracts, travel on passports, call the fire brigade in case of fire or the police in the case of theft, seek a benefit if our income fails and pay for all these services through a variety of methods of taxation, such as income tax, goods and services tax, levies on certain commodities such as petrol, liquor and gambling. It is not surprising, therefore, that the institutions of the state should interact intimately with all sections of society or that the main driving force of government decision-making should be to meet the demands which the system receives from the wider public.

The extent of state activity is itself a matter of political debate. Indeed, part of the social context in which governments operate is formed by the expectations from citizens about what the state's role should be. These public attitudes about the state are part of what is known as the 'political culture' of a society. Some state functions are uncontroversial and follow almost by definition from the meaning of state, for instance, the provision of law, order and defence, and the protection of life and property. In modern democratic societies, it is now also taken for granted that the state has an important role in education, public health and protection of the environment. But on some issues there is disagreement. For instance, the precise extent of state concern for the material welfare of its citizens is a matter of fierce political debate, as is the nature and extent of the state's direct responsibility for the economy and wealth production.

The role of the New Zealand state has been particularly contested in recent years. For over a century, New Zealanders, particularly Pakeha New Zealanders, developed a broad political consensus in favour of a relatively active state (Vowles, 1987; Mulgan, 1993a). From the mid nineteenth century, the state was seen as a major agent of economic and social development. It was the main organisation with the resources capable of developing the country in a way that met the demands of the growing number of settlers. There was widespread support for state initiatives in such areas as economic investment, the provision of commercial services such as insurance and mortgage finance, the control of labour relations, the payment of old age pensions. The state was also seen as an important instrument for achieving social egalitarianism and equal opportunity for all citizens. In the middle decades of the twentieth century this consensus was extended to cover state-provided health and family benefits, as well as state housing and welfare benefits for those in need, a combination of policies later to be grouped under the general heading of the 'welfare state'.

This willingness to use the state as an agent of economic growth and social welfare rather than relying solely on the private sector and individual provision, is sometimes associated with 'socialism' or 'collectivism', a desire to transform society into a more cooperative and united association, based on the collective ownership of property. But most New Zealanders' preference for collective government action did not derive from a commitment to a more collective way of life. The Maori people certainly had a life based on communal ownership and collective enterprise. In contrast, European settlers to New Zealand for the most part had individual, personal goals, particularly the desire to find a more prosperous future for themselves and their immediate families. Collective means and considerable government 'intervention' were simply seen as the most efficient and acceptable methods of achieving these personal goals. 'Social democracy', rather than socialism, is a better term for this willingness to use state action for individual benefit (Chapter 10: 244–5).

These attitudes are still widespread in the community. A recent survey of New Zealand values (Gold & Webster, 1990) showed that when asked about what the government's policy priorities should be, an overwhelming majority gave first priority to the provision of jobs and reduction of unemployment. This was put way ahead of overall economic performance measured in average living standards. This shows the importance that all New Zealanders give to their own economic security and that of their families. Moreover, many people favoured collective state policies as a means of providing economic security. There was considerable support for continuing government ownership of large industrial enterprises such as banks and steel works and even stronger support for tighter government regulation of big companies and multinationals, which were clearly perceived as potentially threatening to the interests of New Zealanders.

These values persisted in spite of recent government moves away from government regulation and the active state. Beginning in the middle 1980s, governments under the influence of market liberal ideas, first Labour and then National, radically reduced the degree of government economic intervention. In addition, through the process of privatising state assets they reduced state ownership and control of service and productive enterprises. Indeed, a new market liberal consensus developed among decision-makers and their advisers, both in government and the private sector, in favour of a much more limited government role in economic management and a significant reduction in direct government responsibility for the material welfare of citizens even if this leads to increased economic and social inequality.

However, this new elite consensus was never fully accepted by the public at large (Vowles, Aimer *et al.*, 1995: Chapter 5). Many voters reject the market liberals' limited state and still hold to traditional social democratic values. This dislocation between the views of the politicians and their advisers and the expectations of many voters provides the main reason why the New Zealand political system has been under unusual strain and why political behaviour has exhibited unusual volatility. The intersections between state and society have become much more contested and the subject of much more open political conflict in the 1980s and 1990s than they were in the earlier post-war decades.

Further reading

New Zealand society in general
Spoonley, Pearson & Shirley (1994); *New Zealand Official Year Book* (Statistics New Zealand, 2002).
Ethnicity
Pearson (1990a); Pearson (1991); Spoonley (1993); Spoonley (1994).
Maori
Durie (2003); Metge (1976); Walker (1987); Walker (1990).
Class
Gold (1992); Wilkes (1994).
Political culture
Gold & Webster (1990); Gold (1992a); Mulgan (1993a); Vowles (1987).

Statistics New Zealand website: <www.stats.govt.nz>

3

The Constitution

The constitution and its sources

The operation of the institutions of the state depends on a number of factors – the structure of society at large, the values and interests of those who wish to influence the state in their favour, historical traditions and expectations of how the state should perform, and so on. One important set of factors is associated with the legal framework in which political decisions are made. This framework is known as the constitution, the basic legal rules and principles which define the institutions of government. In New Zealand, the constitution determines such matters as: the composition of Parliament, how its members are selected, the procedures by which it enacts legislation; the role and powers of the Governor-General; the powers of ministers, both individually and as members of the Cabinet; the structure of the courts and their relation to the other branches of government. The constitution includes major principles, such as the right to vote in general elections or the requirement that the government's budget must be approved by Parliament. It may also cover quite minor matters, such as details of committee procedure in Parliament. As is typical in political analysis, there is no clear line between what is to count and what is not to count as part of the constitution. This is illustrated by the fact that in countries where the constitution is incorporated into a single document, such a document may be quite short, just a few pages like the US Constitution, or a book of up to a hundred pages or more, such as the constitutions of India or Kenya.

Constitutions are often given the legal force of fundamental law, in the sense that they cannot be changed by the normal legislative process but require a more elaborate procedure such as a referendum of all voters. The rationale for legally 'entrenching' a constitution in this way is that the constitution, as the basic law, determines the process by which other laws are passed and amended. It therefore should not be capable of being amended by that process. More broadly, a government which controls the legislature should not be able to use that control to change the basic rules in its own favour. Constitutions also often set legal limits to the actions which governments can take and the laws which they may enact. For instance, it may be unconstitutional for laws to infringe certain basic rights of citizens. In this case, the constitution will provide for a process of 'judicial review' whereby the courts decide whether the legislature or other branches of government are in breach of the constitution.

New Zealand, like the United Kingdom from which its constitution is derived, does not have a constitution of this type. There is no single constitutional document with the force of fundamental law. Certainly, there are some parts of some constitutional statutes which cannot be changed by a simple act of Parliament (see below). Moreover, the New Zealand Bill of Rights Act 1990 allows some judicial review of executive action (Chapter 7: 176–80). But, unlike Australia, Canada or the United States, New Zealand does not have a wide-ranging constitutional document which might generally constrain the legislative power of Parliament. Citizens generally do not have recourse to the courts to have acts of Parliament declared unconstitutional and therefore invalid, a point which is commonly made by saying that New Zealand does not have a 'written constitution'. This is somewhat misleading in that New Zealand does have constitutional laws and conventions which are written down. However, if the concept of a written constitution is taken to imply significant, judicially enforced, limits on the powers of Parliament, then it is true that New Zealand does not have such a constitution.

New Zealand's constitution is to be found in a number of different sources. The document which is commonly referred to as New Zealand's founding constitutional charter is the Treaty of Waitangi. The Treaty marks the historical founding of New Zealand as a British colony and plays a crucial part in determining the legitimacy of New Zealand governments and their right to command the allegiance of New Zealand citizens, both Maori and Pakeha. The Treaty thus serves one of the functions commonly fulfilled by formal constitutional documents, that of providing an historical focus for the citizens' loyalty to their government. However, for most of its history, the Treaty was not recognised as having the force of law or in any way defining or constraining the powers of New Zealand governments. Even now, when it has acquired much more political and legal force (Chapter 7), its legal authority largely depends on its being incorporated into other legal instruments and is not derived directly from the Treaty itself.

Constitutional lawyers distinguish three major sources of constitutional rules – statutes (i.e. laws passed by Parliament), the 'common' law (i.e. legal rules derived from the accumulated decisions of the courts), and constitutional conventions. Important constitutional statutes include the Constitution Act 1986, which brings together a number of rules defining the main institutions of government, and the Electoral Act 1993, which covers the conduct of elections and the composition of Parliament. Certain sections of these acts are 'entrenched', and can only be changed by a three-quarters majority in Parliament or by a referendum. Entrenched sections cover such matters as the 'term' of Parliament (i.e. the maximum period between elections), the composition of the Representation Commission which draws up electoral boundaries and the principles it must follow (Chapter 11), qualifications for voting and the method of voting (Electoral Act 1993, section 268, Constitution Act 1986, section 17). The referendum of November 1993, which approved a new electoral system (Chapter 5: 100) and a new Electoral Act, is an instance of amendment to entrenched legislation. Indeed, such constitutional referendums may be said to constitute a further independent source of constitutional law. The State Sector Act 1988 and the Public Finance Act 1989 also include important constitutional principles about the structure of government agencies and their relationship to ministers and Parliament.

The New Zealand legal system also includes legal rules derived from the English 'common law', law which originates from the accumulated decisions of the courts rather than from statutes. Constitutional rules which are enshrined in the common law include certain rights of citizens, such as the right of free speech, as well as the majority rule in parliamentary procedure and certain powers of the Governor-General.

Finally, there are constitutional conventions which do not have the full force of legally enforceable law. They cover a number of very important rules of the constitution, for instance the rule which requires the Governor-General to act on the advice of ministers who have the support of a majority of Parliament, a rule which is fundamental to New Zealand's system of democratic government. The importance of conventions indicates what is perhaps the most important feature of the New Zealand constitution, and of all 'Westminster' systems (so-called because of their origin in the British prototype at Westminster, London): their formal structure is very much at odds with their informal reality, a feature that can lead to considerable misunderstanding.

The legal structure

The formal legal structure of the constitution is set out in the Constitution Act 1986, which divides the constitution into four elements: the Sovereign, the Executive, the Legislature and the Judiciary. The legal role and function of each of these elements may be briefly summarised:

The sovereign

The role of sovereign, or head of state, is filled by the King or Queen of the United Kingdom (i.e. Great Britain and Northern Ireland), currently Queen Elizabeth II, who also acts as sovereign of New Zealand. Except when the Queen acts as 'the Queen in right of New Zealand', which she does, for instance, when she visits New Zealand, the sovereign's powers are exercised by her appointed representative, the Governor-General. These powers are defined in the Constitution Act itself and in the so-called 'Letters Patent', most recently updated in 1983, which are a list of powers delegated to the Governor-General by the Queen. The main powers of the Sovereign, or 'Crown', include the power to appoint or remove ministers, the power to summon or dissolve Parliament, the power to assent to legislation, the power to make statutory regulations by Order in Council and the power to grant pardons. In all matters, by constitutional convention, the Governor-General normally acts on advice of elected ministers, who have the confidence of a majority in the House of Representatives. If necessary, the Governor-General may need to take independent advice to find out which potential ministers have the confidence of a parliamentary majority. In the case of a serious constitutional crisis or revolution, the Governor-General might be called on to act independently for the sake of preserving the constitution.

The executive

The executive consists of ministers of the Crown, who must be elected Members of Parliament, appointed by the Governor-General to act on behalf of the sovereign or the Crown. Ministers and the Governor General (who presides, if present) constitute the Executive Council which issues executive orders or 'Orders-in-Council'.

The legislature

The legislature, the body which has the function of law-making by enacting statutes, is Parliament. Parliament formally consists of the elected House of Representatives and the sovereign. That is to say, any proposal to make a new statute or to change an existing statute must have the approval of the House of Representatives and the Governor General. Thus, in terms of constitutional law, the House of Representatives is not, strictly speaking, the same as Parliament but only a part of it, the other part being the sovereign. In practice, because the role of the sovereign in law-making is reduced to a formality, Parliament is usually equated with the House of Representatives and the two terms are used interchangeably. The House of Representatives is presided over by the 'Speaker', who is elected by the House from among its members.

The judiciary

Interpretation and enforcement of the law is in the hands of the various courts, headed by the Court of Appeal and the High Court, with the right of final appeal to the Supreme Court. The constitutional independence of the courts from the other branches of government is reinforced by a tradition of non-political appointments and by the very strict protection of their tenure of office. High Court judges and Supreme Court judges, who are also appointed to the High Court, though appointed by the Governor-General, can be removed from their positions only by a resolution of the House of Representatives, for misbehaviour or incapacity. To prevent them from being financially dependent on pleasing the government of the day, the Constitution Act enshrines a constitutional ban on the reduction of their salaries (though, it may be noted, there is no such ban on increasing their salaries).

The Westminster system

The formal legal structure enshrined in constitutional law, particularly in the Constitution Act, gives a reasonably accurate account of one aspect of the constitution, the relation between the judiciary and the other branches. It rightly recognises the fundamental principle of the separation of powers as it applies to the independence of the judicial power from the others. But it seriously misrepresents, or at least obscures, the relations between the other branches, between the Crown, ministers and Parliament. It assumes a much greater role for the sovereign or the Governor-General than in fact that person plays. It makes no mention of the major decision-making body, the Cabinet, nor of the major individual political office, the prime ministership, both of which exist only by convention. Still less does it refer to the fact that the prime minister holds office by virtue of being the leader of a political party or that the Cabinet is drawn from the political party (or parties) which holds a majority of seats in the House of Representatives.

In all political systems, there is a difference between the structure of legal authority as described in formal constitutional law and the actual distribution of political power as determined by the interaction of the various political forces and groups which operate within the system. But this gap between formal structure and informal reality is particularly marked in the case of Westminster systems such as New Zealand's. The reason lies in the history of the British constitution and the fact that the Westminster system is the result of many centuries of historical evolution.

Originally, the main political authority lay with the Crown, the king or queen. To assist them in the conduct of government the monarchs appointed councils of advisers personally responsible to them, a 'Privy Council'. They also needed the support of other important sections of the population on whom they depended both militarily and financially. They would therefore formally consult from time to time with the assemblies representing these other sections, the two Houses of Parliament, the House of Lords, comprising the members of the titled aristocracy or peerage and the leaders of the Church, and the House of Commons, representing the common citizens. Until the reforms of voting rights in the nineteenth century, the 'commoners' represented by the House of Commons were themselves members of the economic and political elite, members of the male property-owning class who were not lords.

The early history of the English constitution (it did not become the 'British' constitution till the political union of England and Scotland in 1707) is a history of struggles to reduce and constrain the power of the Crown. In the thirteenth century, a series of charters, often known as Magna Carta, were agreements to limit the monarch's legal powers in important ways. They have often been seen as the foundation of the English citizen's liberty. In the seventeenth century, there was a period of prolonged constitutional upheaval in which Parliament successfully challenged the monarchs' right to hold absolute power and their claim to be answerable only to God and not to the people. A constitutional settlement was eventually reached, recognised in the Bill of Rights (1689), which decisively placed supreme sovereign power in the monarch and Parliament acting together, the so-called King (or Queen)-in-Parliament. Neither the executive power (the Crown) nor the legislative power (Parliament) could dominate and each checked the other. Many political theorists of the eighteenth century saw this separation and balance of powers as the secret of the relative stability and freedom provided by the British constitution at that time. When the United States became independent their leaders adopted the separation of powers for their new constitution, democratising the British system by turning the monarch into an elected president.

In Britain, however, the hereditary monarch was retained. The balance between Crown and Parliament faced growing pressure for still further popular accountability. In response, the British kept the traditional formal structure while, at the same time, steadily reducing the monarch's powers in relation to the elected branch of the legislature, the House of Commons (the 'lower' house). Certain key constitutional conventions were developed: members of the monarch's advisory body, the council, were to have the support of Parliament, particularly of the popularly elected house, the House of Commons, to which most of them belonged. They would meet on their own, without the monarch, as a cabinet of ministers and have a leader, a prime minister, who would act as the monarch's main adviser. The agencies of the state, though still formally identified with 'the Crown', became effectively under the control of the government of the day. The system of government became one of 'responsible' government, where members of the government, in the sense of the ministers who comprised the executive, were drawn from Parliament and were answerable or responsible to it, while maintaining the confidence of a majority in the elected lower house.

This gradual development of democratically accountable government took place within the structure of the constitutional settlement laid down at the end of the seventeenth century. Though the actual powers of the monarchy (and the House of Lords) were steadily reduced, their formal authority was preserved. The monarchy remained a potent source of historical legitimacy, providing a focus for loyalty to the constitution which transcended partisan political conflict. Those who wielded state power, for instance in the public service, the judiciary and the armed forces, swore allegiance to the person of the King or Queen rather than to the government of the day. Within Parliament itself, those who did not support the government of the day became known as His Majesty's, or Her Majesty's, loyal opposition, signifying that, though they opposed the current government, they supported the underlying system of responsible government and the basic principles of the constitution.

The monarchy's adjustment to increasing democratisation of the system of government helped the British to avoid further constitutional upheaval and revolution. But it meant the emergence of a growing gap between constitutional appearance and reality within the Westminster system. Distinctions needed to be drawn between the formal and the actual structure of power. Walter Bagehot, the perceptive and highly influential nineteenth-century English analyst of the British constitution, distinguished between the 'dignified' and the 'efficient' parts of the constitution (Bagehot, 1867 and 1963: Chapter 1). The monarchy had become largely a dignified or symbolic element of the constitution, while the prime minister and Cabinet were the efficient parts, the professional politicians who actually made the decisions.

This development, Bagehot pointed out in a deservedly famous and much-quoted passage, meant that in the Westminster system, the legislative and executive powers were not so much separated as fused.

> The efficient secret of the English constitution may be described as the close union, the nearly complete fusion, of the executive and legislative powers . . . . The connecting link is the *Cabinet* . . . a combining committee – a *hyphen* which joins, a *buckle* which fastens, the legislative part of the State to the executive part of the State. In its origins it belongs to one, in its function it belongs to the other. (Bagehot, 1963: 65–68)

One further development remained, the rise of organised and disciplined political parties. This occurred towards the end of the nineteenth century, in Britain and elsewhere, as a result of the extension of voting rights to cover all male (and subsequently all female) adults. Before that time Members of Parliament (MPs) were relatively flexible in their allegiances. Governments frequently changed between elections, as MPs shifted their support from one loose coalition of interests to another and from one individual leader to another. When voting rights were extended, organised political parties developed as a means of mobilising the greatly increased numbers of voters. Disciplined political parties met the growing democratic expectation that it should be the voters, not the individual MPs and their close associates, who should make the choice of which leading politicians should form a government. The system of electing the lower house used by the British and most other Westminster systems was the single-member simple-plurality system ('first-past-the-post') system (Chapter 5). When this system, originally designed for electing individual local representatives, was used for nationwide party contests, it had an important unintended consequence. Because each MP had to receive more votes than any other candidate in a given locality or electorate, candidates from minor parties had difficulty in securing enough votes to win any 'seats'. Thus nationwide support for minor parties tended to be under-represented in Parliament and support for major parties correspondingly over-represented. A single party could often gain a majority in the lower house without having the support of a majority of voters. In the twentieth century, the Westminster system thus came to imply not only responsible cabinet government but also, typically, responsible single-party government, i.e. cabinet government in the hands of the leading members of a single political party commanding a majority in the lower house. The lower house itself was typically dominated by adversarial competition between two major parties, one of whom would hold a majority and govern, while the other, acting as the Opposition, sought to replace it at the next election.

The Treaty of Waitangi and the imposition of British sovereignty

The fundamental principles of the Westminster system were introduced into New Zealand in the 1850s in response to the British settlers' demand for self-government. Direct British rule had been in place since 1840, when New Zealand was made a British colony and the British government had appointed a Governor to exercise the Crown's authority. The immediate purposes of the extension of British power to New Zealand were to control the activities of the growing number of British inhabitants, to provide law and order in the small but growing colonial settlements and to regulate the purchase of land from the Maori tribes.

The process of annexation followed well-established international procedures which had been developed by the European colonising powers as means of regulating the worldwide process of colonial conquest (Sorrenson, 1991). Acquiring control over new territory simply by the exercise of brute force or military power was no longer seen as legitimate. While unoccupied territory might be gained by the right of occupation or discovery, where there was a settled indigenous population, the formal consent of that population must be sought to the new rulers and their laws. Hence, the Treaty of Waitangi, by which the Maori chiefs and their tribes gave their allegiance to the sovereignty of the British Crown, was essential to the legitimacy of the new colony and its government.

The Treaty is a relatively brief document and follows precedents already set in similar colonial treaties elsewhere. What was unusual in the Treaty of Waitangi was that it was formulated in two languages, Maori as well as English. Moreover, these two versions differed significantly, the Maori version leaving substantially more power with the Maori iwi than the English version. The Treaty has three main clauses or 'articles'.

THE ARTICLES OF THE TREATY OF WAITANGI

The English Version

Article the First
The Chiefs of the Confederation of the United Tribes of New Zealand and the separate and independent chiefs who have not become members of the Confederation cede to Her Majesty the Queen of England absolutely and without reservation all the rights and powers of sovereignty which the said Confederation or Individual Chiefs respectively exercise or possess, or may be supposed to exercise or to possess, over their respective territories as the sole sovereigns thereof.

Article the Second
Her Majesty the Queen of England confirms and guarantees to the Chiefs and Tribes of New Zealand and to the respective families and individuals thereof the full exclusive and undisturbed possession of their lands and estates, forests, fisheries and other properties which they may collectively or individually possess so long as it is their wish and desire to retain the same in their possession; but the Chiefs of the United Tribes and the individual chiefs yield to Her Majesty the exclusive right of preemption over such lands as the proprietors thereof may be disposed to alienate at such prices as may be agreed upon between the respective proprietors and persons appointed by Her Majesty to treat with them in that behalf.

Article the Third
In consideration thereof Her Majesty the Queen of England extends to the Natives of New Zealand Her royal protection and imparts to them all the Rights and Privileges of British Subjects.

The Maori Version

(Translated by Kawharu (1990): Appendix)

The First

The Chiefs of the Confederation and all the chiefs who have not joined that Confederation give absolutely to the Queen of England forever the complete government (kawanatanga).

The Second

The Queen of England agreed to protect the chiefs, the subtribes and all the people of New Zealand in the unqualified exercise of their chieftainship (tino rangatiratanga) over their lands (whenua), villages (kainga) and all their treasures (taonga). But on the other hand the Chiefs of the Confederation and all the chiefs will sell land to the Queen at a price agreed to by the person owning it and by the person buying it (the latter being) appointed by the Queen as her purchase agent.

The Third

For this agreed arrangement therefore concerning the Government of the Queen, the Queen of England will protect all the ordinary people of New Zealand and will give them the same rights and duties of citizenship as the people of England.

Under the first article of the Treaty, in the English version, the Maori chiefs agreed to cede to the Crown (in the person of Queen Victoria) 'all the rights and powers of sovereignty . . . over their respective territories'. In return for this, the second article guaranteed to the chiefs and tribes (in the English version) 'full exclusive and undisturbed possession of their lands and estates, forests, fisheries, and other properties', while granting to the Crown the sole right to purchase land from the Maori. Article 3 accorded them the rights and privileges of British subjects.

For the Maori version of Article 1, the term 'sovereignty', which in English clearly implied the right of unlimited legal authority, was translated as kawanatanga (literally 'governorship'), a term of vague and doubtful meaning. The Maori version of the second article went further than the English version. It guaranteed the 'unqualified exercise of their chieftainship (tino rangatiratanga) over their lands (whenua), villages (kainga) and all their treasures (taonga)'. Thus, it not only confirmed Maori rights to land and other property but did so in terms which protected their chiefly power, that is, their political independence and autonomy.

The Maori version of the Treaty, then, cannot be said to involve the complete acceptance of British sovereignty in the sense of the imposition of British law and executive power over the whole of the country. Indeed, it is doubtful whether even many of the British authorities considered that the Treaty would inevitably lead to the full extension of British government over all the Maori tribes. The assumption in many people's minds at the time, both Maori and Pakeha, was that the country was divided into two areas or zones, a collection of coastal settlements occupied by British traders and settlers and a large hinterland still under Maori ownership and control (Belich, 1986: 302–3). The immediate purpose was to provide law and order for the British and to regulate dealings between the two peoples. On these terms, many Maori would have supported the Treaty. They welcomed contact with the foreigners, as a source of valuable new technology, but could see merit in some means of controlling the more lawless elements.

The balance of power, however, did not last. The rapid increase in the number of settlers and their demand for land meant that Maori tribal territories were greatly reduced. Tribes who resisted the extension of British authority were subjugated by force and their lands confiscated. A provision in the New Zealand Constitution Act 1852 that 'particular districts should be set apart within which [Maori] laws, customs, or usages should be observed' (Section 71) was never put into practice. By the 1870s, not much more than a generation after the signing of the Treaty, almost the whole of the country was effectively under the control of the new government based in Wellington. The Treaty remained a focus for Maori grievances and a century later, with the establishment of the Waitangi Tribunal, was to offer a means of helping to rectify the unjust situation in which the Maori found themselves (Chapter 7). But at the time, in spite of the guarantees enshrined in the Treaty, British sovereignty had in the end been imposed on the Maori by force.

For the British settlers, on the other hand, their allegiance to the government was simply an extension of their loyalty to the Crown as British subjects. As they journeyed to another part of the British Empire, they assumed, as a matter of course, that they would have the normal duties of British citizens and would accept the authority of British law. But the British also expected rights as well as duties. Direct rule by the Crown through a governor was a denial of the principle of responsible government, which was by now well established in

Britain itself. British settlers elsewhere, most notably in Canada, had campaigned successfully for the right to local self-government under the overall sovereignty of the Crown and Parliament. In New Zealand, these expectations and precedents were to lead quickly to the establishment not just of British law and order but also to representative government on the Westminster model.

The New Zealand Constitution Act 1852 established an elected House of Representatives and an appointed Legislative Council, as well as six provincial councils (subsequently abolished in 1876). Thus, at the national level, the executive power vested in the Governor was to be balanced not only by an appointed legislative council but also by a legislative assembly with responsibility for enacting laws on local matters and elected by male property holders (the basis for voting rights normal at that time). In 1856, the Governor agreed to appoint his advisers from among the elected representatives or councillors and to act on the advice of ministers supported by a majority in the elected lower house. The Westminster system of 'responsible' government had been established. Party government subsequently evolved, as elsewhere, with the extension of the voting franchise to all adults, male and female, in 1893. For most of the succeeding century, and continuously since the mid 1930s, executive power was in the hands of a single majority party. Moreover, the constitutional ascendancy of the parliamentary majority in the lower house was later confirmed in 1950 by the abolition of the Legislative Council, the government appointed 'upper house' or 'second chamber', equivalent to the British House of Lords.

Complete self-government, in the sense of complete independence from United Kingdom governments, was acquired gradually. To begin with, through the agency of the Governors and the troops under their command, the British government continued to have responsibility for military security. The settlers were happy for the British government to foot the bill for the military campaigns against recalcitrant Maori tribes. Even when New Zealand governments had taken over complete internal control within the country's boundaries, membership of the British Empire still implied following the lead of the British government in international affairs, as, most notably, in New Zealand's participation in the two world wars of the twentieth century. The role of Governor, after 1917 known as 'Governor-General', became steadily more formal and ceremonial. However, ties to Britain and allegiance to the British monarchy were reinforced by the convention of appointing titled British people to that office. After the end of the Second World War in 1945, the increase in New Zealand's political independence from Britain accelerated as Britain moved much closer to the European Economic Community (now European Union) and as the British market for agricultural produce ceased to be the central focus of the New Zealand economy.

Constitutionally, New Zealand became effectively independent in 1947, when it finally adopted the British Statute of Westminster 1931 and the United Kingdom Parliament abandoned the right to override the New Zealand Parliament. Important legal links still remained in the authority given to English judgments by New Zealand courts and the use of the Judicial Committee of the Privy Council as the ultimate court of appeal (Chapter 7: 170). The British connection has also been symbolically significant in the continued retention of the British monarch as formal Head of State, acting in her legal capacity as Queen of New Zealand (though the convention of appointing British Governors-General has lapsed, the position now going to distinguished New Zealanders). The New Zealand flag still includes the British Union Jack.

Departures from Westminster

The Westminster system delivers extensive powers to the government of the day. Cabinet ministers not only exercise the executive powers of the Crown but also until 1994, through the first-past-the-post electoral system, could usually count on the support of their own party majority in the lower house. Legislation passed by Parliament is not subject to significant judicial review of its content. In 'unitary', non-federal systems, such as the United Kingdom and New Zealand, central government also has legal control over other tiers of government, i.e. regional and local government. In New Zealand's case, the additional lack of a restraining upper house combined to make New Zealand governments arguably more powerful than governments in any other Westminster democracy. The New Zealand system was more Westminster than Westminster itself (Lijphart, 1984). The only major constitutional check on the government was the requirement that it must face an election in no more than three years' time. Hence the description 'elective dictatorship' (Mulgan, 1992).

Until recently, this system of government appeared quite acceptable to most New Zealanders. As in other Westminster systems, the lack of legal checks on government was balanced by deeply entrenched democratic values and conventions – the obligation on Cabinets to act within the limits set by electoral commitments and party principles; the practice of taking serious note of public opinion conveyed to the party's leaders through the party rank and file both inside and outside Parliament; the closeness of all MPs to their electorates and the opinions of their constituents; the expectation that ministers would consult widely with recognised interest groups (Mulgan, 1995). The Westminster system seemed to offer a unique combination of strong and decisive government backed by equally strong respect for public opinion and the rights of citizens. Its apparent superiority had received endorsement through the wartime success of the British democracies compared with those of continental Europe which had been weakened by multi-party parliaments and coalition governments and which, in many cases, had succumbed to dictatorships.

From the mid-1980s, however, public support for New Zealand's system of constitutionally unconstrained government ebbed dramatically, as both major parties in turn, first Labour and then National, imposed major structural reforms on the state and the economy in open defiance of accepted conventions of democratic consultation. By breaking election promises, ignoring party principles (at least in Labour's case) and ignoring opposition from interested groups, governments appeared to be using their extensive powers against the voters rather than on the voters' behalf. Popular confidence in politics and politicians, previously high by world standards, suffered a sharp decline (Vowles *et al.*, 1995: 131–5). Reform of the electoral system, placed on the public agenda by the report of the Royal Commission on the Electoral System (1986), ceased to be the hobby horse of an eccentric few and began to attract growing popular support. Public suspicion of the existing system was confirmed by the fact that its main defenders were the major party politicians themselves and the wealthy business leaders who had been enriched by their reforms. By the time the National government put the question of electoral reform to the voters, in a prior indicative referendum in 1992, followed by a binding referendum held in conjunction with the 1993 election, a majority of the New Zealand public were ready to put their faith in a radically different electoral system.

The new system, known as Mixed Member Proportional (MMP) and based on the system used in Germany, has removed one of the pillars of the Westminster system. By replacing the first-past-the-post electoral system with a proportional system combining electorate (constituency) seats and party lists (Chapter 5: 101), it eliminates the bias against smaller parties (provided that they can secure 5 per cent of the nationwide vote or win one electorate). It therefore opens the way for a more representative multi-party Parliament and greatly reduces the likelihood that any one party will have a parliamentary majority with which to ram through its government's programme. This has changed the balance of power between Cabinet and Parliament, an effect which was already visible during the transitional Parliament elected in 1993 (Chapter 4: 76; Chapter 5: 102).

New Zealanders had previously shown themselves ready to embrace constitutional innovation and to deviate from the British prototype, for instance in the abolition of the Legislative Council in 1950 and in the path-breaking introduction of the Scandinavian office of Ombudsman in 1962 (Chapter 6: 155). But the change to MMP represents a much more radical departure from the Westminster model. Admittedly, New Zealand governments will still exercise considerable power. Many of the elements of the previous constitution remain intact, for instance the executive powers of Cabinet, the legal supremacy of Parliament and the absence of an upper house. None the less, by introducing proportional representation, New Zealanders have imposed a new, and not altogether predictable, set of constraints on their governments.

The change to MMP also lent momentum to the possible severing of the residual constitutional connection with Britain. The continuing formal and symbolic links with Britain have appeared increasingly anomalous as the two countries move further apart and as different countries and regions become more important for New Zealand's economic and political future. In response to the public support for constitutional change revealed in the 1992 and 1993 referendums on electoral reform, the Prime Minister, Jim Bolger, raised the possibility that New Zealand might soon become a republic instead of a monarchy, with a president replacing the Queen and Governor-General. His government also replaced the traditional honours system of British imperial awards and introduced (but did not proceed with) legislation to end the right of final legal appeal to the Privy Council. These moves faced a mixed reception. In particular, many Maori leaders then as again in 2003 opposed the abolition of Privy Council appeals as potentially weakening their rights under the Treaty of Waitangi. Maori have seen their original compact with the Crown in the Treaty as a highly personal agreement with Queen Victoria and her agents. The custom of referring to the New Zealand government as 'the Crown' reinforces the connection. They still tend to look on the present Queen as in some way personally responsible for guaranteeing their Treaty rights, an impression which was confirmed in

1995 when the Queen herself personally gave the royal assent to the 'Crown's' apology to Waikato Maori for land confiscations in the nineteenth century (Chapter 7). (That the Queen, in assenting to the legislation, was acting solely in her capacity as sovereign of New Zealand and on the advice of her New Zealand ministers, without any formal connection with Britain or the British Crown, was a constitutional nicety which could easily be overlooked.) Though, in practice, the Queen has had no involvement in the decisions of the Judicial Committee of the Privy Council, many Maori see a strong symbolic connection between the two and are still deeply suspicious of the motives of New Zealand governments in seeking to break their ties with Britain.

At the same time, many Pakeha New Zealanders are uninterested in purely formal changes. One British trait which still remains strongly engrained is a reluctance to be literal-minded or overly logical about constitutional forms and traditions. They appear content, for historical and sentimental reasons, to keep certain public symbolic connections with Britain, for instance the monarchy itself and the New Zealand flag with its Union Jack, without taking them at all seriously as signs of dependence. This acceptance of the trappings of empire can be puzzling to people from other cultural traditions. Visitors and migrants from Asia, for instance, may mistake it for a sign of continued subservience to British interests and as compromising New Zealand's commitment to its immediate region.

Support for the republican cause might have been expected to grow as links with Britain continued to weaken and especially had Australia become a republic in the 1999 referendum. Yet there has been little change in public opinion since 1996, and fewer than one third of adults favour New Zealand becoming a republic (Cox & Miller, 2003: 55-59). There are considerable practical problems in the move to a republic, for instance in determining what powers presidents should have and how they should be selected (Stockley, 1996). These difficulties, combined with Maori hostility and Pakeha apathy or opposition, as articulated by the parties of the right, will tend to keep the issue of replacing the British monarchy off the immediate political agenda. In the meantime, under MMP, the substance of the New Zealand constitution, if not its outer form, can be expected to diverge even further from its Westminster archetype.

The legitimacy of party government

As should now be clear, the New Zealand constitution, like all Westminster systems, incorporates a number of constitutional myths or gaps between constitutional appearance and reality. For the most part, the myths are well understood by those who operate the political system and may be seen as sources of symbolic strength for the constitution rather than weakness. But on occasion, the myths can cause serious misunderstanding about the proper functioning of the political system and may therefore lead to mistaken criticism and to the advocacy of inappropriate constitutional reforms. One such myth, already referred to, is the role of the monarch as head of state and as therefore, in some sense, responsible for government policy, a view which has tended to divert some Maori leaders from more effective sources of political and legal redress. Two other mistaken analyses and diagnoses are also worthy of mention.

One concerns the respective roles of individual Members of Parliament and political parties. The formal structure of the constitution has obscured a significant feature in modern parliamentary democracy, namely the essential function played by political parties. Westminster parliamentary procedure treats each MP as an independent individual chosen to represent a particular electorate. It assumes that MPs will speak and vote according to their individual judgement. In fact, as everyone recognises, MPs have been elected as members of particular political parties and are expected to follow the collective opinion of their party colleagues. The party composition of Parliament, that is, the number of MPs belonging to each party, determines who forms the government, who is to be the prime minister and which members are eligible for ministerial office. It is the party organisations which select the candidates and it is the members of the parliamentary party, the caucus, who decide which line MPs will take in debate and how they will vote (Chapter 5: 108–110).

Political parties are a worldwide feature of parliamentary government and fulfil a valuable democratic function (Chapter 10). By grouping together political candidates with similar concerns and interests, parties provide the voter with a means of choosing between alternative political directions for the nation as a whole. They offer the various sections and interests of the plural society a useful channel for seeking to influence government policies in their favour. Parliament is essentially a forum for party political contest and cabinet government is essentially party government. Party discipline, which may be seen as a limitation on the MP's freedom of action, is, at the same time, a guarantee of the voter's choice. The party label gives the voter a say in the choice of government and policies. Party discipline is necessary to see that the party delivers its commitments.

In the Westminster tradition, disciplined political parties with large-scale national organisations are a relatively recent development. Parties were able to transform the constitutional reality of parliamentary government, while the constitutional form remained the same. Under the electoral system of single-member electorates, elections could still be formally treated as the selection of individual representatives of local communities when in practice they had become nationwide competitions between rival party governments. Just as responsible cabinet government had earlier developed within the shell of old constitutional forms which masked its presence, so too did party government.

The constitutional blindness to political parties shown by Westminster systems is in marked contrast to the constitutional practice of many other democracies where representative institutions developed much later, at a time when political parties were already taken for granted as legitimate democratic organisations. In most of continental Europe, for instance, there is much greater readiness openly to admit the existence of parties in constitutional law, as in the use of formal party lists in elections and, more generally, in the construction of electoral systems which will ensure fair results in terms of nationwide party support. New Zealand's new MMP system, which includes a vote directly for a party as well as for a local representative and requires parties to draw up national lists of candidates, is derived from this European tradition. It involves much more explicit recognition of the role of parties in elections than the previous system. Indeed, this was one of the major objections to the change. Many New Zealanders clearly had difficulty with parties selecting lists of candidates even though they happily accepted party selection of individual candidates under the Westminster first-past-the-post system.

Avoiding open reference to political parties, it may be argued, helped to protect the independence of Parliament and the status of individual MPs. But it has had a damaging effect. It suggests that there is something constitutionally illegitimate about political parties and party government and encourages nostalgia for a supposedly non-partisan Parliament of independent MPs. Those disillusioned with what they see as the arrogance and lack of accountability displayed by party governments may see the solution in allowing more freedom for individual MPs. However, though New Zealand has had a problem with excessive executive power and diminishing popular accountability

(Mulgan, 1992), the solution does not lie in returning to a Parliament of independent MPs with loose party ties. Public disillusion with Parliament stems from distrust of the previous major parties and their abandonment of principles and promises, not from parties as such. What is needed is not a weakening but a strengthening of the party system, to make it fairer and more responsive to the party rank and file and to the voters at large. MMP, it has been argued (Royal Commission on the Electoral System, 1986: Chapter 2), will help in this direction. At the same time, by removing the constitutional pretence that parties have no legitimate role in Parliament and parliamentary elections, MMP should help to remind New Zealanders that effective parties and effective party politics are an essential part of their political system.

The separation and fusion of powers

Another misleading constitutional myth concerns the role of the executive and the supposed separation of powers. As has been seen, the formal structure of the constitution treats the various powers of the constitution, the executive, the legislature and the judiciary, as separate and distinct. This may suggest that the appropriate critical standard to apply to the functioning of the constitution is the doctrine of the separation of powers. This doctrine holds that the different branches of government should be held by different people and that their respective constitutional capacities should be so arranged that no one branch can exert absolute power. The rationale behind the theory is that absolute power will lead to the abuse of power and that the constitution should therefore enshrine a system of checks and balances between the various sections of government. In New Zealand, the separation of powers has been particularly emphasised by Sir Geoffrey Palmer, who has asserted it as a major constitutional principle, 'a useful touchstone against which to find the location of powers in the New Zealand Government and judge the propriety of the arrangement' (Palmer, 1987: 5; see also Palmer, 1992: 106–8).

The doctrine of the separation of powers may work well for the role of the New Zealand judiciary in relation to other branches of government, but it mistakes the relation of executive and legislature and the 'efficient secret' of cabinet government. The constitutional reality, as Bagehot pointed out, is not so much a separation of powers as a fusion of powers, because executive and legislative power are linked through the government of the day, that is, through the cabinet of ministers. The Cabinet not only controls the executive branch of government, the various government departments and other state agencies. It also, to a large extent, determines the business of the legislative branch. The prime function of the elected House of Representatives is to legislate the government's programme.

More will be said in later chapters about the respective roles of Cabinet and Parliament (Chapters 4 and 5). But it should be noted that in the Westminster system it is quite legitimate for Parliament's agenda to be largely in the hands of the government and for the government to be able to count on majority support in Parliament for its legislative programme. This does not mean that Parliament should be totally subservient to the executive or should not jealously guard its rights to scrutinise and criticise the government of the day. Nor does it mean that checks and balances on executive power are unimportant. But under the Westminster system, constraints on executive power are not to be sought from an independent legislature. This solution may work for the United States and other constitutions where executive and legislature are intended to check each other's actions. In the Westminster system such checks and balances are better sought elsewhere. The courts have a role to play (Chapter 7). But much more important than legal remedies are political constraints, deriving from the government's need to face public scrutiny in Parliament and from the electoral process itself. Processes of political constraint and accountability, such as a vigorous party system and patterns of government consultation with interested parties, will often be more effective, not less, if governments can count on being able to steer their policies through Parliament.

The change to MMP reduced the likelihood of single-party majority government, and has led to a succession of minority governments (Electoral Commission, 2003: 185). In such cases, Parliament becomes more powerful in relation to the executive because governments need to negotiate with other parties to secure passage for their legislation. On the other hand, MMP is also likely to provide majority coalition governments where the parties of government between them command a parliamentary majority and inter-party negotiation takes place within the executive rather than between the executive and the legislature. The theory that the executive and legislative powers should ideally be separate and that government domination of Parliament is necessarily unsound points the critic in the wrong direction. The theory may remain enshrined in the formal structure of the constitution but it is long since outmoded as an account of constitutional reality or as a beacon for constitutional reform.

Conclusion

New Zealand's constitutional structure, as an offshoot of the British constitution, has had, and continues to have, great strength. By encouraging constitutional development without revolutionary formal change it has shown itself to be highly flexible and capable of being adapted to changing political circumstance without major disruption, not least in the reform of the electoral system which marks a radical break with the Westminster model. The historical continuity with a centuries-old tradition has provided a ready source of political legitimacy, including time-honoured forms and symbols, which the citizens have been able to recognise as helping them to accept the authority of the government of the day and its laws.

The legitimising effect of the tradition has been particularly strong for citizens of British origin, but the potency of the constitutional forms for other ethnic groups, particularly Maori, should not be minimised. The Maori people have been able to draw on the monarchy, and their original compact with Queen Victoria under the Treaty of Waitangi, to particularly good effect. These have helped them both in reasserting their rights and also in reaffirming their allegiance to the New Zealand Crown provided their claims are met.

Traditions and symbols of political legitimacy are essential to political stability. At the same time, the gap between constitutional form and political reality implied by the reliance on historical structures which evolved in another part of the world for a quite different set of political circumstances can bring disadvantages. It may prevent a realistic perception of the essence of the constitution and thus suggest criticisms of present practice and possible lines of reform which do not in fact meet current needs and expectations. In addition, the residual clinging to British forms and traditions may hinder New Zealanders' perceptions of themselves, and others' perceptions of them, as a genuinely independent nation.

Further reading

Constitutional law
Levine & Harris (1999): Part I; Joseph (1993); Keith (1992).

The sources of the constitution
Scott (1962): Chapter 1; Harris (1992); Sharp (2003).
Treaty of Waitangi
Brookfield (1989); Brookfield (1999); Orange (1987); Palmer &
Palmer (1997): Chapter 16; Sharp (1990): Chapters 13, 14;
Sorrenson (1991).
Elements of the constitution
Brookfield (1992); Cox & Miller (2003); Ladley (1997); Palmer &
Palmer (1997): Chapter 3; Wood (1986) *(Monarchy &
Governor-General);* Eaddy (1992): 162–3 *(executive council);*
McGee (1992) *(legislature);* Hodder (1992); Palmer & Palmer
(1997): Chapter 14; Stockley (2003) *(judiciary).*
Establishment of responsible government in New Zealand
Wood (1988): Chapter 1; Dalziel (1992).
Separation of powers and party government
Palmer (1987): Chapter 1; Palmer (1992): Chapters 5–6.

4

The Cabinet and Prime Minister

The central role of the Cabinet

This chapter begins a more detailed description of the New Zealand political system. The pluralist perspective of this study assumes that state and society are in a process of constant interaction and that both within the state and within the wider society there are many institutions, groups and interests which interact and influence each other. No part of the political system is totally independent from any other but all are interrelated. This assumption complicates the task of describing and analysing the system. To be intelligible, description and analysis must necessarily deal with the elements of the system one by one. But each element cannot be fully understood except in relation to all the others. There is therefore no obvious or logical starting point. The order of exposition in the following chapters begins with the main institutions of the state, namely Cabinet, Parliament, the public service, the judiciary and local government (Chapters 4–8), and then moves to the intermediary institutions which link the state with the rest of society, interest groups (Chapter 9), political parties (Chapter 10) and the media (Chapter 12). But the order could equally well have been reversed. Indeed, discussion of one key institutional process, elections (Chapter 11), is deferred until after the account of political parties.

An account of state institutions may naturally start with the Cabinet, a committee of ministers convened and chaired by the prime minister. Cabinet is the apex of New Zealand's system of responsible party government. Indeed, the 'government' is often identified with the Cabinet. The constitutional fusion of powers provides the Cabinet with authority over all the various agencies of government, authority which it may exercise either by direct executive decisions, recognised as binding throughout the public service, or through legislative enactment passed by the Parliament where it has majority support. Cabinet is the central decision-making body to which all major political issues are referred and from which all government policy emanates. It co-ordinates the activities of the various departments of the public service and determines the government's priorities, including the annual budget of proposed public revenue and expenditure which is the government's major statement of policy direction and which needs the final approval of Parliament.

Government departments are under the control of ministers of the Crown with formal authority to decide many matters in their areas of responsibility (their 'portfolios', Chapter 6). However, some of their decisions impinge on the responsibilities of other ministers and on the policies of the government as a whole and need the endorsement of their Cabinet colleagues. In political reality, ministers do not act independently but as members of a team under the leadership of the prime minister, who acts as coordinator and spokesperson of their collective effort. Individual ministerial discretion, in practice, is exercised only with the consent of Cabinet as a whole, consent which may be taken for granted on minor or uncontroversial questions but which otherwise should be explicitly sought.

The Cabinet consists of those ministers of the Crown designated as Cabinet ministers. It is possible to be a minister or member of the 'ministry' (and therefore a member of the largely formal Executive Council, Chapter 3: 53) but not be in the Cabinet (McLeay, 1995: 16–21). The practice of having ministers outside Cabinet, well established in a number of Westminster systems, including the United Kingdom, Canada and Australia, was not introduced to New Zealand until 1987. Before then, all ministers were in the Cabinet, though there were occasional under-secretaries, who performed a subsidiary role similar to that of ministers outside Cabinet, being members of the executive who were not in Cabinet.

If Cabinet is a logical starting point in terms of its pivotal decision-making role, the actual operations of Cabinet, it must be remembered, the political dynamics which determine what it does, can be appreciated only in the light of factors still to be discussed in subsequent chapters. Though Cabinet's authority is extensive, so too are the pressures under which this authority must be exercised. Cabinet decisions are made in a highly political context in which the ministers, both individually and collectively, are subject to influences from a wide variety of sources, from expert advisers within and outside the public service, from their party colleagues, from interest groups and from public opinion. To these influences must now be added the complexities of a multi-party Parliament under MMP and the need to negotiate with coalition partners. Indeed, the desire to force governments into greater consultation with political opponents and with the public generally was one of the main motives behind the move for electoral reform. During the 1980s and early 1990s, Cabinets, both National and Labour, had used their party majority in Parliament as a means of overriding public opinion. Cabinet had operated as a 'fortress' Cabinet (Chapman, 1989: 30–31), resolutely carrying through a programme of radical reform in defiance of those who might normally have expected to have their objections accommodated in a process of consultation and bargaining with the government. The change to MMP, by changing the party composition of Parliament and encouraging coalition government, requires Cabinets to engage in broader and more public discussion about public policy. Other initiatives, such as the Fiscal Responsibility Act 1994 (Boston *et al.*, 1996: 284–90), help to force Cabinets into a more open and 'transparent' approach to policy-making. The extensive constitutional powers of Cabinet remain, however. Though the political environment in which these powers are exercised has certainly been significantly altered, much will depend on the degree of unity between the coalition partners.

Selection of prime minister and Cabinet

In accordance with the constitutional conventions of 'responsible' government (Chapter 3: 52–53), the Governor-General appoints as prime minister a parliamentary leader who has the 'confidence' of a majority in Parliament. The prime minister then recommends the appointment of other ministers from among the members of Parliament. Under the previous electoral system,where a single political party normally held a parliamentary majority, this process was relatively straightforward. Whoever was the recognised leader of the majority party was appointed as prime minister. The remaining members of the ministry were selected from the senior members of the prime minister's party by methods agreed to by the party. With MMP, however, the chances that a single political party will secure a majority have been greatly reduced (Chapter 5: 102). Prime ministers and Cabinets therefore need the parliamentary support of more than one party. This can be achieved in a variety of ways. A single party without a majority may hold office as a 'minority' government, provided that one or more parties outside the government agree not to use their votes to force the government from office by helping to pass a vote of 'no confidence' or by refusing to vote 'supply' (the funds necessary for continuing the business of government) (Chapter 5: 109). Alternatively, two or more parties can combine into a 'coalition' government, in which each party contributes members to the Cabinet. Coalition governments can be either majority governments, where the coalition parties make up a majority in Parliament, or minority governments, governing with the consent of one or more parties outside the coalition. The 1993–6 Parliament, which marked a transition from first-past-the-post to MMP, experienced each of these options in turn, moving from a single party majority government, to a coalition majority government, to a coalition minority government, back to a coalition majority government and back again to a coalition minority government (Boston *et al.*, 1996a: 94–95). The National–New Zealand First government initially formed after the 1996 election was a coalition majority government. It has been followed by a succession of three minority coalitions (Table 4.1).

After an MMP election, it may not be immediately clear which particular option has majority support in Parliament. Much depends on the different strengths of the parties, on their varying degrees of willingness to work with each other and on their capacity to extract concessions, in both policy and government appointments, from potential partners. Negotiations between the parties can be complex and it may be several weeks (as in 1996) or only a matter of days (as in 1999) before the Governor-General, who needs to avoid any appearance of partisan involvement in the process, can appoint a prime minister and Cabinet. In the meantime, the previous government continues in a 'caretaker' role, carrying on the routine business of government but avoiding, as far as possible, any major or politically controversial decisions (Boston *et al.*, 1996a: 110–12; Boston, 2000: Chapter 21).

The prime minister is normally a party leader, a position he or she holds by virtue of the support of party colleagues. In a single-party government, the choice of a prime minister is therefore obvious. Where more than one party forms a coalition government, the prime ministership will usually be offered to the leader of the party in the coalition which has the largest number of members of Parliament, as has happened since 1996. However, the leader of the largest party may be politically unacceptable to potential coalition partners who may therefore insist on the appointment of the leader of a smaller party as a condition for their joining the government, a situation that has not yet arisen in New Zealand (Boston *et al.*, 1996a: 122–3).

The number of Cabinet ministers has previously been decided by the prime minister. The size of New Zealand Cabinets grew steadily through the first century of responsible government. The Seddon government of 1900 had seven ministers, the Savage government of 1935, thirteen, and the Holyoake government of 1960, fifteen. Since the 1970s, the size of Cabinets has normally been twenty at the beginning of the government's term of office, though sometimes dropping to nineteen or eighteen, through resignation or dismissal. Meanwhile the number of ministers outside Cabinet has grown to around six, with an additional one or two under-secretaries.

Table 4.1: Party governments since 1960

Election year	Party in power	Prime minister
1960	National	Keith Holyoake (1960–72)
1963		
1966		
1969		John Marshall (1972)
1972	Labour	Norman Kirk (1972–4)
		Wallace (Bill) Rowling (1974–5)
1975	National	Robert Muldoon (1975–84)
1978		
1981		
1984	Labour	David Lange (1984–9)
1987		Geoffrey Palmer (1989–90)
		Mike Moore (1990)
1990	National	Jim Bolger (1990–7)
1993	National and	
	Right-of-Centre (1995)*	
	National (1995–6)*	
	National and United (1996)*	
1996	National and	
	New Zealand First	Jenny Shipley (1997-9)
	National and	
	Independents (1998-9)*	
1999	Labour and Alliance*	Helen Clark (1999–)
2002	Labour and	
	Progressive Coalition*	

[* minority governments]

There have been periodic calls to reduce the size of Cabinet, perhaps by increasing the number of ministers or under-secretaries not in Cabinet and restricting the Cabinet to a smaller group of senior ministers. Twenty people, it is said, is too large a group for constructive discussion and deliberation. However, political considerations, such as the prime minister's need to reward supporters and to constrain potential dissidents, have been sufficient to override such suggestions. These pressures have increased with the enlargement of the Parliament to 120 members and with negotiations over coalition governments in which each party tries to maximise its number of Cabinet positions. But the somewhat unwieldy size of Cabinet does contribute to the tendency for much of its real work to be done elsewhere, for instance in Cabinet committees, and has facilitated the emergence of one coordinating committee, a 'policy' or 'strategy' committee, as what amounts to an 'inner' Cabinet.

In single-party governments, the method of choosing Cabinet ministers has depended on the methods adopted within the party (McLeay, 1995: Chapter 4). The position of deputy prime minister, the second-ranking cabinet minister after the prime minister, goes to the party's deputy leader. However, the two parties which have formed single-party governments, National and Labour, have differed over the selection of other Cabinet ministers. National has kept more closely to formal constitutional convention, leaving the power to appoint and dismiss ministers entirely with the leader. At the same time, the leader has been careful to consult with members of the party caucus, that is, the MPs elected as National Party members, sometimes asking them for written suggestions about the composition of the Cabinet. Then, with the assistance of the deputy prime minister and other close colleagues, the prime minister has selected the Cabinet, allocating portfolios and determining an official order of ranking or seniority which establishes the place taken by each minister at the Cabinet table, in the House of Representatives and at official functions.

Labour prime ministers, however, have been required to accept the decision of their caucus about which members of the parliamentary party are to be Cabinet ministers. But otherwise they have exercised the same powers as National prime ministers. They have decided the size of their Cabinets, they have allocated portfolios and seniority (again with the assistance of their deputies), and they have been free to select their own preferred appointees to executive posts outside Cabinet, i.e. as under-secretaries and ministers not in Cabinet. Labour prime ministers have also retained the right to dismiss up to three ministers (a limit which no leader is likely to wish to exceed) (Wood, 1988: 18).

In practice, though the difference in methods of selection may have given National leaders more personal power than their Labour counterparts in relation to party colleagues, the outcome, in terms of who is appointed to Cabinet, has been much the same in each party. The need for a politically effective government has required the selection as Cabinet ministers of members who are experienced, competent and representative of different political tendencies within the party. There has also been a need to represent different regions and to include a number of women ministers. There has been pressure to have at least one Maori as Minister of Maori Affairs (not always easy for National) or at least one farmer as Minister of Agriculture (not always easy for Labour) and a lawyer as Attorney-General (less of a difficulty in recent years since the great increase in lawyer MPs). These factors, combined with the restricted pool of talent and experience in a Parliament of less than a hundred members, have meant that the great majority of Cabinet members have virtually selected themselves, confining the room for manoeuvre to be exercised by a National leader or a Labour caucus to no more than two or three junior positions (Chapman, 1989: 19).

Significant differences in Cabinet selection have arisen under the new electoral system. A larger parliament has added to the number of those available for appointment as ministers. More important, the formation of coalition governments requires inter-party negotiation over the composition of Cabinet (Boston et al., 1996a: 123–5). In 1996 and 1999, as is usual in coalition governments, it was agreed that the leader of the smaller of the two parties in coalition should take the position of deputy prime minister. This practice was not followed in 2002, however, when Labour's coalition partner, the Progressive Coalition, having only two MPs, conceded the deputy's role to Labour. After the determination of the position of deputy prime minister, ministerial positions are allocated between the coalition parties, taking note of the comparative size of each party's parliamentary team. In 1996, New Zealand First secured five out of the twenty ministers in Cabinet and four out of the six ministers outside Cabinet, plus an agreement that, in two years' time (1 October 1998), their share would rise to a disproportionate eight Cabinet ministers and three ministers outside Cabinet. Owing to the collapse of the coalition, this increase never occurred. The agreement, however, reflected the initial bargaining power of New Zealand First in the coalition negotiations. The concession that appears to have determined New Zealand First's willingness to join National rather than Labour in a coalition was the creation for Winston Peters of a new ministerial position of Treasurer, senior to the existing position of Minister of Finance. In 1999 close proportionality between the incoming coalition parties was maintained. The Alliance with ten seats in Parliament to Labour's 49 received four of the 20 Cabinet positions, one of the five ministerial posts outside Cabinet and an under-secretaryship. In 2002, with the Alliance eliminated from Parliament, Labour's new coalition partner, the Progressive Coalition, received one Cabinet position.

Within the number of ministerial positions assigned to each party, the appointment (and dismissal) of individual ministers remains in the hands of the respective party leaders. The allocation of particular portfolios to ministers is decided by agreement between the two leaders. Thus the prime minister no longer has the sole right to reallocate portfolios and cannot dismiss ministers belonging to the deputy prime minister's party. The power of the prime minister may thus appear to be significantly reduced and the political dynamics of Cabinet correspondingly altered in ways yet to be discovered. Yet ultimately it is the prime minister who advises the Governor General on the issuing or withdrawal of ministerial warrants. In a political crisis the prime minister's powers remain considerable. In 1998, the National–New Zealand First coalition collapsed when the National prime minister, Jenny Shipley, was able to dismiss the deputy prime minister, Winston Peters, and invite his New Zealand First ministers to split from their party and retain their ministerial warrants. Four did so.

Cabinet meetings

The Cabinet meets weekly, normally on a Monday, beginning in mid-morning and usually continuing into the afternoon. The meetings are chaired by the prime minister or, in the prime minister's absence, the most senior minister, usually the deputy prime minister. Ministers outside Cabinet may occasionally be invited for the discussion of particular items with which they have been closely involved. Also in attendance are the Secretary and Deputy Secretary of the Cabinet, the officials in charge of the Cabinet Office, which is responsible for managing Cabinet business in terms of the policies and procedures set out in the *Cabinet Office Manual* (Cabinet Office, 1996; Harris & Levine, 1993: 265–95). Their role at Cabinet meetings is to formulate and record the Cabinet's decisions and advise on procedure, not to offer policy advice. In addition to the regular weekly meetings, prime ministers also on occasion hold special Cabinet meetings in order to consider a major issue to which the government needs to give particular attention.

The average weekly meeting has twenty to thirty items on the agenda, though the number of items and their political significance may vary widely. Before being referred to a full Cabinet meeting, most items will have already been thoroughly investigated and debated. Planning will usually start in a particular department of the public service, with officials preparing position papers which set out the issues and the various options. Most items will also have been before one of the Cabinet committees (see below). Politically sensitive issues will be referred at some point to the Cabinet's parliamentary supporters in the party caucuses (Chapter 5: 110–18). If the government is a minority government, it may also need to have consulted with those parties not represented in Cabinet on which the government depends for its parliamentary majority. Possible effects on wider government policy will have been investigated. All proposals with economic or financial implications must have a Treasury report included. The State Services Commission must be consulted on all matters impinging on public sector structure or employment policy. Other 'watchdog' ministries, such as Women's Affairs, Maori Development, Consumer Affairs and Environment, also have the right, through their minister, to comment on policy proposals before they go to Cabinet.

Given the careful preparation, many items go through without much discussion at the Cabinet meeting itself. Decisions are usually reached without a vote, often by the prime minister summing up the consensus, a process which allows the meeting to give more weight to the views of some ministers rather than others, depending on their competence on the issue and their general political standing. When decisions are made they are recorded by the Secretaries and then issued as authoritative Cabinet minutes. Where appropriate, they are referred for formal decision to the Executive Council, which meets every Monday afternoon and approves the necessary regulations and Orders-in-Council.

The Labour–Progressive Coalition Ministry
as at 15 August 2002*

THE CABINET
(Labour unless noted)

Rt. Hon. Helen Clark	Prime Minister; Minister in charge of Security Intelligence Service; Minister for Arts, Culture and Heritage.
Hon. Dr Michael Cullen	Deputy Prime Minister; Minister of Finance; Minister of Revenue
Hon. Jim Anderton (Progressive Coalition)	Minister for Economic Development; Minister for Industry and Regional Development; Minister Responsible for the Public Trust; Associate Minister of Health
Hon. Steve Maharey	Minister of Social Services and Employment; Minister of Broadcasting; Associate Minister of Education (Tertiary Education)
Hon. Phil Goff	Minister of Foreign Affairs and Trade; Minister of Justice
Hon. Annette King	Minister of Health; Minister of Food Safety
Hon. Jim Sutton	Minister of Agriculture; Minister of Forestry; Minister for Biosecurity; Minister for Trade Negotiations; Minister for Rural Affairs
Hon. Trevor Mallard	Minister of Education; Minister of State Services; Minister for Sport and Recreation; Minister for the America's Cup; Associate Minister of Finance; Minister Responsible for the Education Review Office, Adult and Community Education
Hon. Pete Hodgson	Minister of Energy; Minister of Fisheries; Minister of Research, Science and Technology; Minister for Crown Research Institutes; Associate Minister for Industry and Regional Development; Associate Minister of Foreign Affairs and Trade; Convenor Ministerial Group on Climate Change
Hon. Margaret Wilson	Attorney-General; Minister of Labour; Minister in Charge of Treaty of Waitangi Negotiations; Minister for Courts; Associate Minister of Justice
Hon. Parekura Horomia	Minister of Maori Affairs; Associate Minister of Social Services and Employment; Associate Minister of Education; Associate Minister of Fisheries; Associate Minister of Forestry
Hon. Lianne Dalziel	Minister of Commerce; Minister of Immigration;

	Minister for Senior Citizens; Associate Minister of Justice; Minister Responsible for the Law Commission; Associate Minister of Education (Special Education)
Hon. George Hawkins	Minister of Police; Minister of Internal Affairs; Minister of Civil Defence; Minister of Veterans' Affairs
Hon. Mark Burton	Minister of Defence; Minister for State Owned Enterprises; Minister of Tourism
Hon. Paul Swain	Minister of Transport; Minister for Information Technology; Minister of Communications; Associate Minister of Finance; Associate Minister of Revenue; Associate Minister for Economic Development; Minister for Small Business
Hon. Marion Hobbs	Minister for the Environment; Minister for Disarmament and Arms Control; Associate Minister of Foreign Affairs and Trade; Associate Minister for Biosecurity; Associate Minister of Education; Minister Responsible for the National Library; Minister Responsible for Archives New Zealand, Urban Affairs
Hon. Mark Gosche	Minister of Corrections; Minister of Housing; Minister of Pacific Island Affairs; Minister for Racing
Hon. Ruth Dyson	Minister for ACC; Minister of Women's Affairs; Minister for Disability Issues; Associate Minister of Social Services and Employment; Associate Minister of Health
Hon. John Tamihere	Minister of Youth Affairs; Minister of Statistics; Minister for Land Information; Associate Minister of Maori Affairs; Associate Minister of Commerce; Associate Minister for Small Business
Hon. Chris Carter	Minister of Conservation; Minister of Local Government; Minister for Ethnic Affairs

MINISTERS OUTSIDE CABINET

Hon. Judith Tizard	Minister of Consumer Affairs; Associate Minister for Arts, Culture and Heritage; Associate Minister of Transport; Associate Minister of Commerce, Auckland Issues
Hon. Tariana Turia	Minister for the Community and Voluntary Sector; Associate Minister of Maori Affairs;

	Associate Minister of Health; Associate Minister of Social Services and Employment; Associate Minister of Housing
Hon. Rick Barker	Minister of Customs; Minister of Justice; Associate Minister of Social Services and Employment
Hon. Dover Samuels	Minister of State; Associate Minister of Tourism; Associate Minister for Economic Development; Associate Minister for Industry and Regional Development
Hon. Damien O'Connor	Minister of State; Associate Minister of Agriculture; Associate Minister for Rural Affairs; Associate Minister of Racing; Associate Minister of Immigration; Associate Minister of Health
Hon. Harry Duynhoven	Minister of State; Associate Minister of Energy; Associate Minister of Transport

PARLIAMENTARY UNDER-SECRETARIES

| Taito Phillip Field | Parliamentary Under-Secretary to the Minister of Pacific Island Affairs, Minister of Justice, Minister of Social Services and Employment |
| Mita Ririnui | Parliamentary Under-Secretary to the Minister of Corrections, Minister of Conservation; Minister in Charge of Treaty of Waitangi Negotiations |

(* For most recent personnel and portfolios see parliamentary website:<www.parliament.govt.nz>)

Cabinet committees

It is at the committee stage that the details of difficult and contentious matters of Cabinet business are thrashed out (McLeay, 1995: Chapter 5). Committees have considerably fewer members than the full Cabinet and usually have fewer items to consider. Officials from the public service departments, though excluded from Cabinet itself, regularly attend Cabinet committees and can contribute to the discussion.

The structure and membership of Cabinet committees is determined by the same process as the allocation of portfolios – in a single-party government, by the prime minister in consultation with senior party colleagues and, in a coalition government, by negotiation between party leaders. In recent years there have been around twelve standing or permanent committees meeting regularly, usually fortnightly. One committee established by all recent governments is a Cabinet Legislation Committee, which organises the government's legislative timetable, determining priorities among the many proposals for new or amending legislation 'bills' put forward by different ministers. This committee also considers all government bills before they are introduced to the House of Representatives. Another regular Cabinet committee is a committee for Appointments and Honours which vets recommendations for major government appointments to statutory bodies as well as the twice-yearly list of honours.

Most of the committees cover broad sectors of government activity with the purpose of coordinating the efforts of different ministers and departments. The ways in which these sectors are defined varies from government to government. Thus the Lange Labour government established a Social Equity Committee, to look at the whole area of social policy, including education. The Bolger National government, however, included education first in an Education, Science and Technology Committee, and then in an Education, Training and Employment Committee, while having a separate Social Policy Committee. Both Clark governments have included a committee for External Affairs and Defence. In order to restrain the incessant demand for increased government expenditure, prime ministers have regularly established a special committee to review all government spending and help prepare the budget (an Expenditure Review Committee in the Palmer government, an Expenditure Revenue Control Committee in the Bolger government and a Government Expenditure and Administration Committee in the Clark governments).

Recent governments have also seen a need to provide better overall control of the government's policy strategy and have established Cabinet committees for this purpose, the Policy Committee under Labour and the Strategy Committee under National. These committees have emerged as the key committees for each Cabinet, in each case monitoring the government's overall economic and social strategy. Under the Lange Labour government, it was the ability of the three finance ministers, Roger Douglas and his associates David Caygill and Richard Prebble (the finance 'troika'), to win majority support in the Policy Committee which was critical to their ultimate success in Cabinet. Those ministers on the Policy Committee who may have had doubts about the finance ministers' proposals would be less able to challenge the committee's collective decisions when they were brought to the full Cabinet. Junior ministers with less important portfolios were unlikely to be in a position to overturn recommendations reached by their senior colleagues after lengthy discussion.

National's Strategy Committee, which included the twelve most senior members of the Cabinet, operated in a similarly powerful fashion, providing a forum in which the major economic and political issues could be discussed, where Treasury advice could be weighed against other political pressures facing the government, and the government's general direction determined. The Committee's influence was enhanced after 1993 when it began to coordinate the government's new strategic management planning process with its Strategic Result Areas (SRAs) and Key Result Areas (KRAs) (Chapter 6: 146). On occasion, such a committee has taken over a significant part of the main work of Cabinet itself, which is to act as the final decision-making body of government business. It has therefore functioned, to a certain extent, as an 'inner' Cabinet, a cabinet within the Cabinet. In a coalition Cabinet, there will also be a need for a high-level committee, consisting of senior members from each of the coalition parties, to work through partisan differences over policy which may arise between the parties (Boston *et al.*, 1996a: 127). The National–New Zealand First Coalition provided for a Coalition Disputes Committee to deal with 'fundamental disputes' between the parties. The Clark governments, however, have relied on an 'agree to disagree' provision in the coalition agreements.

In addition to the regular, standing committees, all governments from time to time set up ad hoc, special-purpose committees to deal with particular areas of current policy which need the degree of detailed examination and high level political commitment that only a Cabinet committee can provide. Thus, the Lange Labour government, when embarked on its restructuring of government departments into state-owned enterprises, set up a State-Owned Enterprises Committee under the chairmanship of the deputy prime minister, Geoffrey Palmer. Similarly the Bolger National government, to facilitate its programme of reform of social welfare, established a powerful Social Assistance Reform Committee under the chairmanship first of the prime minister and subsequently Bill Birch. After the 1993 referendum, an Implementation of Proportional Representation Committee oversaw the changes in the electoral system, and the Clark-led government established a committee to deal with the implementation of complex and, within Maoridom, politically fraught fisheries legislation. Other ad hoc committees may be more short-lived, to deal with an immediate crisis, such as floods, an electricity shortage or toxic infections in the shellfish industry.

The size and membership of committees varies with the degree of political importance of the committee's business and the number of ministers who have an interest in it. All Cabinet ministers are entitled to attend all committee meetings. Where appropriate, ministers outside Cabinet, though not normally entitled to attend Cabinet itself, are full members of Cabinet committees. The prime minister is ex officio (i.e. by virtue of the office) a member of all committees but attends only the most important ones.

The extent to which officials have been present at committee meetings has also varied. Until 1984, the norm was for officials from relevant departments to attend committee meetings with their ministers. They might be expected to leave the meeting when ministers wished to discuss what course of action to recommend to Cabinet but frequently remained throughout the discussion (Galvin, 1985: 78). The Lange Labour government, however, in order to lessen the influence of the permanent public service on policy-making, greatly reduced both the number of officials attending and the extent to which any officials were present during committee meetings. Labour ministers preferred to keep the officials in attendance outside the meeting, but would often invite them in if they were required to answer specific questions. After 1990, with the return of National, there was a move back towards greater involvement by officials in committee deliberations.

Collective responsibility

One of the important conventions of Cabinet government in all Westminster systems is that ministers exercise collective responsibility (this type of responsibility is to be distinguished from individual ministerial responsibility (Chapter 6: 152–8)). All ministers accept responsibility for the collective decisions which Cabinet makes. The main effect of this principle is that ministers must not publicly oppose any of its decisions. Any disagreements they may have with their colleagues – and such disagreements are inevitable and healthy in an effective government – must therefore be kept to themselves. For this reason, secrecy surrounds the proceedings and discussions which take place in meetings of Cabinet or its committees. Confidentiality guarantees that frank disagreements may occur without damaging the public unity of the government.

Though constitutional experts sometimes dispute the precise significance of the doctrine of collective responsibility (Scott, 1962: 113–8; Harris, 1992: 66; Joseph, 1993: 636–7), it is a relatively simple general principle grounded in commonsense and common experience. The presentation of an outer face of unity, it should be remembered, is not unique to Cabinets. It is a common feature of collective decision-making in many bodies and organisations – in boards of directors, juries, appointing committees and so on. Falling in behind a joint decision is a way of confirming that the final decision is now accepted as binding on all parties, whatever their original point of view. It also helps to maintain public confidence in the enterprise, whether it is a business or a public body. Governments, too, need to display unity in order to maintain public confidence in their administration. The media are always on the look-out for potential disputes between ministers and the public airing of such disagreements is usually seen as politically damaging to the government. New Zealand's recent experience with collective responsibility has been with single-party governments where there is a particular premium on unity because of the adverse effect of party disunity on a party's electoral prospects. Under a coalition government, more open disagreement is to be expected between the different coalition partners, particularly in the run-up to an election when individual parties will wish to stress their separate identities and policy preferences (Boston *et al.*, 1996a: 119, 131–2). Even so, as long as all parties in the coalition wish to continue in government they will be under strong pressure to present a united front to their political opponents. Similarly, the prime minister will have an interest in appearing to be in charge of the government as a whole.

The corollary of collective responsibility is that any minister who feels unable to defend his or her government's actions or who breaks ranks and publicly criticises these decisions should no longer remain in the Cabinet and may be dismissed. A classic case of a breach of collective responsibility leading to the departure of a minister from Cabinet was that of Derek Quigley in 1982 (Roberts, 1987: 51). Quigley was Minister of Works and Development in the Muldoon National government. He publicly criticised his government's 'Think Big' policy of supporting large-scale development projects, a policy which was an integral part of the economic policy supported by the prime minister and which had figured prominently in the election held only six months before. The prime minister took immediate offence and offered Quigley the option of either publicly apologising or resigning. Quigley chose to resign. The prime minister was quite within his rights to force a resignation in response to such a clear breach of collective responsibility on such a central issue of government policy. Similarly, in 1991, Jim

Bolger as prime minister was fully justified in dismissing Winston Peters, his Minister of Maori Affairs, who had been a persistent critic of his government's economic and social policy as well as being less than fully loyal to his own leadership.

But the lines which determine what degree of public criticism will provoke dismissal are by no means hard and fast and depend on the political calculations of the party leader and his or her advisers (McLeay, 1995: 198–203). Thus, in the years leading up to the Springbok tour of 1981, when the issue of sporting contacts with South Africa was politically very contentious, Robert Muldoon was quite happy to tolerate his Minister of Maori Affairs, Ben Couch, when he openly opposed government policy of discouraging sporting contacts with South Africa under the 'Gleneagles Agreement'. The prime minister himself had earlier been wholeheartedly in favour of Springbok tours and appeared to pay lip-service only to the policy of opposition. He was therefore not averse to one of his ministers giving comfort to the pro-tour forces.

Again, in dealing with Winston Peters, Jim Bolger tolerated a year of rebellious and damaging criticism from his Minister of Maori Affairs before moving to dismiss him. No doubt Bolger hesitated to move against Peters, fearing that he might come off second best in a public fight with his popular rival. Only when Bolger's own position had become more secure and his other ministers had become more pressing in their demands for disciplinary action against their outspoken colleague, did he move to dismiss Peters. Even then, in order to lessen the inflammatory reaction from Peters, the dismissal was included in a Cabinet reshuffle, as just one among a number of changes to the ministerial line-up. Throughout this drawn-out saga, the issue of whether to dismiss the minister was determined primarily by the prime minister's calculation of the political costs and benefits of so doing. Similarly, Bolger tolerated the outspoken comments of the maverick National minister John Banks, for instance when, in 1996, he publicly opposed on talk-back radio a Cabinet decision to continue culling of wild horses. The prime minister calculated, presumably, that Banks could create even more damage as a disgruntled former minister and potential political martyr than if he continued as an unruly and occasionally embarrassing member of the Cabinet (Chapter 6: 154).

Issues of Cabinet responsibility also arose during the Lange Labour government's second term as part of the clash between the prime minister and his Minister of Finance, Roger Douglas, over the government's overall policy direction (Chapman, 1992). In the months after Labour's return to power in August 1987, Douglas and his supporters had pressed ahead with their own agenda, culminating at the end of the year in the '17 December package', a set of proposed further reforms of economic and social policy including the sale of state assets and a flat rate of income tax. Though this collection of proposals had received Cabinet support, Lange publicly announced at a press conference a few weeks later that he had doubts about one of the key items, the flat-rate income tax, and was intending to defer it, thus effectively scuttling the proposal. This unilateral disavowal of a Cabinet decision was a clear breach of Cabinet collective responsibility. Prime ministers are bound to accept the final executive authority of the Cabinet over which they preside. It is this which distinguishes systems of cabinet government from systems of presidential government, such as the United States, where all executive decisions are taken in the name of the president and where Cabinet members serve simply as the president's advisers.

However, as the prime minister was the sole person with the right to dismiss a minister, the same sanctions did not apply to prime-ministerial breaches of the principle of collective responsibility. While the prime minister could dismiss any recalcitrant Cabinet colleague for breaches of collective responsibility, the other ministers could not dismiss the prime minister. Provided that Lange retained the support of the majority of caucus for his tenure of the party leadership, his position in Cabinet was impregnable. Throughout the year of 1988, the conflict between prime minister and Minister of Finance was carried on behind the defence of Cabinet collective confidentiality. Eventually, it was Douglas's close ally, Richard Prebble, and Douglas himself, not Lange, who were forced out of Cabinet, the former by outright dismissal, the latter by resignation. (The following year, however, Lange himself resigned, having been politically weakened when Douglas was re-elected to the Cabinet. Prebble was re-elected in 1990.)

These incidents show both the strength and the flexibility of the doctrine of collective responsibility in practice. In spite of all the competitive rivalries among them and the fierce arguments that inevitably go on around the Cabinet table and in Cabinet committees, most Cabinet ministers most of the time maintain their collective solidarity to the public. But their silence is as much a matter of political prudence as constitutional convention. All ministers have a stake in the public credibility of their government and in expressing loyalty to its leader, the prime minister, though occasionally they will also see some tactical advantage in airing their disagreements in public. When divisions do become public, it is the party leader, wielding the power of dismissal, who is the arbiter of where the limits of acceptable dissent are to be drawn. When deciding when to exercise this power, a leader will not be guided by constitutional lawyers or by precise precedents. Rather, the decision will depend on an assessment of the political consequences of dismissal in terms of the need to maintain secure and effective leadership and to enhance the electoral fortunes of his or her party. Under coalition governments, the level of open disagreement will increase, as the coalition parties seek to maintain their separate political identities and as ministers who do not belong to the prime minister's party have less to lose from undermining the prime minister's personal authority and can be dismissed only by their own leader, not by the prime minister. A certain degree of disunity in a coalition government will be accepted as legitimate by both politicians and the general public. But, again, the levels of tolerable disunity will be set by the political calculations of the various participants and will not be allowed to escalate beyond a certain point.

The prime minister's role

The position of the prime minister in relation to other ministers is summed up well in the common description 'first among equals'. The prime minister is bound to work through Cabinet and therefore to accept the collective authority of Cabinet colleagues, yet clearly occupies a position of superior authority and influence. As convener of the Cabinet and the more important Cabinet committees, the prime minister controls the Cabinet agenda, deciding what matters will be discussed and when. Being at the centre of the decision-making process gives the prime minister a general perspective over government policy which makes his or her views carry particular weight with other ministers. Besides informal influence, the prime minister has a number of constitutional powers which can be used to bring pressure to bear on ministerial colleagues. One such power that may become of greater importance under MMP is the right to advise the Governor-General to call a general election. New Zealand Parliaments have usually gone the full three-year term (Chapter 5: 102), though Robert Muldoon surprised his colleagues by calling a 'snap' election five months early in 1984. In 2002, Helen Clark, faced with a split in the government's junior coalition partner, the Alliance, and a deteriorating relationship with the government's support party, the Greens, called an election about four months early. In a minority or coalition government, the prime minister's right to call an election will be a major bargaining weapon for keeping other parties in line if those parties have reason to fear the expense of an election or the risk of electoral defeat. The Governor-General, however, before agreeing to an early election, may wish to be assured that no other party leader can form an alternative government with majority support in Parliament (Boston *et al.*, 1996a: 107–10).

Another power, already described, is the power of selection and dismissal, the right of deciding (formally the right of recommending to the Governor-General) who is to be a minister and who should be dismissed from office, as well as which portfolios each minister should hold. The effectiveness of this power varies according to party rules, whether the party leader, when prime minister, is allowed a free hand in appointing ministers, as in the National party, or must accept some direction from the party caucus, as in the Labour party. It will also vary according to whether the government is formed from a single party or from a coalition. In single-party governments, both Labour and National, prime ministers have wielded considerable powers of patronage over their party colleagues through their right to appoint ministers not in Cabinet as well as under-secretaries. As these positions are naturally seen as next in line for full Cabinet membership, in both Labour and National, it has been the prime minister who has often decided which of their parliamentary colleagues will take the first step on the ministerial ladder. At Cabinet level, the issue, in most cases, has been not so much whether a particular colleague is to be included, often a foregone conclusion, but which portfolio he or she will hold. It is in the allocation of portfolios and in the Cabinet ranking, that prime ministers in both parties presiding over single-party governments have had an opportunity to define the direction of the government, to reward supporters, to disappoint opponents and frustrate potential rivals.

In a coalition government, however, the prime minister's powers of patronage are more circumscribed. The prime minister has no control over ministerial appointments from other parties. Matters of portfolio allocations need to be negotiated with the leaders of other parties belonging to the coalition. Conversely, Cabinet ministers, particularly those who are not from the prime minister's party, will have fewer reasons to avoid incurring the prime minister's displeasure. This, in turn, will reduce the prime minister's leverage over Cabinet colleagues.

Even in single-party governments, there may be limits to the prime minister's freedom of movement in allocating portfolios. For instance, after the 1987 election, David Lange tried to weaken the power of Douglas and his market liberal supporters by breaking up the previous finance 'troika' of Douglas, Prebble and Caygill and bringing in a more left-wing minister, Michael Cullen, as Associate Minister of Finance and Minister of Social Welfare. Caygill, the most pliant of the troika, was moved to Health, to replace the hardline Michael Bassett, and Lange himself took over Education. In this way the prime minister was attempting to guarantee that the social reforms, promised for Labour's second term, would be more in line with traditional Labour values than with market liberal principles.

But the strategy was only partially successful. The key appointment was of Douglas himself as Minister of Finance and here Lange was politically powerless to make a change. Support for Douglas's economic strategy had been one of the components of Labour's successful electoral campaign and had brought in pledges of substantial financial contributions (Chapter 10: 255). Dismissal of Douglas would have jeopardised this support.

Similar pressures were on Jim Bolger both when appointing and reshuffling his Cabinet. During the first three years of his government, the confidence of the financial markets in the government's economic strategy was perceived to be closely linked to the appointment of Ruth Richardson as Minister of Finance. Though Richardson might be unpopular with the public at large and the object of criticism within the government caucus, Bolger was clearly reluctant to risk the possible financial repercussions which her dismissal would have caused. At the same time, however, he was able to use other appointments, such as the appointment of Bill Birch to the politically critical portfolios of first Labour and then Health, as a means of responding to caucus expectations and of strengthening his own position within the government. Richardson's position was again at issue after the 1993 election. Bolger signalled his intention of moving National back from an uncompromising market liberal position by removing her from the Finance portfolio and appointing Birch in her place.

In addition to presiding over the general business of their governments and being in charge of the Security Intelligence Service (SIS), which traditionally reports directly to the prime minister, New Zealand prime ministers, until recently, also took on one of the major portfolios. Keith Holyoake was Minister of External Affairs, as were his Labour successors, Norman Kirk and Bill Rowling. However, Robert Muldoon, on becoming prime minister, took Finance, a portfolio which he had held while serving other leaders in previous National governments. Given the strategic position of the Minister of Finance in the formation of a government's economic policy and as supervisor of expenditure by all departments and ministers, this combination of offices was considered by many to constitute a dangerous concentration of power (Palmer, 1987: 67).

The next prime minister, David Lange, reverted to the position of Minister of Foreign Affairs for his first three years, switching to Education after the 1987 election. However, if the combination of prime minister and Minister of Finance had constituted a possible over-concentration of power, the separation of the two in the Lange government, with the determined and skilful Douglas in the Finance portfolio and the prime minister often distracted by other business, produced a dangerous division of power, leading to serious political disunity.

In reaction to the confusion and disarray of the last year of the Lange/Douglas partnership, Lange's successor, Geoffrey Palmer, concentrated on managing and coordinating overall government policy, though he kept responsibility for Environment. The trend was taken further by Jim Bolger who took no portfolio other than the relatively undemanding position of minister in charge of the Security Intelligence Service. Ably assisted by his loyal lieutenant, Bill Birch, Bolger was able to use his control of Cabinet and particularly key Cabinet committees to coordinate economic and other policy. To begin with, the government's agenda appeared driven, as Labour's had been, by the Minister of Finance (Ruth Richardson), and her Treasury advisers. However, after the political unrest caused by Richardson's first budget, her influence was greatly diminished. The assumption that the Minister of Finance would inevitably call the shots, an assumption that seemed to have held good since the first days of the Muldoon government, no longer applied. The prime minister's influence over Treasury was consolidated after the 1993 election by the appointment of Birch as Minister of Finance. The National–New Zealand First coalition government provided yet another variation to the relationship between prime minister and Minister of Finance. While Birch retained the Finance portfolio, the new position of Treasurer, senior to the Minister of Finance, which was created for the New Zealand First leader and deputy prime minister, Winston Peters, offered the potential for continuing conflict over economic policy between two party leaders vying for popular support. However, the replacement of Bolger by Jenny Shipley as National leader and prime minister intervened. A year later Peters was dismissed and the coalition collapsed. Shipley, the first woman prime minister, also took the additional role of Minister of Women's Affairs. In subsequent Labour-led coalitions, Labour has kept a firm grip on the finance portfolios, and Helen Clark has assumed responsibility for the Arts, Culture and Heritage portfolio.

The prime minister's advisers

In order to act as an effective coordinator of Cabinet business and government policy, the prime minister needs an independent source of informed expert advice. For many years a persistent complaint was that prime ministers did not have access to sufficiently full and informed advice to counter that provided for other ministers by their departments. In particular, prime ministers did not have the analytical resources to contest the advice and recommendations emanating from the Treasury, which had a large number of specialist policy analysts on its staff. Treasury used its power to comment generally on the financial aspects of government policy in all departments as a justification for advising on the merits of policy across the whole range of government activity. Particularly under the Fourth Labour government during Roger Douglas's tenure as Minister of Finance, Treasury appeared to adopt the role of the general coordinating agency for government policy and thus helped the Minister of Finance to usurp the general supervisory and strategic role which should properly belong to the prime minister (Boston & Cooper, 1989; Boston, 1989).

In the mid 1970s a small group of advisers, mainly drawn from the public service, was established in the Prime Minister's Department. This group was used effectively by Muldoon as his 'eyes and ears' in the public service and in the community. Under Labour there were various reorganisations of the prime minister's support services, culminating in Geoffrey Palmer's establishment of a Department of the Prime Minister and Cabinet (1989) (McLeay, 1995: 155–9). This incorporated the Cabinet Office, which provides secretarial and administrative support to Cabinet and its committees, and included a significantly expanded group of policy analysts and advisers reporting directly to the prime minister. The Department of Prime Minister and Cabinet is a normal public service department under a chief executive appointed under similar terms to those of other heads of government departments. It is distinct from the Prime Minister's Office, which contains the prime minister's personal staff, political advisers and media staff (Eaddy, 1992: 170–2). The size and importance of the Department of Prime Minister and Cabinet were significantly increased by Jim Bolger and retained by his National and Labour successors (Henderson, 2003: 112). The result has been to greatly strengthen the bureaucratic assistance directly available to the prime minister and to reassert the power of the prime minister in relation to Treasury and the Minister of Finance.

The prime minister and the public

How effectively prime ministers are able to use their constitutional powers of appointing and dismissing ministers, allocating portfolios, organising the committee structure and generally administering the business of Cabinet depends partly on their political standing with the public at large. Above all, the prime minister is a party leader, the public spokesperson not only of the government but also of the party and the guardian of the party's electoral chances. Party governments are strongly identified with party leaders who carry a large share of the parties' electioneering. Election campaigns focus very heavily on the party leaders and a party's relative success or failure will depend critically on the performance of its leader in relation to the leaders of opposing parties.

Once politicians become their party's leader and a potential or actual prime minister, they become public celebrities. While previously they will have been seen regularly on television and their views will have been widely reported in all the media, public interest will have been confined to their political actions and opinions. Once they become the leader, however, media interest expands to cover the whole person, their family background, their friends, their hobbies, where they spend their holidays, and so on. Their partners suddenly become newsworthy and are expected to be seen in public attendance, particularly during election campaigns. When the election is over and a prime minister is established in office, the electoral contest continues in anticipation of the next election. The prime minister's performance in the media, especially television, is under scrutiny both by political insiders and by members of the public at large. Public opinion polls, which measure the popular standing of both the government and the leader, are closely watched, by the prime minister's supporters and opponents alike. The rough and tumble of parliamentary debate provides an opportunity for colleagues and the press gallery to assess the quality of the prime minister's performance in comparison with that of parliamentary opponents and rivals (Chapter 5: 118).

The prime minister's performance in these public arenas, the extent to which it is seen as an electoral strength or a liability, is critical to his or her standing within the Cabinet. After all, the leader serves only with the consent of the party caucus. An unpopular leader presiding over an unpopular government will start losing the confidence of party colleagues fearful about their seats at the next election. Both Muldoon and Lange faced strong, if ultimately unsuccessful, challenges to their leadership from their caucuses. Palmer was ruthlessly dumped by his Labour colleagues only weeks before the 1990 election and Bolger was removed after his and the National Party's opinion poll ratings slumped dangerously. Under MMP, where the prime minister's party does not normally hold a parliamentary majority, the prime minister must also retain the confidence of the members of other parties who are either coalition partners or, in the case of minority government, support the government in Parliament. The extent of this confidence, in turn, will depend very largely on the parties' perceptions of the popularity of the prime minister's leadership and the electoral advantages to be gained from supporting it.

The relative popularity of prime ministers affects the extent to which they can effectively exercise their prime ministerial powers. The two personally most powerful prime ministers in recent times, Muldoon and Clark, were able to dominate their immediate colleagues because they were seen as indispensable electoral winners. Other leaders, such as Palmer and Bolger in his early years, often appeared ill at ease and less than fully competent. The public perception of failure, whether justified or not, was translated into internal weakness and affected their capacity to stand up to Cabinet and caucus colleagues. However, Bolger's success after the 1993 election in managing the transition from first-past-the-post to MMP and in steering the National party through a series of coalition and minority governments, enhanced his electoral popularity and therefore strengthened his position in relation to government colleagues, an asset however that rapidly eroded during the unpopular coalition with New Zealand First.

These factors underline the importance of the political context in the analysis of constitutional relationships. The formal powers of Cabinet and prime minister may be defined by constitutional convention or in the *Cabinet Office Manual*. How these powers are exercised, however, depends on informal political factors, on the performance and interplay of individual personalities, and on the relative weight and effectiveness of pressures exerted by the multiplicity of interests which have a stake in Cabinet decisions. These pressures may be relayed directly to Cabinet by normal sources of political communication, such as party caucuses and Parliament, the public service, or interest group consultation.

Alternatively, their effect may be made more indirectly through the 'anticipated reactions' (Chapter 1: 15), or the unconscious impact of ministers' own political assumptions and values. Generalisations may be made but they must always be treated with caution. Each prime minister has a unique style and each Cabinet its unique political dynamic which in turn varies according to the issues involved and the political standing of leader and government.

Further reading

Cabinet in general
Cabinet Office (1996); (2001); Eaddy (1992); Harris & Levine (1992): Part V; McLeay (1995); (2003); Palmer (1987): Chapter 3; Palmer & Palmer (1997): 60–67; Wood (1988): Chapter 2.
Collective responsibility
McLeay (1995; 2003: 90-92): Chapter 9; Palmer & Palmer (1997): 68-71; Roberts (1987): 50–52.
Prime minister
Alley (1992); Henderson (2003): Chapter 2.6; Palmer (1987): Chapter 4; Palmer & Palmer (1997): 52–57.
Effects of MMP
Boston (2003); Boston *et al.* (1996a): Chapters 6–7; Harris & McLeay (1993); Palmer & Palmer (1997): 11–20.

Parliamentary website: <www.parliament.govt.nz>

5

Parliament

The size and structure of Parliament

In New Zealand's system of responsible party government, Parliament – strictly speaking, the House of Representatives – is the key institution of democratic accountability. Parliament is the only institution of the central state (i.e. excluding local government) whose members are directly chosen by the people. It is the only forum in which the members of the political executive are regularly obliged to answer for their actions. The fact that the prime minister and other ministers are drawn from this elected Parliament and must have the support of a majority of its members ensures that governments are chosen by their citizens and are ultimately responsible to them.

The size of Parliament and the method of its selection are set out in the Electoral Act. Up till 1993, Members of Parliament (MPs) were chosen under a single-member simple-plurality system (commonly known as 'first-past-the-post'), the standard method of election in Westminster systems (Chapter 3: 58). Each MP who won a 'seat' in Parliament was the single representative of a territorial unit, usually called an 'electorate' or 'constituency', being the candidate who won a plurality of votes in that electorate, i.e. more votes than any other single candidate, though not necessarily a majority. Because each MP had to be the most popular candidate in his or her electorate, the system was biased against minor political parties which might have significant support nationwide but whose supporters were too geographically dispersed to win their fair share of seats.

Voters could opt to vote on either the Maori roll or the 'general' roll. The number of MPs was determined by the Representation Commission, an independent statutory body, which redrew constituency boundaries after each five-yearly census. Four parliamentary seats were reserved for members elected by voters on the Maori roll. The number of general seats was fixed at twenty-five for the South Island, with the number for the North Island being adjusted in proportion so that each constituency had roughly the same size of population. Because the population of the North Island has grown faster than that of the South Island, this arrangement, first introduced in 1965, had the effect of producing a gradual increase in the size of the House. The number of MPs increased from eighty, the number at which it had been fixed in 1900, to ninety-nine in 1993. The new MMP (Mixed-Member-Proportional) system was introduced as a result of a nationwide poll or 'referendum' held in conjunction with the 1993 election. In the previous year, voters had been asked whether they supported a change in the electoral system (85 per cent of a 55 per cent turnout of voters opted for change) and, if there were to be a change, which of various alternative systems they preferred (70 per cent opted for MMP). As a result, the 1993 referendum offered a choice between the existing system and the most preferred alternative, MMP, with 54 per cent of a turnout of 85 per cent supporting MMP (Boston *et al.*, 1996a: 20–23; Vowles and Aimer, 1994; Jackson and McRobie, 1998: 232–66). MMP was used for the first time in the 1996 election.

MMP is based on the unique German system which was imposed by the victorious American and British allies on the defeated West Germans after the Second World War and was intended to temper the previous German system of proportional party lists with elements taken from the Anglo-American first-past-the-post system. MMP is a 'proportional' system of election because it aims to produce a Parliament in which the number of MPs for each political party is roughly proportional to the number of voters each party attracts nationwide. Each voter has a party vote which is used to determine the party composition of Parliament which has been increased in size to 120 seats. Seats are allocated proportionately to each party that wins at least 5 per cent of the total vote or at least one of the electorates (see below). (The purpose of this 'threshold' restriction is to prevent the representation of very small single-issue or extremist parties which could have a destabilising effect on Parliament and government.)

In addition to the party vote, each voter also has, as before, a vote in a single-member electorate, helping to choose a local representative in Parliament. Voters are still divided between a general and a Maori roll, inclusion on the Maori roll being decided as a preliminary to the regular redrawing of electoral boundaries which follows the five-yearly census of population. As part of the 'Maori option', voters are asked whether they are of Maori descent and, if so, whether they wish to be included on the Maori roll.

The number of electorate seats is determined by providing sixteen seats for South Islanders on the general roll (instead of 25 as previously) and adjusting the number of North Island general seats accordingly. The number of Maori seats is no longer fixed at four but also varies according to the number of Maori who opt for the Maori roll, the average electoral population for each Maori seat being set to approximate that of the general seats. For the first MMP election in 1996, there were 44 North Island general seats and five Maori seats making a total of 65 electorate seats overall. By 2002 the total electorate seats had risen to 69, including 46 North Island general seats and seven Maori seats. The boundaries for each electorate are drawn up by the Representation Commission, an independent statutory body. In determining boundaries, the Commission is allowed to vary the population of individual electorates by up to 5 per cent more or less than the South Island average, and is required to consider such factors as community of local interests and topographical factors (such as mountain ranges and rivers).

The electorate seats make up just over half the Parliament. The remaining seats are allocated to candidates on 'party lists', lists of candidates drawn up by the parties in order of preference. Parties win sufficient list seats necessary to bring their total number of seats, including electorate seats, up to the number determined by the party vote. In the 1996 election the National party attracted 33.8 per cent of the party vote, which entitled it to 44 seats. As it won 30 electorate seats, it was awarded an additional 14 seats from its list. The Alliance, attracting 10.1 per cent of the party vote was entitled to 13 seats. Having won only one electorate seat, it gained 12 list seats. United attracted only 0.9 per cent of the party vote but won one electorate seat. The basic principle is that the total number of seats won is determined by the party vote and is not normally affected by the outcome of the electorate vote. The electorate vote thus becomes a choice of an individual local representative divorced from the nationwide competition between the parties. There are minor exceptions to this principle: a party that wins an electorate seat without attaining the 5 per cent threshold in the party vote holds that seat (e.g. United in 1996); a party that wins an electorate seat without attaining the 5 per cent threshold in the party vote is entitled to a share of list seats (not applicable in 1996); a party that wins more electorate seats than its party vote would entitle it to, holds the extra seat or seats and Parliament is temporarily enlarged above 120 (not applicable in 1996) (Electoral Commission, 1996: 20–22).

The new system leaves the timing of elections unchanged. An election must be called within three years of the previous election, or, more precisely, within three years of the return of 'the writs' or official results of the previous election. This additional time allowed the dates of elections after the 'snap' election of 14 July 1984 to be at successively later dates, 15 August 1987 and 27 October 1990, thus returning in 1993 to a date in November, the month in which elections have normally been held. A three-year maximum period between elections, i.e. a three-year 'term of parliament', is relatively short by international standards. No western parliamentary democracy has a shorter term and most have a longer one. Calls are regularly made for lengthening New Zealand's term, mainly on the ground that a longer term would allow governments more time for their policies to show results and would therefore lead to more effective, less short-term government decision-making. The question of extending the term of Parliament from three to four years has twice (1967, 1990) been the subject of a constitutional referendum (Chapter 3: 52) and was rejected each time (in 1967 by a 68 per cent majority of those voting and in 1990 by a 66 per cent majority of those voting). Most voters are reluctant to give their governments more leeway or to reduce the attention that governments give to considerations of electoral popularity.

The main effect of the new MMP electoral system is to remove the bias in favour of major parties which existed under the first-past-the-post system. Minor parties, provided they can attract 5 per cent of the total vote, can expect to receive fair representation in Parliament, even if they win few or no electorate seats. The likelihood that any one party will have a majority is greatly diminished. Parliament has changed from being essentially a two-party chamber where a ruling majority party faces a large opposition party which is aiming to replace the governing party at the next election. Instead, there are several parties, some belonging to the government of the day, others distancing themselves from it to a greater or lesser extent (Boston *et al.*, 1996a: Chapter 4). Indeed, this change from a two-party to a multi-party Parliament began soon after the 1993 election. The National government held a very small majority which it subsequently lost through defections and was forced to seek the support of new minor parties (Boston *et al.*, 1996a, 94–5). The other major party, Labour, was made to share the role of opposition to the government with two minor parties, the Alliance and New Zealand First. These parties, though holding only a handful of seats between them, had prospects of much greater influence in the next, MMP-elected Parliament.

Another important effect of the new electoral system on Parliament is the introduction of two classes of MP, electorate MPs and list MPs, whereas formerly all MPs represented an electorate. Many electors are still reluctant to accord the list MPs the same status as the directly elected local MPs. It remains to be seen whether the rise to leadership of Don Brash (National), the first list MP to lead a major party, helps to raise public acceptance of the legitimacy of list MPs. In addition, the substantial increase in the number of MPs, from 99 to 120, has the potential to enhance Parliament's capacity to perform its various functions. (It is worth remembering, however, that the New Zealand Parliament is still relatively small by comparison with other similarly sized OECD democracies (Ireland has 166, Norway 165, Finland 200 and Denmark 179).)

The functions of Parliament

In response to the prospect of electoral reform, Parliament conducted a thorough review of its procedures during 1994 and 1995, culminating in a major revision of its Standing Orders. These changes not only accommodate the challenges of a larger, multi-party Parliament but also respond to a number of long-standing criticisms of Parliament's performance (Boston *et al.*, 1996a: 71–86). The role which Parliament plays, or ought to play, in the political system is a matter of dispute. However, its constitutional functions, the business it conducts and the legal procedures it follows, are relatively straightforward and uncontroversial. Parliament has a number of constitutional functions (Harris, 1992: 62): it has a legislative function, being the institution which enacts legislation by statute, subject to the formal consent of the Governor-General; as part of this legislative function, it also it has an important financial function, because its legislative agreement is necessary for the raising of government funds from members of the public by way of taxation and for the authorisation of expenditure of such funds; it provides from its ranks the leading members of the executive, the ministers of the Crown, supporting their collective right to govern, if necessary through a positive vote of confidence, and requiring them to answer for their conduct in public; it receives petitions from members of the public and is a forum for the airing of citizens' grievances against the actions of the state.

These functions are carried out both by Parliament meeting in full session, with one of its members, the 'Speaker', acting as an impartial chairperson, and also by small groups of MPs acting in 'select committees', under authority delegated from Parliament as a whole. In exercising these functions, MPs are granted certain traditional rights or 'privileges' (Scott, 1962: 61–66), including the right to speak freely without being subject to the normal laws of defamation. The Parliamentary chamber is arranged in a horseshoe, with government MPs and their main opponents facing each other and MPs from other parties occupying the desks in between (see plan, p.119). Senior members of each party sit at the front (on the 'front benches') and the prime minister sits directly opposite the 'leader of the opposition', the leader of the largest party opposed to the government.

The parliamentary year normally begins in February and ends just before Christmas. The 'session' of a newly elected Parliament begins with the formal Opening of Parliament by the Governor-General who reads a Speech from the Throne outlining the government's intended legislation. This ceremony symbolically underlines the fact that the prime function of Parliament is to enact the Crown's, that is, the government's, programme of policies. In subsequent years a statement is made by the Prime Minister. During the year, Parliament is 'in session' for a total of around 30 weeks, usually three to four weeks at a time, interspersed with short breaks. In these weeks the House meets or 'sits' for three days, Tuesday, Wednesday and Thursday, from 2.00 to 6.30 p.m. each afternoon as well as Wednesday evenings (7.00 to 10.00 p.m.) and Thursday mornings (10.00 a.m. to 1.00 p.m.). These sitting times may be extended if the government wishes to 'take urgency' in order to get business through quickly. The meetings of Parliament are presided over by the Speaker, the Deputy Speaker, or one of two Assistant Speakers, in accordance with Standing Orders and Speakers' Rulings. The order of business each day follows a set pattern, beginning, after the formal presentation of petitions and reports, with question time, a period lasting approximately an hour in which ministers must reply to questions from members. About half of all parliamentary time is spent debating government bills, that is, legislation proposed by the government. In contrast, very little time is given to the three other categories of legislation, namely 'members'' (formerly 'private members'') bills, i.e. legislation proposed by members who do not belong to the government, 'local' bills relating to the powers of local authorities and 'private' bills, relating to the legal rights and duties of individuals or private companies, such as trusts or banks. An indication of the relative importance of government legislation is given by the fact that the 1994–96 Parliament enacted 418 government bills, 5 members' bills, 18 local bills and 11 private bills. The parliamentary preeminence of the government is reinforced by the rule that the government may veto any bill which has 'more than a minor impact on the Government's fiscal aggregate' (i.e. its total revenue and expenditure). Nevertheless, the potential exists to allow non-government MPs some initiative in legislation (Boston *et al.*, 1996a, 82–84). Non-government parties also have a say over the Parliament's legislative programme through the all-party Business Committee which determines the order of parliamentary business. The committee is chaired by the Speaker and contains one representative of each party with six or more members, one representative of all parties with less than six members who are in a government coalition and one representative of all other parties with less than six members (Boston *et al.*, 1996a: 73–74).

The passage of legislation follows a set procedure. Each bill comes before the House three times, for three 'readings'. The first reading merely marks the formal introduction of the bill. The bill is debated in general terms during the second reading and then the bill is referred to a select committee for more detailed consideration and to receive submissions from the public. The bill is then considered by the House as a whole sitting as the 'House in Committee', with the Deputy Speaker or one of the Assistant Speakers presiding as 'Chairman of Committees', at which stage particular sections are discussed and detailed amendments suggested. After a bill has passed its third and final reading it is referred to the Governor-General for assent and becomes a legally binding law.

In addition to time spent on debating specific legislation, there are parliamentary debates on general issues of government policy. The Address-in-Reply debate which follows the Opening of Parliament, and a similar debate which follows the prime minister's annual statement, gives members an opportunity to speak on any topic of government policy, as does the debate following the Budget, which is formally a debate on proposed legislation, the Appropriation Bill, but which covers the whole of government's proposed activities for the coming year. There is also opportunity for opposition parties at any time when the House is sitting to seek a snap debate on a matter of urgent political importance. The entire proceedings of Parliament are recorded and published in the official record of parliamentary debates known as 'Hansard'.

What the proper role of Parliament should be, what purposes it should be fulfilling in the course of conducting its daily business, is a question which does not have a straightforward answer. This is evident from the contrasting criticisms that are made of MPs' behaviour and different suggestions which are offered for the reform of Parliament. For instance, many people complain that MPs always follow the party line and that the government is rarely if ever defeated in a vote in Parliament. They may also suggest that Parliament is falling down in its task of checking executive power and should be supplemented by an independent second chamber. These views imply that disciplined political parties have no legitimate place in the constitution and that the main function of Parliament is to check or block the executive. Others criticise MPs because they have not stuck to the commitments their party made during the election campaign or are not sufficiently loyal to the party leadership. This implies that political parties do have a valuable role and that MPs have an obligation to follow their party's line.

Two contrasting sets of assumptions or 'models' of the proper role of Parliament may be distinguished. One is what may be called the 'liberal constitutional' model. It is 'liberal' because it was associated with classic British liberals of the nineteenth century, such as the philosopher J. S. Mill, who sought to restrict the power of the state and particularly valued the freedom and independence of individual MPs. It is 'constitutional' because it places weight on the formal legal structures of the constitution which treats Parliament as largely separate from the executive and individual MPs as independent representatives of local constituencies. According to this model, the main function of Parliament is to act as a deliberative assembly, a meeting place for elected representatives who critically debate the issues of the day, each contributing his or her own individual opinions and judgements to this process. The government of the day should have no right to expect that its proposals will as a matter of course receive the endorsement of this assembly. Indeed, the government's very right to govern can never be taken for granted because Parliament can remove it at any time by a vote of no confidence. This is the model enshrined in the constitutional law of the Westminster system (Chapter 3: 66–69) which makes very little reference to the parliamentary role of political parties and thus preserves the myth that parties are constitutionally disreputable (Chapter 3: 68).

The other model may be described as the 'democratic party' model, 'democratic' because it emphasises the role of Parliament in providing popularly elected governments and 'party' because it recognises the essential place of political parties in modern parliamentary democracies. According to the democratic party model, MPs are elected pri-

Party Composition of Parliament 1960–1993				
Election	Total Seats	Labour	National	Other
1960	80	34	**46**	–
1963	80	35	**45**	–
1966	80	35	**44**	1 (Social Credit)
1969	84	39	**45**	–
1972	87	**55**	32	–
1975	87	32	**55**	–
1978	92	40	**51**	1 (Social Credit)
1981	92	43	**47**	2 (Social Credit)
1984	95	**56**	37	2 (Social Credit/Democrat)
1987	97	**57**	40	–
1990	97	29	**67**	1 (NewLabour)
1993	99	45	**50**	4 (2 Alliance, 2 NZ First)
1996	120	37	**44**	39 (**17** NZF, 13 Alliance, 8 ACT, 1 United)
1999	120	**49**	39	32 (**10** Alliance, 9 ACT, 7 Green, 5 NZF, 1 United)
2002	120	**52**	27	41 (13 NZF, 9 ACT, 9 Green 8 United Future, **2** Prog, Coalition)

(Governing parties in bold; post-1993 parliaments elected under MMP)

marily as party representatives expected to be members of a party team in Parliament. The democratic function of political parties is to appeal to the various sections and interests of the plural society and enable the voters to use their vote to help choose a party-based government and to influence its policies.

Both of these models accommodate the various constitutional functions of Parliament, in legislation, financial authorisation, debate and scrutiny, but they explain their purpose and assess their performance from different perspectives. As is to be expected with a complex and long-standing institution like Parliament, neither model adequately covers all its activities. The 'liberal constitutional' model illuminates some aspects of Parliament which would otherwise remain obscure and unappreciated. In particular, it fits well with the formal procedures of Parliament which were developed in previous centuries before the rise of disciplined political parties and when parliamentary practice was much closer to liberal constitutional assumptions. It also highlights the importance of MPs' role as defenders of the rights of citizens against the power of governments. There are also other aspects of their work where they operate more in the manner prescribed by the liberal constitutional model, for instance in their work on behalf of constituents, in some of the work on select committees and in the occasional 'free vote' in Parliament, times when their partisan party affiliations are put to one side and they genuinely function as independent representatives.

However, the 'democratic party' model provides a more satisfactory overall perspective from which to analyse the workings of the New Zealand Parliament, because it is closer to the expectations which all New Zealanders have of their MPs and which MPs have of themselves. When casting their vote in an election, voters are expressing preferences between nationwide political parties. The main result of an election is the party composition of the new House of Representatives which determines which party or parties can form a government. Accordingly, the MPs themselves know that they have been elected primarily as party members and it is this party membership which determines most of their behaviour in the House. Under the first-past-the post system, the role of parties in elections was sometimes obscured by the fact that elections took the form of selecting individual representatives for separate electorates. In making their selection, however, the great majority of voters were choosing according to the party affiliation of the candidates, not their personal qualities. Some MPs, such as New Zealand First leader, Winston Peters, liked to appeal to public prejudice against political parties by claiming that they were solely concerned with representing the interests of their electorate. But, in practice, it was the partisan function, deriving from membership of a nationwide political party, which was paramount in MPs' parliamentary behaviour.

The prominence of political parties in the New Zealand Parliament will not be affected by the change to MMP and a multi-party parliament. Indeed, the change to MMP underlines the centrality of political parties to Parliament by giving voters a specific party vote which determines the party composition of Parliament. Though many of those who supported electoral reform may have been motivated by liberal constitutional objections to party dominance of Parliament (e.g. Palmer, 1992), evidence from other multi-party systems suggests that party discipline, if anything, is greater than under two-party systems. Small parties, struggling to maintain credibility with the electorate, place a particular premium on unity. Party leaders negotiating deals with other party leaders need to be able to rely on their followers' support (Harris & McLeay, 1993: 122–3). Party dominance of Parliament will continue, even if single-party dominance is less likely than before.

At the same time, MMP may in certain respects bring the New Zealand Parliament closer to the liberal constitutional model. For instance, it is no longer always clear on election night which party forms a government and which party leader is to be prime minister. As happened after the 1996 election, negotiation between the parties and their leaders may be necessary in order to discover a party or parties and a prime minister who can gain the support of a parliamentary majority (Chapter 4: 75). If the government is a minority government, it may have to consult with other parties in Parliament before enacting legislation. To this extent the independent power of Parliament has been increased, partly at the expense of the voters, who no longer have a clear, direct choice between two alternative governments, and partly at the expense of Cabinets, in so far as they cannot take their parliamentary majority for granted.

Moreover, the choice of individual electorate MPs is now clearly separated from the choice of nationwide party. Voters can thus select their local representatives purely on the personal merits of candidates without needing to consider the effect of their vote on the party composition of Parliament. In this respect, MMP may be said to restore an element of the liberal constitutional model, the primacy of the local representation function, for at least half the MPs. Thus, in appearances, the new system certainly departs from the liberal constitutional model, particularly through the use of an explicit party vote and party lists and through abandoning the official assumption that elections are solely concerned with selecting local representatives. In practice, however, it may have brought Parliament closer to the model by returning some power to Parliament and by strengthening the personal ties between local MPs and those they represent (their 'constituents').

If the voters in electing a Parliament have been helping to choose a party government, they can expect Parliament to sustain the party government and to let it govern effectively. At the same time, the government must be subject to constant public scrutiny to prevent it from abusing its power and to keep it accountable and responsive to the public. The need to follow the legal procedures of Parliament requires governments to justify their actions in public and to submit themselves to political criticism. Parliament thus has two broad purposes, which may sometimes be in conflict, to facilitate the people's government and to scrutinise it. In the system of democratic party government, the facilitating role is left primarily, though not exclusively, to parties on the government side and the scrutinising role primarily, though again not exclusively, to parties which oppose the government.

Under the two-party Parliament typical of the Westminster system, the functions of government and opposition have usually been held by a single party. The parliamentary role of the opposition is particularly important as a means of calling the government to account. To symbolise its democratic value, the opposition is sometimes referred to as 'Her (His) Majesty's loyal opposition'. Its leader is known formally as the Leader of the Opposition and is accorded a formal position in the constitution, even though he or she will be an unrelenting opponent of the prime minister and the government. In the multi-party Parliament likely under MMP, the formal position of Leader of the Opposition is given to the leader of the largest party not in the government.

Caucus

The centrality of party affiliation to the operations of Parliament means that the most important organisations in Parliament are those made up of MPs of the same party, the party caucuses. The party caucus has long been seen as a particularly significant aspect of New Zealand's version of the Westminster system (Jackson, 1992; Mulgan, 1989b: Chapter 3). The role which the caucus developed was heavily dependent on the dominance of Parliament by two major parties, Labour and National, which was in turn facilitated by the first-past-the-post electoral system. When one party held a majority of parliamentary seats, its caucus was in effective control of Parliament. How caucus exercised this control, particularly the relationship between the prime minister, Cabinet ministers and other caucus members (government 'back-benchers', as they are called, after their seating position in the Chamber), was therefore a key issue in the relation between Cabinet and Parliament. With the change to MMP and a multi-party Parliament no caucus has as much independent power as single-party caucuses of the past. At the same time, Parliament is still organised primarily on party lines and parties in Parliament need to coordinate their overall strategies and day-to-day parliamentary tactics. The degree of caucus organisation and specialisation depends on the size of each party. With caucuses ranging in size after 2002 from two to 52 MPs the conduct of the meetings obviously varies among the parties. Labour and National continue their former Caucus arrangements and although the smaller parties follow similar procedures, they rely less on caucus committees and sub-committees.

The National and Labour caucuses have operated in a very similar fashion, though Labour, with its historical roots in trade unionism and the organised labour movement, has always been more at home with formally enforcing procedures of collective solidarity while National and the newer parties have relied more on informal conventions. Meetings of each caucus are held weekly during the parliamentary session (on Tuesday mornings) and at other times as needed. The party leader presides. All members of the parliamentary party are expected to be present. (Speakers have usually stayed away, but Jonathan Hunt elected to attend Labour caucuses.) Senior officers of the parties' organisations outside Parliament, the national president of the party and the chief executive also attend regularly as of right. Meetings are held in private and proceedings are meant to be kept confidential, just as for Cabinet meetings and for similar reasons – to allow frank argument and disagreement among colleagues without presenting a politically damaging appearance of disunity to the public.

One of the main powers of the caucus is that of appointing, and, if necessary, unseating the leader. Green Party co-leaders, however, are elected by a general meeting held during the party's annual conference. Labour rules require a vote on the leadership early in the year preceding a general election. In both Labour and National, the issue may be raised at any time. The ever-present possibility of a leadership challenge from potentially disaffected colleagues pervades the relationship between leader and the caucus, providing a constant incentive for the leader to keep in close touch with caucus opinion (Chapter 4: 96–97). The Labour caucus, when in office, has also elected its Cabinet ministers, while National has left this power with the leader, as did New Zealand First in 1996 (Chapter 4: 78–79). The main link between the leadership and the rank-and-file members of caucus is provided by the 'whips', MPs who organise the day-to-day activities of the members of their parliamentary teams, allocating speaking duties, committee attendance, giving or withholding permission for absence from the House and so on.

To assist caucus in the conduct of its business Parliament funds parliamentary research units, responsible to the respective party leaders. Their main function is to collect materials which will help their respective party's causes. Unlike normal members of the public service, they are not constrained by the requirements of political neutrality and can be frankly partisan in their researches. The size of each party's research unit is determined in proportion to its number of MPs.

Both Labour and National have used their research units to service an elaborate structure of caucus committees, covering the various sectors of government and other issues of particular political importance. The number of committees depends on the number of MPs available. Thus, National in 1990–3, with its large majority and large number of backbenchers, had 18 caucus committees, but by 1996 had reduced them to 5. The number of Labour caucus committees, meanwhile, rose from 6 to 10. As with the business of Cabinet and the House as a whole, it is at the committee level, where a few people can give sustained and concentrated consideration to an issue, that most of the detailed work is done. When the party has been in government, caucus committees have provided a useful way for ministers to keep in touch with party opinion on politically controversial issues (Wood, 1992: 303; McLeay, 1995: 116–20). In opposition, when MPs have not had access to public service advice, caucus committees have provided the main means for developing new party policies in preparation for the party's return to government. The newer, smaller parties will not have sufficient members to match the larger parties' committee structure, but will still attempt to allow their MPs to specialise in particular policy areas.

Caucus is the forum in which a party decides the line it will take in Parliament, in the various debates and at select committees. Almost all the business of the House is conducted in terms of predetermined party positions. There are a few occasions when caucus allows its members a 'free vote', that is, the right to vote according to conscience, free from the obligation to keep to a party line. These are usually so-called conscience issues, issues such as abortion or euthanasia or, as in 2003, the legalisation of prostitution, which cut across party lines and where passions run high in the community. Party unity may be unnecessarily threatened if the party comes down on one side or another. But the decision to allow a free vote is one taken by caucus, a collective agreement to relax the rules of collective solidarity in particular cases. Similarly, caucus may allow an individual member to go against party policy where the member feels a need to support the local interests of his or her constituents. But, in the great majority of cases, caucus adopts a position which all members are expected to support.

When a party has been in government, government legislation has been approved by caucus before it is introduced into the House. The government caucus has also usually been consulted on government appointments to statutory bodies. The degree of consultation has varied with the issue and its political importance, its likelihood of affecting the government's electoral chances. In general, the more politically controversial an issue, the more caucus will expect to be involved. The major exception has been the budget. Because of the traditional convention of secrecy surrounding the budget discussions, it has not usually been revealed to caucus members until just before it is announced to Parliament. If the budget has contained politically controversial proposals, as happened with the Bolger National government's first budget of 1991, this can cause serious tensions within caucus between ministers and the rest of caucus. In a coalition government, caucuses of all governing parties will continue to expect to be consulted on all politically significant items of government business. The authority of any one caucus, however, will be limited by the need to secure the agreement of coalition partners and their caucuses.

Once a caucus decision is taken, caucus members are bound to abide by it. In the great majority of cases in both parties, this obligation of collective solidarity is accepted without question. However, there are occasions when the individual MP's loyalty is put to the test and questions arise of what force the convention may have and what sanctions may be visited on rebellious MPs. In the Labour Party, the obligation is built into the party rules, where Rule 226 requires all Labour candidates to pledge that, if successful, they will 'vote in accordance with the decisions of the Caucus of the Parliamentary Labour Party'. Open defiance of a caucus decision would therefore constitute grounds for expulsion from the party and is tantamount to a formal resignation.

The most notable recent instance of the application of this rule was in relation to Jim Anderton when he was a back-bench Labour MP during the Lange government. Anderton opposed the policy of privatising state assets, including the sale of the Bank of New Zealand, which the government embarked on after the 1987 election. He claimed that this policy was contrary to Labour party policy, as indeed it was, at least in relation to the corporations formed out of the former Post Office (Mulgan, 1990: 18). When Anderton subsequently, without caucus permission, abstained on a bill allowing for the sale of the Bank of New Zealand, this led to his exclusion from the Labour caucus. Soon after, he formally left the Labour party and established the

NewLabour party (Jackson, 1992: 241; Gustafson, 1992: 283–4; Chapter 10: 241).

The National party, on the other hand, has prided itself on the relative freedom it allows its MPs, officially subscribing to the traditional, liberal constitutional view of MPs as independent representatives for their particular electorates. However, in practice, the party has placed heavy emphasis on the value of loyalty to the party team. For many years it was able, by means of informal pressure, to achieve virtually the same degree of collective solidarity as Labour had with its formal rule. From the late 1970s, however, the collective bonds began to wear thin. In the latter years of the Muldoon government, a number of rebellious MPs publicly went against caucus decisions by voting against items of government-sponsored legislation (Wood, 1988: 56–60).

Under the first Bolger government, there was even greater restiveness among the caucus back-benchers. The government landslide victory in 1990 produced an unusually large and unwieldy caucus (66 members, excluding the Speaker) and an unusually secure majority (37 members more than Labour and NewLabour combined). In addition, the government began its period in office by pressing ahead with a programme of radical reform which had not been generally anticipated during the election campaign and in some respects was contrary to electoral commitments which the MPs themselves had made on the hustings. These factors caused a quite unusual degree of back bench rebellion in the government's first year (Jackson, 1992: 242). In 1991, two of the rebels, Gilbert Myles and Hamish MacIntyre, left the party and formed a new Liberal party (subsequently affiliated to the Alliance (Chapter 10: 241)). National's most notable dissident was Winston Peters, whose open opposition to his government on a wide range of issues led to his removal from Cabinet in 1991 (Chapter 4: 89), after which he continued to attack his colleagues from the back bench. Exasperation with Peters's continuing undermining of the party leadership eventually led his caucus colleagues to take the unprecedented step of expelling him from the caucus. This precipitated his resignation from Parliament in 1993 and his re-election (in a by-election) as an independent MP, followed by the founding of the New Zealand First Party under his leadership (Chapter 10: 257).

Caucus solidarity thus came under strain in both National and Labour single-party majority governments. This was a symptom of the pressure that governing parties were placed under by governments moving away from traditional party principles and abandoning explicit election promises. In nearly every case of back-bench caucus rebellion, the rebel MPs have been able to justify their opposition to caucus colleagues in terms of loyalty to the party at large, its principles and its policies. The rebels against Muldoon claimed that his policies of economic interventionism and controls were overriding traditional National values of free enterprise and the limited state. Anderton, in opposing the sale of state assets, was clearly defending Labour principles and commitment. The National MPs who refused to support increased means testing of state funded superannuation, were remaining true to their party's electoral promise. Problems of internal discipline also emerge in defeated parties, especially 'broad church' parties like National and Labour, as they attempt to redefine policies and regain lost electoral ground. In 2003, Maurice Williamson was suspended from National's caucus for criticising the party's lagging performance and by implication the performance of the then leader, Bill English. He was reinstated after the leadership change later in the year (p. 240, below).

The disciplinary power of caucus can determine an MP's party political career. Continued membership of caucus depends not only on an MP's conformity to party policy and caucus decisions, however, but also on conducting him or herself in a manner that does not bring the party into disrepute. This was demonstrated in 2003 when the ACT MP, Donna Awatere-Huata, who had been suspended from the caucus pending investigation of her financial dealings, found herself facing charges of fraud. Even before the case came to court, she was expelled from the party's caucus, retaining her parliamentary seat for the remainder of the term as an Independent.

One of the major conventions governing single-party government was that the party would keep to its election policy as set out in the party's 'manifesto' placed before the voters during the election campaign. This was the party's 'mandate', the basis of its democratic right to govern. Though much of the election policy was always deliberately imprecise in its wording and many decisions which government took were not covered in the policy at all, there was a clear understanding that explicit promises would be kept (Mulgan, 1992). The election policy operated not only as the party's contract with the voters but also as a guarantee of the party's own internal unity, the set of policies on which all members of the party were agreed. When both Labour and National governments broke explicit commitments in their election policies they seriously weakened the cohesion of their parties, both in the parliamentary caucus and in the wider extra-parliamentary party (Chapter 10: 260).

More generally, caucus no longer played such a prominent role as the government's sounding-board for testing party and public opinion. Prime ministers such as Keith Holyoake (1960–72) and Norman Kirk (1972–4) were renowned for the close rapport they kept between themselves and their back-bench colleagues and commentators on this period remarked on the extent of caucus influence, both direct and anticipated, on government policy. Admittedly, a government caucus meeting was never a meeting of political equals. The leadership always had the advantage of seniority and experience. Cabinet ministers came fully briefed to the caucus meeting, with the weight of public service advice behind them. In New Zealand's relatively small parliament, most back-benchers have a reasonable expectation of one day achieving ministerial office themselves and therefore have an incentive to stay on side with their leaders and their colleagues generally.

None the less, successful leaders and ministers of an earlier era were careful to anticipate or accommodate likely resistance from their caucus colleagues. The small size of caucus facilitated close personal relations between front and back bench and mutual adjustment on matters of policy. Caucus meetings were often the place where disputes within the Cabinet were finally resolved. Ministers who had been unable to prevail in Cabinet could hope to win in caucus. Thus, Norman Kirk as prime minister had used caucus to defeat unpalatable advice from the Treasury and the Minister of Finance. The Lange Labour government, by contrast, sought to dominate its caucus by force of numbers (Chapman, 1989: 30–31). Cabinet ministers agreed to abide by Cabinet decisions when they were discussed in caucus and the prime minister appointed sufficient Cabinet ministers, undersecretaries and ministers not in Cabinet to ensure that the government side (which also included the two whips) always held a majority in caucus.

The strained relations between Cabinet and caucus in the 1980s and early 1990s reflected changed attitudes of governments and their advisers towards the need to consult caucus and the party on the content of policy, particularly economic policy. From the last years of the Muldoon Government, governments were determined to pursue economic policies which were, at least in certain respects, contrary to their parties' traditional principles and expectations. First Muldoon, as prime minister and also Minister of Finance, particularly in his latter years, set out on a path of economic control and regulation which was increasingly unpopular with his party. Then the Lange government, under the guidance of Roger Douglas as Minister of Finance, embarked on a strategy of deregulation and radical market liberalism which was equally anathema to traditional Labour supporters.

Ministers had now become convinced that they should stick to their own view of the public interest and not yield to opposing views from their colleagues. Robert Muldoon, after many years as a dominant and efficient Minister of Finance, was confident in his own judgement. So too were Roger Douglas and his close colleagues, enthusiastically supported by market liberals in Treasury and elsewhere. They embraced the argument of public choice theory that all political pressure for policies contrary to their own prescriptions was the self-serving expression of vested interests. Once persuaded that the public interest demanded that they stand firm against all political opposition, they felt obliged, if necessary, to use all power at their disposal to override their own parties. The weakness of caucus in the face of a united Cabinet determined to get its own way was revealed.

Back-bench members of the caucus spend more time in the community than ministers and are less subject to the influence of official advisers in the public service. Cabinet sensitivity to caucus opinion could therefore be seen as a means of keeping governments close to the party rank and file and to the general voting public. Caucus thus had a key role in ensuring that the great power which the Westminster system delivered to single-party governments was exercised in a democratically accountable way (Mulgan, 1992; 1995). Conversely, when Cabinets rejected the need to seek caucus approval for their policies and caucuses were unable to make their Cabinets keep faith with party policies and principles, single-party majority governments appeared to be contemptuous of democratic processes and of public opinion. The breakdown of the intimate Cabinet/party relationship in both the Labour and National caucuses led not only to the splinter parties founded by Jim Anderton and Winston Peters (Chapter 10: 241–2) but also to the public rejection of the first-past-the-post electoral system which had encouraged single-party government.

After the 1993 election and referendum, both the National and Labour caucuses were destabilised by the prospect of electoral reform. The reduction in 'general' electorate seats (i.e. excluding the Maori seats) by over a third (from 95 to 60) meant that many sitting MPs would fail to be re-selected as electorate candidates while they could by no means guarantee a winnable place on their party's list for one of the new list seats. Many MPs openly considered breaking away from their former parties, a step which was ultimately taken by 9 National and 3 Labour MPs (Boston *et al.*, 1996a: Chapter 4). Indeed, the National leadership was actively supporting the formation of new, like-minded parties as potential coalition partners. In such circumstances, traditional norms of caucus loyalty were understandably strained. However, the 1993–6 Parliament marked a unique period of political transition from one electoral system to another. After 1996, though the party composition of Parliament will continue to be more varied, it is unlikely to be as fluid as in the three preceding years. MPs will have more incentive to remain loyal to the parties for which they were elected and leaders will have less reason to fear the defection of their backbenchers. Caucus control over ministers will remain crucial to the democratic accountability of politicians and governments. Equally important, however, will be the discussions and negotiations that take place between parties and their leaders.

The debating Chamber

From the general public's point of view, the most noticeable aspect of Parliament's activities is the debates carried out in the Chamber. These debates are broadcast live on radio in their entirety. Though there are very few members of the public listening at any one time, many New Zealanders will have tuned in at some time, perhaps briefly, but long enough to get some general impression, usually unfavourable, of the flavour of parliamentary debates. Since 1990, debates have also been permitted to be televised. However, apart from the annual presentation of the budget, which is broadcast live and in full, televised coverage of Parliament is confined to brief excerpts on news programmes.

The main purpose of parliamentary debates and other business conducted in the Chamber, such as question time, is the pursuit of party advantage by both government and opposition parties. The seating of the House encourages this competitive atmosphere. The main opponents face each other, with the leading members of each side, those on the front benches, closest to each other. Almost every word and also every action – body language is an important weapon in a politician's armoury – is designed to make one's opponents look weak or foolish and one's own side strong and responsible. The party leaders are constantly testing each other's competence and confidence. They know they must maintain the support of their caucus colleagues sitting alongside and behind them. The quality of their parliamentary performance,

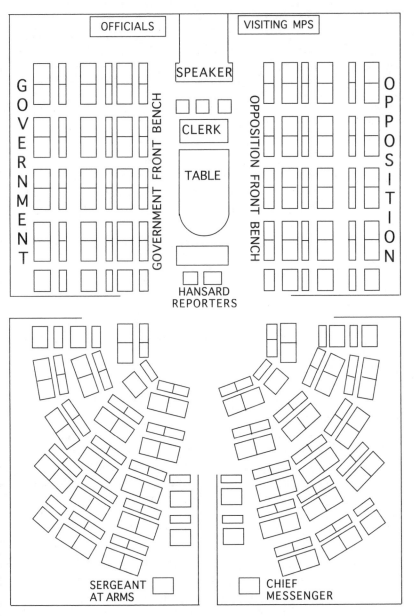

House of Representatives: Seating Plan

whether they dominate their opponents or let themselves be dominated, is a critical factor affecting their standing in the party, second only, perhaps, to their relative performance on television. Both Robert Muldoon and David Lange owed much of their political success to the fact they were outstandingly clever and aggressive parliamentary debaters (as well as television performers) who could deflate their opponents unmercifully and in so doing give heart to their own team. Similar contests for debating supremacy occur between individual ministers and their opposite numbers, the opposition MPs who are designated as spokespersons for their particular portfolios.

The House is thus a major forum for the 'continuous election campaign' (Skene, 1992). An occasional exception is provided by the relatively infrequent 'free' or 'conscience' vote when the parties allow MPs to vote according to their own judgement. Here the atmosphere is quite different. MPs speak much more reasonably and try to minimise not exacerbate their mutual differences. These instances serve only to underline the effect of the partisan party purpose which pervades almost all parliamentary public activities.

Question time, for instance, provides an opportunity for the opposition to probe the actions of individual ministers seeking for points which can be used to embarrass the government politically. Conversely, the government side will use its quota of questions as a vehicle for ministers to announce politically favourable news (Palmer, 1987: 118–22). Debates on government legislation follow similarly predictable partisan lines. The appropriate minister will introduce the bill and seek to justify its intent. Opposition parties, which will usually (though not invariably) have decided to oppose the legislation at least in part, will concentrate on attack, the lead usually being taken by the relevant spokesperson for that particular topic. Speakers follow in turn from each side, in an order determined by the whips. They are required to support their own party's position and to ridicule the position of other parties. A favourite device of debate is to try to identify inconsistencies between the line a party is taking now and what it may have said or done in the past. Where possible, the speakers will seek to convict their political opponents of an embarrassing about-turn, reading out excerpts from a press cutting or from Hansard, material regularly provided for them by the staff of their research units.

Many of the speeches given in parliamentary debates appear repetitive and intellectually impoverished. In part, this is because the parties have a relatively small number of MPs to draw on and MPs are often required to speak without adequate time to prepare what they are going to say. They are therefore forced to fall back on trite polemic and tedious repetition. MPs also get caught up in the highly charged atmosphere of Parliament, which encourages conventions of personal abuse and name-calling which to dispassionate observers seem childish and demeaning.

Advocates of MMP anticipated that the change to a multi-party parliament would modify the adversarial flavour of the parliamentary contest. There is little evidence of this. Although both government and opposition sides now include several parties, each party still seeks to distinguish itself from its allies as well as from its more obvious opponent. Debate is just as much driven by considerations of party advantage and the tone is still usually relentlessly hostile. According to the party government model of Parliament, the party political focus of parliamentary debate is legitimate and justifiable. There is democratic value in forcing the government to face up regularly to hostile scrutiny in a public forum. The outcome of debates, in the sense of which side will win, may almost always be predictable. But the purpose of debates is not to decide the substance of policy but to provide a focus for public justification and criticism of proposed policy.

The existence of this public forum, the government's knowledge that its policies must run the gauntlet of parliamentary scrutiny from a hostile opposition, provides a major, if largely indirect, constraint on the substance of policy. Many policy options that a government might wish to pursue are ruled out in advance through anticipation of the likely hostile reception that they would get from Parliament and the public. Other proposals which get as far as Parliament may be substantially revised by the government in the light of public objections which are highlighted in parliamentary debates. The modifications of policy may not come about through an actual defeat of the government in a parliamentary vote and may not be openly forced on them by opposition parties. None the less, these changes can be said to be caused by the parliamentary debating process and by the partisan critical function performed by opposition parties.

The effects of the critical and constraining function of Parliament are therefore not to be sought in open and outright defeats suffered by the government, of which there are very few. Even in the case of a minority government, proposals which are likely to be defeated will normally be amended or withdrawn rather than introduced and then voted down. The main effects are in the extent to which governments modify their policies in reaction to likely or actual criticism. Here, again, the changing pressures on governments which have made them less sensitive to back-bench opinion may sometimes have reduced the effectiveness of the parliamentary constraints. If Parliament is a forum for the continuous election campaign, then the government must at least be concerned with its popularity and with winning the next election. If politicians become indifferent to electoral success, Parliament's effectiveness is weakened. This was the case with some of Labour's leading ministers after 1987. They had paced themselves for only two terms in government and appeared interested more in making history than in winning again in 1990 (Mulgan, 1992: 520). It is no coincidence that this attitude in the government was accompanied by growing alienation on the part of the public. The desire of politicians for the electoral success of their parties is not, as sometimes thought, a disreputable one. Rather it is a fundamental assumption for a healthy democracy.

Select committees

A very significant part of Parliament's business is now conducted off the main floor of the Chamber within select committees. The use of select committees has been steadily increasing over the last two decades (Jackson, 1987: Chapter 8). The present structure of committees dates back to the reforms instituted by the Lange Labour Government under the guidance of the party's constitutional expert and deputy prime minister, Geoffrey Palmer. It has since been revised to take account of the increase in the number of MPs and the likely end of two-party dominance of Parliament (Boston *et al.*, 1996a). The establishment of select committees and appointment of their members is now in the hands of the new all-party Business Committee chaired by the Speaker. There are thirteen 'subject' select committees (see box), each of which covers a sector of government activity, defined in terms of the spheres of responsibility of one or more government departments or ministerial portfolios, for example Education and Science, and Foreign Affairs, Defence and Trade. Each subject committee has between eight and twelve members and positions are allocated to parties in approximate proportion to their numbers in the House (ministers are not eligible for membership). When single-party majority government was the norm, the governing party could maintain a majority on all committees and was thus able to exercise control over committee recommendations, often through overlapping membership between the relevant caucus committee and the select committee

---

Subject Select Committees

Commerce
Education and Science
Finance and Expenditure
Foreign Affairs, Defence and Trade
Government Administration
Health
Law and Order
Local Government and Environment
Justice and Electoral Law
Maori Affairs
Primary Production
Social Services
Transport and Industrial Relations

Source:<www. parliament.govt.nz/house-committee.html>

(McLeay, 1995: 117). Under MMP, however, committee membership reflects the multi-party composition of Parliament as a whole and it is most unlikely that any one party or caucus will be able to dominate committee proceedings.

In addition to the subject committees, there are a number of special-purpose committees, some of which deal with 'in-house' matters to do with the conduct of Parliament (on some of which ministers may sit): the Privileges Committee, on which senior ministers usually sit, deals with breaches of parliamentary privilege, an ill-defined area of law covering possible abuse by MPs of their powers (usually their right of free speech), attacks on the Speaker or actions by the public which may be seen to hold Parliament and its procedures in contempt (Palmer, 1987: 123–6); the Standing Orders Committee monitors Parliament's rules of procedure; the Regulations Review Committee scrutinises government regulation and the Officers of Parliament Committee, chaired by the Speaker, supervises the various officers of Parliament, the Ombudsmen and the Commissioner for the Environment. Parliament also from time to time establishes temporary ad hoc committees to deal with particular issues, e.g. the MMP Review Committee, 2001. Committees are serviced by staff belonging to the Office of the Clerk of the House.

The main work is done in the subject committees which normally meet at least once a week when the House is in session, Wednesday mornings being kept free for this purpose. If the pressure of work demands, committees also meet in the weeks when the House is not in session and, indeed, this has become the norm for most committees. Committees may also travel outside Wellington to hold public hearings. Their major function is in the review of proposed legislation. Except for certain categories of money bills, that is, legislation on financial matters and bills on which the government has taken urgency, all bills are referred to a committee between their first and second readings in the House. The committee then calls for submissions from members of the public. These submissions are normally made in writing but people making them have the opportunity of appearing in person before the committee to summarise their main points and to answer questions on their submissions.

The select committee stage has become the main point at which interested members of the public have a chance to influence government legislation. The massive scale of the legislative programme associated with the restructuring reforms implemented by recent governments meant that the work of detailed scrutiny had to be divided among a number of committees rather than carried out by the House as a whole. Moreover, much of the legislation required extensive revision after it was introduced. In part, this was a result of the speed at which governments were determined to move. Draft legislation was often poorly thought through and loosely worded. In part, this was also due to a deliberate change in the policy-making style as ministers sought to exclude interest groups from the drafting stage in order to prevent intended legislation from being unduly influenced by 'vested' sectional interests (Chapter 9: 212). The select committee stage often became the first point at which powerful interest groups could mount protests and seek to have an input into government policy.

Many bills attract a large number of submissions, often several hundred. Most bills are changed at the committee stage, often substantially. The committee stage sometimes provides a forum for policy development as the government clarifies its aims in consultation with interested parties. Notable examples have been the Resource Management Act 1991, involving both Labour and National governments (Buhrs and Bartlett, 1993: 123–4), and the Fiscal Responsibility Act 1994, which Ruth Richardson introduced as Minister of Finance and then helped elaborate as chairperson of the Finance and Expenditure Committee

(Boston *et al.*, 1996 : 284–6). At other times, the government may have formulated a clear intention but be forced into making concessions, as happened with a number of the Labour government's major reforming acts, in education and public sector employment. Interest groups, such as unions and public sector professions, who had close links with Labour, were able to put pressure on the government members of the committee to extract concessions from ministers. Professions whose prerogatives are under attack from government may successfully defend their position in front of the select committee. A notable example is the dentists, who successfully deflected a government attempt to deregulate their profession (Burrows & Joseph, 1990: 307).

Under single-party majority government, progress through the committee stage depended on the government's legislative priorities. A frequent complaint was that the time allocated for the preparation of submissions is far too short, often a matter of a few weeks or even days (Burrows & Joseph, 1990: 307). Similarly the time for hearings was sometimes so compressed that people may have had only a few minutes to speak and committee members themselves and their officials could not assimilate the points made to them. In the new Parliament, however, where the all-party Business Committee rather than the government decides the legislative timetable and where government control of committees is less assured, select committees can be expected to be more resistant to attempts to cut short their consideration of bills. By the same token, however, where the government cannot control the committee process, as sometimes occurred after National lost its majority in 1994, it will attempt, where possible, to pursue its policy objectives through executive action which does not require the legislative approval of Parliament.

Besides the review of proposed legislation, the other functions of subject select committees are to scrutinise the annual expenditure for relevant departments, to monitor and conduct special investigations into the various government departments and state-owned enterprises within their area of responsibility and to consider petitions presented to Parliament (more than 2000 petitions were referred to committees during the 45th Parliament, 1996-9). The scrutiny of departmental expenditure includes an examination of estimates for the coming year as well as of the department's report on performance for the previous year. In performing these functions committees are assisted by staff of the Audit Office (Boston *et al.*, 1996: 299–300) and have the opportunity to interrogate the Chief Executives of departments (Chapter 6:

146) and other senior officials on matters relating to the administration of departments. This process is important in underlining the accountability of the public service to the public. Ministers now also regularly appear before committees to outline the policy directions of their departments. An important development has been increased involvement of the Finance and Expenditure Committee in public debate of economic policy through discussion with the Governor of the Reserve Bank concerning the Bank's six-monthly monetary policy statement. The Committee has also questioned the Minister of Finance in relation to the government's budget policy statement, the initial annual statement of general budgetary policy required under the Fiscal Responsibility Act 1994 (Boston *et al.*, 1996: 286).

Since 1985, committees have been able to exercise their own initiative about what areas of government activity they wish to inquire into. High hopes were held that the committees would develop into independent and powerful agencies of scrutiny over the executive. These expectations have on the whole been disappointed, for a number of reasons. One is that the need to process the government's proposed legislation necessarily takes priority over other matters. The sheer pressure of new legislation, together with financial scrutiny, has meant that, with the exception of the Foreign Affairs, Defence and Trade Committee (overseeing an area in which legislation is rare), the great bulk of committee time is given to the other functions.

Another factor which has so far prevented the committees from developing their monitoring and scrutinising function further has been the difficulty of maintaining a sufficiently constant membership which can develop a collective expertise and sense of purpose. Because of the relatively large number of committees, including ad hoc special-purpose committees, and the relatively small number of MPs, many MPs have found themselves serving on more than one committee. More than one committee will often be meeting at the same time and MPs have found themselves double-booked. Together with other urgent calls on MPs' time, this means that there has been a high level of 'substitution'. (Substitution is where the regular member's place at a meeting is taken by another MP from the same party who will usually have little background knowledge of what is being discussed and is there just to keep up the party's voting strength.) While an increase in the number of MPs should relieve the pressures to a certain extent, most MPs will still be unable to devote sufficient time to specialising in their committee areas. Being chairperson of an important committee, particularly the Finance and Expenditure Committee, may bring opportunities for making a mark and for advancing one's political fortunes. But rank-and-file membership carries few rewards in comparison with other demands on MPs' time.

The party basis of Parliament sets limits to the degree of critical independence select committees can adopt. In uncontroversial matters discussed away from the glare of publicity, committees can develop a non-partisan approach in which MPs from different parties cooperate in improving the details of legislation or investigating bureaucratic performance. But as soon as an issue becomes a matter of party policy, committee members must revert to their partisan role. If legislative changes are to be made, committee members will need to consult with their caucuses and, if they are on the government side, with the relevant ministers as well. Some commentators have clearly hoped that the committees could acquire a degree of political independence from the executive similar, for instance, to that enjoyed by congressional committees in the United States. They have deplored the tendency of select committee members to defer to their party caucus (Palmer, 1987: 74–75). It makes sense, however, for the details of politically controversial policies to be thrashed out in caucus committees rather than in the select committee itself. Under a system of democratic party government it is to be expected that the governing parties, if they hold a parliamentary majority, will be able to make the ultimate decision and carry it through Parliament, including through the select committee stage. Nevertheless, a succession of minority governments since 1998 has seen them sometimes under pressure to amend or even abandon contentious bills from select committees prepared to assert a greater degree of independence than before (Boston, 2000: 251).

The question, however, is not whether the select committees can necessarily confront and ultimately defeat the Cabinet or the governing majority. It is rather whether they facilitate the process of public scrutiny and consultation through which governments must pass on the way to enacting their policies and thereby help to make governments more accountable. The function of committees is to assist Parliament's dual purpose of both facilitating and scrutinising the actions of a party government. They should not be expected to act as totally independent checks on government. In this respect, there is no doubt that the committee process, particularly in the review of intended legislation, does provide a valuable adjunct to parliamentary scrutiny. Committees provide a forum in which MPs can work constructively on improving government policy and legislation in the light of submissions from interested members of the public. When issues become politically charged and matters of partisan dispute, the committees provide a focus for mediating this conflict. The discussions behind the scenes between ministers, caucus and the government members of committees, particularly chairpersons, far from undermining the committee process, provide a useful and flexible channel for adjusting government policy in the light of public criticism and thus making governments more responsive to public opinion.

Under MMP, select committees have continued to work within limits set by the party composition of Parliament. At the same time, they reflect the greater diversity of a multi-party Parliament. In so far as legislation requires consultation between different parties, committees provide a forum in which such consultation takes place. Parties not in government, particularly if they provide committee chairpersons (four of the thirteen in 2003), will make use of committees to pursue their own alternative policies and agendas through committee inquiries. In general, the loosening of single-party control over Parliament, together with the increased number of MPs available for committee service, enables committees to be more independent and flexible in their investigations.

MPs as electorate representatives

Under the previous electoral system, all MPs were elected as representatives for a particular electoral district ('electorate' or 'constituency'). They might owe their election to having been selected as party candidates and having attracted sufficient votes from voters wishing to support their party. But once elected, they were expected to be individual representatives of their particular localities, acting for and on behalf of all those living in their electorates (their 'constituents') regardless of party affiliation. Under MMP, around half of the MPs, those elected for electorate seats on both the general and the Maori roll, will have similar responsibilities. The duties expected of the other, list MPs, still remain somewhat uncertain (Boston *et al.*, 1996a: 88). Though not formally linked to any particular electorate, they will also probably take on electorate work for the areas in which they live or for particular groups, for instance women, or farmers, with which they are linked (Vowles *et al.*, 2002: 139–42). List MPs will require endorsement from their party organisations for re-election and may be seeking selection as candidates for electorate seats. Their demonstrated willingness to help those who call on them will be an important factor in securing party support.

MPs' work for constituents covers a wide range of activities and interests. They are required to act as advocates of their electorates with central government. This may take the form of supporting the interests of local organisations, such as local government, local industries or local institutions such as schools or hospitals. If any of these organisations have a problem in their dealings with central government, either with a minister or with some branch of the government bureaucracy, they may call on their local MP to approach the appropriate minister with a request for action or explanation. The minister will pass the request on to the appropriate department or official for reply.

Alternatively, local organisations may wish to exert influence on the political process, either for or against a policy initiative currently or potentially under consideration by the politicians. The local MP will be expected to pass on the opinions of his or her constituents to the MPs concerned, perhaps the minister dealing with the issue, or to caucus colleagues who are members of the relevant caucus or select committees. Sometimes this expression of local pressure may be part of a nationwide campaign. National interest groups, as part of their strategy on a particular issue, will organise their local organisations to contact local MPs (Chapter 9). Thus Federated Farmers, objecting to the raising of charges of rural postal delivery, ensures that local branches in rural electorates make their feelings known to the MPs in their areas. Teacher unions objecting to 'bulk funding' of schools get their members in individual schools to contact their local MPs. Groups of local MPs from a particular city or region will be expected to work together in support of that city's or region's interests, regardless of party affiliation. Thus all South Island MPs have lobbied in favour of cheaper electricity prices for South Islanders. The political parties themselves recognise the importance of the MP's duty to represent his or her electorate, allowing this as one of the few legitimate reasons for an MP to oppose party policy.

Work for electorates also includes acting on behalf of individual constituents. Citizens tend to turn to their MP as someone who can help them in almost any sort of difficulty. Sometimes this will be a problem with a government department. Immigration issues, where people are trying to get entry to New Zealand, for themselves, friends or families, have been a particularly common reason for approaching the local MP. So too are housing and social welfare problems, with

MPs helping constituents who are seeking access to a state house or a benefit. The MP will refer the person to the relevant office or official or, if necessary, will take the case up with the minister.

MPs are often approached about matters which are not to do with central government at all, for instance disputes with local councils or with private firms. Particularly among people who do not have ready access to other sources of professional advice, such as a lawyer, and may not be well informed about their legal rights, the MP is seen as someone whom they can approach and who will give them a fair hearing. The issue may not be related to government at all. Geoffrey Palmer, when MP for the inner city area of Christchurch Central, was often called on to resolve disputes between neighbours (Palmer, 1987: 97–104)!

MPs are expected to make themselves readily available to their constituents. Most live in, or close to, their electorates, returning almost very weekend, usually some time on Friday. They regularly hold 'clinics' or 'surgeries', being available for consultation at times and places advertised in the local press. They will make a point of attending a large number of local functions, such as school fairs, sports days, bowling club openings and so on, and generally be on call throughout the weekend. Most spend Mondays in their electorates, calling on local bodies and branch offices of government departments on behalf of constituents and visiting local industries and institutions. They usually return to Wellington early on Tuesday morning but, even there, they will still attend to electorate matters, following up inquiries, dealing with correspondence, welcoming constituents to Parliament. While MPs are away, their local electorate office, supported from public funds, takes messages and arranges appointments on their behalf.

Ministers have a somewhat different schedule, being based more in Wellington, where the government provides them with houses, and having to devote most of their time to government business. Their Mondays are spent in the capital at Cabinet meetings, for which they must prepare during the weekend. None the less, most return to their electorates at the weekend for at least one day. They make sure not to appear to be neglecting their constituents, keeping in close touch with their local office and having a secretary in their Wellington office responsible for dealing with constituency matters.

Research based on MPs' own assessments of how they spent their time (Anagnoson, 1983; Royal Commission on the Electoral System, 1986: 118) indicated that most MPs spend between 25 per cent and 35 per cent of their time on constituency work while Parliament was in session and slightly more when it was not. Ministers spent about 10 per cent less of their time in this way than did non-ministers. Some MPs, particularly those in 'marginal' seats and therefore particularly anxious about re-election, devoted more than half their time to constituency work, while some in very 'safe' seats were a little less attentive to their constituents (Anagnoson, 1987).

There have clearly been strong pressures on electorate MPs to give high priority to their constituents' problems. Under the previous electoral system, it was the popularity of the nationwide party rather than of the local MP which largely determined people's votes. Even so, the personal vote could have some effect and MPs had an incentive to be helpful to constituents, particularly in 'marginal' electorates where party support was evenly balanced. With MMP, the incentives for electorate MPs will be even stronger. The separation of the electorate vote from the party vote means that voters can choose a local candidate from any party and still give their support to their preferred nationwide party. The personal vote will therefore be worth much more. Moreover, under both systems, the future of all MPs depends on their being reselected by their party. Party members will look unfavourably on a sitting MP who gains a reputation for being unhelpful or offhand to constituents with problems. The 'populist' style of much New Zealand politics, the expectation that MPs should keep close to the values and aspirations of ordinary citizens, places a premium on politicians' willingness to attend to the problems of individual citizens.

Above all, though some MPs may privately agree with complaints about the excessive load of electorate work and about how it deflects them from taking a greater interest in issues of general policy, most find the work itself particularly rewarding. When MPs who are retiring are asked to single out which aspects of the job gave them greatest satisfaction, even those who have held high ministerial office will usually mention electorate work as particularly satisfying. The reason is partly that such work allows MPs to deliver tangible benefits to identifiable individuals. They can thus see the effects of their efforts and receive direct credit and thanks.

In addition, and perhaps more important, electorate work is largely non-partisan. The MP is approached not as a party member but as a local Member of Parliament, constitutionally obliged to help any constituent regardless of party affiliation. While party politics and party politicians in general are the objects of widespread public hostility, the local member, as an individual representing the electorate, may be accorded considerable confidence and respect (Vowles *et al.*, 1995: 161–2). MPs have naturally warmed to this more sympathetic view of their function. They find it a relief from the more torrid climate of party politics and the endless cut and thrust of party competition. In indulging such feelings, both MPs and members of the public indicate the hold that the liberal constitutional model of Parliament and politics still has over them. They still pine for a Parliament which is a chamber of rational debate where individual representatives sensibly discuss each issue on its merits with no reference to party alignments or party commitments.

There is certainly a place for this model in illuminating some aspects of Parliament, for instance some of the detailed work in select committees as well as the great bulk of electorate work. But in so far as it tends to undermine the legitimacy of party politics and party government, which provide the underlying premises for most of Parliament's behaviour, then it may be seen as unhelpful. Excessive support for the value of non-partisan electorate work by individual MPs may impede a proper understanding of the broader democratic functions of Parliament. Without parties, voters would have no opportunity of indicating support for particular national leaders or for particular tendencies in government.

The fact that the local electorate MP is such a valued part of the Westminster parliamentary tradition was a major reason for the Royal Commission's recommendation in favour of MMP. MMP is the only form of proportional representation which also incorporates single-member local electorates (Royal Commission on the Electoral System, 1986: 53–55). At the same time, the move away from a Parliament consisting entirely of constituency MPs to one where nearly half the MPs are elected from party lists will undoubtedly affect the extent to which representing a local electorate continues to be seen as the essential characteristic of being an MP (Vowles *et al.*, 2002: 140). It is to be hoped that MMP will help to strengthen the constitutional legitimacy of parties as democratic institutions.

Parliament and the representation of interests

The central democratic role of Parliament, as an elected assembly of the people's representatives, is to represent the people who elect it. How well does the New Zealand Parliament represent all the different sections of New Zealand's plural society? Which interests are particularly well catered for and which are unduly neglected? Local interests, it is to be noted, are particularly well covered because they are built into the electoral system itself. Each geographical area receives representation through the electorate seats.

Maori interests, too, are protected by the electoral system to the extent that the Maori electorates, first instituted in 1867, have guaranteed Maori voters representation by their own preferred MPs. Until the electoral reforms of the 1990s, the actual implementation of Maori parliamentary representation was less than equal (Sorrenson, 1986; Walker, 1992). The number of seats was fixed at four, regardless of the size of the Maori population or, after enrolment on the Maori roll was made optional, regardless of the number of Maori opting for the Maori roll. For many years the boundaries of the Maori electorates were excluded from consideration by the Representation Commission. Under the new electoral system, however, the number of Maori electorate seats is adjusted in proportion to the same quota as general seats (seven seats in the 2002 Parliament) and Maori voters are at last treated equally with other voters, also since 2002, enabling them to cast an ordinary vote at any polling place in their electorate rather than one designated for electors on the Maori roll (McRobie, 2003: 183). Maori voters also, arguably, suffered political neglect because for half a century all the Maori seats were 'safe' Labour seats for which the National party had little incentive to compete. Labour's monopoly was finally broken in 1993 (Chapter 11: 277). Moreover, in MMP's crucial party vote, every vote counts equally towards the nationwide party totals and no vote is any longer 'wasted' in a safe seat. Thus all parties, including National, now have an incentive to court the Maori vote. Moreover, as the list seats have also produced a significant number of Maori MPs (9 in 2002, in addition to the 7 electorate MPs and 3 Maori MPs representing general electorates), Maori voters have emerged as clear beneficiaries of the new electoral system.

Whether electoral equality is translated into effective equal representation is open to question. Indeed, the meaning of representation itself is not unambiguous (Mulgan, 1989: 97–98). In one sense, Parliament may be said to represent the various sections of society if its members comprise a more or less accurate cross-section of society. This is the 'typical' or 'mirroring' sense of representation. In this sense, for instance, Parliament is said to be unrepresentative of women, as women make up half the population but a substantially smaller fraction of MPs (34 out of 120 or 28 per cent in the 2002 election). However, the introduction of MMP and party lists has increased the typical representativeness of Parliament (McLeay, 2000: 210-15; Karp, 2002: 131-4). When putting forward their lists of candidates, parties are under pressure to make the list appear representative, with, for instance, a fair balance between male and female candidates and between candidates from the various ethnic groups. When candidate selection was purely a matter of selecting individual candidates for single-member electorates, as under first-past-the-post, there was less opportunity to address overall gender and other types of imbalance within a nationwide party. Besides the representation of women and Maori, ethnic representation has also improved with the election of three Pacific Islanders and two Asian MPs in 2002.

But MPs may represent different sections of the population in another sense, as agents acting on behalf of the interests of particular groups, even if they do not themselves belong to these groups or share the characteristics of their members. In this sense, for instance, a female lawyer represents a male client or a trade union official with a university degree represents unskilled workers. Thus a woman MP can represent male AIDs victims or a Pakeha MP can represent Pacific Islanders, in the sense of speaking for them and looking out for their interests.

In a party Parliament, where most influence is wielded by political parties, the most important question is whether the parties act as agents for particular interests. Thus the various Maori iwi need the political parties to take notice of Maori interests when formulating their policies and parliamentary strategies. To this end, the influence of Maori MPs may not be as important as the influence of Maori interest groups, Maori bureaucrats or Maori voters themselves on Pakeha politicians. Similarly, women's groups may use the leverage of women's voting power to try to influence party politicians, who are predominantly male. Women MPs may play a part, as they did in the formulation of Labour's pay equity policy culminating in the Employment Equity Act 1990 (Wilson, 1992). But theirs is not necessarily the crucial contribution.

The question of whose interests are represented by Parliament in general or the parties in particular involves investigation of all the various pressures and influences acting upon MPs. MPs, as professional party politicians seeking re-election, must look primarily to the sources of their party's support in the electorate. But not all types of voter are necessarily paid equal attention by the competing parties (Chapters 10–11). Moreover, there are very strong countervailing pressures, from the bureaucracy or powerful section interests, which will tend to deflect politicians from a simple policy of vote-maximising. None the less, it is in the decisions of politicians as party members rather than as individuals that the most important aspect of Parliament's representative function is to be found.

However, the extent to which Parliament is 'typically' representative of the nation is not without significance. Parliament has an important symbolic function as the nation's elected legislative assembly. In view of New Zealand's claim to be a bicultural society, a significant Maori presence in Parliament is therefore essential. So too is a larger proportion of women, in order to signify the nation's commitment to gender equality. Moreover, there are some occasions in Parliament's proceedings where the presence or absence of MPs from a particular group can make a political difference. This especially applies to issues on which the parties do not take a stand. Thus the women MPs from both major parties have played a key role in abortion legislation, a matter on which the parties allow a 'free' vote. There may also be items of select committee or caucus committee business which are not politically controversial and where individual MPs may have more rein to exercise their own independent judgement.

Further reading

Parliament in general
Harris & Levine (1992): Part IV; Jackson (1987); (2003); McGee (1992); Mulgan (1989): Chapter 3; Palmer (1987): Chapters 7–8; Palmer & Palmer (1997): Part 3; Ringer (1991): Chapters 8–10; Wood (1988): Chapters 4–5.
Functions of Parliament
Palmer (1992): Chapter 5; Palmer & Palmer (1997): 129–30; Royal Commission on the Electoral System (1986): Chapter 4; Skene (1992).
Caucus
Chapman (1989); Jackson (1992); Palmer & Palmer (1997): 121–4.
Select committees
Boston et al. (1996): 336–7; Palmer & Palmer (1997): 137–40; Skene (1990).
Effect of MMP
Boston et al.(1996a): Chapter 5; Harris & McLeay (1993); McLeay (2000).

Parliamentary website: <www.parliament.govt.nz>

6

The Public Sector and the Public Service

The variety of state institutions

In terms of the constitutional analysis of the state, Cabinet and Parliament loom large because they are at the controlling centre. But they make up a very small part of the state itself. Any dealings that citizens have with state officials are unlikely to be with the few elected politicians, of whom there are less than a hundred, but with one of those who work in the various publicly funded institutions of the state, of whom there are hundreds of thousands. The institutions of the state serve a great variety of purposes, from the protection of property to the encouragement of the arts, from the preparation of reliable economic statistics to the preservation of endangered species. They also vary in their organisational structure. They range from institutions belonging to what is often informally referred to as the government 'bureaucracy', that is, government departments directly responsible to ministers and totally supported from public funds, such as the Inland Revenue Department or the Ministry of Social Development, to small institutions which may be only partially funded from public funds and may have considerable independence, such as a kindergarten or a local branch of the Plunket Society.

Different ways of classifying state institutions can be adopted depending on the focus of analysis. If the aim is to understand the role of the state in society, state institutions may be appropriately distinguished in terms of the social function or purpose they serve in society. Thus, some agencies are concerned with law and order, others with economic development, others with social welfare or the well-being of citizens (Rudd, 1991: 147–50). State agencies concerned with law and order include the police, the Ministry of Justice, the Department of Corrections, the armed forces, the Security Intelligence Service. Examples of agencies serving the function of economic development are the Ministry of Agriculture, the Ministry of Economic Development, the Ministry of Research, Science and Technology, and producer boards such as the Wool Board and the Apple and Pear Board. Social welfare agencies include the Ministry of Health, the Department of Child, Youth and Family Services, the Ministry of Education, District Health Boards, schools and kindergartens.

Such functional categories, like most such distinctions, may be blurred and imprecise. Some departments, such as Statistics or Inland Revenue, support all functions of the state. Other institutions, though commonly classified in one category, might also be plausibly included in others. Schools, for instance, may be said to contribute not only to social wellbeing but also to economic growth as well as to law and order. Functional distinctions demonstrate the range of purposes fulfilled by the state and the variety of different types of agency serving each purpose. They will be useful for analyses of particular areas of public policy, such as health or employment, or for studies of particular sectors of society, such as Maori or manufacturers, and of how they interact with state agencies.

However, the focus of this chapter is on how state power is exercised and on how such power may be made accountable to the rest of society. From this point of view, state agencies may be more usefully classified not in terms of their purposes but according to the differing constitutional relationships they have to the central controlling institutions of Cabinet and Parliament (Wood, 1988: 25–6). Such a classification begins with a standard or 'paradigm' case of the typical government department which may be identified as an agency which is publicly funded and directly responsible to a minister placed in charge of it. The minister in turn is subject to overall direction from Cabinet and responsible to Parliament and thus to the public. State agencies of this type make up the departments of the public service, sometimes referred to as the 'core public service'.

Beyond this core is a range of public bodies which differ in various respects from the core public service but which are under a sufficient degree of public control, through a minister or Parliament, or sufficiently dependent on public funding to be counted as part of the overall state. Some state agencies are statutorily independent of direct ministerial or executive control for clear constitutional reasons, in order to guarantee their independence from the government of the day.

For instance, the courts and other tribunals, such as the Waitangi Tribunal or the Complaints Review Tribunal, receive their funding from government but, as required by the principle of the separation of powers, are not subject to government direction in the decisions they make. For similar constitutional reasons, some public officials whose function is to scrutinise and criticise the acts of the executive, for instance the Controller and Auditor-General, the Ombudsmen and the Parliamentary Commissioner for the Environment are formally responsible to Parliament rather than to a minister (Harris, 1992: 69–70).

The major state agencies concerned with law and security, the police and the defence forces, have an organisational structure which differs from that of the standard government department. While their respective ministers are in charge of general policy directions, their day-to-day operations are in the hands of the senior commissioned officers. Members of the police and defence forces swear a separate oath of allegiance to the sovereign and their conditions of employment are different from those of normal public servants.

Other publicly owned organisations may be distanced from government control through being run by independent boards whose members may be appointed by the government but are not subject to direct ministerial intervention. This is the position of public corporations or 'state-owned enterprises' (SOEs), such as Television New Zealand, New Zealand Post and Genesis Power. These bodies are required by the government to return a dividend on investment but are given virtually complete independence about how they achieve this objective. Broadly similar structures have been established for the nine research institutes (Crown Research Institutes), such as AgResearch, Forest Research and the Institute of Geological and Nuclear Sciences. The Reserve Bank is a statutorily independent central bank responsible for the oversight of the national banking and monetary systems. Under the Reserve Bank Act 1989 it is required to pursue the single objective of controlling inflation without ministerial intervention.

There is a wide range of other statutory bodies, advisory boards, commissions, committees and offices, set up by government to fulfil some public purpose, usually of a quite specific nature, such as Sport and Recreation New Zealand (SPARC), the Securities Commission and the Teachers Council. Their functions are usually defined by statute or government regulation, their activities are wholly or partly paid for from public funds, and their accounts are subject to public audit. Such bodies were sometimes known as 'quangos' (literally 'quasi non-governmental organisations') (Palmer, 1987: 90–95) and are now officially classified as 'crown entities' (Boston *et al.*, 1996: 62–4).

Also to be included in state agencies are publicly funded educational institutions, such as schools, colleges of education, polytechnics, universities and wananga. They are run by independent boards or councils, most of whose members are elected or appointed by local communities rather than by the government. However, they are still subject to considerable government direction, through such means as government control of funding formulae and through their need to meet government-determined standards.

The new public management

Since the mid-1980s, New Zealand's state sector has been subject to major restructuring (Boston *et al.*, 1996: Appendix 1). The official impetus behind these reforms has been the attempt to make the public sector both more effective, in the sense of better meeting the objectives sought by the public and its elected government, and also more efficient, in the sense of delivering the best results for a given outlay of public funds. The broader political context has been set by the deregulation of the New Zealand economy which has forced governments to constrain the level of public expenditure in order to maintain the confidence of financial investors (Chapter 13: 313). The reforms are part of an international trend in public sector management, known as the 'new public management' or 'managerialism', which embraces a number of principles, including a general preference for private sector management methods (based on an assumption that there is little essential difference, from a management point of view, between the public and private sector); an emphasis on results and outcomes rather than on rules and procedures; the devolution of decision-making away from the centre ('letting the managers manage') balanced by increased monitoring and accountability of decision-makers; the creation of separate agencies for separate functions rather than allowing one agency or department to combine different and potentially conflicting functions, for instance commercial and non-commercial functions, or policy advice, service delivery and regulatory functions (Boston *et al.*, 1996: 25–6).

The rationale underlying the new public management contains a number of strands (Boston *et al.*, 1996: Chapter 2). Some are drawn from public choice theory and emphasise the tendency of public servants to pursue their own interests at the expense of the public's interest and to prefer policies which suit their own power and position regardless of the cost to the taxpayer. This 'bureaucratic capture' of policy-making is to be countered by removing the public servants' monopoly of service provision or policy advice, by subjecting them to competition ('contestability') or by moving the function altogether out of the public sector. Also influential has been 'agency theory', a branch of institutional economics which analyses the relationships between agents and those whose interest they serve, their 'principals'. In this context, the prime instance of principal–agent relationship is that of ministers and public servants. Particular emphasis is placed on making agents follow the objectives set for them by their principals by means of clearly specified contracts and reliable methods of monitoring performance.

While New Zealand has not been alone in embracing these principles, it has done so with unusual thoroughness and theoretical consistency, particularly in the emphasis on single-purpose rather than multi-purpose institutions, in the use of explicit performance contracts and in the adoption of new accounting principles. This doctrinaire radicalism largely reflects the leading role played by economic theorists in Treasury who approached the question of government structure as one to be organised on first principles rather than on the basis of historical experience (Boston, 1996). Their recommendations met with a sympathetic response from senior ministers keen to impose their priorities on a seemingly immovable public service and willing to use the considerable powers allowed under New Zealand's extreme version of the Westminster system (Chapter 3: 63) to ram through unpopular reforms. Powerful political support was added from business leaders, many of whom benefited directly from the reorganisation (Kelsey, 1995: 127–36), and from representatives of financial markets who claimed that investor confidence depended on continuing reform.

The beginning of the process was marked by the State-Owned Enterprises Act 1986 which established the role of public corporations (SOEs) as commercial organisations and applied both to existing corporations, such as New Zealand Rail and Air New Zealand, and to new SOEs formed from previous government departments, for instance, Electricity Corporation of New Zealand, New Zealand Post and Telecom. After its re-election in 1987, the Lange government adopted an even more ambitious reform agenda, culminating in two major Acts of Parliament, the State Sector Act 1988, which provided a new employment framework for public servants, much closer to that of the private sector, and the Public Finance Act 1989, which introduced a new structure of financial accounting and reporting based on objectives and outputs. The change of government in 1990 did not seriously affect the impetus of reform. Under the same economic imperatives and following the same advice, the Bolger government continued to embed the principles of the 1988 and 1989 Acts through the detailed reorganisation of individual departments and agencies. At the same time, it introduced a few adjustments of its own, particularly a new emphasis on government-wide strategic planning to counter the criticism that the earlier reforms had focused too exclusively on individual ministers and their departments at the expense of the government as a whole. By the mid 1990s, almost all government departments and other public agencies had faced major reorientation and restructuring as functions were hived off to new public bodies, charges were made for services previously freely available to other departments or the public ('user pays'), departments made more use of private firms and consultants rather than their own staff ('contracting out'), and public agencies with a commercial focus, including many of the newly restructured SOEs, were sold to the private sector ('privatisation').

Restructuring the core public service

The basic unit of organisation in the core public service is the individual department responsible to a minister. Around 35 such departments are listed on the State Services Commission webpage. The number is large by the standards of some other Westminster systems, for instance the United Kingdom and Australia. In some countries, individual Cabinet ministers are normally in charge of only one department, which means that the number of departments is in line with the size of the Cabinet. New Zealand, however, has long followed the practice of allocating more than one of the nearly 80 portfolios to individual ministers, particularly if some of the portfolios are considered to carry a relatively light workload. In the coalition Cabinet formed after the 2002 election, for instance, Pete Hodgson was Minister of Energy, Minister of Fisheries, Minister of Research, Science and Technology, Minister for Crown Research Institutes, held two Associate Minister roles and was Convenor of a Ministerial Group on Climate

Change. Marion Hobbs was Minister for Environment, Minister for Disarmament and Arms Control, Minister Responsible for the National Library, Minister Responsible for Archives New Zealand and held three Associate Minister roles (Chapter 4: 82–4).

All departments have the central core function of giving advice to their ministers and to the government as a whole. The whole decision-making process of government, both of Cabinet itself and of individual ministers, is serviced by department officials who prepare background papers and draft recommendations for ministers to act on. Departmental papers typically set out the issues and options and suggest possible courses of action for the ministers to take. For many departments, for example, Defence, Environment, Women's Affairs, this work of informing and advising their minister is the major, indeed, sometimes the sole function of the department (see box). Other departments, however, directly provide public services themselves (e.g. the Conservation Department and Statistics New Zealand), or engage in a trading activity (e.g. the Public Trust Office). Some departments are central agencies concerned with oversight of the public service as a whole (the two most important being the Treasury and the State Services Commission), while the Department of Prime Minister and Cabinet coordinates policy advice. Others are responsible for collecting government revenue (Inland Revenue and Customs) or for monitoring the actions of other departments (the Audit Office and the Education Review Office).

Though the restructuring process left the total number of departments roughly constant, the distribution of departments within the various categories was altered significantly. Under the principles of the new public management, departments with a primarily trading function were corporatised or privatised on the ground that such services could be provided more efficiently by commercially oriented organisations rather than by departments subject to ministerial control and political interference. A number of long-standing departments were removed altogether from the ranks of government departments – for instance, Energy, the Government Printing Office, the Post Office and the State Insurance Office. Other departments, such as Forestry, were radically restructured, with their trading or service activities being corporatised or privatised, and their functions largely confined to the core public-service role of giving ministerial advice. Maori Affairs, which had formerly had direct responsibility for large-scale enterprises, was reduced to a small policy-oriented department. (Maori Affairs was reconstituted by National, in 1991, as the Ministry of Maori

---

Core Public Service Departments

Central agencies

Department of Prime Minister
 and Cabinet
State Services Commission
Treasury

Review and audit functions

Audit Office
Education Review Office

Mainly policy functions

Agriculture and Forestry
Culture and Heritage
Defence
Economic Development
Education
Environment
Fisheries
Health
Housing
Justice
Maori Development
Pacific Island Affairs
Research, Science &
Technology
Transport
Women's Affairs

Significant delivery & policy functions

Foreign Affairs and Trade
Labour
Social Development

Mainly delivery functions

Archives New Zealand
Child, Youth & Family Services
Conservation
Corrections
Crown Law Office
Internal Affairs
National Library
Serious Fraud Office
Statistics
Land Information

**Residual category –
mainly trading
operations (crown entities)**

Public Trust Office
Valuation New Zealand

Taxing functions

Customs
Inland Revenue

Based on Boston *et al.* (1996), and www.ssc.govt.nz

Development (Te Puni Kokiri), initially as a more service-oriented department (McLeay, 1991). Subsequently, however, through National's policy of 'mainstreaming' Maori services, the department was reduced to a more exclusively policy role (Boston *et al.*, 1996: 152–8)).

Departments which combined both a policy and a service function ran foul of the principle that different, potentially competing functions are better performed by distinct institutions. Policy advice, it was held, tended to be distorted by the interests of those providing the service, for instance, teachers (Education), doctors and nurses (Health), the armed forces (Defence), social workers (Social Welfare), prison officers (Justice). A number of such departments were therefore reconstituted into smaller policy ministries while the service providers were grouped into separate public agencies. In some cases, for instance science and health, separate agencies were created not only for the provision of services but also for the purchase of such services on behalf of the government (see below). Departments which retained significant service functions, e.g. Labour and Social Welfare, were encouraged to establish internal policy units independent of the service providers. Similar objections to potential conflicts of interests within departments led to the creation of separate regulatory agencies, for instance the Education Review Office.

Restructuring was often accompanied by a change of name from 'department' to 'ministry'. There is, however, no standard uniformity of titles. Some departments are called 'departments', others 'ministries' or 'offices'. There is a State Services 'Commission' and simply 'The Treasury'. In the restructuring process there was a tendency to use the term 'ministry' to refer to departments concerned solely or largely with giving policy advice to ministers and 'department' for departments which also provided some service to the public. When departments such as Education and Maori Affairs were changed from 'departments' to 'ministries', this was to signify that they were no longer meant to be in the business of directly serving the public (Boston, 1991: 264, n3).

At the same time as the number of trading and service departments has decreased, there has been an increase in the number of 'client oriented' or 'watch-dog' departments (Boston, 1991: 246–7). Groups or interests which have had difficulty in getting their voices heard at the highest levels of policy-making have sought to have a minister and a department charged with representing their point of view at the Cabinet table and in key committees. The first of these new departments was the Ministry of Women's Affairs set up in 1985. It scrutinises policy proposals for their likely effect on women and makes recommendations to the appropriate committees. The ministry has also commissioned its own reports and issued publications aimed to highlight problems faced by women.

The Ministry of Women's Affairs was followed by a Ministry of Consumer Affairs (1986) (subsequently absorbed into the Ministry of

Commerce and then Economic Development), a Ministry of Youth Affairs (1989) (now absorbed into the Ministry of Social Development), and a Ministry of Pacific Island Affairs (1990). The revamped Ministry of Maori Affairs (subsequently Ministry of Maori Development) has also taken on a similar scrutinising role on behalf of Maori interests. A similar role is performed by the Ministry of the Environment on behalf of environmental matters. Most of these client-oriented ministries are very small in terms of their budgets and the size of their staffs – the Ministry of Women's Affairs had a staff of 24 in 2003 and Pacific Island Affairs had 44. There are regular complaints that they are not sufficiently effective in influencing government policy. None the less, they do reflect an attempt to represent those interests which tend to be systematically neglected in pluralist political systems (Chapter 9: 214–5). The groups themselves certainly see some positive benefit from having their own designated minister and departments – moves by politicians to delay the establishment of such departments or to abolish them once they have been established have been vigorously resisted by the relevant interest groups.

While the restructuring of the core public service has been remarkable both for its extent and for its adherence to theoretical principle, it is not without anomalies and inconsistencies (Boston *et al.*, 1996: 82–86). The Treasury, for example, though eager to divide the power of rival departments, has been less willing to weaken its own position. It has retained responsibility for both economic policy advice and financial control of government expenditure, functions which are divided in some other countries. A number of departments, e.g. Foreign Affairs and Trade, Labour, Social Development, still combine significant policy and service functions. The institutional separation of regulatory functions from policy and service delivery functions was followed in education and transport but not in health (where the Ministry of Health retains important supervisory and regulatory roles in health matters).

There have often been good reasons for making exceptions. For instance, while freeing policy advisers from day-to-day administration may enhance the objectivity and independence of their advice, it also makes sense for those with experience in the field to contribute to policy advice. The splitting of functions may reduce internal conflicts of interest but at the cost of less coordination and cohesion. Such considerations, for example, led to the substantial reintegration of the Ministry of Defence and the New Zealand Defence Force which had been institutionally separated a few years earlier (Boston *et al.*, 1996:

92). In general, the recent reorganisation of the public service has led to greater clarity of government functions and to increased efficiencies in the provision of certain services to the public. At the same time, it has been expensive in the amount of resources consumed by the reform process itself and also in the added problems of coordination caused by the greatly increased number of individual public agencies.

Chief Executives and the States Services Commission

A basic principle of democratic parliamentary government is that the public service should be under the control of the elected government of the day. In the State Sector Act, this principle is enshrined in the relationship between ministers and their chief executives (CEs). CEs are required to act as their ministers' agents in much the same way as a chief executive of any major organisation, such as a private company, follows objectives laid down by the owners or directors and is responsible to them for satisfactory performance in meeting these objectives. An annual performance agreement between minister and CE includes a purchase agreement in which ministers spell out what they want their CEs and their departments to achieve (their desired 'outcomes') and CEs specify the particular services ('outputs') the department can provide to meet these objectives from the resources available by the minister (Boston *et al.*, 1996: 110–17). The same structure is carried through into the annual budgetary process in which departments are funded for specified 'output classes'. Subsequently, in their annual reports to Parliament, departments are required to report their success in meeting the agreed outputs by measuring their performance in terms of previously agreed criteria (Boston *et al.*, 1996: Chapter 13).

Since 1994, CEs' performance agreements have been broadened to include reference not only to individual ministers' preferred outcomes but also to the government's overall political objectives. These objectives are defined in terms of 'strategic result areas' (SRAs) and CEs are expected to nominate certain 'key result areas' (KRAs) in which they will be able to contribute to the appropriate SRAs, making progress in terms of specified 'milestones'. The annual performance agreements have thus been integrated into the government's medium-term planning as well as into the more immediate annual budgetary cycle. This helps to meet one of the criticisms made of the State Sector Act's emphasis on individual ministers and CEs, that there was insufficient concern for the effective management of government business as a whole and insufficient recognition that CEs should see themselves as serving the collective interests of Cabinet and the prime minister as well as their immediate ministers (Boston, 1991b: 102–3; McLeay, 1995: 101–7).

An important coordinating role is also played by the State Services Commission, the government department responsible for supervising the public service as a whole. For instance, the Commission is closely involved in the appointment of CEs. While ministers have the right to specify the type of appointee they are looking for, the State Services Commissioner (the Commission's CE) conducts the search for suitable applicants and short-listed candidates are interviewed by a panel including the Commissioner, the Deputy Commissioner and one or more others appointed by the Commissioner. The Commissioner then refers the name of the recommended appointee to Cabinet. Cabinet has the right to appoint its own preferred candidate, but in practice accepts the Commissioner's recommendation. CEs are appointed for limited terms of five years or less with the possibility of reappointment (usually for three years or less). They can also be replaced if there is an irrevocable breakdown in relations with their minister. The most prominent recent such case occurred in 2000, when the CE of the then Work and Income New Zealand, Christine Rankin, lost her job following the restructuring of the ministry. The State Services Commissioner conducts regular reviews of the performance of individual CEs and, after consultation with relevant ministers, is responsible for any recommendations concerning reappointment or transfer.

Under the State Sector Act, the CE acts as the employer of all staff within his or her department. Previously, all public servants had been employed by the State Services Commission under uniform rates of pay and conditions. Working for the public service was seen as a secure, lifetime career. However, according to the principles of the new public management, such a system was inflexible and inefficient. Given that staff salaries usually consume the bulk of departmental budgets, particularly in policy-oriented departments, it made sense for CEs to have control over staffing resources if they were to be responsible for the efficient and effective delivery of their designated outputs. Conditions of employment were also made more flexible in line with those applying in the private sector. Some central constraints still remain. The Act requires CEs to be a 'good employer' in relation to matters such as impartiality and respect for equal employment opportunities (EEO). Moreover, the State Services Commission still retains some general rights of oversight, including the crucial right to negotiate pay and conditions as employer. However, in response to complaints about undue restrictions on managerial freedom, the Commission has since delegated negotiating authority to CEs, while keeping a watching brief to see that settlements do not breach government policy (Boston *et al.*, 1996: 211–16; Chapter 11).

The State Sector Act also provides for the establishment of a Senior Executive Service (SES), made up of the senior managers in each department, those immediately below the CEs, in the mid-1990s numbering about 130 across all departments. This followed a model first introduced in the US and subsequently in Canada and Australia. The intention has been to develop a cadre of senior public servants with generalised managerial skills and committed to the values of the new public management. Some could be recruited directly from the private sector, while others would be promoted from within the public service. Individual members of the SES are employed by their departmental CEs, but the State Services Commission has responsibility for developing the SES as whole. The Commission determines which positions can be filled by SES officers and it must be consulted about individual appointments. So far, the SES has failed to live up to its promise. CEs find the State Services Commission's role an unwarranted interference with their managerial authority. At the same time, perhaps not surprisingly in an era of increased decentralisation and departmental autonomy, the SES has been unable to develop much sense of cohesion or common purpose (Boston *et al.*, 1996: 117–20).

The principle of political neutrality

In treating departmental chief executives (CEs) as the agents of their ministers, the procedures enshrined in the State Sector Act build on two well-established and closely related principles in the Westminster tradition, political neutrality and ministerial responsibility. Political neutrality has been understood in the sense of neutrality in the partisan political conflicts which divide the major political parties (Roberts, 1987: 82–84). Public servants, both individually and collectively, are expected to serve whichever party is in power with equal diligence and integrity. Political neutrality is reflected in the assumption that public servants do not owe their jobs to politicians but are appointed independently, either on the recommendation of the State Services Commissioner, or by their respective CEs. While ministers have some role in the appointment of CEs themselves, they are legally prevented from intervening in the appointment of any other public servants (Boston

1994). By contrast, in countries where the public service is highly politicised, a change in the elected government means a wholesale change in those occupying important positions in the bureaucracy. In the United States, for instance, it is not expected that senior or intermediate officials appointed by one president could loyally serve another. Each new president, on election, is required to make several thousand appointments to the Washington bureaucracy.

Political neutrality does not mean that public servants are political neuters, immune to the political leanings of the government or unaware of the political conflicts between the government and its opponents. The policy environment in which public servants operate is intensely political, particularly at senior levels where major policy is developed. Skilled and professional public servants, in formulating options and giving advice to ministers, will always be alive to the political considerations facing their ministers, such as party commitments or caucus pressure. The point of political neutrality is not that public servants stand aloof from the political purposes of the government but that they are 'impartially partisan', offering the same degree of committed support to whichever party happens to form the government of the day.

From the broader, more critical, perspective provided by theories of structural dominance, the public service is far from politically neutral. To a marxist, the whole apparatus of the bureaucracy is geared to the interests of capitalists and to the exploitation of the working class. Similarly, Maori nationalists would look on government departments as instruments of Pakeha control, oppressing the Maori people through the justice, education and welfare systems. Political neutrality, as constitutionally prescribed for public servants, is narrower in focus, simply requiring neutrality between the different policy perspectives of competing political parties. Where the parties themselves agree on the political directions that all governments should take, there will be little need for neutrality on the part of public servants. There is a general consensus, for instance, that New Zealand governments should foster economic growth and reduce the rate of crime against property and persons. Public servants will not be expected to abstain from expressing their support for such objectives. To do so would not compromise their ability to serve whichever party gains power. Thus, the neutrality in party politics required of the public servant by no means implies complete neutrality about the functions of the state.

In spite of the official commitment by public servants to the principle of political neutrality, politicians have often been sceptical about the commitment of their advisers to following the policy directions being set by the government. Such doubts about the loyalty of the public service were particularly strong among incoming members of the Lange Labour government (Walsh, 1991: 52–53). In part this reflected memories of bureaucratic resistance during the previous Labour government of 1972–5; it was also a natural result of a long period of National government during which senior public servants faithfully serving the government could easily appear to have become personally identified with National's policies. Lange, when still in opposition, suggested that a Labour government might require senior public servants to swear a loyalty oath to the new government (Roberts, 1987a: 100; Martin, 1988: 15). After gaining office, Labour took a number of measures designed to reinforce political control over the public service. One was a significant change in the type of advice available to ministers in their own offices in the Beehive. Previously, ministers had relied on public servants seconded to their offices from the relevant department, advisers who would owe more long-term loyalty to their superiors in the department than to the minister. A number of Labour ministers brought in their own advisers from outside the public service, people who could be relied on to provide alternative advice and help the ministers exert their own control over departments. Increased use was also made of private sector consultants to write reports critical of current public service structures and practices, a trend continued under National.

The need to secure the political loyalty of public servants was also one of the main motives behind the restructuring of the public service in the State Sector Act 1988, particularly in the changes made to the method of appointing chief executives and to their tenure. Previously, the appointment of CEs was wholly the responsibility of the State Services Commission. Though ministers could usually make their preferences known informally, they had no formal right to be consulted, let alone impose a veto. Moreover, the question of reappointment did not arise because chief executives had the right of permanent tenure until retirement (and hence were known as 'permanent heads'). The rationale, dating back to the Public Service Act 1912, was to prevent appointments to public service positions from being subject to political influence and patronage. An independent, career public service was considered an essential safeguard against political corruption and nepotism. It also enabled public servants to offer ministers 'free and frank' advice which might be unpopular but which ministers ought to hear. According to the advocates of the new public management, however, such independence and security of tenure carried too great a cost in terms of the potential for protected public servants to frustrate the wishes of the democratically elected government of the day.

When first proposed, the changes to the tenure and appointment of chief executives gave rise to strongly voiced criticisms that they would lead to the undue politicisation of the public service and thus undermine the concept of a career public service committed to political neutrality (Walsh, 1991: 63–67). These fears have proved exaggerated (Boston *et al.*, 1996: 321–3). Admittedly, there have been occasional arguments between ministers supporting rival candidates (Boston *et al.*, 1996: 100–105). There was also one public disagreement between the State Services Commissioner and the Labour government over the appointment of a CE for the new Ministry of Defence. The Commissioner recommended Gerald Hensley, a highly respected public servant with clear credentials for the job. The government, however, claimed that Hensley was unsuitable because he lacked the necessary resource management skills and asked the Commission to readvertise the position. The real but unspoken reason for rejecting Hensley was almost certainly that he was thought to be unsympathetic to the Labour government's defence policy.

But this was an isolated case which could well have reached a similar conclusion under the former system of wholly informal consultation. In every other appointment made since the Act was passed, the recommendations of the State Services Commissioner have been accepted by the government. Moreover, those appointed under Labour generally showed themselves willing and able to serve the new National government elected in 1990. Talk of large-scale replacements of Labour-appointed CEs, which circulated among National leaders when in opposition, largely evaporated after the new government took office. The new fixed-term nature of CEs contracts does mean that the question of their continuing employment comes up for review periodically. But this review does not necessarily occur at the time when a newly elected government is seeking to introduce changes in policy direction and might therefore look to have a new CE sympathetic to its views. A fully politicised public service would require that all senior positions became automatically vacant on a change of government. Under the present system, incoming ministers are still required, at least in the medium term, to work with the public servants who served the previous government. For their own part, the senior public servants themselves have an interest in maintaining the concept of a career public service and thus have clear incentives to serve the government of the day loyally. Their duty to do so is also reinforced by the new structure of ministerial 'outcomes' and departmental 'outputs' in annual performance agreements which spell out the obligation of CEs to meet objectives set by their ministers. In general, the new public management has tended to emphasise the responsibility of politicians for setting political directions, an emphasis which is reflected in the values of public servants (Gregory 1995). The change to MMP and the need for public servants to respond to the political preferences of more than one governing party has made new demands on the political sensitivities of public servants (Boston *et al.*, 1996a: Chapter 8). But New Zealand's public service will continue to be essentially a career service, operating under traditional conventions of political neutrality.

Ministerial responsibility

The other important principle governing the relations of ministers and public servants is the principle of ministerial responsibility. Under this principle, ministers are answerable to Parliament and to the public for what is done within their departments. Ministerial responsibility means that a minister, being in charge of a department, should take all reasonable steps to see that government policies are being followed in the department, that the department is generally well administered and that faults which come to the minister's attention are remedied.

The concept of ministerial responsibility is the object of some common misconceptions. One is that ministerial responsibility implies that ministers must be personally responsible for everything that is done in their name by any members of their department. This is clearly impossible because no one individual could possibly be aware of everything happening in a large organisation. The concept of ministerial responsibility is therefore said to be a misleading or mistaken doctrine (Palmer, 1987: 82–83).

But this is to misunderstand the doctrine. Ministers are not personally responsible for everything that is done in their name or personally to blame if any mistakes are made by the members of their department. Blame only attaches if the minister could reasonably have been expected to prevent the mistake. There is every justification in the famous words of Bob Semple, Minister of Works in the First Labour Government, when serious incompetence was discovered in his department: 'I am responsible but I am not to blame' (Scott, 1962: 127). However, even where the personal responsibility and blame belongs to officials, the minister still holds overall responsibility (sometimes described as 'vicarious' responsibility) in the sense of being obliged to answer publicly for the action of officials and to initiate any necessary remedies.

Though ministers may not be expected to have known what was happening, this does not allow them to distance themselves totally from what has happened or exonerate them from remedying faults when they come to light. In 1992, when deficiencies came to light in the blood transfusion service run by the Health Department, the minister, Simon Upton, argued that he had been unaware of the problems and therefore was not personally to blame for them. He therefore, mistakenly, denied responsibility. The issue also arose in 1995 in connection with the Cave Creek tragedy when fourteen people lost their lives after the collapse of a viewing platform built by the Department of Conservation. Though the Chief Executive accepted responsibility for administrative deficiencies, the minister properly took responsibility in the sense of seeing that the accident was fully investigated and appropriate measures taken.

In spite of the complications sometimes raised by constitutional lawyers (Scott, 1962: 124–31; Marshall, 1984), ministerial responsibility, like collective Cabinet responsibility, is quite a straightforward concept. It is simply an instance of a more general type of responsibility associated with the duties of anyone managing a large organisation. Ministers are responsible in just the same way as the principal of a school or the managing director of a company is responsible. They answer on behalf of their organisation to their appropriate public, they take charge of the most important or potentially controversial items of policy and they generally see that those under them work efficiently. They are not personally responsible for every action taken but they exercise a general responsibility for the organisation as a whole.

Another misunderstanding concerns the sanction for impropriety or maladministration discovered in a department. It is often claimed, particularly by oppositions, that ministerial responsibility requires the resignation of the minister, whether or not the minister was personally responsible or personally to blame for the misconduct. When ministers do not resign, the media regularly pronounce the principle of ministerial responsibility to be dead. However, there is no obligation to resign when the minister is not personally at fault. In 1986, copies of the Budget were delivered to a number of interested parties around the country before it had been formally announced in Parliament, a mistake made in the Minister's office and a clear breach of important conventions of budget confidentiality. The Minister, Roger Douglas, offered his resignation, presumably because a breach of budget confidentiality was the reason for one of the leading British cases of ministerial resignation (Marshall, 1984: 62). The prime minister, however, refused to accept the resignation. His letter to Douglas clearly set out the New Zealand conventions and precedents about ministerial responsibility (Palmer, 1987: 51–52), indicating that resignation is not required if the minister is in no way personally at fault.

Certainly there can be a strong case for a ministerial resignation if the minister is guilty of personal impropriety. The last instance of such resignation in New Zealand was the case of Sir Apirana Ngata, Minister of Native Affairs (as Maori Affairs was then described), who resigned in 1934 after a commission of inquiry had discovered supposed evidence of financial irregularities in the conduct of his portfolio (King, 1992: 299; Palmer, 1987: 56; Walker, 2001: Chapter 13). Similar accusations were made in the 'Marginal Lands Board loans affair' in 1980 against the Acting Minister of Lands, Duncan MacIntyre, and against Koro Wetere, Minister of Maori Affairs in the Lange Labour government, during the 'Maori loans affair' in 1986–7 (Roberts, 1987: 45–46; Palmer, 1987: 48, 55–56). Both ministers were said to have acted 'unwisely' but neither resigned from Cabinet. John Banks, a minister in the Bolger National government, was involved in a number of discreditable incidents, including conviction for the use of a cellphone on an aircraft while Minister of Police, and attacks on the judiciary which were in breach of *Cabinet Office Manual* rules (McLeay, 1996). The prime minister, however, resisted the frequent calls for his resignation. He did, however, dismiss Ross Meurant, an under-secretary, in 1995 for refusing to resign from a bank directorship (Boston *et al.*, 1996a: 51). In 1999, two of prime minister Shipley's ministers, Murray McCully and Tuariki John Delamere, relinquished portfolios for breeches of administration in tourism and immigration, respectively, while retaining their Cabinet positions. However, Dover Samuels was dismissed from Cabinet by Helen Clark after allegations of past personal misconduct damaging to both him and the government were given wide publicity. Although cleared of the allegations, Samuels remained outside the ministry until after the 2002 election. Three other ministers resigned during the Clark government's first term, Ruth Dyson, after a drink driving charge, and Phillida Bunkle and Marion

Hobbs after questions were raised over the legitimacy of their claims for accommodation allowances. Hobbs returned to Cabinet after being cleared of impropriety, and Dyson was eventually reinstated to her ministerial position outside Cabinet. Bunkle, however, an Alliance minister in the coalition, whose reinstatement would have depended on Jim Anderton's recommendation, did not return.

Whether resignation is required is ultimately a political decision for the party leadership, just as in the case of breaches of collective Cabinet responsibility (Chapter 4: 88–89). In reaching that decision, a prime minister will need to balance the political costs of sheltering a tarnished minister within the embrace of Cabinet solidarity against the costs of dismissing the minister in a blaze of public disgrace. Whatever decision is made, however, does not affect the issue of responsibility. It is simply a decision over what sanction, if any, to apply to a minister who has performed unsatisfactorily, not one about whether the minister was in fact responsible. The lack of ministerial resignations in New Zealand, though it may be regrettable, does not prove that the doctrine of ministerial responsibility is dead.

The principle of ministerial responsibility is an important element in the conventions of parliamentary democracy. It requires ministers to be accountable for their own conduct, to answer publicly for the actions of the bureaucracy and to take appropriate action to remedy mistakes. In its pure form, the principle requires that the minister is the only person held publicly responsible and that the public servants in the minister's department remain out of the public eye and anonymous. However, this extreme version of the scope of the principle no longer applies in New Zealand, if it ever did. In certain circumstances, public servants may be held accountable directly to the public rather than through their minister (Roberts, 1987: 57–62). The Ombudsmen, for instance, have the power to investigate actions of public servants on behalf of members of the public. They have direct access to all departmental records and reports without having to work through the minister and can make public recommendations about remedies in individual cases or about improvements to procedures. At the time when the position of Ombudsman was being introduced, in the early 1960s, doubts were expressed about its compatibility with the principle of ministerial responsibility because it appeared to bypass the minister and thus undermine ministerial authority. However, the Ombudsmen have power only to make recommendations. Moreover, most of the matters with which they deal tend to be at the level of detailed administration rather than major policy. Their recommendations therefore, in practice, do not cut across ministers' responsibility for setting policy and they may be seen as a useful adjunct to ministerial responsibility, adding a further level of public accountability.

The anonymity of public servants has also been decreased by the access to departmental reports and recommendations allowed under the Official Information Act 1982. This is potentially much more at odds with the concept of ministerial responsibility because it provides access to details not only of administration but also of the formation of major government policy. Observers and critics of the government can now know what official advice ministers have received and whether they have acted on it. The Act specifically exempts disclosure of information which would threaten collective and individual ministerial responsibility, the political neutrality of officials or the free and frank expression of advice between ministers and officials. None the less, public servants complain that the ending of official confidentiality impairs their ability to give free and frank advice to their ministers, at least in written reports. At the same time, the public availability of official reports and other documents, though formally a breach in the traditional convention of ministerial responsibility, can be said to enhance public debate by making the information and expertise of the public service more widely accessible.

Some departments have taken advantage of this new freedom by openly publishing their own recommendations. This is most notable in the case of the Treasury. It has been long-standing practice immediately after an election for departments to present incoming ministers with briefing papers, setting out the functions of the department and the main policy issues which will face the department and the minister. The Treasury, after the elections in 1984, 1987 and 1990, took this process a stage further by publishing their briefing papers in the form of book-length policy manifestos in a clear attempt to influence the government and other departments in favour of their point of view.

Public knowledge of a department's views opens a potential gap between the government and its advisers which critics of the government can exploit. Quoting from official papers, they can then require ministers to justify why they have chosen to follow, or not to follow, the advice given to them. Such tactics have been used to good effect by many groups critical of government policy, such as environmentalists and the peace movement. Opposition parties in Parliament have also made avid use of official information requests in attempts to embarrass ministers who have rejected departmental advice. Such use of official information does not, however, infringe the basic assumption of ministerial responsibility, that ministers should be held accountable for the directions their departments take. Indeed, it helps to make ministers more transparently accountable.

The new articulation of the relationship between ministers and CEs under the State Sector Act 1988 has the potential to alter the scope of ministerial responsibility. If ministers are merely responsible for setting objectives or 'outcomes', while the function of CEs is to produce the appropriate 'outputs', then any deficiency in the production of outputs can be laid at the door of the CE rather than the minister (Martin, 1994). Certainly, CEs have become more visible in recent years, defending their department's actions, most notably in the Cave Creek tragedy. In general, however, this model has not been strictly adhered to (Boston *et al.*, 1996: 319–23). Ministers still feel obliged to answer to the public for the detailed actions of their departments. CEs, on the whole, appear willing to let them. The line between the minister's desired policy 'outcomes' and the department's decisions about how to achieve them is not easily drawn. Indeed, the attempt to reduce the aims of ministers and the functions of their departments to clear, unambiguous objectives is fundamentally flawed. The political process in a pluralist democracy requires constant adjustments to a changing social and economic environment and negotiations between competing notions of the public good (Chapter 13: 327). Major policy decisions often arise in the process of determining particular issues, such as the application of a particular regulation or giving the go-ahead for a particular building project. Politics is too complex a task to be neatly distinguished into political ends and administrative means to those ends (Gregory, 1987: 122–4).

As both ministers and their CEs recognise, if the elected politicians are to have control over the overall directions of government policy, they need to retain the capacity to intervene in any particular decision in their departments. (The major exception is decisions about personnel in which ministers are traditionally banned from intervening. This was at issue, in 1994, in the resignation of Perry Cameron, CE of Internal Affairs, after his minister complained publicly about a politically inappropriate appointment over which he, as minister, had not been consulted (Boston, 1994).) In general, while performance agreements may provide a useful opportunity for both ministers and their CEs to clarify their longer-term thinking, there is little evidence of their being used to prevent ministers from taking full responsibility for their departments. When mistakes occur or crises break, it is still the minister who has to answer in Parliament and it is still likely to be the minister, rather than the CE, who will be interviewed by the media. Similarly, while requiring departments to account for their annual performance in terms of defined objectives may help improve their administrative efficiency, it is no substitute for the daily threat of ministerial intervention.

One further limitation on the principle of ministerial responsibility is that public servants may not in all cases be obliged to follow instructions given by their ministers. Most accounts of the professional responsibilities of public servants recognise that they may be asked by a minister to perform some act which is constitutionally improper, for instance, an action involving nepotism, bribery or otherwise infringing the law. In such cases, public servants may be justified in resisting instructions and even in revealing the matter to the public by 'leaking' to the media or 'whistle-blowing' (Martin, 1988: 46; Boston *et al.*, 1996: 325–7). An uncorrupt and law-abiding public service may thus be seen as an important bulwark of constitutional integrity. Though itself part of the executive element of government, it can act as a potential check on the abuse of executive power by the elected members of the government.

The picture implied by the principle of ministerial responsibility is thus not literally accurate. Ministers do not actually decide everything that is done in their name and public servants are not discretionless agents of their ministers' will. The great majority of actions taken or decisions made by government departments are carried out either without reference to the minister or with the merest formality of consultation. None the less, ministerial responsibility provides an important mechanism for holding officials accountable. There are other valuable channels for remedying individual grievances and injustices, for instance the Ombudsmen, watchdog bodies such as the Human Rights Commission and the Race Relations Conciliator, and the courts (Chapter 7). But ministerial responsibility is the ultimate safeguard of public scrutiny of government action. The principle guarantees that ministers are obliged to respond publicly and to explain decisions of their officials. This requirement, in turn, enables the important constraining force of media publicity, both actual and anticipated, to be exerted throughout the bureaucracy.

Politicians and bureaucrats

In relation to the public service's core function of advising ministers and helping the government to reach decisions on matters of general policy, does the balance of power rest with the politicians or the public servants? Constitutional and democratic principle requires that authority should lie with the elected politician, the minister. In reality, however, effective political power may be in the hands of the permanent bureaucracy. Public servants may use this power to pursue their own interests rather than their ministers'. This is the burden of the public choice critique of bureaucracy which was very influential on the new public management restructuring (and received popular endorsement through the BBC TV series *Yes Minister* and *Yes Prime Minister*).

Neither extreme view is correct. Ministers do not do all the directing while public servants simply deliver, as the pure version of ministerial responsibility might suggest. Nor does the *Yes Minister* caricature of the helpless minister being manipulated by senior officials give an accurate picture. The process of interaction and mutual influence between politicians and public servants is complex and subtle and relies much on 'anticipated reactions' (Chapter 1: 15) – officials naturally wish to avoid antagonising their minister, while ministers will often be reluctant to overburden their officials. Individual ministers will bring their own and their government's agenda to the portfolio, particularly where there have been clear commitments to the electorate or the party. On the other hand, the single most important source of new government policy is the public service itself, through initiatives developed in the departments' various policy units or through direct discussion and negotiation with interested parties. Most public servants, especially at the more senior level, see themselves as involved in making policy and not just in advising and implementing. Though, in theory, they may just be engaged in formulating options for politicians to decide among, in practice, they often usually have a clear preference and will hope to steer the minister in that direction (McLeay, 1995: 133–44).

Whether ministers or public servants ultimately prevail depends on a number of factors. One is the type of issue involved (Kellow, 1989). Where a policy is confined to one administrative sector, such as agriculture or health, and is either technical in nature or readily negoti-ated between interested parties, the policy-making process will be mainly in the hands of the public servants, with the minister's role simply that of attaching a final formal approval. On the other hand, where issues are less easily resolved or where other departments or other ministers become involved, the minister may be required to inter-vene more directly. Where major new expenditure is required, indi-vidual ministers and the Cabinet as a whole will become directly involved as part of the annual budgetary process. The capacity of min-isters to determine priorities through the budget has been significantly enhanced by the adoption of 'output classes' as the basis for authoris-ing and reporting expenditure, though the new system still allows con-siderable scope for departmental discretion (Boston *et al.*, 1996: 269–72).

Again, if the issue is one which involves a political commitment, for instance one made by the party in an election campaign or ap-proved by the government caucus, the ministers will expect to take the initiative. Departmental officers will know that the full force of the Cabinet is behind the policy. For instance, under the Lange Labour government, the government's anti-nuclear policy was strongly opposed by many officials in the Department of Defence and the Ministry of Foreign Affairs, particularly when it led to the forced with-drawal of New Zealand from ANZUS. None the less, the policy was implemented by these same officials. However, if the issue is one on which the minister and the party have no clear view, then the public servants have a much better chance of persuading the minister to adopt the department's policy.

Another variable is the competence and strength of individual min-isters. Where a minister wishes to pursue a policy to which his or her department is opposed, officials will raise objections, pointing out the reasons why they consider the minister's option mistaken. Indeed, it is the officials' duty to give contrary advice in such circumstances. They may also find reasons to delay taking action, a tactic which, given the pressure of time in politics, is often sufficient to defeat a proposal. Whether the department is able to prevail will depend ulti-mately on the degree of determination shown by the minister. Some ministers undoubtedly allow themselves to be run by their depart-ments, while others successfully manage to impose their own stamp on their portfolios.

When strong ministers are determined on a particular policy direction, public servants will usually comply loyally. For example, the Treasury has always been an independently influential department, largely because of its strategic role as a central agency responsible for expenditure in all other departments and because of the numbers and quality of its policy analysts (Boston, 1992). Yet when Robert Muldoon was Minister of Finance and in charge of the Treasury, particularly during his last years in office, he regularly overruled Treasury recommendations on matters such as the exchange rate and prices and incomes policy.

Treasury's periods of greatest ascendancy in the major battles over economic and social policy have been when it has been led by a minister who agreed with its views and was able to prevail in Cabinet, as happened in the period when Roger Douglas was Minister of Finance in the Lange Labour government. Indeed, the most effective movements for public sector innovation have usually been spearheaded by a partnership between a strong minister and an enthusiastic department. If the addition of bureaucratic enthusiasm can make a difference, so too the absence of such enthusiasm may make a contrary difference, even if its effect is revealed only in subtle tactics of delay rather than in outright opposition to ministers' preferred policies.

In general, then, the departments of the public service may be seen as independent actors in the political process. They have their own clear policy preferences in many areas and their own extensive resources for exerting political power. However, their political independence should not be exaggerated. In many instances where departmental advisers conflict with ministers they may themselves be acting under pressure from outside sources. Thus Treasury is often acting as the mouthpiece of financial interests in the international markets or the Ministry of Foreign Affairs and Trade is relaying diplomatic pressure from powerful foreign countries. Many departments act as the political agents of social interests or groups. For instance, a watch-dog ministry, such as Women's Affairs or the Youth Development section of the Ministry of Social Development, has a clear role as advocate of their its constituency in the community. Other departments, with close links to a particular economic sector, such as Agriculture and Forestry or Fisheries, will naturally tend to act as advocates for the interests of those sectors. Major interest groups maintain close relations with relevant departments and the political power of the bureaucracy needs to be seen in the context of interest group influence and the role of 'policy communities' which develop around different departments (Chapter 9).

Moreover, New Zealand public servants are significantly constrained by the prevailing principles of political neutrality and ministerial responsibility and by the democratic assumption that final authority rests with elected ministers rather than non-elected officials. Contrary to the assertions of some public choice analyses of bureaucracy, that public servants are motivated solely by self-interest, such values do constitute an important and influential part of the public service ethos (Boston *et al.*, 1996: Chapter 17). How much power public servants exercise within the limits set by this ethos and by pressure from the wider society, is a question which needs to be answered case by case.

State-owned enterprises and other crown entities

While departments in the core public service are under direct ministerial control, other state agencies, known collectively as crown entities, are, for various reasons and to varying degrees, insulated from day-to-day political intervention. One such category consists of state-owned-enterprises (SOEs).

The primary statutory function of SOEs is to act as successful business enterprises, returning a profit on investment. To this end they are organised very like private companies. Ownership is in the hands of shareholders who are members of the government (the Ministers of Finance and State-Owned Enterprises). Control is vested in boards of directors appointed by the government, many of whom, particularly the chairpersons, have had extensive experience in private sector management. Accountability to the public is primarily achieved through the SOEs' commercial sensitivity to consumer preferences as expressed through the market. They are also accountable to Parliament through the requirement of annual reporting under the Public Finance Act and are subject to scrutiny from parliamentary select committees. They are also subject to the Official Information Act and within the jurisdiction of the Ombudsmen.

SOEs were formerly departments, or divisions of departments, which had been engaged in trading activities. The rationale for 'decoupling' them (Roberts, 1987: 14–16) from ministerial direction was that government departments were inefficient providers of commercial services. They were often protected from the discipline of competition by being guaranteed a monopoly in the supply of serv-

---

State-Owned Enterprises (SOEs) past and present

Current SOEs (2003)
AgriQuality NZ Ltd
Airways Corporation of NZ Ltd
Asure NZ Ltd
Electricity Corporation of NZ Residual Ltd
Genesis Power Ltd
Landcorp Farming Ltd
Meridian Energy Ltd
Meteorological Service of NZ Ltd
Mighty River Power Ltd
New Zealand Post Ltd
New Zealand Railways Corporation
Solid Energy NZ Ltd
Television NZ Ltd
Terralink NZ Ltd (in liquidation)
Timberlands West Coast Ltd
Transpower NZ Ltd

Former SOEs, now crown entities
Radio NZ Ltd
NZ Government Property Corporation

Former SOEs, since privatised
Air New Zealand (73 percent government owned since 2002)
Forestry Corporation of NZ
Government Computing Services
Government Supply Brokerage Corporation
New Zealand Railways Corporation
Petroleum Corporation of NZ
PostBank
Shipping Corporation of NZ
Telecom
Tourist Hotel Corporation of NZ

Note: a number of other government-owned enterprises, which were never formally constituted as SOEs, were also privatised, e.g. Bank of New Zealand, Development Finance Corporation, Government Life Insurance, Government Print, Rural Bank, State Insurance.
Based on: Boston *et al.*, 1996: 65-6; Cocker, 2003: 325-6; www.ccmau.govt.nz; www.ssc.govt.nz

---

ices or by having access to state-provided capital at less than market rates. At the same time they were prevented from being fully businesslike by the public's and the politicians' expectation that they would also meet non-commercial, social objectives, such as providing subsidised services in remote rural areas or guaranteeing employment to workers who might otherwise have difficulty finding work. Corporatisation thus accorded with the new public management's preference for single-purpose rather than multi-purpose agencies and with its general support for private sector models of organisation.

The State-Owned Enterprises Act 1986 allowed for the pursuit of non-commercial as well as strictly commercial objectives. SOEs were required to show a 'sense of social responsibility'. A section of the Act (Part 1, Section 7) also enabled the government to purchase services which would otherwise not be provided because they were unprofitable. Here the original rationale was that non-commercial objectives could be pursued so long as they were clearly identified ('transparent') and so long as they were separately paid for rather than being hidden in the total budget and therefore 'cross-subsidised' out of the proceeds of more profitable parts of the enterprise. In the event, non-commercial objectives were almost entirely neglected. The requirement of 'social responsibility', when tested in the courts, was not sufficient to prevent the closure of post offices and has proved largely ineffective (Mascarenhas, 1991: 38). The clause in the Act allowing purchase of non-commercial services was, in fact, used only once, to pay for some banking services from Post Bank, the former banking division of the Post Office, and then only for a transitional period of three years. SOEs have otherwise behaved as fully commercial enterprises.

It is not surprising therefore that the process of corporatisation was closely followed by that of privatisation. There appeared to be little point in state ownership of a fully commercial enterprise which could, virtually by definition, be equally well provided by the private sector. Managers chafed at the remaining constraints due to public ownership, especially at being under the Official Information Act and the Ombudsmen. Corporatisation proved to be, as many of its advocates had intended all along, merely a transitional step on the path to full privatisation. It was politically more palatable than outright privatisation, particularly for a Labour government with strong traditions of public ownership. Corporatisation could be depicted as updating Labour's goal of using the state more efficiently to pursue desirable collective goals (Douglas & Callan, 1987: Chapter 20). In practice, it was a process of restructuring state agencies in a way that would make them commercially viable and attractive to private-sector buyers. Ten years on from the passing of the Act, most of the major SOEs had become private companies.

Corporatisation and privatisation have certainly brought clear gains in efficiency as unprofitable services have been cut back and staffing numbers reduced. Responsiveness to consumer demand has been encouraged by the need to return a profit in competitive markets. However, the policies have been far from universally popular. Long-held expectations that services such as railways, postal delivery and telephones, should be politically accountable through ministers and Parliament have been slow to dissipate. The behaviour of major companies such as Telecom has sometimes seemed high-handed and insensitive to public opinion. The tendency of privatised corporations to come under foreign ownership and control has fuelled political resentment at the loss of economic sovereignty.

Similar principles of distancing public agencies from political and bureaucratic control were also applied by the Bolger National government to government-funded scientific research organisations and to public hospitals. The various research divisions of the former Department of Scientific and Industrial Research and the Ministry of Agriculture and Fisheries, as well as the Forest Research Institute and the Meteorological Service, were restructured in 1992 into independent corporate bodies known as 'Crown Research Institutes' (CRIs). The CRIs bid for government research moneys, distributed by an independent statutory authority, the Foundation for Research, Science and Technology. They are also free to attract research funds from the private sector and to undertake commercial ventures based on their research findings. Conversely, the Foundation is able to purchase research from elsewhere, e.g. from universities or private providers. At the same time, the government's interest in the prudent use of its assets is monitored by the Crown Company Monitoring Advisory Unit, housed in Treasury. The relevant government department, the Ministry of Research, Science and Technology, is now restricted to a largely policy advisory role. The structure of separate institutions for purchasing, providing, owning and advising, is a striking example of the preference for single-purpose agencies (Boston *et al.*, 1996: 83). The aim of the changes has been to make government-funded research more directly oriented to community demand and less subject to central government control. Given the long lead time before the results of research are evident, it is too early to tell whether the restructuring has been successful.

A similar model was adopted by the National government for public hospitals, reconstituted in 1993 as Crown Health Enterprises (CHEs). For many years, public hospitals were under the immediate control of locally elected hospital boards, though central government, which provided most of the funds through the Department of Health, also exercised considerable authority. During the 1980s, area health boards replaced hospital boards and were in turn replaced by four appointed regional health authorities (RHAs). The RHAs acted as the government's purchasing agents, purchasing health services from the newly independent CHEs. The separation of functions was reflected in the creation of dual ministerial portfolios. The Minister of Crown Health Enterprises was responsible for the government's interest as the owner of hospitals, appointing members of the CHEs and monitoring their performance. The Minister was advised by the Crown Company Monitoring Advisory Unit (CCMAU), which is a division of Treasury but gives advice independent of Treasury's advice to the Minister of Finance. The Minister of Health, meanwhile, as the minister responsible for the purchase of health services, oversaw the RHAs through the Ministry of Health which has general responsibilities for providing health policy advice. The intention was to increase efficiency and accountability by clarifying lines of responsibility and removing the mixed and conflicting directions which hospitals received under the former structure when they were responsible for determining health priorities as well as for efficient management and were subject to both local and central control. However, the creation of separate institutions with narrower functions, while it reduced the problem of conflicting purposes *within* institutions, also created major new problems of co-ordination *between* institutions. For the general public, the issue of accountability, of whom to blame when things went wrong, became more confused not clearer (Boston *et al.*, 1996: 173–7). As with SOEs, the public still expected their health institutions to be politically accountable, through elected politicians subject to the verdict of the ballot box. The unpopularity of National's restructuring of the health sector encouraged Labour and its coalition partner, the Alliance, to undertake another extensive revamp of the health sector, including a return to partly elected District Health Boards.

How publicly funded services are to be provided most efficiently and in a way which meets expectations of public accountability remains an open question. Various channels of public influence are available, whether through direct consumer choice, through locally elected boards or councils, or through bureaucracies responsible to elected politicians. Which channels are more effective depends on the nature of the service and the community being served. Where members of the public are well informed and have a genuine choice between alternative providers, competition and consumer choice can be relied on to provide the most efficient and popularly responsive type of service. This applies, for instance, to some aspects of health and education services, particularly in larger urban areas. But where there is no effective choice, for instance in the rules and standards applied in allocating welfare benefits or state housing, the public may need to look to the politicians and the public servants for redress, particularly if they have fewer resources of their own to call on. Removing the dead hand of Wellington may, in some circumstances, simply amount to removing the best means of protection available to the more vulnerable sections of society.

Further reading

The public service in general
Boston *et al.*(1996); Palmer & Palmer (1997): Chapter 5; Ringer (1991): Chapters 5–6; Shaw (2003); Wood (1988): Chapter 3.
The new public management
Boston *et al.*(1996): Chapters 1–2; Easton (1997).
The core public service
Boston *et al.* (1996): Chapters 3–6; Whitcombe (1992).
The Treasury
Boston (1992); Goldfinch (1997).
Ministers and chief executives
Boston *et al.* (1996): Chapters 5, 13; Martin (1988): Chapter 4; Martin (1994); Palmer (1987): 45–56; Roberts (1987): Chapter 4.
State-owned enterprises and crown entities
Boston *et al.*(1996): Chapters 3, 8.

Website of Crown Company Monitoring Unit, which gives access to all Crown Research Institutes, SOEs, Crown Owned Companies, Crown Entities:<www.ccmau.govt.nz>

7

Courts and Tribunals

The legal system

The other traditional branch of the constitution, after the legislature and the executive, is the judiciary, the judges of the various courts. Their function is to interpret and apply the law laid down in parliamentary statutes and in the precedents of the common law. The legal system also includes, in addition to the judges, officers of the courts, such as court registrars, members of the probation service and the prison service, and the police. Unlike judges, these other officials are constitutionally members of the executive branch. They are responsible to ministers, the Ministers of Justice and of the Police, though, in the case of the police, there are limits to the minister's right to direct their operations (Chapter 6: 138). The legal system also includes members of the legal profession. Though lawyers are mostly in private rather than public employment and, in that sense, outside the state, they are formally part of the court system and are important agents of state power.

The social effects of the legal system are profound. In many respects the law acts on behalf of the powerful forces of society and thus reinforces prevailing social and economic inequalities. Theories of structural dominance, such as marxism, feminism and anti-colonialism, therefore point to the legal system as an important set of mechanisms by which dominant groups maintain their power under the ideological guise of providing impartial justice for all. Those prosecuted and imprisoned for breaches of the criminal law are predominantly from the less well-off sections of society, especially Maori and Pacific Islanders. The cost of legal proceedings enables wealthier sections of society to make better use of the law in defence of their own interests (Chapter 12: 303–4). In matters where legal redress may in theory be open to all, formal equality before the law does not guarantee actual equality of treatment. Women, too, have been discriminated against by a male-dominated legal system in areas such as rape, domestic violence and pornography.

On the other hand, it may be argued that the law provides some protection against the abuse of political power. There are certain basic assumptions of the legal system, sometimes grouped under the general concept of 'the rule of law', which provide valuable safeguards of individual liberty, safeguards which are absent in undemocratic regimes. For instance, governments and their agents must themselves act in accordance with law. Every citizen accused of a crime is entitled to a fair and open trial. These requirements may not guarantee true equality but they prevent many of the worst forms of abuse. The openness of the legal system can be, and has been, used by relatively powerless groups and individuals to gain advantages denied by other branches of government. For example, many of the gains won by Maori interests in the last two decades have been achieved through the courts. Legal processes, including the actions of quasi-judicial bodies such as the Human Rights Commission, have also been used to reduce discrimination against ethnic minorities and women, as well as against vulnerable individuals such as refugees.

The overall social impact of the law and the legal system is thus a complex matter and a subject for legal sociology rather than political science. The focus of political analysis generally is on political decision-making processes, on the formulation of public policy. From this point of view, the most relevant aspects of the legal system are therefore those in which judges and the courts do not simply apply and enforce policies and laws made elsewhere in the political system but actually themselves contribute to the substance of policies and to the meaning of laws. The important political question is which interests in the plural society are most served by judicial policy-making.

The structure of courts and tribunals

The courts of general jurisdiction hear a wide range of cases in both criminal and civil law (Ringer, 1991: Chapter 14). They are arranged in a hierarchy or tier of ascending authority – the District Courts, the High Court, the Court of Appeal and the Supreme Court. The great bulk of cases are heard by District Court judges, who number around a hundred and sit in a large number of cities and towns throughout the country. More serious cases, together with appeals from the District Courts, come before the High Court. The Court of Appeal, as its title suggests, is mainly concerned with hearing appeals against judgments by other courts, particularly the High Court. From 2004, the final authority on New Zealand law rests with the Supreme Court, which in that year replaced the Judicial Committee of the Privy Council in London. Judges of the Court of Appeal, High Court and Supreme Court share similar status, with their method of appointment and tenure of office, unlike those of District Court judges, being protected by the Constitution Act (Chapter 3: 54). This reflects their uniquely important role in guaranteeing the constitutional independence of the judicial process.

The repatriation of the court of final appeal by the implementation of the Supreme Court Act (2003) which set up the Supreme Court and ended appeals to the Privy Council was a significant step in the evolution of the legal system. Use of the Privy Council reflected the fact that New Zealand law is historically grounded in English law and that New Zealand courts still follow precedents set by English courts. However, the direct influence of the Judicial Committee of the Privy Council on New Zealand law has been relatively slight. Few New Zealand cases were actually heard by the Committee – on average between one and two per year (Hodder, 1992: 411) – and, in matters which turn on issues of broader public values rather than fine points of law, the Committee usually preferred to follow the New Zealand courts. However, the Committee's judgments have occasionally impinged significantly on public policy, as, for instance, when it ruled on claims by Western Samoans to New Zealand citizenship (*Lesa* v *Attorney-General* 1981) and on the extent to which ministers could be liable for negligence (*Rowling* v *Takaro Properties Ltd* 1988).

Such cases indicate that recourse to the Privy Council compromised New Zealand's political independence (Palmer, 1992: 90). By the turn of the century most other Commonwealth countries, including Canada and Australia, had already dispensed with the right of appeal to the Privy Council even if they had kept the British monarch as Head of State. Defenders of the Privy Council argued that it had the practical advantage of providing access to another tier of judicial skill and experience which would be hard to duplicate within New Zealand. Moreover, because the Judicial Committee usually showed restraint in relation to policy matters, it met with favour from those who supported the supremacy of Parliament and feared the consequences of giving final jurisdiction to a resident court which, like the Court of Appeal, might show increasing readiness to enter politically controversial areas (Hodder, 1992: 411). The politically most important opposition to change, however, came from Maori leaders who saw continuing links with Britain as important for safeguarding their rights under the Treaty of Waitangi (Chapter 3: 59–60, 65).

Therefore, although ending appeals to the Privy Council had been foreshadowed for some years and was regarded as 'inevitable' (Stockley, 2003: 67; Chapter 3: 65), the final passage of the legislation was still controversial. The government was unsuccessful in achieving broad cross-party support and the legislation passed with a narrow majority, amid calls by its opponents for the change to be submitted to a referendum. The Act establishes a Supreme Court comprising the Chief Justice and at least four or no more than five judges, all of whom are to have the status of High Court judges. All four judges appointed to the inaugural Supreme Court were senior judges sitting in the Court of Appeal, to which they had originally been appointed by a previous National government. This somewhat allayed suspicion among the new Court's opponents that it might be unduly infected by the incumbent government's political bias.

Besides the courts of general jurisdiction, a number of specialised courts administer particular branches of the law which call for a particular type of legal approach or experience. They are the Maori Land Court and Maori Appellate Court, the Employment Court, the Family Courts and the Youth Courts. Family Courts deal with domestic matters concerning matrimonial disputes and the welfare of children, while Youth Courts hear cases concerning offenders under the age of seventeen. The Maori Land Court and Maori Appellate Courts have their origin in nineteenth-century policies whereby ownership of Maori land was to be determined according to Pakeha methods of legal title. They decide a number of types of dispute which may arise over Maori land, relating to such questions as the terms of leases and the powers of trustees.

The role of the Employment Court is historically of great political significance. The Court was established under the Employment Contracts Act 1991 to replace the Labour Court, itself established in 1987 as a successor to the Arbitration Court. The Arbitration Court heard cases involving disputes between individual workers and their employers. More important, it had power to register and enforce industrial 'awards' covering wages and other conditions of employment for all workers employed in a particular category of work. It could also make 'general wage orders', setting basic wage levels across all the awards under its jurisdiction. Thus the Arbitration Court was intimately involved in the broader political function of national economic management.

However, in the 1970s and 1980s, the Arbitration Court came under criticism as an unduly constraining force on wage bargaining and contrary to market liberal principles that wages should be a matter of agreement between individual employers and workers. The present Employment Court, together with a separate Employment Tribunal set up to deal with disputes and personal grievances between individual employers and employees, is largely concerned with adjudication of employment contracts which have already been agreed on. In this respect the Court functions in much the same way as any other court dealing with commercial disputes and no longer occupies a central place in economic and industrial policy-making.

In addition to formal courts presided over by judges, there are many other 'quasi-judicial' bodies, variously described as tribunals, boards, commissions and committees, which conduct hearings and make decisions or recommendations. They may share some of the characteristics of courts, for instance, sometimes holding their proceedings in public and allowing the parties to be represented by lawyers. At the same time, they may be more relaxed than courts in their procedure and are not bound by their own precedents. All tribunals, however, are required by law to follow the rules of 'natural justice', for instance the rule that each party to a dispute has a right to be heard. In terms of public policy-making, one of the most important such tribunals is the Planning Tribunal, which has power, under the Resource Management Act 1991, to settle disputes about land and water use arising out of resource management plans made by local bodies. Influential in the public control of private business is the Commerce Commission, which decides whether mergers and takeovers of commercial companies unduly reduce the benefits of competition and are therefore to be prevented as contrary to the public interest. In respect of Maori issues, the Waitangi Tribunal has played a critical role in the reassertion of Maori claims against the Crown (see below).

There are also certain watch-dog bodies established to investigate complaints and make recommendations on matters of individual rights. The Human Rights Commission, in tandem with the Complaints Review Tribunal, deals with unlawful discrimination on a number of grounds such as ethnicity, gender, marital status, religion, ethical belief, age or sexual orientation. The Office of the Race Relations Conciliator has similar functions in respect of race relations. The Privacy Commissioner deals with improper invasions of personal privacy. These bodies may have an influence on public policy by making general recommendations to governments and contributing to public debate. Some were established as a result of government responses to United Nations initiatives. The UN has made a number of policy statements on human rights issues which it has invited member countries to adopt and which New Zealand has ratified as international treaties. Thus New Zealand introduced the office of Race Relations Conciliator as part of its adoption of the International Convention on the Elimination of all Forms of Racial Discrimination. Similarly the Human Rights Commission was established to advance the protection of rights enumerated in the UN Inter national Covenant on Human Rights, which New Zealand has ratified. International treaty obligations, even when not explicitly incorporated into domestic law by act of Parliament, have increasing influence on judicial interpretation of domestic law. They also have considerable moral force. New Zealand governments usually pride them selves internationally on the country's human rights record and are therefore susceptible to criticisms that they are in breach of international standards.

The courts and public policy-making

How far do the courts of general jurisdiction actually make the law as well as simply applying it? The New Zealand legal system, like the English system from which it is derived, gives a prominent role to the courts as a source of law. Much of the substance of the law is derived from the 'common law', the law based on the accumulated decisions of courts. Admittedly, the doctrine of parliamentary sovereignty requires that statutes passed by Parliament take precedence over common law. There has also been a general trend to consolidate areas of the law previously covered by the common law into statutes. However, in many parts of the law, for instance the law relating to the enforcement of contracts or the claiming of damages in civil disputes (torts), the main legal principles are still those derived from the common law. Many of the legal rights which define the basic liberties of the individual New Zealand citizen, so-called 'civil liberties', were first enunciated by the English common law. For instance, one fundamental common law right is that of *habeas corpus* (Latin for 'have the body'), under which the individual may not be unlawfully detained by the state (Rishworth, 1992: 151).

Moreover, even within statute law itself, while the general principles themselves may be set out in legislation, the interpretation of these principles and their application to particular cases is often determined by decisions of the courts. Given the complexity and unpredictability of human behaviour and social life, law-makers will always be unable to anticipate every possible contingency when drafting a law. Whichever court is responsible for applying the general rules to particular cases will be called on at some point to exercise discretionary judgment, to decide how the law should apply to a new situation not clearly covered by existing law. The issue, therefore, in statutory interpretation is not whether courts do or should decide the law — that is inevitable — but the extent of their discretion.

The considerable law-making power of the courts is subject to a number of restrictions. One is the doctrine of precedent, by which judges are bound to follow decisions made on similar cases by courts of the same or higher jurisdiction. To differ from established precedent a judge must be able to claim with justification that the relevant facts of the case under discussion are different from those pertaining in earlier cases. This justification must be able to withstand appeal to a higher court. Thus, while the court system as a whole may, over time, have a major say in law-making, the discretion allowed to an individual court on a particular occasion is usually very limited.

Moreover, even where existing law is deficient in meeting the situation of a particular case and clearly needs to be supplemented or reinterpreted, the courts may refrain from making the decision themselves but may instead refer the issue to Parliament as the supreme law-making body. This is particularly the case with matters of broader social or economic policy where the courts accept the superior democratic authority of an elected government and Parliament (Richardson, 1985). The principle of parliamentary sovereignty, as demonstrated by the rule that parliamentary statutes are of supreme legal authority, together with the decisive control that New Zealand governments exercise over the legislative process, encourages the courts to hand politically controversial questions to the executive arm of government. New Zealand governments have had the power, if needed, to introduce and pass legislation at very short notice. Inaction by the courts need not lead, as it can in other political systems, to damaging delay and uncertainty about the law or to general political paralysis. This has facilitated an attitude of legal conservatism on the part of the judiciary, allowing them to stick closely to the letter of the law, leaving legislative innovation to the government and Parliament.

An example of the courts' willingness to defer to the authority of the elected government is provided by the frequently quoted constitutional case (e.g. Palmer, 1987: 186–90; Hodder, 1992: 421; Keith, 1985) of *Fitzgerald* v *Muldoon*. This arose out of a statement made to the press by Robert Muldoon, shortly after he became prime minister when National won the 1975 election. As part of its election campaign National had promised to abolish the previous Labour government's contributory superannuation scheme and replace it with one paid directly from taxation revenue. In his press statement, Muldoon claimed that, from that date, employers would no longer need to make contributions as required under the existing Superannuation Act. Fitzgerald brought a legal case against Muldoon, claiming that this instruction was illegal on the grounds that a law could be repealed only by Parliament, which had not yet considered the question. In his decision, the Chief Justice agreed that the prime minister's instruction was illegal under the English Bill of Rights 1689, which is part of New Zealand law (Chapter 3: 56) and provides that only Parliament itself can suspend its own laws. However, the judge also effectively upheld the legitimacy of the government's action by adjourning for six months that part of proceedings which called for measures to remedy the illegality. He explicitly recognised the likelihood that Parliament would meet within that time and make the necessary legislative changes. Constitutional principle was reasserted but so too was constitutional and political reality, that public policy is determined by the government of the day, particularly when it is backed by an electoral mandate.

During the 1980s, however, the Court of Appeal, particularly through Sir Robin Cooke, who became President of the Court in 1986, indicated a readiness to exercise greater discretion and to be more independent in relation to Parliament. The force of the doctrine of precedent has been weakened as the Court of Appeal, following the House of Lords, claims no longer to be bound by its own previous decisions or those of any English courts, apart, that is, from Privy Council decisions on New Zealand cases (Hodder, 1992: 415–6). The Court has been prepared to take a broader view of statutory interpretation, looking beyond the letter of the law and paying more attention to the stated general purposes of particular pieces of legislation, to the parliamentary debates which accompanied their enactment and even to international covenants on human rights which Parliament has ratified (Keith, 1985: 35–38). The Court has also been prepared to indicate possible limits to parliamentary sovereignty derived from the common law, for instance on Parliament's capacity to restrict the citizen's right of access to the courts or to use a barbaric method of compulsion such as torture (Keith, 1985: 33). The Court has thus emphasised that the ultimate authority for the doctrine of parliamentary sovereignty is, in fact, the common law recognition of this doctrine by the courts. Continued acceptance of this doctrine depends on Parliament's continuing respect for fundamental community and constitutional values (Rishworth, 1992: 148–9).

A most notable example of the Court's encroachment on matters usually left to the government was in its judgment on the State-Owned Enterprises Act (*NZ Maori Council* v *Attorney-General* 1987), in which it used the requirement in the Act not to breach the 'principles of the Treaty of Waitangi' as a means of requiring the Crown to safeguard possible Maori interests in assets being transferred to state-owned enterprises. In a subsequent case (*Tainui Maori Trust Board* v *Attorney-General* 1989), the Court later claimed the right to be the final arbiter of the meaning of the Treaty's 'principles', a claim treated by the prime minister, Geoffrey Palmer, as an unwarranted attack on government authority and parliamentary sovereignty (Hodder, 1992: 425, n18). Another legal ruling with considerable political ramifications was made in 2003 when the Court of Appeal overturned restrictions on the jurisdiction of the Maori Land Court, enabling it to hear Maori claims of customary ownership of the seabed and foreshores. This enhanced a growing perception of the Court as an 'activist' body and the most important court from the point of view of the impact of judicial authority on government policy. It remains to be seen whether the new Supreme Court acquires a similar reputation

The advent of MMP and the end to single-party majority government as the expected norm may encourage the courts to continue in a more active policy-making role. The rationale for judicial restraint in Westminster systems has partly depended on the existence of an elected government with a clear mandate and the capacity to pass legislation quickly and decisively. Under MMP, the uncertainty of a government's command of Parliament and the fact that its policies are open to interparty negotiation may provide the courts with an apparent policy vacuum which they may be tempted to enter. On the other hand, the increased democratic legitimacy of a proportionately elected Parliament may discourage the courts from appearing to trespass on the rights of the legislature. Moreover, with the abolition of the right of appeal to the Privy Council, the Court of Appeal and Supreme Court may be tempted to consolidate public acceptance of the change by exercising a more cautious approach in relation to government policy. Judicial behaviour tends to follow historical cycles with periods of greater activism succeeded by periods of relative conservatism.

The Bill of Rights

The courts have always played an important role in defending individual citizens against the misuse of public power by the other branches of government. One area of legal remedy is through the procedures of 'administrative' law which allow the courts to review particular decisions of the executive, usually public officials, which affect individual members of the public. The courts usually keep clear of judging the merits of the case, leaving matters of 'policy' to the government. However, they are able to decide whether the decision followed the proper legal procedures, including the principles of 'natural justice'.

Another innovation which will encourage the courts to offer greater protection is the introduction of a bill of rights through the Bill of Rights Act 1990 (Harris, 1992: 72–73). This Act sets out basic civil and political rights, including the right of free speech, freedom of religious belief and practice, freedom of association, the right to vote (see box, p. 179). The rights are not absolute but are subject to 'such reasonable limits prescribed by law as can be demonstrably justified in a free and democratic society'. Unlike bills of rights in some other jurisdictions, such as the United States and Canada, New Zealand's Bill of Rights does not allow for full-scale 'judicial review' whereby the courts can overrule any act of Parliament which is held to breach one of the stipulated rights.

Such a fully fledged bill of rights with judicial review was proposed for New Zealand in a White Paper published by the Labour Government in 1985 (*A Bill of Rights for New Zealand: A White Paper,* 1985) with the strong support of Geoffrey Palmer, then Minister of Justice and Deputy Prime Minister. The proposed bill of rights specified the major civil and political rights and also incorporated the Treaty of Waitangi. This bill of rights, like the key sections of the Electoral Act (Chapter 3: 52), was to be entrenched beyond the power of a mere parliamentary majority to amend it. Courts would have the power to review the actions of other branches of government and declare them invalid if they were in breach of the stated rights.

However, a number of objections were raised to the proposal (Chapman, 1985; Palmer 1992: 51–58): it was undemocratic in preferring the decisions of unrepresentative judges (overwhelmingly male, Pakeha and middle class) over those of a Parliament elected by all adults; it would lead to a more politicised judiciary with judges appointed for their political views rather than professional competence; it would favour the interests of those wealthy enough to afford the expense of litigation; it gave undue priority to civil and political rights over other equally, if not more, important economic and social rights, such as the rights to employment, health and education. Maori opinion was dubious about incorporating the Treaty of Waitangi in a document susceptible of amendment by referendum. The positive advantages of safeguarding basic civil and political rights against incursions from governments failed to arouse any widespread public enthusiasm. In contrast to the movement for electoral reform, there was no obvious area of public disquiet round which support for change could form.

As a result, the original proposal for an entrenched bill of rights with full judicial review was dropped and, in its place, the Labour Government enacted an unentrenched version, without the Treaty of Waitangi. However, the revised Bill of Rights, though not infringing parliamentary sovereignty, does require that Parliament take basic rights into account when passing legislation. Each piece of proposed legislation is to be scrutinised by the Attorney-General (a Cabinet minister), who is to inform Parliament whether the draft legislation is consistent with the Bill of Rights or in breach of it. In practice, the minister acts on advice of officials in the Ministry of Justice (or officers of the Crown Law Office in the case of legislation promoted by the Minister of Justice). This process has led to changes in draft legislation both at the preliminary drafting stage (Fitzgerald, 1992: 140) and at the select committee stage (Palmer, 1992: 59). Because the rights specified in the Act are generally considered to be valuable and important, ministers and governments are unwilling to risk the adverse publicity surrounding an intended breach of one of the rights.

The Bill of Rights, though having only persuasive force in relation to the substance of legislation, has a more direct role in statutory interpretation. Where more than one meaning can be given to a statute, the courts are required to prefer a meaning which is consistent with the Bill of Rights. This may add little to existing practice, because the courts have traditionally preferred interpretations which favour the preservation of citizens' rights (Rishworth, 1992: 148). However, the additional authority given by the Bill of Rights to such a preference may help to reinforce the importance given to these values in the wider community. Similarly, many of the rights enshrined in the Bill of Rights are traditional common-law rights of citizens, for instance the right not to be arbitrarily arrested. But added weight is given to these rights by the fact that the courts may now quote the authority of the Bill of Rights and associated international precedents when upholding the rights of individual citizens against agents of public power, such

---

Summary of the civil and political rights protected under the New Zealand Bill of Rights Act 1990

Life and Security of the Person

* Right not to be deprived of life
* Right not to be subjected to torture or cruel treatment
* Right not to be subjected to medical or scientific experimentation
* Right to refuse to undergo medical treatment

Democratic and Civil Rights

* Electoral rights: Every New Zealand citizen over 18 has the right to vote in elections by secret ballot and is qualified to be a member of the House of Representatives
* Freedom of thought, conscience, and religion
* Freedom to express one's religion or belief
* Freedom of association
* Freedom of movement

Non-Discrimination and Minority Rights

* Freedom from discrimination
* Rights of minorities

Search, Arrest and Detention

* Right to protection against unreasonable search and seizure
* Right not to be arbitrarily arrested or detained
* Rights pertaining to those persons arrested or detained
* Rights pertaining to those persons charged with an offence
* Rights in relation to criminal procedure for those who are charged with an offence
* Right to protection against retroactive penalties and double jeopardy
* Right to the observance of justice in respect to the procedures of public authorities

For full specification, see Bill of Rights Act 1990, Levine & Harris, 1993: 44–47

---

as the police. For instance, the existence of the Bill of Rights allowed the Court of Appeal to establish a new right of damages for victims of improper police searches (Harrison, 1995). So far, judges have been keen to use the Bill of Rights in their judgments whenever possible. They appear to share the expectation of the Act's author (Palmer, 1992:

58–70) that the Bill of Rights, though unentrenched, will gradually acquire sufficient legal and political authority to allow the courts to exercise at least some of the powers of scrutiny and control that they would have had under a system of full-scale judicial review.

Admittedly, the Bill of Rights covers only some of the rights that most New Zealanders would consider fundamental to a just society. As critics of the original bill pointed out, it does not cover social and economic rights, such as the right to adequate food and housing or the right to work. Such rights involve major decisions of taxation and expenditure and are best left to elected governments and politicians rather than to independent courts applying judicial methods of reasoning. It is therefore a mistake to overstate the importance of the particular rights in the Bill of Rights, as if they were the only basic rights of New Zealanders rather than simply some of these basic rights. Even so, they are rights which New Zealanders from all sectors of society, privileged and marginalised, may at some time need to rely on.

The Waitangi Tribunal, the courts and Maori rights

One area of public policy where the judicial process has been particularly influential is in the political recognition of Maori rights. While the courts themselves, particularly the Court of Appeal, have made a significant contribution, the main role in defining Maori rights and bringing them on to the political agenda was played by the Waitangi Tribunal. The Tribunal was originally established in 1975 and consisted of the Chief Judge of the Maori Land Court and two other members. Its function was to enquire into claims brought by Maori that they had suffered from government action or inaction contrary to the principles of the Treaty of Waitangi. It had the power only to make recommendations to government, not to make final decisions and, to begin with, was limited to the investigation of grievances that had occurred after the establishment of the Tribunal in 1975. A decade later, however, in 1985, in response to a further electoral commitment by the Labour Party, the jurisdiction of the Tribunal was extended to cover claims arising out of events which had occurred since the inception of the Treaty in 1840. The membership of the Tribunal was increased to seven. In 1988, following the Court of Appeal's judgment in the State-Owned Enterprises case, the Tribunal was given the power to decide matters relating to assets controlled by state-owned enterprises and to mediate between disputing parties. As a result of a large increase in the number of claims before the Tribunal, membership was increased to seventeen, allowing the Tribunal to sit in up to three divisions at a time.

The Tribunal's method is to deal with individual claims one by one or in groups (where they cover similar issues), conducting an investigation into the history relevant to the claim or claims. It then issues a report which summarises the historical background and assesses the extent to which the Crown has acted in a way contrary to its Treaty commitments. The report may include specific recommendations about possible remedies for past injustice or may recommend that the parties negotiate directly with government.

The Tribunal has deliberately adopted a bicultural method of procedure, conducting much of its hearings on marae, combining marae protocol with courtroom practices and recognising both the Maori and the English languages (Durie & Orr, 1990; Sorrenson, 1989). Many of the claims have involved the Tribunal in commissioning extensive research, using both oral and written evidence. As most of its work has been taken up with conducting inquiries and making recommendations rather than issuing judgments, the Tribunal is sometimes said to be more like a commission of inquiry than a court (Sharp, 1990: 125; Ringer, 1991: 40). On the other hand, because many of its reports are couched in a broadly legal style of argument, particularly in so far as the Tribunal has set out to interpret the Treaty of Waitangi itself, the Tribunal has directly contributed to the increasing use of the Treaty by the courts themselves and to the development of a 'Maori jurisprudence'.

In its findings, the Tribunal has carefully and skilfully steered a middle course between those, usually Maori, who claim that the Pakeha must offer full restitution of past wrongs, and those, usually Pakeha, who argue that the past cannot be undone and that restitution is either impossible or unjustifiable (Sharp, 1990). It has stressed the Maori understanding of the Treaty (Chapter 3: 60), particularly the Maori version of Article 2 which guaranteed tino rangatiratanga (full chiefly authority) over lands, villages and taonga (treasured possessions). It has also documented the many breaches of the Treaty's provisions committed over the years by governments and by government officials. Governments acted in the belief that the Treaty had no legal force at all. At most, the Treaty had authorised British sovereignty over the country and therefore sanctioned all acts of the New Zealand Parliament and its legally appointed agents.

At the same time, however, the Tribunal has also taken note of the instruction in its enabling statute that it should concern itself with the 'practical application of the principles' of the Treaty (Treaty of Waitangi Act 1975: preamble). Building on the Maori notion of the wairua (spirit) of the Treaty which is 'always speaking', the Tribunal has been able to reinterpret and adapt the Treaty to fit present-day circumstances. For instance, assertion of rangatiratanga does not necessarily mean rejection of the sovereign authority of Parliament. Reparation for past wrongs is to be sought from the Crown only, not from private owners, even if privately owned land has been unjustly acquired. The level of compensation recommended to government should be set by considering the present needs of the iwi concerned, not the full present value of the assets unjustly acquired. In addition, the protection of taonga (treasured possession) has been extended to cover possessions which were clearly not at stake in 1840, for instance, the Maori language and Maori culture itself.

In effect, the Tribunal has been using the Treaty as a constitutional document which could be adapted to new circumstances in much the same way, for instance, as the two-centuries-old United States Constitution has been adapted by the US Supreme Court to apply to situations unforeseen by the founding fathers who drew it up. The US Constitution was written by men who took slavery for granted and did not contemplate the extension of equal political rights to women. Yet the same document has recently been used to justify the elimination of racial and gender-based discrimination. The extent of creative reinterpretation of the Treaty by the Waitangi Tribunal was not always explicitly recognised by those involved. The habits of thought of both Maori and the legal profession place weight on the authority of tradition and tend to stress continuity rather than innovation in the use of time-honoured concepts. Much of their talk seems to imply that the present application of the Treaty implies honouring the actual intentions of those who signed it a century and a half ago. Not surprisingly, many plain-minded Pakeha took fright at what they mistakenly saw as an intended return to the status quo of the 1840s. In fact, the practical recommendations made by the Tribunal were little different from those that could be arrived at quite independently of the Treaty through concern for the currently disadvantaged position of the Maori and through application of the principles of human rights (Mulgan, 1989a: Chapter 4). Use of the Treaty, however, gave impetus to these demands by publicly recognising the status of the Maori as first inhabitants of the country and their history of unjust colonisation.

The success of the Waitangi Tribunal in bringing Maori claims on to the public agenda encouraged Maori leaders in the middle 1980s to unite behind the Treaty as a vehicle for advancing Maori interests. Hitherto, Maori attitudes to the Treaty had been mixed. Though revered by the iwi of the north, the region where it had been first signed, the Treaty had been belittled by other iwi, particularly those such as Te Arawa and Ngati Tuwharetoa near Rotorua and Taupo, who were never full signatories to the Treaty. At the same time, Maori radicals had previously tended to consider the Treaty as a 'fraud', a hypocritical instrument of colonial conquest. The Lange Labour Government responded to the new-found authority of the Treaty among Maori by making the concept of the 'principles of the Treaty of Waitangi' the cornerstone of its attempt to remedy Maori disadvantage. The Cabinet decided, in June 1986, that all future legislation should 'draw attention to any implications for recognition of the principles of the Treaty of Waitangi' (quoted by Williams, 1990: 30). During the restructuring of the state sector undertaken by the Labour government (Chapter 6), the principles of the Treaty of Waitangi were regularly mentioned as one of the guiding principles. References to Treaty principles were included in a number of pieces of legislation, including the State-Owned Enterprises Act 1986.

It was the requirement in this Act (Section 9) that 'nothing in this Act shall permit the Crown to act in a manner contrary to the principles of the Treaty of Waitangi' which allowed the Court of Appeal to consider the principles of the Treaty. The Maori Council brought a case expressing concern about the possible effects of the transfer of Crown assets to SOEs when these assets could still be the subject of Maori claims before the Waitangi Tribunal (*NZ Maori Council* v *Attorney General* 1987). The court required the government to prepare a scheme which would allow adequate safeguards of Maori interests in the event of claims arising over resources transferred to SOEs. In doing so, the judges took the opportunity to discuss the Treaty at length, consciously beginning a process of determining the contemporary legal interpretation to be given to Treaty principles. This process has been continued in subsequent cases arising out of the same and similar legislation which incorporates reference to Treaty principles in relation to state assets. The Court of Appeal's lead has been followed not only by itself and the High Court but also by other quasi-judicial bodies such as the Planning Tribunal and the Waitangi Tribunal itself (Williams, 1990: 27).

The landmark judgment of the Court of Appeal in the SOE case also stimulated wider government and bureaucratic interest in the concept of the principles of the Treaty. Treasury included a section on the implications of the Treaty in its 1987 post-election briefings, *Government Management.* In 1988, the government established a Treaty of Waitangi Policy Unit within the Department of Justice which was responsible for drafting the government's own statement of the principles of the Treaty published the following year. These principles, which emphasised the authority of the government and the legal equality of all New Zealand citizens, were criticised by some Maori activists as diluting the Treaty promises and giving insufficient weight to Maori authority (rangatiratanga) in relation to that of the Crown. However, the principles as enunciated were a reasonable summary of the approach adopted by the Waitangi Tribunal and the courts. Though too little for some Maori, they were clearly too much for many Pakeha who were opposed to any legal recognition of separate Maori rights, claiming that 'we are all New Zealanders'.

The courts have been particularly active in the reassertion of Maori traditional fishing rights and their reinterpretation to include Maori access to the profits of modern commercial fishing. In this area there was additional legal ammunition available to those advocating the Maori cause, because Maori fishing rights, unlike other Treaty rights, were already legally recognised. These rights had been protected in legislation since the nineteenth century, though they had usually been understood in terms of customary rights to recreational fishing or fishing for local consumption rather than highly capitalised commercial fishing. However, when the Labour government introduced a system of transferable fishing quotas for commercial fishing, Maori advocates claimed access to such quotas, a claim which was upheld by the High Court. This resulted in further legislative recognition of Maori fishing rights, for instance in the Maori Fisheries Act 1989, and eventually in the settlement by the Bolger National government in 1992 by which a half share in a major fishing company, worth $150 million, was transferred to Maori interests. Again, the work of the Waitangi Tribunal was an important part of this process, not only in its path-breaking method of interpreting Treaty rights in terms of late-twentieth-century conditions but also in its historical investigations of Maori fishing practices, particularly in the lengthy Muriwhenua Report 1988, which documented the successful commercial exploitation of fisheries by Maori in the decades immediately before and after 1840.

Additional legal support for fishing and other claims was found in the concept of native or aboriginal rights. At the time when New Zealand and other similar territories were being colonised by the British, the English common law recognised certain rights belonging to the aboriginal or indigenous peoples whose lands were being colonised. These rights included customary rights to resources such as traditional lands and hunting grounds. These rights were subsequently ignored and overridden by New Zealand courts but they have recently been resurrected by legal scholars and recognised by the courts, for instance in some recent eases about Maori fishing rights (e.g. *Te Weehi* v *Regional Fisheries Officer* 1986). However, it is the Treaty and its principles, perhaps because they are unique to New Zealand and of especial significance for the Maori, which have been most prominent in the protection of Maori interests.

The constitutional significance being accorded to the Treaty was evident in the fact that it was incorporated into the draft Bill of Rights as part of a proposed fundamental law for New Zealand (see above). Even though that proposal lapsed and the Treaty was not included in the subsequent unentrenched Bill of Rights, the courts are still showing a willingness to develop the constitutional application of the Treaty wherever possible. Reference to the Treaty by the courts usually depends on its having been explicitly referred to in legislation, as in the State-Owned Enterprises Act 1986, the Conservation Act 1987 and the Resource Management Act 1991. However, in a number of cases the courts have ruled that the principles of the Treaty of Waitangi should be taken into account in the adjudication of certain matters, such as land and water rights and fishing rights, even when the relevant legislation does not explicitly mention the Treaty or Maori interests generally. This reflects the growing importance of the Treaty as part of the legal and political context within which Maori interests are discussed. Expanding reference to the Treaty by the courts also arises out of the courts' greater willingness in recent years to interpret all legislation much more broadly, with reference to its wider social impact and not just to the strict letter of the law (Keith, 1990: 60; Joseph, 1996: 11–14).

Judicial processes, both through the Waitangi Tribunal and the courts themselves, have certainly helped to bring issues of Maori rights and the general situation of the Maori people to the attention of governments and the wider public. Whether this recognition has led to an adequate response from governments in terms of redistributing material resources to the iwi is another question. The Tribunal can only recommend solutions to Maori claims; it is for governments to make the actual decisions. Similarly, the courts may require the government to take note of Maori interests or to negotiate in good faith, but they leave it to the Crown, that is, the government, to make the final dispensation.

In reaching settlement of Treaty claims, both Labour and National governments have found themselves facing intense political pressures. The need to prevent further ethnic conflict and to preserve New Zealand's reputation for relatively harmonious race relations requires that Maori grievances and aspirations are treated honourably. On the other hand, full reparation, even in terms of the present and future needs of Maori iwi, has appeared economically unsustainable at a time when governments have been under pressure to contain public expenditure. Moreover, governments must also take into account the negative political reaction from non-Maori sections of the community (the so-called 'Pakeha backlash'). As newspaper correspondence columns and talk-back radio indicate, many New Zealand voters fiercely resent any suggestion that Maori should be granted what appear to be special privileges based on ancestry and ethnic identification.

The National party, in particular, has been always been suspicious of ethnic 'separatism' and many of its members were opposed to the prominence given to the Treaty under the Lange Labour government. (It was the capacity of Winston Peters, as a Maori, to articulate this opposition which fuelled his growing popularity in the late 1980s (Chapter 10: 257).) The Bolger National government was much more cautious than Labour, for instance, about encouraging separate Maori institutions (Boston *et al.*, 1996: Chapter 7) and about incorporating references to the Treaty into legislation. Though the Waitangi Tribunal was allowed to continue its investigations, the government determined to impose a final limit of both time and funding on the settlement process.

In 1994, the government announced a policy, widely known as the 'fiscal envelope', which set aside a total of $1 billion over ten years for the settlement of all Treaty claims. Beyond that period, no new claims would be heard and the Tribunal would have effectively competed its work. Though one major iwi, the Tainui, reached an agreement under this policy, settling for $170 million and a formal apology, the concept of the fiscal envelope was angrily rejected by most iwi and sparked a series of violent confrontations between

Maori activists and public authorities. The lack of consultation with Maori leaders in formulating the policy was seen as an affront to Maori rangatiratanga. The attempt to set a final limit on Treaty claims not only offended Maori aspirations but also threatened their major source of political leverage, the capacity to manipulate Pakeha guilt about the injustice of the past (Mulgan, 1996). Maori leaders realised that the government's main motive in pressing on with settling Treaty claims was a desire to leave the past behind. In the event, the government was forced to conciliate Maori opinion by softening the implication that all grievances could be finally settled within the stated limits. By mid 1996, fewer than 20 claims had been settled while the Tribunal had still to report on over 500 claims lodged with it. Six years later, the workload had increased to more than 900 registered claims and the Tribunal itself estimated that it would be 2010 – 2012 before it had reported on all of them. The work of the Tribunal and the settling of claims will no doubt continue well into the century. The pace of the process is bewildering for many people who see it as part of a Maori 'grievance industry'. Consequently, it has become a divisive political issue, one of several which have raised the salience of race relations in New Zealand politics. While Labour, the Greens, the Alliance and the Progressives have expressed tolerance of the Tribunal's work, the parties of the right, National, ACT and New Zealand First, have called for an end to it, National nominating 2008 as a deadline for the settlement of all historic claims.

How far Maori have benefited from the legal processes involving the Treaty of Waitangi is a matter of dispute. Some Maori nationalists and their supporters have claimed that few, if any, substantial advances have been made by Maori. Adopting an anti-colonialist perspective, they argue that the effect of the Tribunal and court processes has been merely to divert Maori claims for sovereignty and justice, while leaving the structure of Pakeha domination, legal, political and economic, intact (Kelsey, 1990; 1993: Chapters 17–21). The concept of the 'principles of the Treaty' pays lip-service to Maori rights while denying Maori the right to their own sovereignty, their tino rangatiratanga, which was guaranteed by the Treaty.

Certainly, the need to operate within an economic system of international capitalism sets substantial limits to the degree of economic redistribution which New Zealand governments are able to contemplate. Moreover, Maori, along with Pacific Islanders, have on average suffered more harshly from the effects of economic retrenchment. Maori are disproportionately to be found in the ranks of the unemployed and the imprisoned (Chapter 2: 27). Perhaps, as some argue, the major beneficiaries of the new initiatives have been the members of the Maori professional middle class who are involved in administering iwi-based corporations rather than the genuinely disadvantaged Maori whose plight provides the main political rationale for redistribution of resources (Levine & Henare, 1994). None the less, few dispassionate observers would deny that in its creative use of the Treaty of Waitangi and judicial processes, the New Zealand state has been able to make a significant response to Maori demands. At any rate, threats to disband or drastically limit the activities of the Waitangi Tribunal, such as those implied by the fiscal envelope policy, have been greeted with genuine dismay by Maori spokespersons as likely to undo genuine advances made since the mid 1980s.

In bringing Maori issues on to the political agenda, the mainstream democratic processes of party government have also played a crucial role. It was the Labour Party's links with Maori voters and Maori interests which committed the party first to establishing the Waitangi Tribunal in 1975 and then to extending its jurisdiction in 1985. It was the Lange Labour government's sympathy for biculturalism which encouraged it to incorporate references to the Treaty into legislation. It is governments, both Labour and National, which have ultimately been called on to deliver resources. But, in between, it was the judicial element of government which made the major contribution to reshaping public policy. The Tribunal and the courts articulated and gave authority to the concept of biculturalism and partnership, the view that Maori have a unique place alongside the Pakeha in New Zealand public life. They also insisted, in opposition to most Pakeha public opinion, that biculturalism involves a recognition of past injustices to the Maori and a willingness to remedy them. In doing so, the Tribunal and the courts demonstrated the capacity of legal processes to protect and advance the interests of those who might otherwise be neglected by democratically elected governments.

As democratic theorists have often pointed out, democratic principles require that the rights and interests of minorities should be safeguarded as well as those of majorities. These minority rights and interests are in particular danger in democracies when, as in the case of the Maori, they are likely to be opposed by an intolerant majority. An independent judiciary, committed to the rights of minorities and prepared to stand up to the government of the day, is therefore an essential element in any functioning democracy. Admittedly, the courts are better at protecting some rights than others and the resources of the law are in many instances more readily available to the wealthier citizens. Some supporters of the Westminster system and the tradition of parliamentary sovereignty may be uneasy at the recent trend for courts to exercise greater discretion and initiative in policy matters. They will welcome the failure to enact an entrenched bill of rights. At the same time, they must recognise that the power of Parliament, controlled by a determined executive, is often used to override the interests of the more vulnerable sections of society. As the example of Maori rights indicates, a bold judiciary can make an important contribution to the political process.

Further reading

The court system
Harris (1992): 70–74; Palmer & Palmer (1997): Chapter 14; Ringer, 1991: Chapters 14–15; Stockley (1997); Stockley (2003).
Political role of judges
Hodder (1992).
Bill of Rights
Harris & Levine (1992): 44–7; Joseph (1993): Chapter 26; Palmer (1992): 51–70; Palmer & Palmer (1997): Chapter 15.
Waitangi Tribunal and Maori rights
Brookfield (1999); Hayward (2003); Kawharu (1989); Palmer & Palmer (1997): Chapter 16; Sharp (1990); Sharp (1992); Ward (1999); Waitangi Tribunal website: <www.waitangi-tribunal.govt.nz>

8

Local and Regional Government

Local government and the central state

The most prominent institutions of the state are those associated with central government – Cabinet, Parliament, the central bureaucracy, the courts and the police. But the state, in the sense of the set of legally coercive institutions performing public functions, also includes institutions of regional and local government. Their role is considerably less extensive than central government's. Services provided by local authorities amount to a fraction of those provided by central government (Bush, 1995: 235–6). Local government also tends to attract less political controversy and media attention than central government. None the less, local bodies are responsible for a number of basic services, such as roads, water supply, sewerage, rubbish disposal, parks and libraries, which all New Zealanders expect the public authorities to provide. Local bodies also administer various sets of regulations covering the use of property, for instance planning schemes and building codes, and other matters such as the control of noise and licensing of dogs. More generally, local government displays a style of non-partisan, consensual politics which is different from that associated with central government and which has important effects in reinforcing the political dominance of certain interests, particularly those associated with the ownership of landed property. A comprehensive account of the New Zealand state and its politics should therefore include reference to this important, though often overlooked, sector of government activity.

Constitutionally, the institutions of local government are subordinate to central government, their structure and functions being established by various acts of Parliament and until 2003 their powers limited to those expressly permitted by Parliament. In this respect, New Zealand has a 'unitary' system of government, as distinct from a 'federal' system, such as those of Australia, Canada or the United States. In federal systems, the constituent states or provinces retain certain independent legal powers which the central, federal government is constitutionally barred from infringing. In a unitary system, on the other hand, the central legislature, i.e. Parliament, is legally sovereign and is free to determine the structure and powers of subordinate levels of government as it sees fit. The constitutional dominance of central government in New Zealand was demonstrated during the far-reaching reforms of local government undertaken by the Labour government in the 1980s, culminating in the wholesale amendments to the Local Government Act 1974 passed in 1989. The structure of local government was radically redrawn, in many cases against the wishes of local communities as expressed through their local body members (and only after the government had abolished the right of local communities to object to restructuring through voting in a local poll).

Such ruthlessness towards local sentiment, though constitutionally justifiable, was politically untypical. Local government certainly acts within limits laid down from the centre, though the precise extent of these limits has become a more open question after local authorities were granted power of general competence in 2002. Central government exercises a certain degree of regular control over local bodies, particularly in the financial area, for instance by prescribing the methods by which local authorities may raise revenue. But within these general limits, local bodies are usually left free to make their own decisions in direct response to their local communities. Because local body members are directly elected by the residents of the communities they serve, they have their own independent channels of democratic accountability to their local electors. This gives them the right to speak as the legitimate representatives of their communities, a right which has usually been respected by central government. Local and regional rivalries are a continuing feature of New Zealand life and local bodies one of their most important means of expression.

Deference to the independent democratic rights of local bodies was also evident in procedures dealing with proposed reorganisations and amalgamations of existing local bodies, a recurring issue in the history of New Zealand local government. Formerly, amalgamations could not occur if the residents of the local communities themselves petitioned for a local poll and voted to prevent the change. Though this right of veto was removed by the Lange Labour government in its restructuring zeal

(Wood, 1988: 142–51), conventions of community consultation and of deferring to local sentiments could not be totally discarded. For this reason, in spite of the reformers' determination to redesign the system of local government according to first principles, the structure of the system still owes as much to tradition as to rational principle and needs to be understood in the context of its history (Bush, 1995: Chapters 1–2).

Historical development

Belief in the value of local government institutions which were politically independent, though legally subordinate, was part of the political culture brought to New Zealand by the British settlers. There was a natural expectation that local communities would form their own local institutions and that these would follow the time-honoured British distinction between urban municipalities, the larger being cities and the smaller boroughs, and rural districts, known as counties. To begin with, under the New Zealand Constitution Act 1852, New Zealand was divided into six provinces – Auckland, New Plymouth (renamed Taranaki), Wellington, Nelson, Canterbury and Otago. The larger towns were incorporated within the provinces as distinct municipalities. Four further new provinces were subsequently added – Hawke's Bay, Marlborough, Southland and Westland. However, improved communications and moves for more concerted and more equitable national development led to the abolition of the provinces in 1876. The system of territorial local bodies was revised, consisting of municipalities (cities and boroughs) and counties. Each such body had an elected council, while municipalities also elected a separate leader (a 'mayor') who presided over the council's meetings. In accordance with nineteenth century assumptions linking voting and property ownership, the right to vote in local elections was given to ratepayers, that is to those who owned landed property within the area and who could be called on to pay the 'rates', or local taxes levied on such property. Moreover, votes were allocated in proportion to the value of property owned and rates paid, with the more wealthy exercising up to five votes each. Apart from subsequent changes to the voting rights in line with developing principles of democratic equality, this structure of territorial local government remained unchanged in broad outline until the reforms of 1989.

Over the years, new municipalities were added and existing boundaries adjusted by mutual consent. Boroughs became cities if their population exceeded 20,000. Special purpose ('ad hoc') bodies were introduced to deal with local needs which were considered beyond the expertise available to the general purpose territorial bodies. These included harbour boards, hospital boards, water catchment boards, rabbit boards (subsequently animal pest destruction boards), electric power boards, museum trust boards, licensing trusts. Most consisted of members who were directly elected by members of their communities. In some cases, members of special purposes bodies were chosen by the territorial councils in their areas, a process of 'indirect election'. Voting rights for all local bodies were gradually extended beyond the ranks of ratepayers to match, more or less, the adult residential qualification used for general elections. However, though plural voting was abolished for municipalities before the end of the nineteenth century, some remained in force in counties until 1974. Moreover, ratepayers were entitled to a vote in more than one local authority provided they owned property and payed rates in each locality, a form of plural voting for multiple property owners. Ratepayers also had an advantage at the enrolment stage. Until the consolidation of local electoral rolls and the general electoral roll in the mid 1980s, ratepayers were automatically listed on the local roll while non-ratepaying residents were required to take active steps to enrol personally.

The system as a whole was formed by historical accretion and pragmatic adjustment to perceived needs (Bush, 1995). Thus, particular functions, such as drainage or electricity power supply, could be met by special purpose bodies in some parts of the country and by general purpose territorial bodies in other parts. As towns and cities grew, local bodies and their boundaries did not always keep pace. General support for principles of local autonomy underlay the legislative requirement that local bodies could not be amalgamated without the consent of the communities concerned. A series of Local Government Commissions, beginning in 1946, recommended the rationalisation of functions and the amalgamation of small, supposedly inefficient local bodies, but to little avail. Many communities preferred to retain their identity and resist amalgamation, particularly if joining a larger body was likely to lead to an increase in rates. The result, in the early-established 'metropolitan' cities, or 'four main centres' (Auckland, Wellington, Christchurch and Dunedin), was the uneasy coexistence of city councils (in the case of Auckland and Wellington, several city councils) with small boroughs or counties all servicing the population of a single urban area.

The interests of larger regions, relatively neglected since the abolition of the provinces, were catered for, almost a century later, by a new tier of regional government. This began with the Auckland Regional Authority, founded in 1963. In 1974, as part of a major overhaul of local government, the Labour Government introduced a nationwide structure of regional government centred on 'regional' and 'united' councils. 'Regional' councils were directly elected by voters and could levy rates directly. The Auckland Regional Authority was subsequently joined by the Wellington Regional Council (in 1980) and the Northland Regional Council (in 1987). The remainder of the country was covered by 'united' councils, which were indirectly elected, being selected by members of the territorial local bodies in their region, and totally reliant on these bodies for funds. The 1974 reforms also introduced new types of smaller unit within territorial local bodies, community councils and district community councils, which lacked the legal and financial powers of territorial bodies and acted mainly in an advisory capacity to their parent bodies.

The reforms of 1989 were engineered by a reforming Local Government Commission which had been given much strengthened powers and was backed by a determined radical government. As a result, the structure of local government was considerably simplified (Bush, 1990; 1995: 78–94). The sharp distinction between urban municipalities and rural counties, which had been gradually weakening over the last decade, was largely superseded. Many of the smaller boroughs were abolished and their territories incorporated into larger districts. The united councils were replaced by a more uniform system of regional government. The category of special purpose local body was almost eliminated. The management of all local bodies was restructured in accordance with the principles of the new public management. The reforms embodied in the Local Government Act of 2002 left the structure of local government intact while raising its functional status by extending to local government the power of general competence. In other words, local and regional councils are no longer restricted to specifically authorised activities, but can do anything unless it is specifically proscribed. The potential for local authorities to extend their range of activities, however, is hedged by the Act's demanding procedural requirements involving extensive consultation and conformity to elaborate planning processes (Mitchell, 2003).

The three levels of local government

There are three levels of general purpose local government. In descending order of size, they are region, district (and city), and community. Their boundaries have been decided by the Local Government Commission after exhaustive local consultation. In determining boundaries, the Commission is required to consider how particular services could be provided most efficiently and effectively. It is also to have regard to 'community of interest', that is, the extent to which groups of people in particular localities share common interests which would best be met by their being incorporated into a single unit.

The most important level of local government is the middle level, that associated with the standard territorial authority of which there are now two types only, cities and districts. Indeed, the term 'city' is a courtesy title only, applied to fifteen authorities (including four each within the urban centres of Auckland and Wellington) and now restricted to mainly urban districts with more than 50,000 inhabitants which form a distinct entity. In all essential respects, the fifteen cities and 59 districts are treated as similar and are subject to the same laws and regulations. All have elected councils and all now have a separately elected mayor.

The functions performed by territorial authorities are various and wide-ranging (Bush, 1995: 129–30). They include the provision of local roading, sewerage, local land use and building controls, water supply, parks and reserves, libraries, cemeteries, civil defence, pensioner housing, dog licensing. Some of these functions are shared with other branches of government. For instance, roading is also a responsibility of central government, in part through government funds dispersed by Transit New Zealand (formerly the National Roads Board). Civil defence and resource management involve regional councils as well as cities and districts.

At the regional level, the country is now covered by twelve regional councils, all directly elected. Each region is divided into a number of electoral constituencies, the boundaries normally following those of the constituent cities and districts. There are also four 'unitary authorities' where the functions of regional councils are carried out by territorial councils. The main function of the regional councils is the management of natural resources, including the management of water catchments and harbours (other than commercial port facilities), regional resource management, protection of the environment and pest destruction. Regional councils also have a statutory role in civil defence. In Auckland and Wellington, which have had a longer experience with elected regional government, the regional councils have had responsibility for certain functions elsewhere provided by cities and districts, for instance, parks and reserves, water supply and passenger transport.

The future role of regional councils generally remains unclear. Though a regional perspective is certainly needed for resource and environmental management, a population of less than four million may not require a fully fledged separate tier of elected government for this purpose. The growing number of 'unitary authorities', originally, in 1990, only Gisborne, but, since then, Marlborough, Tasman and Nelson, suggests a weakening of support for regional government in provincial areas. Even in Auckland and Wellington, the case for separate regional government has been weakened by the reorganisation of the constituent local bodies into a smaller number of larger and more effective councils. The Auckland urban region, for instance, is covered by four city councils and three districts compared with the previous eleven cities, sixteen boroughs and four counties. In 1991, National's Minister for Local Government proposed the abolition of regional councils and their replacement by much more modest resource management boards. This proposal met with strong opposition from the regional councils and was not pursued. However, in 1992, the powers of regional councils were further curtailed, a change which, in the case of Auckland, necessitated the transfer of the management of the Council's considerable trading functions to a separately elected Regional Services Trust.

Both regional and city and district councils have the power, within certain legally specified limits, to make local regulations, known as 'by-laws', which have the force of law. They may raise revenue by levying various forms of rates which are set annually at a certain fraction of the value of landed property. Councils can choose not only the fraction or rate of value levied but also the basis on which the value is determined – whether the value of the land alone, total capital value (land plus buildings) or annual rental value. They can also strike differential rates, for instance distinguishing between commercial and non-commercial property. In addition to levying rates, councils also receive proceeds of an additional taxes levied on the sale of petrol for the purpose of subsidising public transport. They can engage in certain trading activities, for instance, in the sale of utilities such as water, or of public services, such as transport or housing. They frequently raise loans for major capital developments, for instance new drainage or water schemes.

In all their financial dealings, local authorities are subject to controls laid down by central government. Certain common forms of revenue raising are not permitted, for instance income tax or consumption tax. Some local body loans are still subject to authorisation by the Local Authorities Loans Board (and to a poll of ratepayers if 15 per cent of the registered voters petition for one) Central government determines the maximum levels of remuneration which council members are entitled to pay themselves.

Councils are also subject to the same processes of financial scrutiny by the Controller and Auditor-General which apply to central government departments, as well as to investigations by the Ombudsman. In general, central government has sought to impose on local government the same managerial principles it has applied to its own activities (Boston *et al.*, 1996: 191–202). Financial planning and accounting is now organised around the achievement of designated objectives. The role of Chief Executives as individual managers and employers has been emphasised (and their remuneration increased). Provision of many services has been contracted out to the private sector. Trading enterprises, such as public transport departments, have been corporatised into 'Local Authority Trading Enterprises' (LATEs) on the model of SOEs (Chapter 6: 161–6) or privatised.

The restructuring of local government also required local bodies to incorporate a Maori dimension. Unlike Parliament, local bodies have never had statutorily guaranteed Maori representation. The concentration of local government on the material development of landed property according to Pakeha economic values has often been at the expense of Maori interests. However, under the Resource Management Act 1991, regional councils are required to consult the interests of local Maori when making planning decisions. A number of regional councils, as well as cities and districts, have established Maori advisory committees. Provision was made in 2002 to extend and formalise these procedures and also to help correct the under-representation of Maori in local government by enabling local and regional councils to establish designated Maori wards or constituencies, thus following the historical practice of separate Maori parliamentary seats. By 2003, however, only one authority, the Bay of Plenty regional council, had taken up this option, and in another the proposal was thrown out in a citizen-initiated local referendum on the matter (Drage, 2003).

The lowest, and least powerful, level of local government is occupied by the 157 community boards within individual cities and districts. Community boards are an optional, additional form of organisation intended to provide a focus for more localised identity and more localised interests within the larger, more disparate area covered by a city or district. Some community boards represent small country towns situated within predominantly rural districts, thus recognising the long-standing differences between the interests of town-dwellers and country-dwellers which have always been a feature of local government. Community boards are also found within the larger cities, where they represent smaller suburbs or localities, in many cases areas which had had their own independent councils before the enforced reorganisation and amalgamations of 1989. Where the city or district is divided into a number of separate wards, the boundaries of the community board or boards usually coincide with ward boundaries.

At least half the members of each community board are directly elected by local voters but the balance may consist of members appointed from the council of the particular city or district in which the board is located. The functions of community boards are largely consultative and subsidiary to those of the parent council. Community boards have no power to levy funds or raise loans or make by-laws. Though other powers and funds may be delegated from the parent authority, in most cases the activities of the boards are restricted to giving advice to the council and to acting as a sounding board on behalf of localised interests (Bush, 1995: 114–5).

Perhaps the most striking effect of the 1989 local government reforms and subsequent restructuring was the almost complete elimination of special purpose local bodies, for so long a very significant category of New Zealand local government. In many cases, their functions were given to the most relevant multi-purpose bodies, a transfer made possible by the strengthening of regional councils and the reorganisation of cities and districts. Indeed, some special purpose functions, such as drainage, were already being provided by some territorial bodies and by regional councils. The functions of water catchment (catchment boards) and pest destruction (animal pest destruction boards) now belong to regional councils.

Other trading functions carried out by elected harbour boards and electric power boards have been transferred from elected local bodies to government-appointed corporations or have been sold to private enterprise. Efficiency and accountability to the citizen, it was argued, are better served by offering individual consumers a choice between competing providers of services rather than through public monopolies answerable to elected councils. For similar reasons, the restructuring of the health services saw for a time the abolition of popularly elected area health boards (which incorporated former hospital boards).

Hospital services were thus completely removed from the traditional local government sector (Chapter 6: 165) until the reintroduction in 2001 of partially elected District Health Boards. Only a few special purpose bodies survived the restructuring process, being deemed inappropriate either for transfer to multi-purpose bodies or for corporatisation or privatisation. These include twenty-four elected licensing trusts, which control the sale of liquor in certain designated areas, and a small number of museum trust boards, such as the Otago Museum Trust Board.

Conduct of elections

Elections for all local bodies are held together every three years on a fixed date, the second Saturday in October. In recent decades this date has fallen in the year before general parliamentary elections (though general elections, unlike local elections, can be called at the prime minister's discretion before the three-yearly term is completed (Chapter 5)). The right to vote is open to all those enrolled on the parliamentary electoral roll as resident within the relevant region, city, district or community. Candidates for election need not be resident in the locality concerned. Candidates are forbidden from standing in more than one division of the same authority, though they may stand for the positions of mayor as well as councillor. Whether candidates should be elected for electoral divisions ('wards') or 'at-large' for the whole local body area has been subject to political dispute. The Labour government in 1989 imposed mandatory wards for cities and districts with populations over 20,000 as well as for regional councils while National has allowed cities and districts to decide for themselves, and this discretion has remained under Labour-led governments since 1999. Political controversy has also surrounded the separate ratepayers' franchise which allowed people to vote in more than one territory if they owned property and paid rates in each territory (for instance, if they owned a holiday house as well as a residential home). This right was abolished in 1986 but restored in 1992. Since 1989, voting in almost all local bodies has been conducted by postal ballot. Voting papers are posted to all enrolled voters several weeks before the election date. Voters fill them in and return the votes by post in time for them to be counted on the election day itself. The method of counting votes has been first-past-the-post; i.e. the candidate (in the case of mayors), or the candidates (in the case of local bodies), with the most votes win.

However, after the introduction of MMP in national politics, advocates of proportional representation lobbied for the introduction of the single-transferable-vote (STV) in local authority elections. A sympathetic minister, Sandra Lee, in the Labour-Alliance government after 1999 added weight to the issue. As a result, since the Local Electoral Act (2001), councils have been able to choose whether to use STV or first-past-the-post. They may also be forced to switch to STV by local referendum. Despite the enabling legislation, conservatism reigned and there was no rush among local councils nor their electors to abandon long-practised first-past-the-post elections. For the 2004 local elections, only ten of the 86 local authorities chose STV (Drage, 2003: 13).

Levels of voter turnout at local elections have traditionally been well below that of general elections. For many years, turnout in the metropolitan cities, for instance, was around 40–50 per cent, about half that normal in parliamentary elections (Chapter 11: 269–73; Bush, 1980: 201). Turnout for the more obscure special purpose bodies could fall lower still, particularly if relatively few positions were contested. Recent reforms have improved the levels of voting turnout somewhat. Restructuring has removed most of the more low-profile special purpose bodies. More important, postal voting has produced increased levels of participation. (The effect of postal voting is indicated in the experience of the Lower Hutt City Council which restored the traditional voting-booth mode of voting in 1992 and saw turnout decline to 29 per cent compared with the then 49 per cent average for cities (Bush, 1995: 283).) But turnout is still significantly below that achieved at general elections. In the 1998 elections average turnout was 51 per cent for cities and 61 per cent for district councils (Bush, 2003) .

Politics without parties

Political activity at the local government level is significantly different from that associated with central government. The contrast can be illustrated in terms of the alternative models used earlier to analyse the functions of Parliament (Chapter 5), the 'liberal constitutional' model and the 'democratic party' model. In comparison with Parliament, local body councils behave in a way which more closely resembles the 'liberal constitutional' model. This is the model enshrined in the constitutional and legal account of Parliament, though not in current parliamentary practice. It emphasises the political independence of individual elected representatives and the deliberative function of Parliament as a debating chamber where policy is freely discussed and decided. Whereas parliamentary politics tend to be partisan and controversial, centring on conflict between clearly identifiable political parties, local politics are more often personal rather than partisan and are given more to a mode of political consensus than to open political conflict.

Most elected local body members stand for election as independents rather than as members of a recognised political party (Bush, 2003), a tendency which is particularly marked in rural districts. The main exception is in the larger cities and urban regional councils, where the Labour party has sponsored party candidates, usually unsuccessfully. Local elections have also been contested by the environmentalist parties, first Values and then the Greens (Chapter 11), demonstrating their concern for local environmental and planning issues (in accordance with the international Green slogan to 'think globally, act locally'). Not surprisingly, given both its Labour roots and until 1998 its Green members, the Alliance (Chapter 10) has entered candidates in local elections. The National party, in contrast, is conspicuously absent from local politics. However, Labour's entry into local politics in the early twentieth century provoked the emergence of 'citizens" or 'ratepayers" associations, which contain many National members. These associations sponsor candidates who are opposed not only to Labour party candidates but also more generally to the intrusion of party politics into local government. Their opponents often accuse them of being the National party in disguise, a charge which has some substance given the principles and policies often supported by their members. On the other hand, outside their three-yearly electioneering activities, these associations have little of the formal organisation normal for political parties, such as policy-making committees or conferences. They make a point of stressing the political independence of their individual candidates and are prepared to endorse members of any political party as their candidates. They thus function in the paradoxical, but politically popular, role of being a party against party.

On the whole, candidates from the mainstream political parties do not fare particularly well in local elections. Labour regularly attracts a smaller proportion of votes than it does at general elections in the same localities. This reflects the widespread support for the view, successfully exploited by the citizens' associations, that party politics should have no place in local government. This assumption is regularly reflected in the media coverage of local government, particularly during local election campaigns, when it is a common theme of editorials, letters to the editor and talkback radio. Party politics tends to be seen as unduly divisive, particularly in small communities where people know each other personally. Local body politicians prefer to see themselves as representing the community as a whole and not simply one section of the community, which allegiance to a particular party seems to imply. In this respect, they are able to act out the liberal constitutional ideal of the free independent representative. It is an attractive role, more comfortable and less unpopular than that of party politician. Parliamentary MPs reflect the same point of view when they find particular satisfaction in their work as non-partisan local constituency representatives (Chapter 5: 131–2).

The unimportance of party in local politics is reflected in the relative unimportance of election policies and manifestos in local elections (Mulgan, 1989: 140). For the most part, election statements, whether issued by individual candidates or parties, are brief and general. Elected councils therefore conduct their business without the limitations set by explicit mandates. The major exception is a general embargo on excessive rate increases. Ratepayers are very conscious of the level of their rates and almost all candidates and parties pledge themselves to keep the rates down, or at least to keep increases within the overall level of inflation. There are occasional mandated policies, as for instance in Wellington in 1986, when the incoming Labour mayor and council majority had pledged to introduce an alternative sewerage scheme. For the most part, however, incoming council members are not bound by any clear electoral commitments, so long as they keep the rates in check.

Similarly, there is rarely any regular caucusing or holding of party colleagues to a disciplined party line. Local body members in general, whether or not they formally describe themselves as 'independent', behave very much as independent representatives, debating issues on their merits and not as members of any united group or party team. Political differences certainly occur, often centring on the mayor and the chairpersons of committees, but they rarely solidify into permanent alliances. Debates in council meetings or in committees are more likely to be genuine discussions and exchanges of view rather than partisan altercations or repetitions of already determined party positions. The parallel at the parliamentary level is with the occasional 'free vote' or uncontroversial select committee meeting, when MPs can ignore the normal constraints of party discipline and can deliberate in the manner prescribed by the liberal constitutional view of Parliament.

Lack of party identity and party mandates may certainly add to the deliberative seriousness of council meetings and provide a welcome contrast with the tedious rantings of MPs in parliamentary debates. On the other hand, the fact that few policies are clearly endorsed by the voters means that elected councillors are deprived of a major source of leverage against their bureaucratic advisers. At the central government level, public servants recognise the overriding political authority of the government's party policy (Chapter 6: 160). Apart from the general pledge to keep the rates down, incoming local politicians have few policy initiatives which they can insist on implementing and which their permanent staff will accept as binding.

The lack of party identification also tends to weaken the links of accountability between voters and elected members. Voters cannot easily identify who is responsible for particular decisions and it is therefore less clear whom they should reward or punish at election time. On occasion, individual members, particularly mayors, may become clearly associated with particular policies and may be held to account by the voters for them. But when decisions have been taken by an unidentified group of councillors, electoral accountability is less effective. Unless there is an identifiable opposition group or party to act as a focus for disgruntled voters, councillors are likely to feel under little threat from the likely reactions of the electorate. This is underlined by the fact that incumbent local body members have a very high electoral success rate when they offer themselves as candidates and, not infrequently, are returned unopposed (Bush, 1995: 289–90). In the absence of party identity and responsibility, the most important factor in securing votes is the level of individual name recognition, a factor which is increased through publicity gained while holding office. Once elected, therefore, local body members, apart from mayors, are hard to dislodge.

The generally non-partisan style of local government helps to keep the political temperature low and encourages public apathy about local politics. News coverage of political debate in local government is intermittent at best. The news media tend to devote more attention to the more adversarial and therefore more newsworthy political processes surrounding central government. Television, which is the main mass medium of political communication, is compelled by its cost structure and commercial pressures to concentrate on issues of interest to a mass nationwide audience (Chapter 12). Newspapers cover the major councils in their circulation areas, the main city and regional councils in the case of urban daily newspapers. The more localised 'giveaway' newspapers carry news items from their various local bodies and often try to stimulate debate about local issues. But the journalistic resources available to them for proactive and critical reporting are severely restricted.

At the local level, therefore, many of the types of pressure which surround parliamentary politicians – party conflict, media criticism and electoral competition – are weak or non-existent. Organised political conflict is by no means unknown. Many local bodies have faced vigorous opposition from environmental and Maori groups (Bush 1995: 266–72). However, the main channels of political influence and accountability are informal and personal. In forming their political judgements, local councillors rely primarily on their own individual experience and the opinions of their personal acquaintances. Similarly, the influence of organised interest groups at the local level is much more likely to be conveyed through personal contact than through the more formalised structures of persuasion applied to central government (Chapter 9). Rural councillors will pick up the views of local farmers through their daily contacts with friends and neighbours. In towns, organisations such as Rotary clubs and other 'service' clubs provide a regular forum for personal interchange and influence. Local body politicians are distinguished by being 'joiners', the type of people who are heavily involved in community organisations, such as churches, service clubs, women's organisations, sports clubs, and so on (Bush, 1995: 198). It is in these social contexts, among networks of usually like-minded people from similar social backgrounds, that they conduct their regular political consultation and lay the basis of their political judgements. The social characteristics of local body members therefore become particularly significant for assessing the interests which are served by local government.

The contrast with central government can be expressed in terms of different senses of political 'representation' (Mulgan, 1989: 144–5; Chapter 5: 134–5). Elected politicians may represent their constituents in the sense of sharing the same characteristics, being a typical or 'representative' cross-section of their constituents. On the other hand, politicians may represent their constituents by acting for them as agents or delegates appointed to pursue their interests. This function can be successfully performed whether or not politicians are typical of their constituents in the sense of sharing the same characteristics. It is this agency sense of representation which is dominant in Parliament, where MPs are chosen by political parties competing for electoral support. Relatively high voter turnout and publicity for party polices give parties an incentive to appeal to all sectors of the voting public (Chapter 11). This incentive operates whether or not MPs, acting as agents of the parties, actually belong to the sector groups being targeted. A party can offer policies to appeal to voters under thirty without having any candidates in that age group. At the local level, however, much more depends on the personal background of the individual politicians. It is correspondingly more important whether elected politicians are typically representative of their constituents.

In practice, local bodies are far from being representative cross-sections of their communities. Those who become elected to local bodies are overwhelmingly middle class in social background and closely associated with local property interests. Farmers have always predominated in rural areas, while the towns and cities have seen a disproportionate number of members drawn from the ranks of local business and professional people. Maori have also been under-represented, less than 6 per cent of councillors in 1998 identifying as Maori (Drage, 2003: 13). Though Maori iwi are significant landowners in many parts of the country, it is the Pakeha and their interests which have been predominant. Men have outnumbered women in local government, though not so decisively as in Parliament. Being a part-time responsibility which does not require living away from home, local body politics has been more compatible with public expectations of women's domestic role. Moreover, in the larger cities where competing parties put forward lists of council candidates, women have benefited from the pressure on parties and citizens' groups, when making up lists of candidates, to include at least a reasonable proportion of women candidates in any list. Whereas choosing a male rather than a female candidate for a single office may appear justifiable, choosing several males and no females for a number of vacancies appears much more discriminatory. The introduction of party lists under MMP produced a similar effect in favour of greater gender balance at the national level with Parliaments elected since 1996 containing an increased proportion of women (Chapter 5: 134). It is in the smaller communities, where parties do not operate and independent candidates are the norm, that male property holders, such as farmers and businessmen, are particularly dominant.

The politics of consensus

Among the plurality of interests that exist within local communities, some are systematically excluded from influence over local government. The bias inherent in local government is masked by the degree of consensus and the absence of deep-seated controversy which surrounds local decision-making. This is partly a result of the types of function which local government undertakes. They tend to be functions and services which are widely accepted as necessary and desirable. The provision of roads, water supply, sewage disposal, parks, rubbish collection and so on are aspects of modern living which almost everyone takes for granted. There may be argument about how much should be spent on particular services or about where certain facilities, such as parks or rubbish tips, should be situated, but there will be little dispute over the general need for such services or about their being a proper charge on the rates.

The dominance of political consensus is reinforced by the general reluctance of local bodies to involve themselves in activities which are likely to generate political controversy. For instance, most local councils have been very cautious about embarking on the extensive provision of social welfare services or housing (beyond a modicum of relatively uncontroversial pensioner housing). Such services are prohibitively expensive, given the restricted basis of local government revenue. Moreover, they involve a politically contestable degree of income distribution from some classes or sections of the community to others. For this reason, responsibility for major policies in social welfare, as in education and health, is willingly conceded to the party politicians in Wellington. Similarly, in the area of economic policy, though local bodies may act as advocates of local economic development and may even offer financial inducements to encourage local industries, these initiatives are usually restricted to policies which have wide community support and would not be contested between local members of rival political parties.

That consensus rather than controversy is the norm for local government does not mean that all interests are equally served by local government decisions. It is rather an indication that certain interests dominate and others are systematically excluded. Local government has its origins in the material development of localities, in the provision of services which enhance the profitability of local enterprises and the value of property. It is inextricably linked to the interests of ratepayers, those who pay a tax on their property and expect something in return. While some councils have looked for a broader community role in 'community development' and all accept some responsibility for recreational and cultural needs, the interests of ratepayers dictate an emphasis on material services such as roads, drainage and water supply, which will add value to private property. The same interests provide the overriding constraint within which local councils act, the need to keep the rates down. The importance of property interests is indicated by the persistence of the ratepayer franchise. This franchise is based on the assumption that voting rights belong particularly to those who own property and pay taxes thereon, an assumption which has had no place in parliamentary elections for a hundred years.

Such open political conflicts as do occur within local government tend to be within limits set by the general objective of protecting and enhancing private property. They are usually conflicts between different groups of property owners, for instance between farmers and home owners in towns, between owners of commercial properties and home owners, between home-owners in one locality or suburb and those in another. But the interests of those local residents who own no landed property at all, such as state house tenants and the unemployed, are of marginal concern to local bodies. If they are to be the responsibility of any government authority, it is of central government not local government. Thus 'keeping politics out of local government' is in effect a licence to prefer certain sections of the community, the owners of landed property. It is a deceptive cloak for the systematic pursuit of certain political interests ahead of others. While the politics surrounding central government are far from an equal contest, with some sections of the plural society faring much better than others, local government provides an even less hospitable arena for the interests of the most vulnerable.

Further reading

Local government in general
Boston *et al.*(1996): Chapters 8–9; Bush, 1995; Bush (2003); Drage (1999); Drage (2002); Palmer & Palmer (1997): Chapter 12; Ringer (1991): Chapter 18; Wood (1988): Chapters 9–10.
1989 restructuring of local government
Bush (1990).
2002 reform of local government
Drage (2003); Mitchell (2003).
Democracy and consensus in local government
Mulgan (1989): Chapter 5.

Local Government New Zealand website:<www.lgnz.co.nz>

9

Interest Groups

The importance of interest groups

One of the basic assumptions of a pluralist theory of politics is that the political system operates within a plural society made up of different groups with differing values and interests (Chapter 1: 9). Much of the activity of the state needs to be understood in terms of the influences it receives from the various aspects of this wider society. An account of New Zealand's pluralist society has already been given in Chapter 2 and the succeeding six chapters have covered the main institutions of the state. The focus of the next four chapters is on the interaction between the two, particularly on how the plural society affects the state and on how political institutions respond to pressures and influences from the various sections of the public.

This chapter concentrates on the role of interest groups in the political system. An interest group is to be understood as an organised group representing to government the views of those who share a common interest. In this sense, an interest group is not the same as a social group with interests, that is, one of the various classes, ethnic groups, geographical localities and so on which make up the plural society described in Chapter 2. In the context of political analysis, interest groups are formal organisations with a political function, organisations which represent the interests of particular groups and seek to influence governments to their point of view.

Pluralist theories of politics have often been closely associated with an emphasis on the role of interest groups. The early, classic versions of pluralism, as developed particularly in the United States, formulated a view of the state as the more or less passive recipient of pressure from organisations representing various sections of society (the 'cipher' or 'weather-vane' state). These organisations were known as 'pressure groups' or 'interest groups' and politicians were cast in the role of balancing or 'brokering' the different groups against each other. Political analysis consisted in identifying and assessing the respective methods of group influence on political actors and institutions.

As already indicated (Chapter 1: 13), this model of the state as a passive cipher responding only to pressure from sectional interests is inaccurate and one-sided. It ignores the possible independent influence of state institutions and, in some formulations, may also overlook the role of wider social forces, such as dominant ideologies, social structures or international economic pressures. Moreover, it is more applicable to the United States than to Westminster systems such as New Zealand. In Westminster systems, governments control Parliament and are able to exert strong countervailing power against powerful sectional interests. Even under MMP and the greater degree of consultation which multi-party government generates, a government supported by a parliamentary majority will still exercise considerable power. In the United States, however, the legislative power of Congress is separate from the executive and political parties are much less disciplined. It is much easier for lobby groups to affect the policy-making process through influence over individual members of Congress. None the less, though the political importance of interest groups must not be overstated, they certainly play a highly significant part in determining both the agenda and the outcomes of political decision-making in New Zealand as in other liberal capitalist democracies.

In each sector of government activity, the policy-makers in Parliament and the public service have to take account of interest groups pressing for, or against, certain policy options. Ministers of Finance will need to listen to groups such as Federated Farmers, the Business Roundtable, Business New Zealand and the Bankers' Association. A Minister of Education will be under pressure from teacher unions (e.g. the NZ Educational Institute, the Post Primary Teachers' Association and the Association of University Staff), from boards of trustees (the School Trustees' Association), from school principals (the Principals' Federation) and other educational groups such as the Independent Schools Council and the Education Forum. A Minister for the Environment will need to steer a middle course between pressure from producer groups, such as Federated Farmers and the Forest Owners' Association, and environmental groups, such as the Forest and Bird Protection Society of New Zealand, the Environmental Defence Society and the Ecologic Foundation. Similar networks of interested parties surround other ministers and their departments.

Such interest-group activity is an inevitable and healthy part of a demo-cratic political system. In an open democratic society where people are free to organise for lawful political purposes, like-minded members of the public wanting certain results from government, whether central or local, will often wish to take concerted action to influence governments to their point of view. Governments, for their part, will tend to take no-tice of such groups and their opinions. Elected governments want to retain the support of voters and will therefore have an incentive not to alienate sections of the voting public who express strong views on cer-tain issues. Governments may also need the active support and coopera-tion of certain groups, such as bankers or doctors, on whom they depend to implement their programmes successfully. They will therefore seek their consent by involving them in the decision-making process. In each sector of government, 'policy communities' tend to develop, consisting of ministers, public servants and key interest groups who share a con-cern for policy in that area. However, though interest groups are a vital source of popular influence on governments, it must also be conceded that some groups can organise themselves more effectively and have a greater impact on governments than others. One of the proper functions of a democratic government is therefore to protect interests which are neglected and to take countervailing action on their behalf.

Models of interaction between interest groups and governments

There are differing institutional structures for managing the interac-tion of interest groups and governments and differing views about the proper stance to be adopted by governments towards interest-group influence. These can be understood in terms of different theoretical models of the relationship between interest groups and governments. As is normal with the use of generalised models in social science, no one model or theory encapsulates the whole complexity of interest-group behaviour but each can help to illuminate certain aspects.

One model is that assumed in the classic versions of pluralism and which may be described as the open or 'laissez-faire pluralist' model. The political system is likened to an open economic market in which private individuals wishing to pursue the interests they share with oth-ers organise themselves into competing interest groups in order to gain benefits from government (Mulgan, 1989: 105). Interest groups are essentially non-state, private organisations which come into being or fade away depending on the level of support they can generate from private individuals or institutions. They may influence the state but are in no way sustained or controlled by it. This is the standard pattern of interest-group politics in pluralist democracies and applies to the great bulk of interest-group activity in New Zealand.

A second model is derived from a species of pluralism known as 'corporatism' (Mulgan, 1989: 104–5), where interest groups are formally incorporated into the system of government. The political system is less like a free market and more like a state-run command economy. Interest groups are legally recognised by the state as the sole legitimate representatives of their respective economic or social sectors. The state may confer certain monopolistic powers on them and help to sustain them financially. Leaders of the various groups cooperate with each other and with state officials in negotiating public policies which will affect them and their members.

This corporatist model has been particularly prominent in certain European countries, such as Sweden and Austria, where governments have negotiated overall economic policy directions with representatives of the various industries and trade unions. New Zealand has had strong elements of corporatism in its history, in matters such as the state regulation of wage bargaining through the Arbitration Court and the national award system (Chapter 7: 171–2). There have also been periodic attempts to involve the major economic sector groups in indicative economic planning (1968–73), an economic summit (1984) and a 'compact' or 'growth agreement' (1988–90) (Vowles, 1992: 359–61). Corporatist elements have been, and continue to be, particularly evident in the relations between New Zealand governments and the most important export sector, farming. Corporatism was also reflected in government handling of Maori interests through the state-created New Zealand Maori Council and its constituent district councils (Fleras, 1986).

While the laissez-faire pluralist and corporatist models of interest group politics differ over the extent to which governments formally incorporate interest groups into the legal structure of government, both accept that interest-group influence on government is valuable and legitimate. Both assume a view of politics in which public policy emerges out of a process of negotiation between different groups of society with different sectional interests and different conceptions of the public interest. (It is for this reason, because it shares a pluralist view of society and politics, that corporatism is best seen as a variety of pluralism rather than as an alternative to it (Jordan, 1990: 296–7).)

More sceptical pluralists or 'neo-pluralists' (Chapter 1: 19) recognise that the interest-group system is seriously biased and that there is therefore need for the government to act as an independent defender of neglected interests. But with that proviso they accept the democratic value and legitimacy of interest-group influence. Such pluralist assumptions about the duty of governments to consult with organised interests have been a long-standing part of New Zealand's political culture (Mulgan, 1993: 47–49).

There is a third model of interest-group politics which rejects the pluralist view of politics and the legitimacy of interest-group influence. This may be called the 'market liberal' model because it is associated with market liberal or 'new right' theories which seek to limit the role of the state and place more reliance on the unregulated choices made by individuals and private firms operating in a free market (Chapter 1: 18). Building on an influential public-choice analysis of interest-group politics, the model depicts interest groups as self-interested 'vested' interests seeking special advantages or 'privileges' for themselves which are contrary to the public interest and to the long-term prosperity of the country (Olson, 1982; Vowles, 1993). The political influence of sectional interest groups produces damaging policies such as tariffs protecting certain industries from external competition and state-enforced monopolies preventing competitors from providing needed public services more efficiently. These policies may benefit members of the groups concerned but at the expense of the public at large. Economies such as New Zealand's have stagnated through protecting established and powerful sectors of the economy while stifling economic initiative and investment in new enterprises. Whether interest groups behave according to the laissez-faire or the corporatist model, the consequences of allowing them to affect government decisions are uniformly dangerous. The duty of governments is therefore to resist all interest-group pressure and to stick to implementing the market liberal view of the public interest, that is, to enforcing the general rules needed to regulate the operations of a free market ('the level playing field') and a free society.

This view of interest groups has been an important part of the market liberal ideology dominant in English-speaking democracies since the 1980s and is frequently used to help explain why New Zealand's economic performance declined during the 1960s and 1970s. It has also, by changing the ideological environment in which groups must operate, had important effects on the actual dynamics of interest-group politics in New Zealand. These changes, in turn, by helping to alienate many of those group members who had formerly expected to be listened to by politicians and governments, contributed to the general disillusion with single-party government reflected in the public support for MMP.

Varieties of interest group

Interest groups vary in a number of respects. One is in the type of interests which they represent. In part, the range of organised interest groups reflects the range of social groups in New Zealand's plural society. Economic divisions are particularly important in New Zealand society and, given that economic policy is a major area of government attention, economic interest groups are particularly prominent in the political system. There are well-organised interest groups representing the various sectors of the economy, such as farmers (Federated Farmers), bankers (the Bankers' Association), as well as cross-sectoral groups representing different class interests, for instance employers and manufacturers (Business NZ), managers of large companies (Business Roundtable) and unionised workers (Council of Trade Unions). There are also a large number of occupational and professional associations, such as the Law Society, the Medical Association, the Nurses' Organisation, the Post Primary Teachers' Association, the Society of Accountants. With respect to ethnic and gender divisions, there are organisations acting on behalf of those groups whose interests tend to be politically neglected, for instance, Maori (the New Zealand Maori Council and the Maori Congress), Pacific Islanders (e.g. the Samoan Advisory Council) and women (the National Council of Women). In the areas of leisure and recreation there are countless interest groups representing, for instance, motorists (the Automobile Association), the various sports (e.g. the New Zealand Rugby Football Union, the New Zealand Amateur Athletic Association), musicians (e.g. Chamber Music New Zealand, Musical Theatre New Zealand) and members of churches (e.g. the National Council of Churches and the various public-issues committees of the individual churches).

The range of organised interest groups is not a simple reflection of the range of diverse elements in society itself, though it is in many respects parallel to it. Some sections of society are hardly organised at all and must rely on others to represent their interests. Those who are in some way incapacitated, such as children, the chronically ill, certain classes of beneficiaries, prisoners, refugees, are unable themselves to support a politically effective organisation. If their voices are to be heard, it will usually be through the mouth of some agency, either private or public, which is organised to speak on their behalf. On the other hand, there are other sections of society whose power is so pervasive that they have no need for specially designated organisations to represent their interests. This is particularly the case with ethnic and gender differences. There is no group specifically established to look after the interests of Pakeha, no Pakeha Congress parallel to the Maori Congress or the various Pacific Islands groups. There is no National Council of Men along the lines of the National Council of Women. This reflects the fact that most political institutions and structures are already biased in favour of Pakeha and males.

From this perspective, looking at the interest-group system as an offshoot of the plural society, the standard case of an interest group is an organisation formed by the members of one of the sections of that society to represent their interests. However, not all interest groups are sectional interests of this type. There are other organised interest groups which do not, strictly speaking, represent the interests of a social group in the sense of a section of society with its own separate identity outside the political system. Instead, they are formed to support a particular public cause or government policy, such as electoral reform (the Electoral Reform Coalition), the banning of abortion (Society for the Protection of the Unborn Child) or the protection of public radio (Friends of the Concert Programme). The environmental movement contains a number of such groups, for instance, Greenpeace, the Forest and Bird Protection Society, the Friends of the Earth and the Ecologic Foundation. Their purpose is essentially political and their members are identified primarily by the fact that they share a common view about what governments should do. Such groups are sometimes referred to as 'cause' groups, as distinct from 'interest' groups, 'interest group' being thus confined to groups based on an identifiable social group with a sectional interest. A preferable usage is to refer to all groups which pursue a shared interest as 'interest groups' but to distinguish between two types of interest group, 'sectional' interest groups, which pursue a sectional interest, and 'public' interest groups, which are concerned with the interests of the community as a whole and not just the interests of one section.

The line between a 'public interest' group and a 'sectional interest' group is sometimes hard to draw. Some sectional interests, such as the women's movement, are so broadly based that they may seem to represent a public cause. Moreover, sectional interests regularly use the language of the public interest in pursuit of their own advantage and can indeed sometimes genuinely claim to be seeking a public as well as a sectional benefit. Sectional economic interests, such as farmers or manufacturers, can argue that what will be of immediate advantage to themselves will also be of general benefit to the community, providing economic growth and increased employment. Doctors and nurses campaigning to maintain or improve their own conditions of work argue that it is the patients who will benefit as much as themselves.

The tendency to prefer the rhetoric of the public interest has been considerably strengthened by the growing prevalence of the market liberal view of sectional interests. When organised sectional interests are, virtually by definition, seen as 'vested' interests attempting to divert the state from its proper purpose of legislating for the public interest, there is a strong incentive for groups to pose their demands in terms of the public interest as the only legitimate concept for public policy. This has led to the emergence of a new form of interest group, such as the Business Roundtable, the Education Forum and the Maxim Institute, groups which are formally united round a conception of the public interest and a set of policies rather than membership of a particular sector or occupation.

However, the view of the public interest and the policies which such groups favour are clearly in the interests of a certain section of society and it is this section from which most of their support is derived. In the case of the Business Roundtable, which is made up of executives of major businesses, the sectional interest is that of large businesses and their investors, particularly those which have benefited from financial deregulation and the privatisation of state assets, policies advocated by the Roundtable. In the case of the Education Forum it is the interest of elite schools catering particularly for parents who want traditional academic success for their children as measured by high performance in external examinations. The Maxim Institute lobbies and mobilises support for a socially conservative stand on a range of issues. An earlier example was the Coalition for Public Health, which was organised by doctors in the public hospital service and others opposed to the further privatisation of hospitals (Easton, 1994: 227–9). Though such groups are formally organised around policies rather than interests and though these policies have a possible public as well as a sectional effect, the groups have more affinity with traditional sectional interest groups than with public interest cause groups. Their main aim is to press for the sectional interests of their members. They may have adjusted better than traditional groups to an ideological climate which denigrates vested interests but their claim to have risen above the pursuit of sectional interests must be treated with scepticism.

Interest groups also vary in the extent to which their purpose is to influence government policy. Though the significance of interest groups for political analysis depends on their interaction with government agencies, in many cases this is only a minor and incidental part of what they do. Many organised interest groups are formed for essentially nonpolitical purposes, to coordinate activities which have no direct relation with government. For instance, nationwide religious organisations are mainly concerned with matters of their own internal organisation, their doctrines and forms of worship. It is only occasionally and incidentally that they raise issues which require them to focus specifically on trying to influence government policy. The same applies to leisure or recreation groups whose national organisations are almost entirely concerned with administering their members' activities. They may go for long periods without being concerned with governments at all.

On the other hand, there are some interest groups whose whole reason for existence is to put pressure on governments. This is the case with political action groups such as Defence Action, which campaigned against government military spending, and the superannuitants' groups, such as the Superannuitants'Association. Such groups perhaps most deserve the original name 'pressure group', sometimes preferred to 'interest group' as a generic term for any group which seeks to influence government. Used in this way, however, 'pressure group', implies, misleadingly, that all groups are primarily oriented towards lobbying government. Moreover, the term 'pressure' may suggest the attempted use of undue or illegitimate influence. Like 'vested interest' or 'lobby group' it is often used in political debate as a means of disparaging the political activities of interest groups. As a general term of political analysis, 'pressure group' may therefore wrongly imply that there is something inherently improper or illegitimate about any group's attempts to influence a government to its point of view.

Most of the politically important groups, such as the major economic groups, fall in between these two extremes. They are heavily involved in political lobbying at every point in the policy process, while at the same time providing services to their individual members or coordinating nationwide activities which have no direct political purpose. Thus Federated Farmers provides its members with a journal and organises local meetings on topics of practical interest to individual farmers. At the same time, particularly through its national organisation, it gives a lot of attention to government policy and to lobbying politicians and public servants. Similarly, most local trade union officials are involved with negotiating wages and other working conditions and with trying to settle individual disputes. On the other hand, the national body, the Council of Trade Unions (CTU), concentrates on larger political issues of government policy.

Indeed, this combination of activities on the part of an interest group may be a useful way of recruiting and retaining members at the grass-roots level. Interest groups face the potential problem of 'free-riders', a problem frequently discussed in public choice accounts of collective action and interest groups (Olson, 1965). How can people be induced to contribute towards the costs of achieving some collective benefit, such as a pay increase negotiated by a union, when they can enjoy the same benefit whether they contribute or not? In such cases, selfish individuals have an incentive to take a 'free ride' at the expense of their more collectively conscientious colleagues.

However, if, in addition to such general benefits, an interest group can offer specific benefits exclusively to individual subscribers, then there will be a stronger incentive for people to join. Thus trade unions offer protection for individual workers in conflict with their employers and access to various goods and services at a discount. Federated Farmers keeps individual members in touch with the latest developments in farming, for instance, through its fortnightly newspaper, *Straight Furrow*. In some cases the individual benefit is often the only reason for joining and the lobbying activity is of concern only to office-holders. Thus individuals join the RSA (Returned Services' Association) in order to belong to a convivial social club but indirectly support the lobbying activities of the national executive on issues such as war pensions and defence policy, activities which they would be unlikely to pay for directly. Similarly, motorists pay subscriptions to the Automobile Association for the breakdown service, maps and so on, not necessarily intending to contribute to the Association's lobbying in favour of better roads and reduced petrol tax.

Narrow self-interest is not the only motivation behind group membership. Many people contribute to interest-group activities, at least in part, out of a sense of social obligation and an unwillingness to be seen to take a free ride at the expense of colleagues, friends and neighbours. Some groups, such as politically oriented cause or single-issue groups, make a virtue out of the altruism of their members and their orientation to the good of the community as a whole. For instance, the environmental pressure groups such as Greenpeace or constitutional reformers such as the Electoral Reform Coalition appeal directly to people's sense of public spirit, in the same way as private charities persuade people to contribute to worthy causes. In many cases, such groups are working against the interests of the market liberal supporters of the limited state, such as the Business Roundtable. Indeed, it can be argued that the environmental movement and certain sections of the women's movement have replaced the sectional trade unions as the main source of political opposition to the interests of business (Deeks, 1992: 12–13).

Methods of organisation

Most interest groups have an organisational structure based on principles of democratic representation. Key decisions, such as the appointment of officers, approval of accounts, changes to the constitution itself, are in the hands of a general meeting or conference, usually held annually, and attended by all subscribing members or, more usually, by delegates chosen by subscribing members. An elected national executive will, typically, meet regularly through the year to handle more routine matters and deal with political issues as they arise. Depending on the size and resources of the group, there will also be paid administrative assistance to help run the group's affairs. The major economic sector groups and professional organisations maintain substantial head offices with full-time salaried administrative, research and public relations staff. Less well-funded groups, such as many of the public-interest cause groups, may have to rely more on the voluntary assistance of enthusiastic members.

The typical national interest group is federal in structure, being made up of a number of constituent units, each of which in turn has its own members and democratically elected officers. Indeed, in many cases, it is the constituent organisations which existed first, having been formed to meet the more specific needs of their members. The national organisation then developed later as a 'peak' organisation, a structure designed as a more effective means of communicating with government on matters of common interest. A single body which can speak with one voice on behalf of a large number of members will always be taken more seriously by governments than a large number of smaller groups with differing points of view. This is the rationale behind national federations, such as the Council of Trade Unions, Business NZ, the National Council of Women and the Maori Congress. Each unite and coordinate many disparate organisations, bringing together and articulating their common concerns, while respecting their independence.

Most such peak associations combine both regional and functional divisions. The National Council of Women, for instance, has affiliated to it a wide range of organisations serving the differing interests of women, such as the Federation of University Women, the Maori Women's Welfare League, and the Women's Division of the Federated Farmers. The Council also has local branches made up of members from the various affiliated women's organisations. At the same time, all of these affiliated groups have their own local and national organisations.

Similarly, the Council of Trade Unions (CTU) is a federation of (in 2003) 34 individual trade unions, each of which has its own local and national organisation serving the interests of workers in a particular occupation or groups of occupations, such as meat workers, postal workers, nurses or firefighters. The Council also has fifteen district councils attended by local affiliates from the different unions which themselves have their own local branches and national organisations. These regional bodies facilitate the process of identifying matters of common interest to trade unionists and relaying them to the central office. Business NZ, which contains a large number of individual trade groups, such as furniture manufacturers, footwear manufacturers, toy manufacturers and so on, also has five regional associations (Northern and Central Manufacturers' Association, Canterbury Employers' Chamber of Commerce, Canterbury Manufacturers' Association, Otago-Southland Employers' Association). In each case the structure may appear complex but the rationale is clear and sensible – to meet the differing needs of members and pursue their differing interests, some specific to their particular trade or occupation and some shared with others in related trades and occupations, some confined to a particular locality and some common throughout the country.

A prime illustration of both complexity and effectiveness is the interest-group structure provided by the peak association Federated Farmers, the organisation which serves the interests of farmers (Mulgan, 1989: 106–9; Bremer, 1993). It contains a general organisation which is divided into twenty-three separate regions or 'provinces', each of which has a large number of local branches. In addition to the general organisation, which looks after matters common to all farmers in that particular locality, there are also special produce sections, dealing with particular types of farming – meat and wool, dairy, and agriculture (in the specialised sense of cropping, e.g. wheat growing). Each of these produce sections, as well as the general organisation, has a regional and a national structure, with regular meetings, annual conferences and elected officials. At the head of the whole organisation is a national executive chaired by a national president who can speak for all farmers.

The structure is built on the recognition that any individual farmer will share concerns and interests with differing, overlapping groups of other farmers. There may be a purely local matter, for instance the retention of a local school, which will be appropriately dealt with by the local branch. There may be matters of wider local concern, such as measures to alleviate drought, which will require action at the regional level, but do not necessarily affect all farmers nationally. Similarly, a dairy farmer will have some interests in common with other dairy farmers locally and nationally, interests not shared by neighbours who are in a different line of farming. In turn, there are issues on which all farmers are agreed, such as the reduction of costs of manufactured farm supplies. Here the weight of the whole organisation will be used to press for measures such as the reduction of tariffs on imported manufactured goods.

The representative, federal structure of the typical peak association helps to maintain the political standing of the association and the credibility of its arguments with government. If the leaders can claim the active support of their rank-and-file members, conveyed to them through local office-holders and local meetings, they will carry more weight with the politicians and public servants whom they wish to influence and their views are more likely to be reported as authoritative in the media. However, this expectation of authority depends on an assumption that governments have an obligation to pay attention to representations from important sections of the community. This assumption is itself rejected by the market liberal critique of interest groups. According to market liberals, any sectional interest is an illegitimate vested interest seeking undeserved 'privilege' (Douglas, 1990). Claims by a group to be fully representative or to speak for the whole of its particular sector or occupation do not impress; they simply reinforce the criticism that the group is attempting to exert improper influence.

In response to such criticisms of interest-group politics, as already mentioned, some sector groups, such as the Business Roundtable, have depicted themselves as concerned with the public interest rather than with the sectional interests of their members. This has also been reflected in their organisational structure. Numbers are kept small (the Business Roundtable has only 61 members, the Education Forum eleven) and there is thus no large rank-and-file membership electing an executive or endorsing its policies. Rather than being open to all members of a certain sector or occupation, membership is by invitation only and is confined to those who generally support the groups' policy standpoints. In the past, certain prominent business people eminently eligible for membership of the Business Roundtable, such as Hugh Fletcher, the former managing director of Fletcher Challenge, have publicly distanced themselves from the organisation. In 1987, the president of the then Manufacturers' Federation resigned from the Roundtable in protest against its opposition to protective tariffs (Mulgan, 1989: 123).

Like other public-interest groups, the Business Roundtable concentrates on publishing policy discussion papers similar to those provided by government advisers and therefore readily assimilable by politicians and public servants. Not having to consult a large and diverse membership means that the group can support much more clear-cut and intellectually coherent policies. This was noticeable, for instance, in the early 1980s when the Business Roundtable was able to take the lead in supporting a much more radical industrial relations strategy than the more broadly representative Employers' Federation (later Business NZ) could at that time. The need to be representative is not ignored altogether. If charged with being a self-selected clique, the Business Roundtable can claim that its members manage companies which together represent a large majority of the share capital listed on the New Zealand Stock Exchange (Vowles, 1992: 346). None the less, it is the individual's support for the policy direction, not eligibility derived from holding a particular position in business, which ultimately determines membership.

Methods of influence

The methods by which interest groups seek to influence government policy are as diverse as the interest groups themselves. At one extreme are the methods used by the well-established and well-resourced groups, the 'insider' groups, who are treated as part of the political system and can expect to be consulted and listened to as a matter of course. At the other extreme are the methods resorted to by 'outsider' groups, those groups who do not have easy access to ministers and government officials, who are often poorly resourced and who will have to rely on staging protests or demonstrations in order to get attention. In between, most groups hope to be treated as trusted insiders as much as possible but they may on occasion have to resort to more provocative methods of exerting pressure if they consider themselves unduly neglected.

For the insider established group, the most important point of influence is in maintaining a general predisposition in its favour on the part of politicians and officials. If the policy-makers are already sympathetic to the interests of a group and to the policy directions it supports, then this should reveal itself in the choice of which issues get on to, and which are kept off, the crowded government agenda and in the final decisions which are made. A group which can only seek to exert influence after a policy has been publicly proposed by the government, is much less likely to affect the outcome than one which can influence the prior process of policy formulation. To help create and maintain a climate of sympathetic support for their interests, all the major interest groups cultivate good relations with the policy-makers, preparing written material in the form of reports and media releases and backing them up with regular personal contacts with politicians and public servants.

The broad influence interest groups may have on the agenda of government policy is illustrated by the role played by certain business interest groups in the transformation of government economic policy away from economic intervention and controls and towards deregulation and greater reliance on market forces. The main economic reforms were introduced by the Lange Labour government in its first term, through the powerful advocacy of the Minister of Finance, Roger Douglas, his Cabinet colleagues and public service advisers (Chapter 4: 85; Chapter 5: 117; Chapter 6: 160). But the climate in which such sweeping and radical reforms would prove politically acceptable had already been set by the major business interest groups. During the later 1970s and early 1980s, leaders of the New Zealand business community gradually coalesced behind the set of internationally influential ideas associated with radical market liberalism (Roper, 1992; Roper, 1993: 155–64; Easton, 1997). This process was facilitated by regular meetings of the leaders of the major business and industry groups, the so-called 'top tier', including Federated Farmers, the Manufacturers' Federation, the Employers' Federation, the Retailers' Federation and the Chambers of Commerce. Though some groups were in favour of more and faster deregulation than others, they were all able to agree on some detailed issues, such as an approach to taxation reform which closely parallelled that eventually enacted by Labour (Vowles, 1992: 350). Throughout the restructuring process, the vigorous public support of sympathetic interest groups, such as the Business Roundtable, the Employers' Federation and the Chambers of Commerce, was an important factor in sustaining the government's momentum.

Such support is conveyed partly through carefully cultivated networks of personal contacts and partly through media publicity and the reported comments of interest group leaders. Leaders will look to have access to the relevant ministers and to be regularly consulted by them, or at least to be able to see them if they have a particular issue to raise. 'Policy communities', of politicians, public servants and relevant interest groups, are an important part of routine government decision-making. Such access is not easily gained, especially in a political climate where interest groups are suspected of being vested sectional interests (McLeay, 1995: Chapter 8). Moreover, economic deregulation, including the phasing out of import controls and farming subsidies, has decreased the opportunities for representatives of specific industries to seek special benefits.

The end of state involvement in wage-fixing has reduced the participation of the trade unions in corporatist-style negotiations with employers and government. Indeed, trade unions have been the major losers from the changing style of interest-group organisation. Trade unions are indisputably representatives of a sectional interest. This did not matter when government consultation with major sectional interests was considered prudent and legitimate. Trade union leaders could expect to be invited by the government to sit down with employers' representatives and to negotiate a common position on matters such as a national wage rise. But once sectional interests were delegitimised, unions found themselves excluded from the corridors of power.

As formal consultation of groups has declined, informal contacts and personal networks have become correspondingly more important. While Labour was in power (1984–90), the unions, like the women's movement and teachers, could still exert some pressure by exploiting their personal contacts in government and the party. But these links no longer existed under the subsequent National government (Jesson, 1992). Employers and business leaders, on the other hand, have retained their rights of access regardless of the party in power. Their support is critical to the overall performance of the economy on which any government's popularity depends. The greater exposure of the economy to international financial markets and the increased importance of maintaining business confidence, requires any minister of finance to meet regularly with representatives of the banking and financial community.

Leading business people can usually count on seeing key ministers, including the prime minister, when they wish to. Especially during the Lange Labour and Bolger National governments, considerable influence passed to informal elite networks of key figures in government and business, such as the members of the Business Roundtable, who were closely linked to Roger Douglas and heavily involved in the corporatisation and privatisation of state assets (Venables, 1988). For instance, Alan Gibbs, chairman of Ceramco and Freightways and a member of the Business Roundtable, was a personal friend of Roger Douglas and became chairman of the Forestry Corporation and convener of a committee recommending commercialisation of the health services ('the Gibbs report'). Sir Ron Trotter, former chairman of the Business Roundtable, was also chairman of Telecom and then, under National, was a key figure in organising the restructuring of hospitals. The influence of these personal networks between business leaders and politicians has been increased by the reliance of political parties on substantial donations from individual businesses and businessmen (Chapter 10: 255). While such donations may not be made in return for personal favours, they are expected to buy access to politicians and reinforce the government's commitment to providing a favourable climate for business.

The Clark governments, however, have distanced themselves further from the Business Roundtable than their Labour and National predecessors. Indeed the CEO of the Business Roundtable, Roger Kerr, is a relentless critic of the government's economic policies and was excluded from the forums generated by the government's 'Knowledge Economy' initiative. Business itself is more pluralistic, with prominent businessmen like Stephen Tindall (Warehouse) and Dick Hubbard (Hubbards Foods) and organisations like the New Zealand Business Council for Sustainable Development and Business for Social Responsibility playing more prominent roles in business–government relations.

Leaders of groups who do not enjoy such good personal contacts and find it hard to penetrate the government's defence may resort to the services of professional public relations consultants or lobbyists. This profession has mushroomed as previous expectations of regular access and consultation have diminished. Mostly former journalists and public servants themselves with an intimate knowledge of the inner workings of government, such political consultants can help their clients by telling them who the key decision-makers are and how and when they should best be approached.

Structures of formal, corporatist consultation have not disappeared completely. For instance, corporatism still flourishes in the farming sector, where Federated Farmers is widely represented on a network of quangos. The producer boards, such as the Dairy Board and the Wool

Board, are still largely controlled by farmers and the state still guarantees their considerable powers, including, in some cases, the sole right to market and sell the products concerned. Though governments no longer engage in the corporatist economic management planning through negotiating incomes policy with employers and unions, they have also drawn back from the extreme laissez-faire approach favoured by market liberals. The Bolger National government set up an Enterprise Council consisting of fifteen leading business people and sector leaders (including Ken Douglas, then president of the CTU). The Council was chaired by the prime minister and met about every two months to discuss major issues of government policy. However, in most areas of economic management, formal consultation with sectional interest groups has been replaced by informal personal contacts buttressed by media campaigns using the language of the public interest. Most major interest groups, including Federated Farmers and the Council of Trade Unions, employ their own economists to generate economic policy analysis favourable to their sectional interests. The broadcast media make frequent use of such analysts, particularly economists employed by trading banks, as sources of economic and political comment (Chapter 12: 300).

Apart from maintaining links with ministers and public servants, interest groups will also try to keep in close touch with the political parties, both inside and outside Parliament. Under MMP, where issues of policy are more likely to be negotiated between parties in Parliament, interest groups can be expected to increase their attempts to influence MPs (Boston *et al.*, 1996a: 160–2). Back benchers can play a critical role in caucus and on select committees and are inundated with a constant stream of propaganda material from interest groups. Opposition MPs are fed information which can be used to criticise the government in debates. Parties outside government, having only their small parliamentary research units to help with developing new policies (Chapter 5: 112), welcome additional input from interest groups, many of which have their own professional research teams. Such cooperation is particularly common with groups which have a traditional connection with the party or whose members tend to be strong supporters. Thus trade unionists, with their institutional connection with Labour, expect to have an influence on Labour's policies. So too do teachers, who are traditionally prominent among Labour activists. For instance, when Labour was elected in 1984, it came to power with commitments to restore compulsory unionism and to abolish the sixth-form university entrance examination (a change advocated by the Post Primary Teachers' Association

(PPTA)). Similarly, in the lead-up to the 1990 election, the then Employers' Federation, which had natural affinities with the National Party, played a significant role in developing National's industrial relations policy of deregulating the labour market. This subsequently became the basis of the Employment Contracts Act 1991. Much reviled by trade unions, however, the Employment Contracts Act was one of the first to be repealed and replaced by the more union-friendly Employment Relations Act by the Labour-Alliance coalition in 2000.

When government policy is being introduced in the form of new legislation, an important opportunity for interest-group influence is provided by the select committee stage (Chapter 5: 122–8). One of the main functions of the head office staff of a major interest group is to examine all parliamentary bills as they are introduced into the House and to organise the preparation of submissions on those bills considered relevant to the group's interests. For groups which have not been involved in previous discussions surrounding the bill, the committee stage may offer the first and best chance of affecting the outcome. Though the more powerful 'insider' groups will hope to have influenced policy well beforehand, they will usually also make a submission. They will try once more to persuade the government to move closer to their own preferred policies; if they are satisfied with the government's proposals, they will seek to strengthen the government's resolve in the face of hostile opposition from other groups.

Select committee hearings on controversial and politically contentious legislation like the Employment Relations Bill, the Smoke-free Environments Bill or the Prostitution Reform Bill are often reported in the media and attract hundreds of submissions from individuals and groups both for and against the bills' proposals. The web pages of major interest groups also declare their positions on contentious issues. Select committee hearings thus provide important opportunities for groups to publicise their opinions and mobilise support in the wider community.

There are some groups which are able to make little headway through the normal channels of political influence. These are the typical outsider groups, those who lack the resources to mount sophisticated public relations campaigns or those whose views are too radical or eccentric to be taken note of by the mainstream political organisations. For such groups, the main method of political action is the public demonstration or protest (Harris, 1989). Some New Zealand groups have had considerable political success through this method. For instance, the anti-apartheid groups were able to prevent New Zealanders from having sporting contacts with South Africa in the 1970s and 1980s. The movement began as a fringe movement, without majority support in the community, and was ardently opposed by those determined to retain New Zealand's links with its traditional rugby rivals, the South African Springboks. The protesters' main political weapons were the street march and the public demonstration at key locales, such as sporting venues or outside the Rugby Union headquarters. These techniques, which had also been used by the anti-Vietnam War campaigners of the 1960s and early 1970s, were designed to capture media attention, to demonstrate depth of support (through numbers of people prepared to march) and to harass opponents. The Labour party was persuaded to their point of view in the 1970s, banning the Springbok tour of 1973, and the issue became one which divided the two major parties. In 1981, the National government allowed the Springboks to tour New Zealand but the violence of the demonstrations and the sheer number of protesters convinced National that the experience was not to be repeated. Opposition to sporting contacts became a matter of bipartisan consensus (until contacts were renewed, with the support of the African National Congress, in 1992).

Similar success met the anti-nuclear movement, which demonstrated against visits by US naval ships. Their policy was adopted first by Labour and then by National. Maori activists, too, have made good use of the protest as a means of gaining political attention. The Land March of 1975 is generally seen as the starting point of the modern Maori political renaissance. Subsequent protests, at Bastion Point in 1977–8 and then at Waitangi during annual Waitangi Day celebrations, provided the background for the work of the Waitangi Tribunal and the increased attention to Maori issues (Sharp, 1990: 1–20). A further wave of Maori protests was sparked by the Bolger government's 'fiscal envelope' initiative in 1994–5 (Chapter 7: 186–7). Ceremonies at Waitangi were again disrupted, a number of public parks and buildings were forcibly occupied and the government was forced to modify its plan of setting limits to Maori claims under the Treaty.

Protests and demonstrations are not always successful. For instance, in 1991, the union movement sought to organise massive resistance to the Employment Contracts Act and many unionists marched in protest at the attack on union rights and the abolition of compulsory unionism. However, the government was unmoved and the Labour Opposition was unenthusiastic about being seen to embrace the unions too closely. In this case, the protesters were unable to withstand the countervailing power of the business groups who supported the government's policy and the financial markets who would have treated any reversal of policy as a reason for diminishing confidence in the New Zealand economy.

Protest is not the sole preserve of outsider groups. It may also occasionally be used by well-established organisations when they have failed to influence government through the normal channels of influence. Farmers, for instance, though members of an interest group with excellent access to governments, are also prepared to take to the streets. During the process of deregulation in 1985–6, when subsidies were being removed and interest rates raised, some farmers, particularly those with high levels of debt, were fiercely opposed to the government's policies. Stock were publicly slaughtered at the farm gate in front of the television cameras. The leadership of Federated Farmers was forced into mounting a march on Parliament (Mulgan, 1989: 110). In 1992, secondary school teachers, whose union (the PPTA) has usually enjoyed close relations with education ministers and officials, staged a number of strikes and public demonstrations in protest against government policies of bulk funding and in defence of national salary awards. In neither case did the public demonstrations appear to have any significant impact on government policy. More recently, however, when farmers again took to the streets in 2003 to demonstrate against the Clark government's proposed levy on livestock to help fund research into reducing animal emissions (which contribute significantly to environmentally damaging 'greenhouse' gases), the government responded by withdrawing the proposal.

Whether the resort to protest and demonstration is successful or not will depend on the circumstances and on the constellation of political forces. Provocative and disruptive measures, while they may attract the media, may sometimes alienate the wider public and merely indicate the lack of mainstream support for the cause. On the other hand, they may also bring home to governments the degree of opposition to their policies and the potential political damage from persisting with them, as was the case with the farmers' protest in 2003 when public opinion was heavily on the side of the farmers against the so-called 'fart tax'. Protest by extremists may strengthen the hand of more moderate elements within the same sector. For instance, violent demonstrations by Maori activists have enabled the more moderate Maori leaders to extract important concessions from governments. Moderate leaders can offer to contain the unrest and prevent the more radical Maori from gaining ground within Maoridom. But to do that they need to be seen to be delivering tangible benefits to their people (Mulgan, 1989a: Chapter 5).

To exercise effective leverage on government, an interest group must be able to threaten some sanction against the government if its demands are neglected. Business groups can point to a possible loss of market confidence and decline in valued economic activity. Groups with large numbers of members or supporters, such as the super-annuitants' groups, Grey Power and Age Concern, can threaten loss of voting support at the next election. Some disadvantaged groups have the potential to damage the government's and the country's reputation for social justice – a weapon skilfully used by Maori activists and other aboriginal minorities around the world (the so-called 'politics of embarrassment'). Where there is no political sanction, or where the government judges that greater damage will be sustained by being seen to give in to pressure, protests and demonstrations may make the television news and the front pages of the newspapers but ultimately they will have little effect.

Persistent inequalities

The political effectiveness of interest groups varies considerably. Democratic principle would require that each group have equal influence or, at least, influence in equal proportion to the number of its members. In practice, certain groups are always more influential, and others less influential, than they should be. In general terms, as might be expected, those with more material resources at their command are able to wield more influence. Interest-group influence costs money, for instance to fund executive meetings and travel, salaries for research and administrative staff, printing costs for attractive propaganda, and so on. Person for person, individual employers can afford to contribute more to such activities than can individual workers or the unemployed. More important, in a capitalist economy like New Zealand, which is open to international economic forces and dependent on maintaining business confidence, the business interests which help to determine this confidence occupy a privileged position (Deeks, 1992; Roper, 1993). Voters seek economic security and prosperity for themselves and their families and are likely to punish governments who do not deliver such prosperity. This gives crucial political leverage to groups such as farmers or forestry companies on whom the country depends for its exports. Even more, it places power in the hands of financial investors who, unlike farmers, can move their capital in and out of the country at will, depending on the comparative return offered on their investment (Chapter 13: 312–3).

The extent of this power is not to be overstated. There are many important and controversial areas of government activity, for instance issues of law and order, school curricula, women's rights and so on, where questions of market confidence or export performance are involved only marginally, if at all. None the less, the need to conciliate those who control economic investment and production in New Zealand does set crucial limits to government activity. For instance, even if the views of the markets do not dictate precisely how governments should spend their resources, they do affect the overall levels of taxation and expenditure that governments can set. Interest groups which represent these key economic forces can always expect to receive a serious hearing from New Zealand governments anxious to encourage business confidence.

As well as advantaging the economically powerful, interest-group politics also tends to favour long-standing interests which have had time to establish their organisations and political contacts. Conversely, new interests which have difficulty breaking into the circles of influence are disadvantaged. Thus the structure of Federated Farmers, for instance, has tended to be less accommodating to the interests of farmers engaged in growing newer export products, such as fruit and horticultural products, compared with those in traditional beef and cattle farming (Mulgan, 1989: 120). Similarly, government moves towards restructuring of state-owned institutions, for instance in the education or health systems, has met organised resistance from existing groups defending entrenched positions; but the new institutional structure has not yet given rise to new groups on which the government could rely to support restructuring. There is thus evidence to support the market liberal criticism that interest-group influence is conservative and a cause of political inertia and economic stagnation.

The interest-group system also tends to favour sectional interests at the expense of the interests of consumers and of the public at large. People are more likely to contribute to the cost of a group which supports their occupational interests than to one which represents their interests as consumers. Occupational interests loom large in people's lives and individuals are more likely to see some tangible return for their contribution. By contrast, interests which people have as consumers and as members of the general public are thinly spread and shared with countless others. There is therefore less incentive for the individual to contribute to groups aiming to support such interests. Thus interest groups supporting sectional economic interests and particular occupations and professions, such as doctors and teachers, are strong; consumer groups are weak (Mulgan, 1989: 127–9). Moreover, the leaders of any interest group may not always represent the views of their rank and file as accurately as opinion polls. Governments may therefore be tempted to rely on their own polling rather than listen to groups themselves (Atkinson, 1989).

These criticisms of interest groups are well-founded: interest-group politics clearly do tend to favour the wealthy against the poor, the established against the up-and-coming, and sectional interests against the public interest. Democratic governments should not adopt a purely passive role towards interest-group pressure, along the lines of the 'weather-vane' state envisaged by some versions of pluralism. But nor need they follow the market liberal model and refuse on principle to have anything to do with organised interests. While the call on governments to ignore vested sectional interests and concentrate only on the public interest may have a certain rhetorical appeal, in practice it leads to even greater political inequality. It does not remove interest-group activity altogether but simply displaces it. It gives even greater power to those sections of society most able to benefit from limited state involvement in economic and social activity and most able to identify their particular sectional interests with the particular view of the public interest favoured by international financial markets (Mulgan, 1992). At the same time, if governments rely on pollsters rather than interest group leaders for their input of public opinion into decision-making, this will only serve to increase the alienation between politicians and the wider community.

Given the economic inequalities inherent in liberal capitalist societies, some degree of political inequality is inevitable in pluralist democracy. However, inequality is likely to be less if governments recognise the legitimacy of all groups and seek to interpose independent, 'countervailing' power on behalf of weak interests, including weak sectional interests, which would otherwise go unprotected. Such attempts to equalise the balance of forces in society will always be inadequate. But they will lead to less unequal results than the market liberal attempt to discredit all interest-group activity. This in fact has been the normal stance taken by New Zealand governments in relation to interest group pressure and is one of the justifications for the Westminster system of strong single-party government. All interest groups are to be listened to and their views taken into account. But the government reserves the right, and the power, to override powerful interests in the name of poorly organised sections of the public or on behalf of the voting and taxpaying public as a whole. However, since the mid 1980s, New Zealand governments have to a certain extent abdicated from the dual role of broker between different interests and defender of weaker interests. In doing so, they appear to have placed the great power of the Westminster executive at the disposal of the more powerful rather than the more vulnerable sections of society. As a result they helped to undermine the democratic legitimacy of the Westminster system itself.

Further reading

New Zealand interest groups in general
Deeks & Perry (eds) (1992); Mulgan (1989): Chapter 4; Palmer & Palmer (1997): 198–202; Tenbensel (2003); Wood (1988): Chapter 7.
Economic sector groups
Deeks (1992); Deeks (1997); Perry (1992); Roper (1992, 1993); Street (2003); Vowles (1992).
Changing patterns of interest-group consultation
Jesson (1992); McLeay (1995): Chapter 8; Mintrom (2003); Vowles (1993).
Outsider groups
Dann (2003); Devere & Scott (2003); Harris (1989).

Websites: most major interest groups have their own sites.

10

Political Parties

The changing party system

As already indicated, political parties play a key role in New Zealand's system of parliamentary government (Chapter 3: 66–69; Chapter 5: 106–10). Like organised interest groups, political parties form an institutional link between the various groups and interests of the wider plural society and the institutions of government. However, political parties have a specialised function. Their purpose is not just to influence government action but to do so in a particular way by endorsing and supporting parliamentary candidates at elections. Political parties are a universal feature of modern representative democracy. In New Zealand, historians usually trace the beginning of the modern party system to the Liberal Party which, coinciding with the introduction of full adult suffrage in 1893, held power for a long period (1891–1912). During that time, their conservative opponents formed themselves into the Reform Party, which in turn held power for many years (1912–28, 1930–35), sometimes joining in coalition with the Liberals in opposition to the newly emerging Labour party. After Labour came to power in 1935, the Reform and Liberal parties formally united into the National party.

The emergence of organised parties offering clear political options increased the power of the voters. Voters could use their vote not only to elect a local representative but also to influence the choice of government more directly. The parties' need to coordinate a nationwide campaign encouraged the development of party organisations outside Parliament (the 'extra-parliamentary' party), with paid party officials and subscribing members willing to contribute time and money to help the party to electoral success. In return, rank-and-file members of the party expected some say in the direction taken by their parliamentary representatives and in the policies they supported. To be successful, political parties needed to keep faith with their supporters and to appear reliably united behind their leader. Internal party discipline thus became essential for electoral effectiveness and, in turn, helped to guarantee the outcome of the voter's choice.

Party systems are commonly categorised according to the number of significant political parties which they contain. While most democracies produce a wide range of party labels, most self-styled political parties are politically irrelevant, being the creation of political eccentrics and attracting only a handful of supporters. Political parties only become politically significant if they can secure enough votes to affect the overall election result, either by winning seats in Parliament or, at least, by determining which other parties win seats. Political scientists distinguish two main types of party system – two-party systems and multi-party systems (Duverger, 1964; Sartori, 1976). In two-party systems, one party normally has a majority of seats and elections are essentially competitions between two alternative single-party governments. In multi-party systems, no single party has a majority and governments are typically formed by coalition between two or more parties. As with most such distinctions in thesocial sciences, the boundaries are not hard and fast and individual countries may have elements of both. In Australia, for instance, one party (Labor) can form a government but its opponents (Liberal and National) must govern in coalition and either side normally faces an upper house in which other, smaller parties hold the balance of power.

The structure of a party system is the result of a number of factors, including the country's social and political history. It is also affected by the electoral system itself, the method by which individual votes are converted into seats in Parliament. For instance, in single-member plurality ('first-past-the-post') systems, each successful candidate must win more votes than every other competitor in a given locality. This tends to reduce the chances for smaller parties to win seats and thereby encourages the development of two-party systems. Conversely, in systems of proportional representation such as MMP, seats are allocated to parties in proportion to the votes cast for each party. This allows smaller parties to win seats and encourages multi-party systems.

For much of the previous century, under the first-past-the-post electoral system, the New Zealand Parliament was dominated by competition between two political parties, first the Liberal and Reform parties, and then, after the success of the Labour party, by Labour and the National party. From the 1940s to the 1980s, New Zealand was a remarkably 'pure' and stable instance of a two-party system (Aimer, 1992: 326–8). Admittedly, there were other significant 'minor' parties besides the two 'major' parties, Labour and National, notably Social Credit, which scored over 10 per cent of the valid vote in 1954, 1966, 1978 and 1981 (when it reached a peak of 20.7 per cent of the valid vote). But even at its peak, Social Credit did not win more than two seats and was unable to break the two major parties' monopoly of power. In the elections between 1946 and 1990, National and Labour between them won a total of 1284 parliamentary seats, losing only seven to other parties (six to Social Credit (renamed the Democratic Party in 1985) and one to NewLabour).

The 1993 election marked an historic turning point. The minor parties attracted an unprecedentedly high percentage of the total vote (30 per cent) and won four seats (two each for the Alliance and New Zealand First parties). New Zealand voters were not only voting for a new electoral system which would reduce the dominance of the major parties in the future but many were already prepared to give minor parties greater representation in a first-past-the-post Parliament. The 1993–6 Parliament underwent a process of transition, as existing political parties and individual politicians positioned themselves for MMP and a multi-party Parliament. The result was a remarkably fluid party structure in which an unprecedented number of MPs (13 out of 99) left their former parties to form new parties or to join other existing parties. Such fluctuations were not expected to continue once MMP was in place and many of the newer parties had been proven to be electorally unsuccessful. However, the effects of such a radical change took more than one election to work their way through the system. Even after the third MMP election in 2002, the structure of the party system was still unstable, particularly with respect to the parliamentary status of the smaller and newer parties.

Party origins and electoral history

An account of the historical origins of New Zealand's political parties must begin with the two former 'major' parties, Labour and National. They are no longer as electorally dominant as before, attracting an average of only 65 per cent of total votes in the elections since 1990 and the term 'major' itself is no longer so appropriate. In 1996 Labour's party vote fell to 28 per cent, and in 2002 National's was even lower at 21 per cent. However, their history provides the context in which other, newer parties have developed. Indeed, two of them, New Zealand First and the Alliance (at least its dominant NewLabour component), were founded by disenchanted members of National and Labour respectively.

TABLE 10.1 *Party voting in general elections, 1960–2002*

Election	Labour	National	SocCred/ Democrat	Values	NZ Party	NewLab	Green	Alliance	NZ First	ACT	Christian	United/ FutureNZ	Other
							% valid vote (number of seats)						
1960	43.4(34)	47.6(46)	8.6(0)	N/A	N/A	N/A	N/A	N/A	N/A	N/A	N/A	N/A	0.4(0)
1963	43.7(35)	47.1(45)	7.9(0)	N/A	N/A	N/A	N/A	N/A	N/A	N/A	N/A	N/A	1.3(0)
1966	41.4(35)	43.6(44)	14.5(1)	N/A	N/A	N/A	N/A	N/A	N/A	N/A	N/A	N/A	0.4(0)
1969	44.0(39)	45.4(45)	9.1(0)	N/A	N/A	N/A	N/A	N/A	N/A	N/A	N/A	N/A	1.5(0)
1972	48.4(55)	41.5(32)	6.7(0)	2.0(0)	N/A	N/A	N/A	N/A	N/A	N/A	N/A	N/A	1.5(0)
1975	39.6(32)	47.6(55)	7.4(0)	5.2(0)	N/A	N/A	N/A	N/A	N/A	N/A	N/A	N/A	0.2(0)
1978	40.4(40)	39.8(51)	16.1(1)	2.4(0)	N/A	N/A	N/A	N/A	N/A	N/A	N/A	N/A	1.3(0)
1981	39.0(43)	38.8(47)	20.7(2)	0.2(0)	N/A	N/A	N/A	N/A	N/A	N/A	N/A	N/A	1.4(0)
1984	43.0(56)	35.9(37)	7.6(2)	0.2(0)	12.3(0)	N/A	N/A	N/A	N/A	N/A	N/A	N/A	1.0(0)
1987	48.0(57)	44.0(40)	5.7(0)	0.1(0)	0.3(0)	N/A	N/A	N/A	N/A	N/A	N/A	N/A	1.9(0)
1990	35.1(29)	47.8(67)	1.0/1.7 (0/0)	N/A	0.0(0)	5.2(1)	6.8(0)	N/A	N/A	N/A	N/A	N/A	2.4(0)
1993	34.7(45)	35.1(50)	N/A	N/A	N/A	N/A	N/A	18.2(2)	8.4(2)	N/A	N/A	N/A	3.6(0)
1996	28.2(37)	33.8(44)	N/A	N/A	N/A	N/A	N/A	10.1(13)	13.4(17)	6.1(8)	4.3(0)	0.9(1)	3.2(0)
1999	38.7(49)	30.5(39)	N/A	N/A	N/A	N/A	5.2(7)	7.7(10)	4.3(5)	7.0(9)	2.4(0)	0.5(1)	3.9(0)
2002	41.3(52)	21.0(27)	N/A	N/A	N/A	N/A	7.0(9)	1.3(0)	10.4(13)	7.1(9)	1.4(0)	6.7(8)	4.0(1)

TABLE 10.2 *Party voting in Maori electorates, 1960–96*

Election	Labour	National	Soc Cred/ Democrat	Values	Mana Motuhake/ Alliance 1993–2002	NZ Party	NZ First	Mana Maori	ACT	Other
					% valid vote (number of seats)					
1960	62.4(4)	21.1(0)	15.0(0)	N/A	N/A	N/A	N/A	N/A	N/A	1.5(0)
1963	65.1(4)	29.0(0)	2.2(0)	N/A	N/A	N/A	N/A	N/A	N/A	3.7(0)
1966	67.5(4)	22.5(0)	10.0(0)	N/A	N/A	N/A	N/A	N/A	N/A	N/A
1969	73.8(4)	19.3(0)	6.5(0)	N/A	N/A	N/A	N/A	N/A	N/A	1.5(0)
1972	80.4(4)	12.8(0)	5.3(0)	2.0(0)	N/A	N/A	N/A	N/A	N/A	1.5(0)
1975	75.5(4)	15.3(0)	5.8(0)	2.2(0)	N/A	N/A	N/A	N/A	N/A	1.2(0)
1978	77.6(4)	10.3(0)	10.8(0)	1.3(0)	N/A	N/A	N/A	N/A	N/A	N/A
1981	64.8(4)	9.3(0)	10.1(0)	N/A	15.1(0)	N/A	N/A	N/A	N/A	0.7(0)
1984	77.6(4)	7.1(0)	2.4(0)	N/A	9.6(0)	2.7(0)	N/A	N/A	N/A	0.6(0)
1987	70.9(4)	8.2(0)	3.0(0)	N/A	17.2(0)	0.3(0)	N/A	N/A	N/A	0.7(0)
1990	65.4(4)	10.8(0)	N/A	N/A	22.4(0)	N/A	N/A	N/A	N/A	1.4(0)
1993	50.5(3)	3.0(0)	N/A	N/A	18.3(0)	N/A	20.6(1)	5.1(0)	N/A	2.6(0)
1996	31.9(0)	6.1(0)	N/A	N/A	8.5(0)	N/A	42.3(5)	3.3(0)	1.1(0)	6.9(0)
1999	55.0(6)	5.7(0)	N/A	N/A	6.7(0)	N/A	13.2(0)	4.4(0)	0.8(0)	14.2(0)
2002	53.7(7)	4.2(0)	N/A	N/A	2.6(0)	N/A	14.9(0)	4.0(0)	1.0(0)	19.5(0)

Leading 'Other' party: 1996 Aotearoa Legalise Cannabis (3.7); 1999 Greens (4.0); 2002 Greens (10.7)

The Labour party has the longest continuous history in New Zealand, having been formed in 1916. Its origins were in the trade union movement and in growing support for socialist principles which had already led to the election of a number of MPs with labour sympathies. In order to coordinate this parliamentary effort, the Labour Party was officially established as the political wing of the labour movement. The party quickly secured a foothold in Parliament, based on support in the poorer sections of the four main cities and the South Island West Coast, but was unable for many years to win more than a quarter of the seats. By 1935, however, after a lengthy economic depression which the other parties had failed to counteract, together with a steady modification of the more radically socialist elements in its programme, Labour had become sufficiently attractive to the voters to win a clear majority under its leader Michael Joseph Savage. During the following years, Labour introduced a number of reforms in industrial relations, economic management, health, education, housing and social security, which were to become part of the generally agreed basis of government policy for the next half century, until the restructuring of the 1980s.

Labour increased its majority in 1938 and remained in power throughout the Second World War (1939–45) and the immediate post-war period. Savage was succeeded in 1940 by Peter Fraser, who remained prime minister till Labour's defeat by National in 1949. A significant factor in Labour's support was its securing of the support of the (then) four Maori electorates, in part through an agreement with the Maori Ratana church (Sorrenson, 1986). Labour's monopoly of the Maori seats, though not unchallenged (particularly by Mana Motuhake), remained secure until the loss in 1993 of Northern Maori to New Zealand First, which went on to win all Maori electorates in 1996, then lose them to Labour in 1999.

For the next twenty-five years, after being ousted in 1949, Labour was mostly in opposition, winning only two one-term periods in office, under Walter Nash in 1957–60 and Norman Kirk (succeeded by Bill Rowling) in 1972–5. In 1984, however, under the leadership of David Lange, Labour was able not only to defeat National but also to attract sufficient support to win a further term of government in 1987. Once the second election was safely won, however, the strains imposed by the government's espousal of radical market liberal doctrines erupted in sustained political conflict. There was an open feud between Lange and the Finance Minister, Roger Douglas, leading to the resignation first of Douglas and then of Lange (Chapter 4: 89–90). The deputy prime minister, Geoffrey Palmer, took over as prime minister in 1989, only to be himself replaced a year later by Mike Moore less than two months before Labour's devastating defeat in the 1990 election. Within weeks of Labour's further loss in 1993, Moore was replaced as party leader by his former deputy, Helen Clark, who led the party back into government in 1999 in coalition with the Alliance. Despite the electoral collapse of the Alliance in 2002, Labour's continuing status as the predominant party enabled it to continue in office in coalition with the two Progressive MPs and a guarantee of support in confidence and supply votes by United Future.

The National Party was formed in 1936 but its origins lie much further back in the two major parties of the pre-Labour era, the Liberal and Reform Parties. After Labour's success in 1935, the remnants of these two parties, United (as the Liberals had become) and Reform, formed themselves into a new party, the National party. The logic of the electoral system encouraged the unification of the two anti-Labour parties and a reassertion of a two-party Parliament.

During the long period of the Savage/Fraser Labour government, the new National Party gradually consolidated its organisation and support under the leadership of Sidney Holland, who led them to eventual victory in 1949. In 1951, in the aftermath of a long and bitter dispute between waterside workers and their employers, Holland capitalised on Labour's links with an unpopular union movement by calling a snap election and increasing National's majority. National was also to benefit from the long period of post-war prosperity, keeping Labour's protected economy and welfare state essentially intact and delivering a steadily increasing standard of living to all sectors of society.

Holland won again in 1954 but was replaced by his deputy, Keith Holyoake, shortly before the 1957 election, which Labour lost to National. Holyoake went on to lead National to four consecutive victories in 1960, 1963, 1966 and 1969, before eventually retiring in favour of his deputy, John Marshall. Marshall lost the 1972 election to Norman Kirk and Labour and was soon replaced by Robert Muldoon, another powerful and successful leader, who helped National to victory in 1975, 1978 and 1981. By this time, however, New Zealand's international economic position was steadily weakening and so too was National's support in the electorate. Indeed, in the elections of 1978 and 1981, National attracted fewer votes overall than Labour, only managing to win more seats because Labour's votes were more heavily concentrated in safe seats. In keeping with international trends, pressure for financial deregulation and increased exposure of the economy to international market forces was building up within the business community and among the government's economic advisers (Roper, 1992; Chapter 9: 222–3). As both prime minister and finance minister, Muldoon was able to resist this pressure right up until he met defeat in the 'snap' election he called four months early in July 1984. During the next six years in opposition, National had some difficulty adjusting to Labour's radical adoption of its own principles of the free market and private enterprise, switching leaders from Muldoon to Jim McLay in 1984 and then to Jim Bolger in 1986. Ultimately, however, the economic policies of the mid and late 1980s sat more comfortably with National than Labour and National was able to return confidently to power as Labour was routed in 1990.The Bolger National government continued the process of state restructuring, by introducing increased targeting and means-testing of welfare spending, ending centralised wage bargaining and re-organising health administration. In the 1993 election, however, National won the barest of majorities, 50 out of 99 seats, and subsequently, as a result of defections by National MPs, was forced to govern in coalition and, for a time, in a minority coalition government, moderating its reforming drive (Boston *et al.*, 1996a: 94–5). After the 1996 election, it remained the largest single party in Parliament and formed a coalition with New Zealand First.

The coalition was an unexpected and unpopular combination, which soon saw Labour surpass National in opinion polls. Concern with the trend and with the growing popularity of Labour's leader, Helen Clark, provoked a leadership coup in National. In November 1997, Jenny Shipley replaced Bolger to become New Zealand's first woman prime minister. Ousted from government by the Labour-Alliance coalition in the 1999 election, National experienced a period of instability. In October 2001, Shipley's deputy, Bill English, toppled her as leader. The party's electoral support remained low, however, and in the 2002 election, it sank to only 21 per cent of the party vote, the lowest in its history. Continued low ratings in the opinion polls fuelled dissatisfaction with English's leadership and in October 2003 the National caucus elected Dr Don Brash, the former governor of the Reserve Bank, and a first-time MP to lead the party.

Though the first-past-the-post electoral system favoured the two major parties, other, 'minor' parties were an important and continuing feature of New Zealand elections. The most significant minor party in the postwar period was the Social Credit Political League (renamed the

Democratic Party in 1985). Formed in 1953, it immediately attracted 11 per cent of the nationwide valid vote in the 1954 election. Over the next three and a half decades, until its eclipse to less than 2 per cent at the 1990 election, it averaged 11.1 per cent. It reached its highest points in the elections of 1978 (16.1 per cent) and 1981 (20.7 per cent), when its leader, Bruce Beetham, held a seat in Parliament (Rangitikei, 1978–84). As a party within the Alliance from 1992, the Democrats retained a parliamentary presence of two list MPs after 1996, though their party background would have been invisible to most electors. With the collapse of the Alliance in 2002, the Democratic Party again lost representation. A persistent advocate of proportional representation for many years, it is ironic that the party's apparent demise should occur under MMP.

During the 1970s, the Values Party, sometimes claimed as the world's first environmentalist party, attracted a significant share of the vote, peaking at 5.2 per cent in 1975. Mana Motuhake, founded in 1980 by a Labour Party MP and former Minister of Maori Affairs, Matiu Rata, attracted a relatively small percentage of the total vote nationwide but became a significant force in the Maori seats. In 1983, during the last term of the Muldoon National government, a former National party member and wealthy property developer, Robert Jones, formed the New Zealand Party in opposition to Muldoon's increasingly interventionist approach to economic management. The party won 12.3 per cent of the vote at the 1984 election, drawing votes from National and helping Labour to power, though winning no seats. It quickly faded, however, once both major parties became committed to economic deregulation. In 1989, the Lange Labour government's willingness to privatise state assets, including the Bank of New Zealand, led Jim Anderton, a Labour MP and former party president to form the breakaway NewLabour party. The party won 5.2 per cent of the vote at the 1990 election, while a resurgent environmentalist party, the Green party, won 6.8 per cent.

After the initial referendum on electoral reform in 1992 had indicated a strong likelihood of a change to MMP, minor party activity increased significantly. The 'Alliance' was formed under the leadership of NewLabour's Jim Anderton, a coalition of Green, NewLabour, Democratic, Mana Motuhake and Liberal (a party formed in 1991 by two dissident National MPs). It secured 18.2 per cent of the vote and two seats, making itself a contender for substantial representation in a MMP-elected Parliament. The other important new party was New Zealand First, which was founded in 1993 by dissident National MP,

Winston Peters, and won 8.4 per cent of the votes and two seats in the election of that year. The transitional period between the 1993 decision in favour of MMP and the first MMP election in 1996 saw a further proliferation of small parties hoping to achieve parliamentary representation under the new system (Boston *et al.*, 1996a : Chapter 4). Some were founded by MPs belonging to existing parties, such as the Right of Centre (subsequently Conservative) and Christian Democrats, both formed by ex-National MPs, and the United party formed by a group of ex-National and ex-Labour MPs. Labour's former Minister of Finance, Sir Roger Douglas, with financial support from leading business people, established the Association of Taxpayers and Consumers (ACT), later passing on the political leadership to another former Labour minister, Richard Prebble. The new Christian Democrats joined with the older Christian Heritage party in a Christian Coalition. The Progressive Greens were formed to represent the more economically conservative wing of the environmentalist movement. Many of the new parties were not represented in Parliament after the 1996 election. The requirement, under MMP, that a party must secure over 5 per cent of the total vote or at least one electorate in order to win any seats in Parliament restricted representation to four parties besides National and Labour – New Zealand First, the Alliance, ACT and United.

After 1996, the form of the post-MMP multi-party system began to emerge more clearly. The Greens withdrew from the Alliance to contest the 1999 election in their own right. Winning seven seats in 1999 and nine in 2002, and consistently rating above the 5 per cent threshold in opinion polls, the Greens appear to have established themselves as a significant party on the left of the political spectrum. After the parliamentary demise of the Alliance following its rancorous split in 2002, and pending their electoral recovery, the Greens are a potential coalition partner for Labour. In 2002, however, bitter disagreement between Labour and the Greens over the issue of the release of genetically modified material into the environment extinguished any likelihood of an agreement. Instead, a splinter of the Alliance, the Progressive Coalition, led by the founder and former leader of the Alliance, Jim Anderton, took the Alliance's place as Labour's coalition partner.

New Zealand First and ACT, representing respectively the populist centre and the neo-liberal right of the party spectrum, retained their representation in Parliament after the 2002 election. The Christian Coalition, however, which had only narrowly missed crossing the 5 per cent threshold in 1996, collapsed and the two parties followed separate unsuccessful paths in 1999. In 2000, the descendants of the Christian Democrats, Future New Zealand, merged with the United party to create the United Future New Zealand party, led by United MP, Peter Dunne. The fledgling party surprised both itself and the country by winning eight seats in 2002. Positioning itself firmly in the centre of the party system, United Future promised to support the Labour-led minority government in order to maintain stability, while making it clear that the party was equally prepared to be a true pivotal party and support an alternative government of the right.

Principles and supporters

To attract voters and maintain their support, parties need to establish a recognised identity. They must be seen to support certain political interests and to stand for certain political values. At the same time, a party cannot afford to be too inflexible in its ideology and must be able to adapt to changing circumstances and the changing concerns of the electorate. A democratic system in which political parties compete for the highest segment of the vote may be compared to an economic market where rival firms compete with each other for market share. Indeed, this comparison is the basis of a highly influential academic analysis of modern democracy, the 'economic theory of democracy' of Anthony Downs (1957), in which economic assumptions of public choice are applied to the behaviour of both voters and parties. Voters are likened to consumers wishing to spend their vote on purchasing a product, in their case a party government. Parties are seen as entrepreneurs seeking to attract the custom of voters and so maximise their profit, in their case tenure of political power, by appealing to as large a segment of the voting public as possible.

How far this model applies to the behaviour of New Zealand voters will be discussed in the following chapter. As far as the political parties are concerned, the model does provide a generally accurate account of their aims and actions. Their major aim is to attract votes and win seats in Parliament. The principles and values they espouse are intended to strike a chord with like-minded members of the public. Much of what the party organisations do, for instance election advertising and door-to-door canvassing for votes, is exactly parallel to the activities of a commercial sales campaign. The better resourced parties even follow commercial companies in engaging commercial market consultants to poll the electorate on what the voters think about various political issues, on the image they have of their parties, and so on.

Tensions may exist within a party about how best to appeal to the electorate and, indeed, about how far party principle should be compromised for the sake of immediate electoral advantage. Some party members, particularly the more doctrinaire party activists, will not necessarily agree with the need to trim the party's sails to match shifts in the electorate. This may be particularly the case with strongly 'programmatic' parties, parties formed to promote a particular political programme or cause, where loyalty to the cause may, for some members, take priority over short-term electoral success. In general, however, the need to attract support of voters is the dominant motive of most individual party members and of the party organisations as a whole.

Parties can be categorised according to their different approaches to the role of government. The most common classification is in terms of the contrast between 'left-wing' and 'right-wing' (terms which are derived historically from the seating arrangements in the French revolutionary assembly of 1789). Being on the left has usually been taken to imply support for greater equalisation of wealth and power and an active role for the state in economic management, while being on the right implies greater reliance on the private sector of the economy and a more limited role for the state. In the economic voting theory of Anthony Downs, for instance, individual voters are located on a single left/right continuum or spectrum from extreme left to extreme right and parties are seen as competing for as large as possible a slice of this continuum. More generally, political analysts and commentators often describe parties or individual politicians as being on the 'extreme' or 'moderate' 'left' or 'right' or, indeed, 'centre'.

For most of New Zealand's history, as for most other western countries, the dominant set of political ideas were those associated with the political 'left', the ideas linked to the socialist tradition of radical reform. The Labour party began as a programmatic radical party seeking to serve the interests of workers through 'socialist' reform. Socialism is a political tradition with many varieties and the Labour Party itself always contained a wide spectrum of views. All forms of socialism share a hostility to unbridled capitalism and a willingness to use the state to help build a fairer and more cooperative society. But they differ about the extent of change necessary and the political means justified in making changes. On the whole, the Labour Party positioned itself toward the more moderate end of the socialist spectrum, for instance banning members of the Communist Party from Labour Party membership as early as 1926. Its roots were in Christian and liberal humanitarianism more than in doctrinaire marxism. It stood for the 'social democratic' strand in New Zealand political values, the readiness to use the collective mechanisms of the state for the pursuit of prosperity for individual citizens and their families (Chapter 2: 48). Labour's political aims were more to modify capitalism than abolish it altogether and the party remained committed to the use of democratic rather than revolutionary means.

In this moderating tendency Labour reflected the immediate concerns of most of its core supporters in the trade union movement and among the poorer sections of society. It was also responding to the imperatives of electoral competition. Labour could not expect to win office unless it broadened the basis of its support to include middle income and rural voters. Residual commitments to 'socialism' remained but were gradually diluted (Gustafson, 1992: 268–73). The commitment to 'socialise the means of production, distribution and exchange' was removed in 1951 and by the 1980s the party's socialist objective had been transformed into a vaguely defined concept of 'democratic socialism'. Its leaders were more at ease with concepts such as 'social justice' and 'equity' which carried no necessary connotations of state economic intervention.

In contrast to Labour, National for most of its history was much less concerned with doctrine and principle. Its major reason for existence was opposition to Labour and the supposed need to keep the country free from socialism. A number of positive principles and values were regularly appealed to, for instance conservative values of support for the Crown and the maintenance of close ties with traditional allies, Britain and the US. The party also frequently endorsed general principles supporting the interests of private property, such as freedom and free enterprise. These could be counted on to appeal to National's core basis of support among farmers and business people.

In practice, however, National was extremely flexible and pragmatic in how it applied such principles, presiding over a managed and regulated economy and largely consolidating and indeed expanding the welfare provisions introduced by the Savage/Fraser Labour government. In this, too, it reflected the interests of its supporters in the rural and business sectors. Farmers were generally content with the corporatist structures which regulated much of the marketing and sale of farm products (Chapter 9: 224–5). Many business people depended on key elements of the regulated economy, such as import controls and tariffs. National, on the whole, was willing to see itself in contrast to Labour as a broadly based and non-doctrinaire party of competent managers, content to govern pragmatically without bitter ideological debate. If the main purpose of the party was to keep Labour out, there was less room for conflict between the demands of principle and electoral success (Wood, 1992; Mulgan, 1989: 61).

The previously familiar contrast between Labour as the more ideological party of the centre-left and National as the more pragmatic party of the centre-right was severely shaken by the actions of the Lange Labour government after its election in 1984. Labour set about restructuring the economy and the public sector within a well-developed theoretical perspective, that of market liberalism, dubbed 'Rogernomics' after Labour's Minister of Finance, Roger Douglas. However, these economic theories did not derive from within Labour's democratic socialist tradition of thought. Indeed, they were diametrically opposed to the socialist preference for collective action and state management of the economy. The guiding principles of the reformers, such as the value of individual choice and the superiority of the private over the public sector were, in fact, principles much more likely to appeal to Labour's traditional opponents than its supporters. The contradictions implicit in the Labour government's conversion to an alien ideology eventually erupted in open conflicts within the party after the 1987 election, leading to the Lange/Douglas clash and the formation of the splinter NewLabour party (Chapter 4: 89–90; Chapter 5: 113–4).

National's position as the party of conservative anti-socialist pragmatism was also undermined by the upheavals of the 1980s. The Lange Labour Government was certainly not a socialist government. Indeed, in some respects, it was clearly less socialist than previous National governments, particularly those led by Robert Muldoon who exercised extensive government intervention in the economy. Therefore, the mission of keeping the country safe from socialism no longer had any plausibility as a unifying force. Some sections of the party responded by following the party's normal instinct to behave as a middle-of-the-road party of pragmatism and cautious conservatism. Others, however, were sympathetic to the ideas of market liberalism and wanted the party to press ahead with even more doctrinal purity and enthusiasm than Labour. They sought to 'finish the job' which Labour had left uncompleted in the areas of industrial relations and social welfare. The market liberals largely set the agenda for the Bolger National government, especially in its first term, thus confirming the traditional position of the National party on the right of Labour.

However, because the dominant ideology about the role of the state in the economy is now right-wing market liberalism rather than left-wing socialism, National has become the more doctrinaire and ideological of the two parties. While Labour's market liberals, under Sir Roger Douglas's leadership, joined the extreme right-wing Association for Taxpayers and Consumers (ACT), Labour itself gradually repudiated the extremism of Rogernomics and sought a more pragmatic, less ideological approach to economic management. Labour now occupies a central position, to the left of National and ACT but outflanked on the left by the Alliance and the Progressive Coalition which have reasserted a more traditional interventionist role for the state in the economy. Survey research also locates the Greens clearly to the left of Labour (Vowles *et al.*, 2002: 86; 2004: Figure 2.1). Like the Alliance, New Zealand First has also concentrated on the negative effects of the economic restructuring pursued by both Labour and National governments, opposing overseas ownership of New Zealand assets and attacking individual business leaders who have benefited from the changes. At the same time, New Zealand First is hostile to trade unions and supports further tax cuts, positions which align it more with parties on the right. Its signature themes since 1999, however, have become the more populist issues of immigration, law and order and race relations.

While the general approach to state intervention in the economy, encapsulated in the left/right spectrum, remains the main basis on which parties differentiate themselves (Boston *et al.*, 1996a: 9; Vowles *et al*, 2002: 84-6), it is not the only ground of difference. Parties also respond to public concerns about non-economic areas of government policy. Of particular importance in the last two decades has been a range of issues associated with a number of new social movements representing the 'new politics', such as environmentalism, feminism, anti-racism, the peace movement and the movement for gay and lesbian rights (Vowles *et al.*, 1995: Chapter 6). These movements, common throughout the economically developed world, are sometimes described as 'post-materialist' (Vowles *et al.*, 1995: 71–8) in the sense that most of their supporters have taken material prosperity for granted and have had little interest in economics or economic policy. A new political divide has arisen between 'social liberals' who favour greater personal freedom along with greater social diversity and social conservatives who emphasise more traditional conformist values. In New Zealand, the first political effect of the new politics was the founding of the Values party, a precursor of the Green party, in the early 1970s (Miller, 1992: 315–9).

The Labour party also adopted a number of social liberal causes, including opposition to nuclear weapons and nuclear power, opposition to sporting contacts with apartheid South Africa, support for women's rights and for honouring the Treaty of Waitangi. The National party, meanwhile, generally maintained a conservative approach on social issues, though some of its younger and more urban members were more liberal in their attitudes.

Attitudes on social issues cut across attitudes on economic issues. Thus, some groups who are right-wing economically combine their market liberalism with social liberalism. This 'neo-liberal' standpoint was adopted by many of those who led the 'Rogernomics' revolution in the 1980s, including members of Robert Jones's New Zealand party. It has support both on the right of the Labour party and in National's liberal wing and has been reasserted in extreme form by ACT. Other market liberals, however, are social conservatives, joining hostility to state intervention in the economy with strong support for traditional patriotic and 'family' values. This combination is commonly identified as the 'new right' and is found, perhaps most clearly, in the United Future party as well as in National's conservative wing. Conversely, some on the economic left are social liberals, such as the Alliance, Greens, Labour's left wing and perhaps the Progressives. Others on the economic left are social conservatives, for instance the left-leaning members of New Zealand First, which has opposed Asian immigration and appealed particularly to superannuitants. This is the combination of values represented by National's former leader, Robert Muldoon, who was the mentor of Winston Peters and the idol of many of his elderly supporters in the 1990s. New Zealand First, however, has also attracted a strong following among Maori voters who generally favour generous settlements under the Treaty of Waitangi, a social liberal stance.

A fourfold classification can therefore be constructed along two axes, economic (left/conservative–right/liberal) and social (conservative–liberal) (see box, p. 249). Such a classification inevitably involves a degree of over-simplification and overlooks important variations both between and within individual parties. But it does indicate the range of significant political interests in New Zealand's pluralist society and the need for a multi-party system to represent them adequately. Labour and National, it may be noted, appear in more than one category, reflecting their history as more broadly based parties buttressed by the previous electoral system. However, under the new system which is less discouraging to smaller parties, Labour and National will find it harder to maintain party unity over a wide range of interests and policies. They may well continue to lose supporters to more focused alternatives, such as ACT and the Alliance. New Zealand First is not easily categorised in any one category, as it has supported policies associated with all four. This reveals the tensions within the party which contributed to the split in 1998 when faced with the reality of government instead of the less demanding role of negative protest. The fact that New Zealand First appealed particularly to Maori voters, winning all five Maori electorate seats in 1996, suggested that it could become a predominantly Maori party. However, this now seems an unlikely role. In 1999, all the Maori seats returned to Labour, and in 2002 New Zealand First with an average of 15 per cent of the party vote in Maori electorates was again a distant second to Labour. Moreover, in that election New Zealand First did not stand candidates in the Maori electorates to back up its advocacy of abolishing the separate Maori seats, a policy that coupled with the party's intolerance of Treaty of Waitangi issues is likely to limit its appeal to Maori voters. There is therefore continuing potential for an independent Maori party. In this case, ethnicity would become another dimension in New Zealand's party system, in addition to distinctions based on economic and social values.

Political Parties and Political Attitudes

Social liberal

Social Democrats	Neo-liberals
(Labour left; Alliance;	(Labour right;
Greens?, Progressive)	National liberals; ACT)

Economic conservative ———————— **Economic liberal**

Interventionist conservatives	New right
(Muldoon National; NZ First?)	(National conservatives;
	United Future)

Social conservative

Organisational structure

Membership of a political party provides citizens with an opportunity to participate actively in the political process. Each party needs rank-and-file members who will endorse the party's principles and support its electoral campaign. Members pay subscriptions and contribute to party funds and can play a part in the party's organisation. In order to be registered as a political party under the Electoral Act, and thus qualify for nominating candidates for party lists, a party must have at least 500 financial members who are eligible to vote as electors (Electoral Commission, 2002: 29). However, the actual number of party members is not generally known because many parties tend to keep their memberships and finances confidential. Research conducted for the Electoral Commission in 1994 indicated that 6 per cent of adult New Zealanders were at that time members of a political party whereas three times as many (19.2 per cent) claimed to have previously belonged to a political party. This decline in membership has continued. By 2002, estimated total party members had fallen to about 105,000 or approximately 3.8 per cent of the adult population (Vowles *et al.*, 2004: Table 2.5). Although conforming to trends in a number of other developed democracies, falling party membership in New Zealand is also explained by local factors. Both National and Labour suffered a very severe decline in membership as a result of rank-and-file disillusion with their performance in government. National is estimated to have gone from a peak of over 200,000 to less than 40,000 members (Wood, 2003:255). In early 1993, Labour was reported as having less than 10,000 individual members, down from a high of around 80,000 in the early 1980s. At the same time, the number of unions and union members affiliated to the Labour party dropped sharply with the decline in trade union activity resulting from the Employment Contracts Act 1991 (Kelsey, 1995: 187). No reliable estimates can be made of the membership of the smaller less established parties, whose numbers fluctuate along with their electoral fortunes.

The organisational structure of parties varies according to their size and history. National and Labour, as the two longstanding major parties with mass memberships, developed elaborate structures to handle large numbers of members. On the other hand, the smaller recently formed parties have had much less time to organise and the role of their rank and file is less well-established. None the less, to be politically credible and electorally effective, all parties aim to achieve as substantial an organisation as possible. The structures created by Labour and National remain the models which others generally follow, if only because Labour and National are the parties in which many current New Zealand politicians and party activists gained their first political experience.

Both Labour and National parties have four levels of organisation – local branch, electorate, regional and national. Rank-and-file members normally join an individual branch based on a particular locality. The branches collect subscriptions, organise meetings and social occasions, elect a committee and appoint delegates to other parts of the party structure. As electorate boundaries are redrawn every five years, a branch may find itself moved from one electorate to another. Thus the branch tends to be the local fixed point and the electorate organisation, though crucial at election times, is less permanent. The number of branches and their size varies with the level of support for the party. In places where the party has been strong there will usually be several highly active branches in each electorate but elsewhere, where party support is weak, the local organisation will often be very thin and some branches may be virtually defunct.

Besides the normal type of branch which is open to anyone, both parties have branches for specified categories of member. In the areas where Labour is strong, particularly the large cities, the party has separate branches for women, Maori, Pacific Islanders, and youth members. National, too, has a well developed Young Nationals organisation. In addition to individual branch members, Labour has members who belong through membership of a trade union affiliated to the party. This arrangement stems from the party's origin as the political wing of the trade union movement. Affiliated trade unions pay a levy to the party for each of their members and have their own designated representatives at various levels of the party organisation.

The political activity of local branches and their members is focused particularly on the local electorate. Each party has a structure of electorate committees to assist in the selection of electoral candidates and the running of election campaigns. Beyond the electorate level are the regional organisations, with Regional Councils in both parties comprising delegates from local branches (and affiliated unions in the case of Labour). These have regular meetings, including an annual regional conference, and generally provide a useful point of liaison and consultation between the local and national organisations.

At the national level, final authority rests with the parties' annual conferences. The right to attend and vote at conferences is carefully regulated in order to ensure reasonable representation of the various sections of the parties. The Labour conference, for instance, includes specified numbers of delegates from each of the Labour Regional Councils, the Labour Electorate Committees, the branches and the affiliated unions. The number of delegates for each branch is determined by the number of subscribing members in that branch. Similarly, the affiliated unions may send delegates and cast votes in proportion to their members. Though each individual union member is weighted at less than half of the weight given to individual branch members, the large numbers of union members involved means that the union delegates wield considerable influence within the party. From 1993, Labour replaced its annual conference (and regional conferences) in election years with party 'congresses', aimed solely at coordinating election strategies and tactics.

While the leader and deputy leader of each party are elected by the parliamentary parties (in National the caucus choice of leader also requires ratification by the Board of Directors), it is the conferences which elect the party's leading officers. In the case of Labour, these include a president, two vice-presidents and an executive, as well as members of a larger Council which has representation from each region as well as of the various sections, such as youth, women, Maori and Pacific Islanders, and the affiliated unions. The Labour Party also has a full-time permanent General Secretary, who is a member of the executive and responsible for running the party's head office.

National elects a party president and has a General Manager as chief administrative officer. Between conferences, authority is in the hands of a nine-person Board of Directors which includes the leader and one other member of the party's parliamentary team, the party president and another six members elected by conference.

The organisations of the smaller parties follow essentially similar lines, combining national office-holders and executives with more local groups within the electorates. Local branches ('groups' in the case of the Greens) may also be combined into a regional level of organisation between the local units and the central bodies. However flimsy the parties' local structures, they will hold an annual conference as a bonding and morale-boosting occasion for their members, and to generate publicity and provide a platform for the leaders. Party conferences also elect the organisational office holders, and to varying degrees steer the direction of party policies. However, more definitive policy is likely to have its source in the party leadership or a designated policy committee on which the different organisational elements of a party are represented.

More than any other party's, the Alliance's organisation has had to adapt to changing political circumstances. Its original federal structure crumbled as constituent parties withdrew, beginning with the Greens in 1997 and ending when the last significant party, the Democrats, left in 2002. For a time the Alliance boasted a significant rank and file mem-

bership, reporting 25,000 members in 1996, significantly more than Labour at that time. In that year, the party won 10 per cent of the party vote
and thirteen seats. In 1999 it entered government as Labour's junior
coalition partner. But by 2002 it had split, lost its founding leader (and
the electorate seat he held), and was eliminated from parliament in the
general election that year, winning less than 2 per cent of the party vote.
The Alliance's revised constitution of December 2002 reconstitutes the
party as a unitary organisation, in some respects reflecting its original
Labour heritage and commitment to democratic procedures. As well as
local branches, there is provision for sector representation among
women, youth and industrial groups. Branches are organised into nine
regions. The ruling body is the annual conference on which branches
and sector groups are represented according to their numbers of members. Between conferences, a council representing all sections of the organisation is the party's governing body. The conference votes on
policy proposals, approves election policies, elects officers and also the
party leader and deputy leaders (a function usually delegated to party
caucuses). In a further gesture to traditional labour doctrines of checking the oligarchic tendencies of party caucuses, the Alliance council is
to confirm Cabinet minister appointments nominated by the leader.

The development of New Zealand First's organisation has been more
closely identified with its leader, Winston Peters, than with its members
or their values. Control of the party has largely remained with Peters
himself and his close advisers. In this case, the main function of the
party organisation has been to rally supporters and provide assistance
with campaigning. With a small active membership, the party's electorate branch structure is thin. The country is divided into twelve regions,
each of which holds an annual convention of delegates from constituent
electorates. The main organisational showpiece, however, is the annual
convention of the party as a whole, which elects the office-holders and
seven of the members of the managing body, the board. Typically the
board brings together the party's parliamentary leadership, party officers, and representatives of the organisation. Unlike the Alliance, however, New Zealand First does not forbid the election of MPs to
organisational roles, such as the party presidency.

ACT was founded by Sir Roger Douglas with the backing of wealthy
business people and has had little need for grass-roots support, except at
election time. Organisation at electorate level is minimal. Like other
parties, however, ACT holds a series of regional conferences in addition
to its annual general conference. The main decision-making body is a

board of trustees, which brings together the parliamentary leadership, party officers, a caucus representative and seven regionally elected members. The board is a powerful body with a final say in policy matters, election strategy and candidate selection.

The Greens, like the Alliance, attempt to combine organisational effectiveness with grass roots democracy. Members are organised into groups (vaguely defined as 'a collection of persons which has sufficient sense of identity and community to be able to work together to achieve the aims of the Charter' (Constitution and Rules, clause 6.1). The groups are collected into nine provinces (regions), similarly broadly defined, which elect representatives to the party's executive. The annual conference is the 'supreme body', which functions as a policy forum and elects party officers. Gender equality is written into the constitution, which requires that the key officers of two convenors, two policy convenors and the party co-leaders, all elected by conference, are to be one male and one female. These and other elected and appointed members comprise the executive responsible for the running of the party between conferences. The Greens' executive, therefore, is the equivalent of the Alliance's and Labour's councils, New Zealand First's board, ACT's board of trustees and National's board of directors. Perhaps more than the party's organisational structure, it is the Greens' culture of internal democracy that most distinguishes it from other parties. In addition to its prescribed gender equality, it requires decisions at all levels of the party to by consensus, meaning 'by the agreement of most participants' (clause 14.1), and where a vote is necessary, it must be carried by a 75 per cent majority. The Greens' participatory style extends also to candidate selection (see below).

Parties need considerable resources to pay for their normal administrative costs and to mount election campaigns. Parties which are represented in Parliament have valuable access to MPs' allowances for such items as air travel, postage and telephones. They can also use the assistance of publicly funded party research officers (Chapter 5: 112). Parties with no MPs thus face considerable handicap unless they have substantial independent resources. At election time, parties receive an allocation of public funds, based on their levels of popular support as assessed by the Electoral Commission, to cover television and radio advertising. Though parties are prohibited from purchasing additional broadcasting time out of their own funds, they may contribute towards the production of television and radio advertisements which can be very expensive. They must also raise money to cover the cost of campaign posters and other printed material and postage, as well as other transport and administrative costs associated with conducting a nationwide electoral campaign. Statutory limits are set on how much parties and individual candidates may spend on advertising in the three months leading up to an election (Electoral Commission, 2002: 31–36) but these are set at relatively high levels which allow considerable variation in the amounts actually spent by different parties.

Parties raise their funds from a variety of sources. Individual party members contribute through paying an annual subscription, often set at a modest level in order to encourage as many people as possible to join the party. Party members may also be called on for additional contributions to assist with particular election campaigns. With declining membership numbers, however, most parties have come increasingly to rely on substantial contributions from organised interests groups or wealthy individuals.

Both National and Labour, when in office, have encouraged business leaders to pay substantial donations to their party funds in exchange for invitations to be briefed by senior ministers (Gustafson, 1993: 79). Many businesses make a practice of giving donations to several parties, partly as a public service but more importantly in order to purchase general good-will and access to ministers. For instance, Fletcher Challenge donated $50,000 to both National and Labour in 1990. Organisations whose interests are more closely aligned with one party are less likely to be even-handed, though, with the conspicuous exception of trade unions affiliated to Labour, interest groups are usually careful to avoid open identification with one party. Links between parties and sympathetic interests tend to be informal and personal, but no less influential for that reason. Thus individual members of Federated Farmers will also support the National Party in the expectation that National will favour the interests of farmers. In recent elections there has been a tendency for individual business people to give very large donations not just to the party but in support of particular policies. In 1987, wealthy individuals who supported the policies of Roger Douglas gave large sums to a party fund controlled by Douglas himself, on the clear understanding that they hoped his policies would be followed after the election (Gustafson, 1992: 281). The most notable donation was $250,000 by Equiticorp's Allan Hawkins. Similarly large and less than unconditional donations were reported to have been made to National before the 1990 election. The backing of wealthy individuals can be particularly important when new parties are founded. Thus, the New Zealand party,

which had a significant impact on the defeat of the Muldoon government in the 1984 election, relied extensively on the financial support of
its millionaire founder, Robert Jones. Similarly, the fact that ACT was
generously supported by certain members of the Business Roundtable
and other business leaders must account, in part, for its being the only
party formed after the 1993 referendum to win more than 5 per cent of
the vote in 1996.

Candidate selection

The main function of political parties is to secure the election of party
candidates to Parliament. Candidate selection is therefore a vital aspect
of party activity. Under MMP, parties must select two classes of candidate, electorate candidates and list candidates. Parties are required by
the Electoral Act (Section 71) to follow democratic procedures in candidate selection, involving all financial members in the process, either directly or indirectly through selected representatives. Methods for
selecting electorate candidates follow those used under the former first-
past-the post electoral system in which all candidates stood for individual territorial electorates. In such selections, local party members
can expect to play a key role in choosing the candidate for whom they
will campaign and whom they hope to see as their local member. At the
same time, the party leadership has a legitimate interest in the election
of capable candidates who can contribute to an effective and well-
balanced parliamentary team. The two former major parties, Labour
and National, developed their own procedures for selecting electorate
candidates, with Labour giving more weight than National to the central
party interests.

In the Labour party, selection takes place after a meeting attended by
local party members at which the various candidates for selection address the meeting and answer questions. The final decision is made by a
committee consisting of three members appointed by the New Zealand
Council, representing the interests of the central party, one or two members elected by the local Electorate Committee (depending on the
number of local party members), and one elected by the local party
members present at the meeting. Members present at the meeting also
vote directly on whom they think should be selected and their collective
opinion is conveyed to the selection committee where it is formally
given the weight of one additional vote. The balance of votes is usually
slightly in favour of the local members as against the national office and
representatives from the centre are usually anxious not to appear to be

overriding clear local sentiment, though their influence can be decisive if the local electorate is divided.

In the National party, the local party members have a larger say in candidate selection, the role of the central party organisation being restricted to an initial vetting process. All nominees for selection must first be approved by the Board of Directors. In the case of Winston Peters in 1993, the then National Executive ruled that he was ineligible for renomination as National MP for Tauranga because of his inability to work with his caucus colleagues, a decision which precipitated Peters's resignation, his re-election as an independent at a by-election and his subsequent founding of the New Zealand First party. However, the use of central vetting to exclude an unpopular candidate was quite exceptional. A final short-list of three to five possible candidates is chosen by a pre-selection committee consisting of five local members elected by the electorate and four people appointed by the regional chair and party president (two each). The final selection is made at a meeting of branch representatives chosen by the branches, and numbering at least 60 people. Normally, the local electorates jealously protect their right to have the final say and heavy-handed pressure from the centre may backfire, as it did at the Tamaki by-election in 1992, caused by the retirement of Sir Robert Muldoon. The leadership clearly wanted the presentable former All Black, David Kirk, as candidate but he was passed over in favour of a local party stalwart, Clem Simich.

The balance between local and central choice in other parties depends mainly on the capacity of their local organisations, regardless of what their constitutions might say. Newly formed parties may have difficulty in establishing effective local organisations recruiting prospective candidates in all the electorates in which they want to field candidates. Regional or national officers must therefore make the selection if there are insufficient numbers of local party members. This may mean nothing more than vetting and accepting willing volunteers to stand in electorates which they have no chance of winning. ACT combines both central control and grass roots democracy. The management Board vets applicants and decides which electorates will be contested. The final selection is by secret ballot of party members in the electorate, provided that there are sufficient numbers of members in the electorate and sufficient numbers attend the selection meeting. Prospective candidates for the Alliance and Greens enter a candidate pool, specifying the electorate they wish to contest. This choice and the candidates' credentials are vetted by a selection committee appointed by the executive, in the case of the Greens, and in the Alliance by the party's Council. Final selection of Green electorate candidates is made by party members in the electorate. The Alliance follows the Labour model, in which selection is by a panel representing central and local interests and comprising a Council-appointed chair, two regional representatives, and a maximum of five local representatives, depending on membership numbers. As with Labour, the opinion of those present at the selection meeting is given the weight of one additional vote.

Parties must now also select and rank candidates for their national list. Indeed, for the smaller parties, the rank ordering of party lists is the crucial element of candidate selection, since with few exceptions their candidates are unlikely to win the first-past-the-post electorate contests against National or Labour candidates. Party lists are an innovation in New Zealand elections and have been the subject of adverse criticism on the ground that they allow parties rather than voters to determine who becomes an MP (an objection which overlooks the fact that, under first-past-the-post, parties also had the major role in deciding who became MPs for local electorates).

In making up their lists, party office holders have been anxious to avoid the charge that selection is in the hands of a central party elite and so have sought to involve the party rank and file in the process. However, it is also important to ensure that the finished list is balanced and representative in terms of characteristics such as region, gender and ethnicity. Parties therefore have an interest in maintaining central oversight over the final composition of the list. Labour, National and the Alliance, have all adopted a roughly similar approach to list selection. Initial nominations are called for from individual branches and party members. Candidates in each region are then ranked by especially established regional meetings. The final list is then drawn up by a central Moderating Committee (Labour), or List Committee (National and Alliance). The rank ordering of the Greens' list is done by preferential ballot of all party members, after a preliminary ranking by the candidates and the executive. This is circulated to all members along with biographical details of the candidates. The candidate selection committee appointed to oversee the process is also authorised to make minor adjustments if necessary to achieve a balance of gender, ethnicity, age, region and skills. Other parties have followed more centralised procedures. ACT's Board has the final say in ranking the candidates after sending the list to members and inviting them to indicate their twenty preferred candidates. The ranking of New Zealand First's candidates has been strongly influenced by the leader and his close advisers, as was the construction of United Future's first list in 2002.

Individual candidates may stand for an electorate as well as on the list. (If they win their electorate, their list seat is allocated to the next person on their party's list.) Parties must therefore decide, when drawing up their lists, how many electorate candidates to include. All parties have adopted the practice of placing the party leaders and deputy leaders at the top of their party list, even when they are also standing for electorates, which, in most cases, they could expect to win. Because parties are so closely identified with their leaders, it makes sense for the party leader to be seen as leading the party team. Indeed, the leader's name may be the only name on the list which voters can recognise. In addition to the leaders, a large proportion of other electorate candidates are also included on lists. Indeed, of the 69 electorate MPs elected in 2002, only thirteen (ten Labour and three National) were not also on their party's list. Smaller parties, which can expect to win list seats rather than electorate seats, none the less aim to field candidates in as many electorates as possible as part of their overall election strategy. Willingness to stand in an electorate is therefore likely to be a condition of securing a winnable place on the party list. Indeed, New Zealand First has restricted its party list to those who were also standing in electorates. In 2002, when the party was still rebuilding after its electoral slump in 1999, it nominated a list of only 23 candidates, compared to lists of 60 – 80 for other significant parties.

Parties and policy-making

When party leaders and other candidates campaign in elections, they not only proclaim the general values and principles associated with the party but also propose specific policies which they promise to support if elected. When a single party formed a majority government, as was normal under the first-past-the-post electoral system, it could be expected to use its parliamentary majority to enact its preferred policies. The parties' election policies thus became seen as a form of electoral commitment between voters and government, a binding 'mandate' which party governments were obliged to follow (Mulgan, 1990). The major parties developed the practice of putting forward comprehensive policies for all areas of government activity combined into a single election 'platform' or 'manifesto'. In the 1970s, Labour's prime minister Norman Kirk and National's Robert Muldoon gave particular emphasis to their parties' manifestos, in part as means of keeping their Cabinet and caucus colleagues united under their leadership but also to reinforce their governments' popularity with party supporters and voters.

Since the 1980s, however, party manifestos have been less significant as predictors of how parties will act in government. The restructuring agenda of the Lange Labour government was not foreshadowed in it election policies and, indeed, involved the breaking of a number of election promises, a pattern followed by the Bolger National government after 1990. The change to MMP, which was precipitated by the failure of governments to keep their election promises (Chapter 3: 64), has removed a precondition for the straightforward enactment of election mandates by discouraging the election of single-party majority governments. Governing parties must now negotiate over which of their policies will be accepted and which will be rejected, although so far the predominance of either National or Labour has limited the extent of the major parties' policy trade-offs in coalitions since 1996. However, voters can no longer expect that governing parties will be able to enact all their policies. None the less, at least some of a governing party's policies will be enacted and all its policies will be relevant to the party's election campaign and to its dealings with potential coalition partners. The post-election discussions between the various parties interested in forming a government focus closely on the details of each party's policy. The issue of how party policy is decided thus remains important for all political parties.

Within all political parties there is a natural tension over who should have the final authority on party policy. Ordinary members of the party may justifiably claim that they provide the basis of the party's support, without which MPs would not be elected, and should therefore be the ultimate source of the party's policy. MPs in the party caucus, on the other hand, as full-time politicians, are in closer touch with the various sections of the government policy-making process in Wellington and may have a better grasp of the political practicalities involved. They can also claim to be more representative of public opinion than party activists whose views often tend to be more extreme (Vowles *et al.*, 1995: 85). Within the caucus itself, the leader and other senior members, as ministers or prospective ministers, may consider that their judgment and experience should carry more weight than that of junior colleagues. When parties are in government, policy making initiatives tend to gravitate to their parliamentary wings, shifting back towards the organisational membership when they are in opposition.

Historically, the Labour party tended to give greater weight to the extra-parliamentary party in policy-making, the MPs being seen as the agents of the wider labour movement. Conventions of collective solidarity, which played an important part in the ethos of organised labour and trade unions, carried an expectation that policy would be debated and decided democratically and that party policy decisions would be binding on the party's leadership. Discussion of policy within the party, with proposals ('remits') being forwarded to the annual conference where they were debated and voted on, was always seen as central to setting the party's political direction.

Labour has diminished the party's policy-making role by treating the annual meetings in election years as morale-boosting congresses rather than decision-making conferences. Moreover, the policy that really counts as party policy is that presented to the voters during the election campaign. Labour party policy is formulated by a Policy Council, consisting of representatives chosen by the annual conference, an equal number of representatives of the parliamentary caucus, together with national office-holders and representatives of the party's various sectional councils, such as Maori, Pacific Islanders, industrial affiliates, and women. The final policy must then be confirmed by both the New Zealand Council of the party and the parliamentary caucus. Though the extra-parliamentary party has more members formally involved, the party's parliamentary leadership is usually able to ensure that it goes into an election campaign with policies it can happily support. But party policy has sometimes been a matter of fierce debate. In the lead-up to the 1984 election there was sharp disagreement within Labour on the party's economic policy between those who favoured a traditional interventionist approach and those, such as Roger Douglas, who were more in favour of economic deregulation. In the end, the conflict was not resolved and the party went into the election with an inconclusive compromise (Oliver, 1989).

The National party, by contrast, arose out of a parliamentary coalition and its main purpose was mainly electoral, to work for the return of a non-Labour government. Part of National's anti-Labour ethos was support for the rights of individual MPs to exercise independence of judgement and an antipathy to rules requiring binding support of majority decisions. This was reflected not only in National's official tolerance of dissent within its parliamentary caucus and rejection of Labour's Rule 226 (Chapter 5: 113–4) but also in a broader recognition that the parliamentary team as a whole could not be bound by its party. Thus, annual conferences of the National party, though they too involve the discussion of remits and the taking of votes, have never been treated as anything other than a sounding board for the parliamentary party, an indication of party opinion but in no way binding on the party's leadership. For instance, during the Holyoake and Muldoon years, National party conferences regularly passed motions in favour of abolishing compulsory unionism but this issue was not taken up until well into the Muldoon government's last term (Industrial Relations Amendment Act 1983). Consequently, from time to time, there have been complaints from the extra-parliamentary side that their views and those of the party at large have not been given sufficient weight. Such objections were frequent in the latter years of Robert Muldoon's leadership and in the early years of the Bolger government. In response, while National was in opposition during the Lange/Palmer government, the parliamentary leadership took care to involve party members in the formation of party policy through a structure of specific policy committees at electorate, regional and national level.

In opposition again after 1999, National in 2003 revamped these committees, introducing a number of policy advisory groups comprising members with a particular policy interest or expertise as a primary source of policy development. It also replaced its long-standing policy committee with a policy consultation committee, to ensure , like the former committee, cooperation between the caucus and the party's organisational wing. Its women's and Maori advisory committees, and the Young Nationals were also to be directed towards policy development. Approval of policy lies with the Board of Directors.

The other, newer parties are evolving their own policy-making procedures. The Alliance and Greens have broadly representative policy committees including members from the caucus (if there is one) and the organisational wing, which initiate and facilitate policy development, providing the channels for upward movement of policy proposals, with final ratification at central level. In the case of the Alliance, this requires a minimum of 66 per cent vote by the Council. New Zealand First's approach to policy-making has been more fluid and less open, in keeping with the personal dominance of its leader, Winston Peters, and with his formative experience in the National party under Robert Muldoon. In ACT, responsibility for party policy is firmly in the hands of the Board of Trustees, though, if the party has three or more MPs, the party caucus must first be consulted. This insistence on central control reflects the party's origins as a programmatic party committed to the extreme neo-liberal ideas espoused by Sir Roger Douglas.

All New Zealand political parties are still adjusting to the new electoral system and to the new multi-party composition of Parliament. The role of party policy has changed from a potential mandate binding on an elected government to an initial bargaining position from which parties may expect to negotiate with each other. Though political leaders may be under pressure from supporters to declare some policies non-negotiable, the logic of coalition and minority government compels them into compromising on their preferred policies. Parties which refuse to compromise, like the Alliance in 1996, rule themselves out of a chance to share in government.

The fact that party policy now becomes a matter of post-election bargaining further weakens the role of the extra-parliamentary party in party policy-making. Inter-party negotiations are conducted by the party leaders and their senior parliamentary colleagues. In the 1996 coalition discussions, party presidents were also included as a means of involving the wider party organisation. However, control of the outcome was firmly in the hands of the party's parliamentary leadership reporting to the party caucus. Because MMP has tipped the balance of political power more towards the institution of Parliament (Chapter 5: 109), it has also increased the influence of parliamentary representatives within political parties. To the extent that rank and file members feel further excluded from influencing their parties' policy directions, they may have even less incentive to maintain their membership. MMP may be revitalising New Zealand's party system by opening up opportunities for new political parties. But whether it can enhance public participation in politics and reverse the decline in mass membership of political parties now appears doubtful.

Further reading

The New Zealand party system
Aimer (1992; 2001); Boston *et al.* (1996a): Chapter 4; Gustafson (1993); Mulgan (1989): 56–78; Wood (1988): Chapter 6.
The National Party
Gustafson (1986); Wood (2003).
The Labour Party
Gustafson (1992); Miller (2003a).
ACT
Reid (2003).
Alliance
Jesson (1997); Trotter (2001).

Greens
Bale (2003).
New Zealand First
Miller (1997a); Miller (2003a).
United Future
Aimer (2003).

Party websites: <www.[name of party].org.nz> [act; alliance; greens; labour; national; nzfirst; progressives; unitedfuture].

11

Elections and Voters

The electoral process

Regular elections are the central, fundamental feature of a democratic system of government. From the citizen's point of view, the act of voting expresses the principle that governments are the chosen agents of the people. The average voter may give very little attention to politics from day to day and may accept that the business of government is in the hands of politicians and public officials. None the less, every three years or so, at election time, he or she will take the trouble to cast a vote for the party and candidate of his or her choice, participating in a process that culminates in a collective decision about which party (or parties) will form the government and which party leader will become prime minister. This three-yearly choice not only determines who is to be the government but may also affect the decisions which the government takes.

The administration of the electoral process begins after each census with the Representation Commission determining the number and the boundaries of the electorate seats (Chapter 5: 99). A necessary preliminary is the holding of a nationwide Maori option to determine who wishes to vote on the Maori roll and how many are to be included in the 'Maori electoral population' and how many in the 'General electoral population' (Electoral Commission, 2002: 21–22). Once the electorate seats are finalised, the next stage is the compiling of the electoral rolls for each electorate. Forms are mailed to all currently enrolled voters and extensive media campaigns encourage those not already registered to do so. To qualify for the vote one must be either a New Zealand citizen or permanent resident and have reached the age of eighteen (Electoral Commission, 2002: 28–29). For many years the voting age was twenty-one but it was lowered to twenty in 1969 and then to eighteen in 1974. Registration is legally compulsory for those eligible to vote, though failure to register is not actually prosecuted by the authorities.

The date of the election is effectively determined by the prime minister, who advises the Governor-General accordingly (Chapter 4: 91). A day is set for the nomination of candidates and the election itself, which must be a Saturday between 20 and 27 days after nominations close.

The parties will have begun their preparations well before the election. Candidate selection often begins the year before, allowing the candidates plenty of time to become known in their electorates. Under MMP, not all candidates will be contesting an electorate. Some will be standing for their parties as list candidates only. Once parties have submitted their full list of candidates by nomination day, they cannot change the order of candidates on the list. By the time the official campaign period begins, parties will expect to have finalised their policies and advertising campaigns as well as their fundraising. The formal campaigns, lasting last three to four weeks, begin with televised opening addresses by the party leaders and then continue with a carefully constructed schedule of daily meetings and 'photo opportunities' for the leaders, designed to make good copy for the news media. The media provide extensive coverage of the election (Rudd, 1993), television concentrating on the nationwide party contest, particularly the party leaders and party policies. The parties are also provided with free radio and television time in which to run their advertisements (Chapter 10: 254). Newspapers are able to provide more comprehensive reports and analysis than television and radio and traditionally give detailed accounts of the contests in each of the individual electorates in their circulation area.

Meanwhile, on the ground level, candidates and their party supporters campaign vigorously in their electorates. The parties traditionally attempted to 'canvass' each household, determining where their likely supporters live and asking whether they would like help in getting to the polls or in casting a special vote. They also deliver campaign literature, usually pamphlets which extol the virtues of the candidate and the party for which they are standing. Computerised letters are mailed to targeted groups of key voters. Individual candidates will also hold their own meetings, though in the age of television politics these tend not to attract large audiences. Partly because of the larger size of electorates since the adoption of MMP, and partly because of the decline of party membership, household canvassing by parties has also declined in recent years (Vowles *et al.*, 2002: 91, 106–7).

On the election day itself, media advertising and campaigning are banned. Polling booths are established at convenient local points, such

as schools and church halls, and run by temporary staff under the super-
vision of a returning officer appointed for each electorate. Voters have
their name marked off on the electoral roll and are given a ballot paper
on which, in a private booth, they tick the name of their preferred candidate for their electorate, and the party they wish to vote for from the
party lists. Voters may choose whether to cast both their electorate and
party votes or either one of them. Allowance is made for voters who are
unable to attend to vote in their own electorate to make 'special' votes.
The parties may appoint scrutineers who observe that the process is
properly carried out. The polls close at 7 p.m. after which the ballot papers cast in each electorate are assembled and counted, again in the
presence of party scrutineers. Preliminary results are announced during
the evening, relayed to the broadcast media, who monitor the national
party contest, and placed on the Internet. Final results of the election are
returned some weeks later, after all the special votes have been counted
and the rolls checked for possible double voting.

Electoral power

From the politicians' perspective, the fact that they must face an election in three years or less is a dominating factor in their activities. Overall strategy, for all parties, is determined by the goal of doing well at the
next election. Individual decisions will be routinely assessed by politicians and their advisers for their possible impact on the party's standing
with the voters, whether any significant sections of the electorate are
likely to approve or disapprove. The electoral motive is sometimes depicted as an unworthy one on the ground that issues should be decided
'on their merits' and not for 'political' reasons. However, this is to misunderstand the basic mechanism of public accountability in a representative democracy. If governments did not care about their popularity
and parties did not compete to maximise their votes at the next election,
governments would not be responsive to public opinion and the wishes
of the voters. The strength of representative democracy is that it har-
nesses the self-interest of politicians, their natural desire to seek and
maintain power, to the pursuit of the collective interest as perceived by
the voters (an assumption encapsulated in the 'economic' theory of democracy (Chapter 10: 243)). Indeed, the growing disillusion with electoral politics can in part be traced to the Fourth Labour government's
second term (1987–90), when many ministers appeared to lose interest
in winning the next election (Chapter 5: 122).

The electoral motive may vary in its importance depending on the issue and the political context. For instance, governments may be more inclined to risk taking unpopular decisions early in their term than they would in an election year. Some issues may be quite routine and have little or no electoral impact whenever they are decided. However, almost any issue has the potential to become politically controversial and to affect the electoral popularity of individual politicians and their party. Politicians will therefore take care to avoid creating adverse reactions from the electorate. Many policy options are rejected and many issues never reach the policy-making agenda, because they are seen as electorally suicidal. For instance, major increases in taxation or the introduction of significant new charges for public services, though often favoured by politicians and their advisers, are regularly ruled out as politically impossible. Such avoidance is a good example of the power of 'anticipated reactions' (Chapter 1: 15) and an important means by which the voters control their elected rulers, even though the control is indirect and exercised without the voters' being aware of it.

Electoral power is an essential element in a democracy because it is one aspect of political power where each person's views and interests should count equally. The more wealthy and established sections of society may have political advantages elsewhere, for instance through superior interest-group influence on politicians and public servants. But in so far as politicians and parties seek to win the support of the voters, they have an incentive to treat each person, rich or poor, male or female, Pakeha or Maori, as equally important.

How much electoral power is exercised by the average voter depends on a number of factors, including the effectiveness of the media in informing the public (Chapter 12) and the extent to which each voter's decision to vote is a considered reaction to the governing parties' performance and potential compared with that of the alternative parties. Only if voters are thought by politicians to react positively or negatively to particular policies will the voters exercise electoral power. This in turn raises the complex question of why voters vote the way they do.

In academic research about New Zealand politics, voting studies make up by far the largest body of published work (Wood, 1991: 9) and have attracted most of the research funding from external sources. This interest in electoral research is stimulated by the widespread public and media interest in elections. Elections are the central public event in modern democracies and the focus of much media activity. Expert views are sought about the likely outcome of forthcoming elections and about the explanation of results as they become known. Political activists, such as politicians and party organisers, also have an obvious professional interest in understanding the factors which cause voters to support one party rather than another. Election results provide the researcher with a large body of quantitative data which can be elaborately analysed. These results can also be supplemented by survey research in which randomly selected citizens are questioned about their social background, political attitudes and voting patterns. As a result, the study of voting behaviour has become the most professionalised and technically sophisticated branch of political science, an international trend which is reflected in New Zealand (Aimer & McAllister, 1992; Vowles *et al.*, 2002: Appendix A).

Voter turnout

The electoral power of the voters obviously depends, in the first place, on their being willing to exercise their vote. If certain sections of the voting public are known to be regular non-voters, then parties and governments will be less inclined to take account of their interests. The great majority of adult New Zealanders do exercise their right to vote. Indeed, turnout figures for New Zealand have been among the world's highest, indicating a high degree of support for the democratic process.. Between 1981 and 2002, for example, the average turnout of those registered on the electoral roll was 86.8 per cent. In 2002, however, it had fallen to 76.9 per cent. Not everyone who is eligible to vote actually registers to vote in the first place. A comparison of the electoral roll with the number of those aged eighteen and over as recorded in the quinquennial census shows that in 2002 6 per cent of the eligible population were unregistered. The effective turnout figure for 2002 is therefore around 72 per cent. Voter turnout fluctuates between elections. 1996 marked a slight increase over 1993, perhaps attributable to the interest generated by the new MMP electoral system. More notable is the long-term trend. Average effective turnout declined steadily through the post-war period from over 90 per cent in the 1940s to 75 per cent in 1999 before reaching a new low in 2002 (Vowles & Aimer, 1993: 43; Vowles *et al.*, 2002: 99–100; Electoral Commission, 2002: 174).

Why do some people not bother to register or to vote? From some perspectives it is the decision to vote, rather than non-voting, which may be more difficult to explain. When the electoral process is looked at collectively, from the perspective of the system as a whole, the outcome is naturally seen as the 'people's decision' or the 'voters' choice'. But from the point of view of the individual voter, the casting of his or her individual vote may have a negligible effect on the eventual outcome and may not in any realistic sense be seen as contributing to a 'decision' or a 'choice'.

This problem is the so-called 'paradox of voting' generated by the theory of rational voting elaborated by Anthony Downs (1957). According to this theory, individual voters are motivated only by their own interest in affecting the result and voting is seen as involving personal costs, such as time, travel expenses and so on. The rational voter will therefore do a cost/benefit calculation, balancing the undoubted costs of exercising a vote against the likelihood that his or her vote will be decisive in electing a government of his or her preference. In any large group, such as a nationwide electorate, the chances that one particular vote will determine the outcome are infinitesimal and so, in an electorate made up of rational individuals, no one will vote. (This is an instance of the wider 'collective action' problem generated in public choice theory, a problem which also arises in accounts of interest-group behaviour (Chapter 9: 217). Rational individuals, in theory, will not contribute to the expenses of lobbying activities if they can get the same benefits through taking a free ride.)

The fact that voters still vote in their hundreds of thousands shows the deficiencies of public choice explanations of collective processes such as elections. It also means that motives other than narrow personal advantage in the outcome must be found to explain the act of voting itself. Commitment to the interests of a social group to which individual voters belong may be a motive in deciding which party to vote for. Unionists may vote Labour because they perceive Labour to be the party which benefits unions, just as farmers may support National because it is perceived to favour the interests of farmers. But in deciding to cast a vote at all, even for the party which fosters their group's interests, voters must be motivated by something other than their own personal advantage. Indeed, most people accept that they have a duty to vote even if their own individual vote makes no difference (Vowles & Aimer, 1993: Table 4.1; Vowles *et al.*, 1998: 157; Vowles *et al.*, 2002: 110). This suggests that they recognise the self-defeating consequences which result if everyone attempts to take a free ride and abstains.

Moreover, for many people the act of voting is not a costly or burdensome chore but satisfying and enjoyable in itself. To differing degrees, voters become caught up in the growing excitement of an election campaign which increasingly dominates the media in the days leading up to the election. Like sports fans cheering on their team, voters with strong partisan feelings welcome the opportunity to express their support and to share in their party's performance, even when they know that their own support will not affect the outcome.

That most people vote out of a sense of public duty or satisfaction in civic participation is indicated by the fact that in the past levels of turn-out were roughly uniform in all electorates. Under the first-past-the-post system, the outcome of the election turned on the results in 'marginal' seats, that is, those electorates where the levels of support between the two major parties were closely matched and where both parties appeared to have a realistic chance of winning the seat. Voters in marginal electorates had a more decisive effect on the result of the election than voters in safe seats whose votes had no effect at all. One might therefore have expected comparatively high levels of turnout in marginal seats and very low levels in safe seats. There was some tendency in this direction, but it was relatively minor (Vowles & Aimer, 1993: 56), probably due more to the fact that parties put greater effort into campaigning in marginal electorates rather than to any difference in the attitude of voters to the value of their vote. Voters in safe seats clearly felt an equal desire to register their preferences, even though their vote was irrelevant to the outcome. Under MMP, however, the distinction between safe and marginal seats becomes much less significant because it applies only to the less important, electorate vote (Vowles *et al.*, 2002: 103). For the party vote, which determines the party composition of Parliament, each person's vote counts equally regardless of which elec-torate they live in.

More relevant to whether people bother to register and vote than the chances of their vote affecting the outcome is their social position. Broadly speaking, those who are well integrated into the dominant structures of society, those who have well-paid jobs (or have retired from well-paid jobs), those who are looking after children and those who own, or are purchasing, their own homes, are much more likely to participate in elections (Vowles *et al.*, 2002: 227–8). By contrast, the social outsiders, the young, the unemployed, the single, though they may have as much of a stake, if not more, in the results of elections, are much less likely, because they are socially marginalised, to think voting is worthwhile.

Non-voting is particularly high among Maori and Pacific Islanders and the Maori seats have consistently had much lower levels of turnout than the general seats (Vowles & Aimer, 1993: Table 4.5; Electoral Commission, 2002: 70). In 2002, turnout (as a percentage of registered voters) was 58 per cent in Maori electorates compared with 79 per cent in 'general' electorates. Low turnout in the Maori seats has been linked to Labour's domination of the seats and the relative lack of party competition for the Maori vote. Maori participation may yet increase under the new electoral system which gives greater scope for Maori representation (Chapter 5: 101), and as Labour's dominance in Maori seats is challenged by New Zealand First or the future appearance of a viable Maori party. However, in spite of the 'Maori renaissance' and the greater political prominence of Maori issues in the 1980s (Chapter 7: 185), Maori voters are still disaffected comparatively from the political system.

So too are the young. Those under eighteen are totally disenfranchised even though they may already be making an independent contribution to the economy and society generally (Royal Commission on the Electoral System, 1986: 233–6). Young adults, including potential first-time voters, are on average less likely to vote. In 2002, 38 per cent of 18–24 year-olds did not vote, compared with 16 per cent in the 50–59 age group (Vowles *et al.*, 2004: Appendix table 2.1). Politicians may therefore have less incentive to consider the interests of the young (in stark contrast to the over fifties, who are the most assiduous voters as well as the group particularly active in political organisations, including political parties).

The growing number of socially and economically marginalised citizens who do not bother to exercise their right to vote marks a general decline in democratic responsiveness of governments to voters. Some of the increased abstention in 1990, and to a lesser extent in 1987, was undoubtedly due to the Labour government's repudiation of the party's traditional principles, which led large numbers of disaffected Labour supporters to abstain (Vowles & Aimer, 1993: 47). This could have been seen as a temporary phenomenon which could be expected to disappear if Labour and the party system generally restored closer contact with the expectations and aspirations of the voting public. On the other hand, if economic conditions continue to encourage the growth of a socially marginalised underclass, the underlying trend of falling levels of turnout is unlikely to be reversed. This will mean that these sections of the population are also deprived of their fair share of electoral power, in addition to other social and political disadvantage, because politicians will be able to neglect their interests without suffering adverse reactions at the polls. Despite briefly responding to the advent of MMP in 1996, turnout has continued to decline since 1990. The reasons for the decline are complex, and include a variety of attitudinal and social structural effects, many of which New Zealand shares with other advanced (post-industrial) democracies (Vowles *et al.*, 2002: 111–13).

Investigating the voters' choice

The extent to which parties and governments respond to the voters' interests also depends on the extent to which the voters themselves are perceived as reacting to what politicians say and do. But do voters so react? When voters decide to cast their vote for one party or candidate rather than another, what motivates their choice? Academic researchers investigate this question from two differing, though complementary, perspectives. One perspective takes an aggregate approach, looking at the voting statistics for different districts, for instance different electorates or polling booths within electorates. These can then be compared with known social characteristics of the districts in question and a cause or motive for voting inferred from this correlation. Thus, if electorates in rural areas have tended to vote National, it can be hypothesised that farmers and rural workers generally tend to support National because they perceive it to be the party which favours the rural interest. However, this is a blunt and inconclusive method. It is blunt because it ignores all the variations of individuals' circumstances and attitudes which are masked by generalised statistics. It is inconclusive, because even to establish a correlation between, say, a voter's occupation and how he or she votes, does not establish that he or she voted for a party because of a belief that the party's policies favoured the interests of people in his or her particular occupation more than the policies of other parties. The main reason for voting may be attitudes of partisan loyalty acquired through family socialisation and may have little to do with immediate perceptions of the party and its policies.

Aggregate research therefore needs to be supplemented by survey research into individual voters, their personal background, social and political attitudes, views of the parties, their leaders, policies, and so on. Survey research asks such questions of a random sample of voters and thus builds a much more complex set of correlations of different possible factors (or 'variables') with voting patterns. By the use of the statistical techniques of 'multivariate' analysis, it is possible to isolate variables which are good predictors of voting decisions and to distinguish them from variables which are irrelevant. Even then, however, one must be cautious in interpreting the results. Surveys are based on answers to questions which different respondents may not fully understand or may answer inaccurately. However carefully and conscientiously surveys are administered, they always contain a margin of error. The New Zealand Election Study surveys, the most elaborate election surveys conducted in New Zealand since 1990 (Vowles *et al.*, 2002: Appendix A), still received replies from less than 73 per cent of those surveyed. These figures are high by international standards and, once appropriate adjustments are made, are sufficient to guarantee reliability for the general trends discovered. But, as with all such surveys, the detailed percentages must be treated as approximations only.

The result of academic research on elections has been to emphasise the complexity of voting behaviour. The more is known, the more scepticism is required about any single theory of political motivation. Each voter is a unique individual, subject to a variety of different pressures, including long-term social factors, such as family background, partisan loyalty and occupational position, as well as more immediate effects such as perceptions about the prime minister and government of the day or about the policies of the competing parties. Generalisations are possible about what factors tend to be more relevant than others in explaining or predicting how people vote and this may be sufficient to indicate the relative power of differing section of the voting public. But such generalisations are simply statements of probability which always have to be understood in a context where there are many exceptions and idiosyncrasies of behaviour which may not show up in the statistics.

Socio-economic factors

Given what has been New Zealand's essentially two-party system, voting research has concentrated particularly on reasons for supporting the two former 'major' parties. In so far as voting is the result of longstanding historical and social factors, many people are still influenced by their attitudes towards the two old adversaries, Labour and National, even if the electoral system no longer entrenches these parties' virtual monopoly of Parliament. The obvious starting point for research has been the contrasting socio-economic profile for each party as revealed in aggregate analyses of each party's safe seats. The basis of Labour's support has been in urban electorates which have a higher proportion of those on lower incomes. National's core support is in rural areas and in the wealthier city suburbs. Elections have been fought out in marginal electorates which contain a socio-economic mix of these factors, such as middle-income city suburbs or the smaller cities and large towns. This social cleavage at the axis of the two-party system reflects the historical origins of the two parties, with Labour the socialist party of unionists and workers and National the anti-socialist party of farmers and business people.

This divide, which has been reflected in the economically left-wing and right-wing orientations of the parties, has provided the basic assumption on which political activists and commentators have estimated where each party's supporters are to be found. For instance, when the political complexion of a city electorate was being assessed, the areas of expensive housing were normally seen as National in sympathy and poorer areas, such as blocks of state housing, are classed as Labour. These assessments were usually borne out by reports of party canvassers and analyses of results in individual polling booths; National won the 'blue ribbon' districts and Labour the run-down districts.

The importance of this socio-economic division has also been confirmed in academic studies in which the class composition of each New Zealand electorate was estimated, using the proportion of employers recorded in the census as resident in each electorate (Vowles, 1989; Vowles *et al.*, 1995: 16–18). A high correlation was discovered between the tendency of an electorate to have more employers and a tendency for it to vote for National. Conversely, the fewer employers and the more employed workers or unemployed, the more likely the electorate was to prefer Labour. The percentage of employers in an electorate may be a convenient single-measure indicator of the class composition of a particular electorate, but the concept of class itself is more complex and disputed, being related to a number of factors (Chapter 2: 38–41), including occupational status, whether manual or non-manual workers, being self-employed or not, and so on. Survey research allows a more sophisticated examination of class factors in voting. A tendency to vote National has been particularly associated with having a high income, being self-employed, being a farmer or a salaried manager, working in the private rather than the public sector and owning a mortgage-free house. Labour voters were more likely to have had a low income, be union members and live in state houses.

Simple correlations may paint a misleading picture if they suggest that each factor is an equally significant predictor of voting behaviour. Statistical 'regressions' can assess whether a particular factor has any independent predictive value or whether it simply varies in tandem with some other factor or factors. This is done by holding other factors constant and then adding in the factor in question to see if it makes a difference. For instance, if we know someone's occupation and housing status, does adding in their income level alter the chances that they will have voted National or Labour? In fact, income on its own tended to be a relatively insignificant indicator of voting patterns. Of the class-related variables, the most significant factors appear to have been occupation, in the case of farmers (pro-National), union membership (pro-Labour), housing status and receipt of several welfare benefits (pro-Labour) (Vowles & Aimer, 1993: Table 3.3).

The aggregate generalisations about electorates in terms of socioeconomic profile still generally hold true but they are generalisations only. After all, 'blue ribbon' National seats may have been 'safe' for National but they still contained considerable numbers of Labour voters, just as Labour's economically depressed inner city heartland contained many National supporters. None the less, there has always been a strong tendency for significant numbers of voters to vote against what might be thought of as their normal class interest (Bean, 1988) and the number of such voters appears to have been steadily increasing since the 1960s. The decline of class voting accelerated during the term of the Fourth Labour government when Labour attracted an exceptionally large number of well-off voters in 1987, and by 1990 had also alienated many of its working class supporters. (Vowles, *et al.*, 1995: 17). As Labour distanced itself from the radical economic reforms of those years, class voting between Labour and National returned by 1999 to about the same level as 1984, only to plunge again in 2002. In that election, Labour's support was only weakly rooted in social structure, reflecting the party's broad appeal to the 'centre' of New Zealand politics (Vowles *et al.*, 2004: ch. 2).The socio-economic profiles of other parties are also blurred and overlapping. The Alliance, for instance, in 1993, was unable to make good its claim better to represent Labour's traditional supporters among unionists and manual workers and was almost indistinguishable from Labour in the class of voters it attracted. New Zealand First supporters, though slightly more representative of the elderly, Maori and church-goers, were, in terms of social class, generally typical of the electorate as a whole (Vowles, *et al.*, 1995: 25–26). The rise in popularity of the smaller parties like Alliance, ACT, the Greens and New Zealand First suggests that under the more proportional and less distorted MMP system both Labour's and National's links with their traditional class support will be still further attenuated.

In general, then, though socio-economic class is by no means a universal predictor of which party voters will prefer, it has still been an important element in the distinction between Labour and National voters.

To this extent, electoral competition between the major parties has articulated and reflected the main socio-economic division within New Zealand society and can be seen to have provided an avenue of political influence for competing class interests. However, the significance of class division in voting decisions has been slowly declining over several decades and may decline still further under MMP with the rise of new parties less grounded in class conflicts of the past.

What of the other divisions which distinguish the different elements of the plural society (Chapter 2)? Are factors such as ethnicity, gender, locality or religion relevant to explaining how people vote? According to the results of survey research, ethnicity is electorally significant in that Maori and Pacific Islanders have been far more likely to vote for Labour than for other parties, while, since 1993, New Zealand First has also sometimes attracted Maori (though not to Pacific Island) voters (Vowles & Aimer, 1993: 34–39; Vowles, *et al.*, 1998: 171–83). In 1993, New Zealand First captured one Maori seat from Labour, and in 1996 won all five, though lost them again in 1999 (Vowles *et al.*, 2002: 66–72). Maori and Pacific Islander support for Labour is not just a consequence of the fact that they are disproportionately members of the lower socio-economic groups. Even when class factors are held constant, a Maori or Pacific Islander has been more likely to vote Labour than has been a Pakeha in the same class position (Vowles & Aimer, 1993: 34–39).

Gender has emerged in recent elections as a factor in vote choice. While there is now no gender gap in turnout of men and women, there is a difference in their party choices. Over the longer term, women in New Zealand have followed the trend in many Western democracies, moving from greater support for parties on the right to greater support for the left. Women may have a slightly more positive attitude than men to state spending on education, health and education as well as to the environment (Aimer, 1993). ACT party voters are disproportionately men, but the most electorally significant gender gap since 1996 has been the greater support for Labour among women, a trend accentuated by Helen Clark's leadership (Boston *et al.*, 1997: 140-1; Vowles *et al.*, 2002: 93-4, 227) Locality, the part of the country one lives in, is not a major indicator of party preference. Given New Zealand's lack of deep regional divisions, this is hardly surprising. Apparent regional differences between the parties are to be accounted for by other factors, though there has been some very minor advantage for Labour in Wellington and the Canterbury-West Coast region of the South Island and for National in the central North Island (Vowles & Aimer, 1993: 31).

Another factor which has been politically very significant in many countries but has had relatively little political effect in New Zealand is religious sectarianism. Support for one religion or religious denomination rather than another is not reflected in political allegiance, with the minor exception of a slight tendency for Roman Catholics to prefer Labour (Vowles & Aimer, 1993: Table 13.4). However, regular attendance at any church as distinct from no regular church attendance is electorally significant. Church-goers of whatever religion or denomination tend to favour National, New Zealand First or Christian parties, and those with no religious affiliation Labour, the Alliance or the Greens (Vowles *et al.*, 1995: 27–30; Vowles *et al.*, 2002: 227). MMP has encouraged a more visible electoral manifestation of religious affiliation through the Christian Heritage and Christian Democrat parties which joined in a Christian Coalition for the 1996 election and secured 4.3 per cent of the vote though winning no seats. The Coalition collapsed, but in 2000 the former Christian Democrat wing of the Coalition merged with United to form United Future, which won eight seats in 2002. Although avoiding the label 'Christian', United Future attracted most of its voters from among active church-goers (Aimer, 2003: 299).

Party identification and electoral volatility

For many voters, voting for one or other of the major parties has been a matter of long-term, often life-long, commitment. 'My family has always been National' or 'we are all Labour people' are commonly shared sentiments, indicating a sense of loyalty and personal identification which transcends any rational calculation of interest or advantage to be gained from one party rather than another. Such sentiments are more like the feelings of partisan loyalty which people have for their school, their home town or their local sports teams. Supporting one's party and voting for it is like backing one's own side and wanting to see it triumph over traditional rivals. Such loyalties are often first picked up in the home, in which children acquire their political attitudes through listening to the political opinions of adult family members and their friends.

Party identification has been claimed to be a dominant factor in New Zealand voters' choices (Lamare, 1984, 1992; Aimer, 1992: 332–5). Voting researchers ask standard 'party identification' questions such as 'Generally speaking do you usually think of yourself as National, Labour, Alliance, New Zealand First [etc] or some other party?' A majority of those questioned usually answer in the affirmative. This can be further linked with the party preference of people's parents. Usually up to nearly half of those who identify with one of the parties in this way report that one or both parents had a preference for the same party.

The theory of party identification has been the subject of considerable controversy and debate, internationally as well as in New Zealand (Lamare, 1992; Aimer, 1992; Vowles & Aimer, 1993: Chapter 2; Vowles *et al.*, 1995: 35–38). Scepticism has been expressed about the extent to which answers to questions about party identity, for instance 'do you think of yourself as Labour etc.', give reliable information about long-term attitudes which may be said to have caused, or at least influenced, the voter's decision. The answer, particularly when it is given in a questionnaire administered soon after an election, may be little more than a restatement of the voter's decision to vote for that particular party or, at most, a statement of short-term political attitudes.

Such doubts are even stronger when positive answers to the much weaker question, whether people feel 'a little closer' to one party rather than the other, are included as evidence of party identity (Lamare, 1992). In this case, to claim that voters have voted Labour or National because they identify with Labour or National may be no more than to say that people have voted Labour or National because they voted Labour or National. This is an empty pseudo-explanation which simply repeats what has to be explained without offering any independent explanation of it.

However, scepticism about the evidence of party identification may be overstated. The hypothesis that deep-seated party loyalties can be an important factor in people's political opinions and voting decisions fits with our commonsense perceptions of many people we know, sometimes even ourselves. Many people do have sentiments of loyalty and partisanship which are distinct from more rational and immediate perceptions of the parties' policy directions. Questions about party identification in public opinion surveys may be somewhat crude and blunt instruments for measuring what is often a subtle and complex interplay of motives. None the less, the phenomenon is a real one, if not easily measured.

Perhaps the clearest survey evidence of the existence of such partisanship as an independent factor is from those who accept a general preference for a particular party but admit that they did not vote for that party. Thus, the 1990 survey discovered that nearly a third of those who generally preferred Labour did not actually vote Labour in that election (Vowles & Aimer, 1993: 21). This finding, which indicates the alienation of Labour's traditional supporters from their party, also shows that many voters do have a general disposition to vote for a particular party and that this disposition is not just a reflection of how they actually vote. At the same time, however, these instances where people vote against their party identification prove that party identification in itself is often not a determining factor in people's voting behaviour.

Similarly, in the 1993 election, a large proportion (around a third) of those voting for the Alliance and New Zealand First indicated an identification with one of the older 'major' parties (Vowles *et al.*, 1995: 35–38). This was to be expected in that both newer parties originated as 'splinter' parties, breaking away from Labour and National respectively (Chapter 10: 241–2). At the same time, compared with Labour and National voters, voters for the Alliance and New Zealand First parties included far fewer people who identified with those parties. That the newer parties, having been in existence for a relatively short time, have not yet had the time to develop the psychological bonds associated with strong party identification was further demonstrated by United Future, contesting its first election in 2002. A substantial proportion of United Future voters retained their National identification and a smaller share their Labour identification (Aimer, 2003: 297). This suggests that support for such parties is relatively unstable and unreliable compared with the core support of established parties like Labour and National.

Political partisanship, a general preference for one party rather than another, is therefore to be accepted as one important factor in voting, particularly when it is linked to the partisan preference of parents. However, the importance of this influence is declining. An increasing number of voters show no strong partisan attachment to any political party (Vowles *et al.*, 2002: 92). As for parental influence, though it is an important factor in determining strong feelings of partisanship, its overall effect on the electorate is weak. In fact, only a third of the voters in 1993 (32 per cent) reported voting the same way as one or both of their parents.

These trends are part of a larger trend towards greater volatility among voters. Declining sentiments of partisanship mirror the declining force of socio-economic class factors in influencing party voter preference for Labour or National. Survey research suggests that, since the 1970s between 30 per cent and 40 per cent of electors have voted differently in two consecutive elections. With the advent of MMP and the wider party choices offered, individual volatility has risen further. In 1999, 41 per cent and in 2002 nearly half the electors who were eligible to vote in both elections chose a different party from the one they had voted for in the previous election (Vowles *et al.*, 2004: Fig. 2.5). Volatility is becoming the norm and stable party preference the exception.

Issues

If long-term allegiances are less strong, does this mean that voters are paying more attention to more immediate factors, such as the parties' election campaigns and policies or the respective quality of their leaders? The effect of voters' views on particular issues on their voting decisions is extremely difficult to assess. Though the parties put forward very detailed and comprehensive election manifestos, voting research has confirmed that most voters are unaware of most of the detailed commitments made by parties. None the less, when prompted by survey questions, most voters are prepared to say which major issues or sets of issues, such as law and order, unemployment, Maori rights, are important to them and which of the major parties are closest to their own views on these issues (Levine & Roberts, 1992; Vowles *et al.*, 1995: 63–64; 2002: 22–24). In mostcases there is a correlation between a voter's views of which issues are important, which party is closest to their views and how they vote.

Voters for all parties register significant interest in economic issues, health and education but interest in other types of concerns varies with party support, and from election to election. There are always substantial minorities of voters who vote against the party which they claim is closest to their views on the issues of greatest importance. Moreover, even when there is coincidence between voting direction and views on important issues, this does not prove that the party's stand on an issue or issues has been the determining factor in the voter's decision. The voter's view of the party's stand on issues could equally well be a consequence of the voter's decision, resulting from a natural wish to see one's preferred party as the party most sympathetic to one's own interests.

An alternative approach to trying to gauge the effects of policies and issues on voting choice is by examining correlates at the aggregate level. This has been done most systematically in relation to economic policy. On the hypothesis that good performance would favour incumbent parties, while poor performance would lead to greater support for the opposition, support for parties has been correlated with the performance of the national economy. Economic performance does have some significant relation to voting support but a weak one only. There is no evidence to sustain the widespread view that governments stand or fall on economic performance and that governments which cannot deliver buoyant economic indicators will necessarily suffer at the polls. This generally negative finding is confirmed by a study (Crothers & Vowles, 1993) in which trends in public opinion poll support for the parties were compared with results of polls measuring economic confidence. Some significant correlation was discovered but, again, it was a weak one. In particular, when the Labour government was in trouble with the voters, from 1988 to 1990, its unpopularity was relatively impervious to improvements in economic confidence. Other factors were clearly at work.

The generally weak correlation between economic conditions and voting choice in recent New Zealand elections fits with findings in other similar countries where there tends to be a looser connection between economic performance and voting when the economy is weak than when it is strong. That is, governing parties are more likely to be rewarded for prosperity than punished for hardship (Crothers & Vowles, 1993: 107–8; Vowles *et al.*, 1995: 63–73).

The overall importance of issues in voting behaviour remains elusive. There is no doubt that many voters are concerned about certain issues and that these concerns are significant in determining the votes of certain voters. In the expanded party system under MMP, the newer parties have become associated with different types of issues, ACT with law and order and taxation, New Zealand First with immigration and Maori issues, the Greens with environmental and trade issues. However, in the case of voters for the former 'major' parties, views on issues are still likely to be less significant as predictors of voting choice than either political partisanship or socio-economic position (Vowles *et al.*, 2004: Fig. 12.2). On the other hand, with the gradual decline in the importance of these long-term structural factors, voters in general may be becoming increasingly likely to decide their vote in the light of the parties' stands on particular policy issues (Bean, 1992).

Leaders and candidates

Another influence on voting, generally more potent than attitudes to particular issues, is people's perceptions of the respective party leaders. Party electioneering material emphasises the personality of the leader and much of the media coverage of election campaigns involves debate with and between the rival party leaders. Survey research indicates that leaders do have a significant effect, particularly when they have strong personalities. For instance, both Robert Muldoon, initially at any rate, and David Lange were influential in their parties' victories. In 1990, Labour changed its leader from Geoffrey Palmer to Mike Moore, in the hope that Moore would appeal more to traditional Labour supporters, a move which had some success (Vowles & Aimer, 1993: 193–6). Even more, Labour's electoral recovery in 1996 and return to government in 1999 owed much to perceptions of Helen Clark as leader (Vowles *et al.*, 2002: 22). Independent perceptions of the qualities of leaders remain less significant than general attitudes towards parties as a whole, though the latter must be influenced to some extent by the performance of the leader as the party's main spokesperson. For instance, during most of the first term of the Bolger National government, Jim Bolger was less popular than the Labour leader, Mike Moore, and also than Winston Peters, yet the National party remained ahead in the opinion polls and won the 1993 election (Vowles *et al.*, 1995: 154–5). Again, the declining force of party partisanship and class voting may be expected to throw greater weight not only on issues but also on leadership as a separate factor in people's voting decisions (Bean, 1992a). In particular, electoral support for new parties which have not yet established strong social roots in the community is likely to be especially dependent on the public profile of their leaders. Thus, the success of the Alliance and New Zealand First was closely linked to the popularity of their leaders, Jim Anderton and Winston Peters (Vowles *et al.*, 1995: 155–8).

Under the previous electoral system, all party voting took place through voting for individual local candidates. In most cases, the qualities of the particular candidates had little perceptible effect on the outcome because most voters used their vote to express preferences about nationwide parties, their policies and their leaders. However, the 'personal' vote for a popular a candidate could sometimes be worth an increase of a few per cent, sufficient to make the difference between success and defeat in a close, 'marginal' electorate (Bean, 1992a). Under MMP, however, the separation of the electorate vote from the party vote encourages voters to take greater account of the personal qualities of local candidates while it also diminishes the extent to which support for a party need be influenced by judgments about individual party candidates. Indeed, up to nearly 40 per cent of voters have shown themselves to be very willing to 'split' their votes, that is vote for the candidate of a party other than the one they have given their party vote to (Electoral Commission, 2002: 174; Vowles *et al.*, 2004: Chapter 2).

Despite all the intensive research, the balance of factors in people's voting decisions still remains hard to fathom. This should be hardly surprising when we consider the complex processes we go through ourselves when deciding how to vote. Generalisations about hundreds of thousands of individual voting choices are bound to be crude and imprecise. But some firm, if mainly negative, conclusions can be reached.

One is that the model of the totally rational voter is a myth. Few, if any, voters make up their minds purely on the basis of informed calculation of the respective costs and benefits to be gained from each party's policies. On the other hand, it is equally mistaken to see the voting public as essentially irrational, as influenced only by unthinking habit or media images. Most voters have views about what they want from government and what they expect their elected politicians to deliver. One of the lessons of the late 1980s and early 1990s is that governing parties which break their commitments and abandon their principles can expect retribution from their supporters. Some voters may remain loyal to a party regardless of how it behaves. But sufficient numbers of others can be counted on to change their vote and damage the party's electoral chances. Electoral power in a representative democracy requires the harnessing of the party politician's desire for electoral success to serving the interests of the voters. In the end, New Zealand voters generally vote with enough informed flexibility to keep the politicians on their toes. The difference between electoral success and failure may lie in only a small percentage of votes. Politicians and political parties cannot afford to neglect the interests of any significant group in the voting public. All main sections of the plural society can therefore expect to have their interests considered by at least one, if not all, of the political parties.

The major, and worrying exception, is that growing section of the public, the political underclass, who consistently do not vote and whose reactions can therefore be safely ignored by the politicians, particularly when their interests conflict with those of the assiduous voters, such as the middle-aged and elderly members of the Pakeha middle class. For the rest, however, elections are confirmed as the single most important method of exercising political power in a pluralist democracy. The change to MMP, by ending the two-party monopoly of Parliament, has altered the assumptions on which electoral choice and electoral power are based. Elections are no longer competitions between two alternative party governments, one of which forms a government and, in theory at least, can therefore be expected to implement the policies it presented to the electorate. The choice of government and the choice of which major policies it will adopt is now more likely to be a question of post-election negotiation between the parties. To this extent, the new electoral system has reduced the power of voters to determine their government while correspondingly increasing the power of Parliament (Chapter 5: 109). At the same time, it can be argued that the last single-party governments had to some extent abandoned their obligation to enact their election policies and had thus undermined the effect of the voter's choice (Mulgan, 1995). By contrast, the change to multi-party Parliament, by offering the voters a more effective choice of political options and forcing more political negotiation between political parties, may be expected to increase the degree of indirect electoral influence over government decision-makers. This was certainly the expectation not only of those who supported MMP in the 1993 referendum but also of those who opposed it. Opposition to MMP came particularly from members of business elites who feared the damaging economic consequences which would flow from having governments unable to take electorally unpopular decisions. The extent of this electoral power should not be exaggerated. There are many other countervailing influences on politicians which will continue to have an impact, not least the pressures from international financial markets and from the bureaucracy. Even so, no New Zealand government is now able to ignore the views of voters to the same extent as did the Labour and National governments from 1984 to 1993.

Referendums

As well as voting in elections, voters may also have the opportunity to vote in referendums (or 'referenda'), that is on specific questions of policy. One category of referendum is the constitutional referendum, which is one of the methods of changing the 'entrenched' clauses of the Electoral and Constitution Acts (Chapter 3: 52). The most notable such referendum was the 1993 referendum on the electoral system. Constitutional referendums have also been held on extending the term of Parliament from three to four years (Chapter 5: 102). Governments have also in the past occasionally chosen to hold referendums on particular policy issues, such as liquor licensing and gambling, where public feeling is running high and where the government has not wished to provoke internal party divisions by coming down on one side or the other. In these cases, the referendum can be seen as a more democratic version of the parliamentary 'free vote' (Chapter 5: 112) when parties allow their MPs to vote according to their consciences (Mulgan, 1989: 99–102).

Until recently, all referendums were held at the initiative of the government of the day. In 1993, however, the National government honoured an election commitment to introduce a form of citizens-initiated referendum (CIR), by which citizens can petition for a referendum to be held (Citizens Initiated Referenda Act 1993). According to the Act, the precise wording of the question (often a contentious issue) is determined by a parliamentary officer, the Clerk of the House, in consultation with the proposer.

For the referendum to be held, the proposer must secure the signatures of over 10 per cent of registered voters (i.e. 267,000 using the 2002 electoral roll) within a year. The referendum will be indicative rather than binding, i.e. the government will not be obliged to enact the majority's decision. This may seem to be a serious qualification to the voters' democratic power. But it is a reasonable restriction, given the well-known dangers of majority decision-making, especially in relation to minority rights. For instance, a referendum fired by Pakeha anti-Maori sentiment might call on the government to abolish the Waitangi Tribunal or to take some other step obviously directed against Maori rights. In this case a government would be expected to act as a defender of Maori rights and should refuse to allow the measure to proceed.

Up to the end of 2002, 27 petitions had been approved on a wide variety of topics, such as the prohibition of egg production from battery hens, the ending of parole for murderers sentenced to life imprisonment, the prohibition of discrimination and preference on the basis of ethnic origins and the reduction of the size of Parliament under MMP from 120 to 100. All except three petitions have lapsed or been withdrawn through failure of their supporters to gain the requisite number of signatures within the year (Electoral Commission, 2002: 40–42). The first petition to proceed as far as an actual referendum was sponsored by the Firefighters Union and asked the question: 'Should the number of professional firefighters employed full-time in the New Zealand Fire Service be reduced below the number employed on 1 January 1995?' The referendum attracted a turnout of 27.7 per cent of registered voters, a large majority of whom voted in the affirmative. However, the government refused to take any notice of the result, citing the loaded wording of the question, the low level of participation and the general inappropriateness of dealing with a complex issue of industrial relations and budgeting priorities by such a blunt Yes/No question. These are all standard objections to the use of referendums (e.g. Harris, 1992a) and served to discredit the process. Two other referendums were held concurrently with the 1999 general election. One again demanded a reduction in the size of Parliament (to 99 members), the other called for a reform of the justice system to introduce tough sentencing options (Electoral Commission, 2002: 42). Being held on election day ensured a high turnout of 85 per cent. Both proposals secured very strong support but were not directly acted on by subsequent governments, though public opinion was clearly taken into account in later provision for longer sentences for serious criminal acts under new sentencing and parole legislation in 2003.

CIR offers disaffected groups in society the opportunity to force new items on to the political agenda. Given the need to attract over 260,000 signatures, the process is most likely to be used effectively by organised interest groups, particularly 'outsider' groups (Chapter 9: 221) with large memberships which have difficulty in otherwise attracting government attention, or by citizens exploiting a temporarily highly emotional issue. Whether governments do take note will depend on a number of factors, including the size of the turnout and of the majority supporting the proposal, as well as a general judgment on the political advantages and disadvantages of ignoring a popular vote. If referendum decisions are seen as simply a means of interest group protest they are likely to be discounted as no more than one factor which governments should take into account in making their decisions. However, if a referendum is held on an issue which is clearly separable from the mainstream of economic and social policy and if the people appear to speak with a loud and united voice, a government will find the result hard to overlook.

Further reading

Electoral administration
Electoral Commission (1996; 2002).
Voting behaviour and elections
Boston *et al.* (1997; 2000); Gold (1992b); Holland (1992); Levine & McRobie (2002); Levine & Roberts (2003); McRobie (2003); Vowles (1994; 2003); Vowles & Aimer (1993); Vowles *et al.* (1995, 1998, 2002, 2004).
Referendums
Catt (1996, 2003).

Websites: Electoral Commission: <www.elections.org.nz>; New Zealand Election Study: <www.nzes.org>.

12

The Media

The role of the mass media

Communication is an essential part of all political activity, as people exchange information and try to persuade others to their point of view. Within small political groups, such as the Cabinet, Cabinet committees or caucus, such communication is conducted by the circulation of agendas, minutes and discussion papers, supplemented by face-to-face discussion. Within the wider society, when it is a matter of informing and persuading large numbers of people, other methods of communication come into play, such as newspapers, computerised mail, radio and television. These are known as the media of 'mass' communication or 'mass media' or, more commonly, simply 'the media'.

The various sectors of the media are the result of innovations in technology which have been exploited for commercial and political purposes. Printing is a centuries-old process but it was the perfection of high-speed rotary presses in the late nineteenth century which opened the way for the modern mass-produced daily newspaper. Advances in electronic technology brought the telegraphic cable which gave newspapers instant access to news from around the world. This was followed, in the early twentieth century, by the invention of radio and, in the middle of the century, by television. New developments in technology, for instance satellite transmission and computerised information technology, continue to bring changes in the structure of the media, particularly when combined with greater centralisation of ownership and control. Information technology and the opportunities it offers for increased commercial profit are one of the main driving forces behind the increasing globalisation of economics and politics.

In a modern democracy the media have an essential constitutional role. They are the means by which government and citizens communicate. They provide voters with information on which to base their judgements of politicians and policies. In turn, public reaction reflected in the media helps to provide politicians and public servants with feed-back about their performance and to keep them responsive to public opinion. The media are not necessarily just passive means of communication. Ideally, they can also have an active role, providing the information and critical perspectives about policies and policy options to help the citizen to reach independent and well-grounded judgements. This is recognised in the familiar description of the press as 'the fourth estate' (a reference to a pre-modern view of the political community as divided into three sections or 'estates of the realm', the nobility, the clergy and common citizens).

Indeed, the media are more than observers of the political process; they are themselves an integral part of that process. They help to set the agenda of political debate, deciding which issues are given prominence and which overlooked (Leitch, 1992: 50-51). An interview on TV or radio with a minister about a particular issue will often play a vital part in how that issue is decided. It will not be just a report on the discussions leading up to a decision but will itself be part of those very discussions. Indeed, the broadcast media, especially television, have in some respects displaced Parliament as a potential forum of political debate and public scrutiny.

Ideally, according to the principles of democracy in a pluralist society, the media should reflect all values and interests in the community equally. They should provide a forum, or set of forums, in which all competing points of view can be debated and in which everyone can have a fair chance of contributing to the formation of public policy. In practice, as elsewhere in the political system, there are certain interests which are systematically favoured in the media, while others are regularly treated prejudicially.

Television

Politically, the most important medium is television. At present, New Zealand has three main nationwide 'free-to-air' television channels (that is, channels which can be received without cost by any television set), TV1, TV2 and TV3. Of these, TV1 and TV2 are operated by Television New Zealand (TVNZ). Television New Zealand, along with Radio New Zealand, was created in 1988 in place of the former Broadcasting Corporation (BCNZ) which had had responsibility for both public television and public radio and had been required to balance commercial aims with the public interest. While this balance had been retained by Radio New Zealand on the basis of a Charter specifying the company's objectives,

TVNZ operated for fourteen years as a state-owned enterprise (SOE, Chapter 6: 161–2) which required it to operate on commercial principles and return a dividend to the government. However, with the introduction of its own Charter in 2003, TVNZ (like Radio New Zealand) is again enjoined to weigh commercial performance against specified public broadcasting objectives (www.tvnz.co.nz). The third channel, TV3, established in 1989, is privately owned, and now controlled by the Canadian-based company CanWest Global Communications, which also runs C4 (formerly TV4) as a youth music channel and a stable of private radio stations (see below). As well as the main networked channels, a number of regional stations provide limited local or minority interest programmes, for example, Triangle Community TV in the Auckland region. In addition to the free-to-air services, a pay-television service, in which reception of the programmes is confined to subscribers, is provided by Sky Television (NZ) offering a range of channels including overseas news programmes, mainly the 24-hour news programme produced by the United States company CNN (Cable News Network) but also programmes from the BBC (British Broadcasting Corporation).

The state's interest in the electronic media is expressed through the publicly-funded Broadcasting Commission, known as New Zealand On Air. The function of New Zealand On Air is to pursue some of the public-interest objectives previously undertaken by the now-defunct BCNZ, objectives which are not likely to be provided by broadcasting companies run according to strictly commercial imperatives. Thus New Zealand On Air is required to subsidise the extension of television (and radio) reception to the more remote areas It also helps to fund programmes which reflect and develop New Zealand identity and culture, including Maori culture, and has a responsibility to provide for the interests of women, children, persons with disabilities and minorities in the community, including ethnic minorities. To this end, it has subsidised programmes such as the current affairs programme, *Sunday*, the documentary series *Inside NZ* and *Documentary NZ,* the rural magazine programme, *Country Calendar*, the historical series, *The Way We Were*, and the popular 'soap' serial, *Shortland Street*. Part of New Zealand On Air's funds now go directly to the Maori broadcasting agency, Te Mangai Paho, which in turn funds Maori television programmes such as the news programme, *Te Karere*.

Television production is extremely expensive, both in equipment and personnel, and is largely funded from the companies' own commercial operations, particularly from advertising. Apart from pay-television, the number of television stations is thus determined by the level of demand by advertisers for television time. The nature and quality of programmes shown is set by the need to attract as large an audience as possible – the higher the 'ratings' for a particular programme, the more can be charged for showing advertisements which accompany it – at the lowest possible cost. Hence the dependence on imported overseas programmes, which are much cheaper than the equivalent locally produced programmes. Though the television companies can claim that the amount of local content has increased since the deregulation of the industry in 1988, this has largely been through the overall increase in television broadcasting with the advent of TV3. The proportion of total television programming time taken up by locally produced programmes has, in fact, declined over the last fifteen years. The Labour-led coalitions after 1999, however, have attempted to stem this trend by introducing a Charter to TVNZ obliging it to increase the amount of local content programmes, a move which critics saw as being in conflict with the SOE's commercial objectives.

Television contributes to the public life of New Zealand in many ways, by the messages it conveys and the values it projects, not least through the advertisements themselves, which make up a substantial share of air-time (up to fifteen minutes in the hour in prime time). Of particular importance for political communication are the nightly news programmes, especially the early evening news, which is the focal point for television viewing and programming. Also important, though attracting fewer viewers, are the occasional current affairs magazine programmes, such as *Foreign Correspondent* and the former *Sunday* programme. Television also mounts special programmes for major political occasions, such as elections or the annual announcement of the budget. In addition, television advertising is the main medium of mass political persuasion, especially during election campaigns but also at other times, for instance when governments wish to build public support for controversial policies.

Quite apart from the content of television programmes, the very fact that most people spend so much time watching it and rely on it as their main source of political information has had a profound effect on the practice of politics. For instance, because people no longer have to leave their homes to see and hear their political leaders, television has replaced the public meeting as the main forum of political communication. Indeed, during election campaigns, television becomes the main arena in which the parties set out their policies, the leaders debate with one another and the final results are reported and discussed.

Radio

By contrast with television, radio broadcasting is cheaper and more flexible. New Zealand is able to sustain a large number and variety of radio stations, particularly in the major metropolitan areas, where particular stations are targeted at particular sectors of the listening audience ('niches' in the marketing jargon). Listeners in Auckland have around 50 stations to choose among and Wellingtonians over 30. Radio is partly state-owned and partly private. State-owned, public radio is controlled by the state-owned enterprise, New Zealand Public Radio (Radio New Zealand), funded mainly through New Zealand On Air in accordance with government policy conveyed in a 'ministerial directive'. New Zealand Public Radio provides the National and the Concert programmes, both of which broadcast a single nationwide programme on a national network. New Zealand on Air is responsible for the 'AM Network', which broadcasts Parliament and nationwide sports and is available as 'Access Radio' to various community groups. New Zealand on Air also supports two Pacific Island community stations (one in Auckland and one in Wellington) as well as a number of Maori language stations, funded through the Maori broadcasting agency, Te Mangai Paho.

As with television, which developed within the institutional structure designed for radio, the state formerly exercised monopoly ownership and control of radio broadcasting, from the late 1930s to the mid 1960s. But private radio is now well established, with their own national association, the Radio Broadcasters Association, representing approximately 200 radio stations. Private radio was augmented in 1996 by the sale of the former publicly owned commercial 'community' stations. Comprising the second largest radio group in New Zealand, Radio-Works NZ Limited is now owned by CanWest Global Communications. To compete with Radio New Zealand's national news coverage, the private stations support their own national news and sports network through Independent Radio News.

In the broadcasting of news and current affairs, radio operates as a supplement to television. Its major strengths are the immediacy of its news coverage and the fact that people listen to the radio while doing other things, such as driving a car or cooking. While television attracts the mass audience for evening news and for major events such as elections and budgets, radio dominates the early-morning slot. Some of the private stations run informative breakfast programmes, while National Radio's *Morning Report* ishighly influential among policy-makers (Palmer, 1992: 205). Radio's greater flexibility and immediacy allow it to get news to air very quickly and major news stories often break first on the regular hourly news bulletins run by most radio stations, public and private.

Another politically very important aspect of radio broadcasting is talk-back radio, a type of programme where listeners phone in and discuss their opinions on issues of the day with the resident talk-back host or a guest expert (McGregor, 1996). Politics provides much of the subject matter of talk-back radio and politicians are frequent guests on such programmes. Indeed, some politicians, notably the controversial former National minister and later mayor of Auckland City, John Banks (Chapter 4: 89; Chapter 6: 154), have hosted their own talk-back programmes. Talk-back radio provides one of the best indicators of the opinions of disaffected average members of the public, giving an insight into what issues voters may think are particularly important and what aspects of government policy they find particularly troubling.

Newspapers and magazines

The longest-standing medium of mass communication is the newspaper. Newspapers were an integral part of New Zealand's developing political life in the nineteenth century and have remained an essential medium of political communication, as they are in all modern democracies. In contrast to radio and television, newspapers have always been privately owned and controlled. The structure of the newspaper industry has changed greatly, both as a result of technological innovations within the industry itself and in response to competition from the newer rival electronic media of radio and television. Whereas in earlier periods the country could sustain many newspapers with quite small circulations, the high costs of modern printing presses and the commercial advantages available to large-scale publishing businesses have led to a reduction in the number of newspapers and a greater concentration of ownership.

The daily newspaper market is dominated by the metropolitan morning dailies which serve not only their home cities but also their surrounding provincial regions. Largest is Auckland's *New Zealand Herald* with a circulation of over 200,000. The others are the *Dominion-Post* in Wellington, the *Press* in Christchurch and the *Otago Daily Times*. Major provincial centres also support daily newspapers, some of which are morning papers, for instance the *Southland Times* (Invercargill) and the *Daily News* (New Plymouth). Most provincial dailies are evening papers complementing the morning metropolitan paper, for instance the *Waikato Times* (Hamilton) and the *Manawatu Evening Standard* (Palmerston North). Television's dominance over people's evenings, together with reducing use of public transport by daily commuters, has meant that many evening papers have been unable to survive. All four metropolitan areas have lost their evening papers.

Besides the daily press, there are also several national weekly newspapers, including the *National Business Review* and *The Independent* which have an influential readership among the business and political elite. Two Sunday papers are on sale nationally – the *Sunday News* (circulation: 110,000) and the *Sunday Star Times* (circulation: 204,000). There are also many local 'giveaway' papers published once or more a week and distributed free to particular suburbs or localities. Relying largely on material supplied by local organisations and often with minimal editorial content, these 'community' newspapers support themselves solely on the proceeds of advertising aimed at their local market.

The newspaper industry is characterised by local monopoly. Each of the main daily newspapers, both metropolitan and provincial, is well established as the only newspaper serving its market. This is the result of a number of factors, including economies of scale in printing a larger number of copies, the higher advertising charges that can be levied on a larger circulation, and the inability of New Zealand's relatively small population centres to sustain the differentiation between upmarket 'broadsheet' newspapers and mass circulation 'tabloid' newspapers found in larger centres overseas. An attempt in the 1980s to establish an alternative morning paper to the *New Zealand Herald* within the largest market, Auckland, was unsuccessful – the *Sun* was forced to close after less than a year.

Though individual newspapers may attempt to extend their sales into the territory of their neighbouring rivals, they normally prefer to accept the benefits of coexistence and cooperation. All the main papers subscribe to the New Zealand Press Association, a cooperative organisation which allows the individual papers to pool news-gathering resources. News items are routinely exchanged between newspapers and all can benefit from jointly funded Press Association correspondents stationed in Wellington and overseas. At the same time, there has been increasing concentration of newspaper ownership (Molineaux, 1995). The great bulk of the country's major newspapers are now in the hands of just two companies – Wilson and Horton and Independent Newspapers Limited (INL). Between them they control the newspapers read by over 90 per cent of those buying metropolitan newspapers. Wilson and Horton (now controlled by Independent News) own the *New Zealand Herald,* while INL owns the Wellington *Dominion–Post* and the Christchurch *Press.* This leaves the *Otago Daily Times* as the only metropolitan newspaper in independent ownership. Wilson and Horton and INL are also significantly involved in the ownership of provincial newspapers, owning respectively 33 per cent and 53 per cent of the readership. INL also owns both Sunday newspapers.

Consolidation of newspaper ownership has been accompanied by growing overseas control – INL is half-owned by the international media conglomerate, Rupert Murdoch's News Ltd, while Wilson and Horton was taken over in 1995 by Tony O'Reilly's Independent Press. Overseas ownership of the media has been a controversial issue in New Zealand politics. In the 1960s, when the Canadian and British company, Thomson Newspapers, attempted to take over the *Dominion,* the National government of the day passed legislation (the News Media Ownership Act 1965) to uphold the principle that the nation's newspapers should be kept in New Zealand hands. This measure suited the newspaper's owners, who had close links with the government, but it was also supported as a valuable means of protecting New Zealand's political independence. However, as with television, where legislation curbing foreign ownership was altered to allow the sale of TV3, this principle of national media independence has proved to be untenable in the face of increasingly international technology and increasing globalisation of media markets.

While television and radio may offer greater drama and immediacy in the presentation of news, newspapers have the advantage of being able to provide a much broader and more detailed coverage. There is far more information in a daily newspaper than in any radio or television news bulletin. Newspapers can also offer background and interpretation of the news, helping the reader to place the news of the day in a wider context and to reach a more informed judgement of its significance. Newspapers contribute directly to political debate through the writing of 'editorials', articles in which the paper's editor and senior writers anonymously express what is taken as the newspaper's collective opinion on political and other issues. Correspondence columns of letters to the editor offer members of the public an opportunity to express their points of view and to contribute to political debate.

Newspapers provide indispensable information for those seriously engaged in politics, for politicians and their advisers, for members of elites in both the public and the private sector who must interact with government and for those members of the wider public who take an active interest in politics. However, people read newspapers for many different purposes and with differing degrees of thoroughness. For many readers, the main interest may lie in the sports news or the classified advertisements and the political news may be worth only a cursory scanning of the major headlines. For instance, it must be doubted whether many readers actually read a newspaper's editorials with any degree of critical attention. Readership surveys over the last ten years have shown a steady decline in newspaper readership, especially among the young. The trend, however, was halted in 2002, though for how long remains to be seen. As a mass medium of political communication, newspapers have clearly been eclipsed by television and radio. Their specifically political role is directed much more towards the interests of the politically active minority. In this area, however, they play a vital part in informing and stimulating critical public debate on political issues.

Also of relevance for political communication are national magazines which carry news and opinion about political issues. Pride of place for many years belonged to the *Listener,* a weekly magazine published by the former Broadcasting Corporation and reaching a very wide readership (estimated to be 1,337,000 at its height in 1982). However, its circulation has been declining and its role as the leading journal of in-depth political reporting and critical comment has been partly usurped by the newer breed of 'glossy' monthlies, particularly *Metro* and *North and South.* Magazines, too, have been subject to greater concentration of ownership. The *Listener* is now owned by Wilson and Horton, while *Metro* and *North and South* belong to the Australian Kerry Packer's Australian Consolidated Press.

Besides magazines published locally, there are some overseas weeklies which have a small but influential readership among New Zealand decision-makers and business leaders. For instance, the US-based *Time* magazine publishes a New Zealand edition concentrating on international news with a focus on the Asia/Pacific region. The Sydney *Bulletin* incorporates material from *Time*'s US rival, *Newsweek.* The London *Economist,* which is a fervent purveyor of market liberal ideas, has been particularly influential among business people and economic advisers. The *Far Eastern Economic Review* provides news and comments on Asia and the *Guardian Weekly* on world events generally.

Being wholly in private ownership, newspapers and magazines have not been as subject to political control as the electronic media. The main legal constraint on press freedom is the law of defamation which protects individuals against libellous attacks on their reputation. Most newspapers and magazines regularly consult their legal advisers on proposed items which are potentially defamatory and some take out insurance policies to protect them against the high costs of defamation proceedings (Booth, 1992).

Government and the media

The main channel for political news about the government and its activities is the parliamentary press gallery. This is a formal association of journalists who specialise in political reporting and who are accredited to cover the activities of Parliament and ministers. In return for certain privileges, such as access to the MPs' restaurant and bar (Bellamy's), members of the press gallery submit to rules which require the approval of the Speaker (Palmer, 1992: 214). They elect an executive to deal with parliamentary officers on issues such as accommodation. There are approximately 45 fully accredited members of the gallery, from television and radio as well as the print media. About the same number, 48, are associate members, journalists who are not engaged full-time in the political reporting but who have a need for regular access to Parliament and ministers.

Members of the gallery attend ministerial news conferences, and receive press statements issued by ministers and other MPs, both Government and Opposition. When Parliament is in session they attend and report its proceedings. They accompany ministers to outside speaking engagements and on other official occasions. Gallery journalists also talk informally to MPs, hoping to gather inside information about what is going on behind the scenes, for instance evidence of possible policy clashes in the Cabinet or caucus room or grumblings about the parties' leaders. They will report 'leaks', that is, items of confidential political information which are unofficially but deliberately divulged to the media, a technique of attempting to influence public debate which is used by politicians from both sides and also, sometimes, by disaffected public servants.

The relationship of politicians and journalists is a tense and uneasy one, mixing both mutual need and mutual suspicion (Maharey, 1996). Politicians need to communicate with the public and gallery journalists need newsworthy stories and pictures to satisfy their editors and justify their existence. But politicians naturally seek publicity which casts them in a good light and aim to control the media's agenda. Journalists, on the other hand, concentrate on stories which will make arresting headlines, looking particularly for areas of difficulty in policy-making or for political conflicts behind the politicians' facade of confidence and unity.

In this constant battle for supremacy, the government has a natural and decided advantage. For much of the time, the government has the initiative over when and how news of its actions is communicated to the media. A government's activities are inherently of interest to members of the public and will therefore usually be seen by journalists and their editors as newsworthy. The occasion may have been carefully stage-managed for television, with the prime minister in an authoritative setting in his or her office backed by leather-bound law volumes and flanked by flags, or in an outside location, perhaps wearing an engineer's hat or surrounded by smiling children. But any journalist who refused to report an important statement made in such surroundings, or any editor who refused to carry it, would rightly be criticised for preventing the country's leader from communicating with the citizens (Harvey, 1992: 139).

This natural advantage, the government's control over the timing and presentation of its announcements, helps the government to manage the news in its own favour. All politically successful governments pay great attention to media management, to seeking to maintain a favourable media image for themselves while denying their political opponents the chance to make effective criticism. Each minister's personal staff contains at least one full-time press officer and the Prime Minister's Office has several. Government press officers are sometimes assisted by public relations consultants brought in for specific projects, such as a particularly ambitious media campaign, e.g. the Labour Government's selling of its tax reforms, the promotion of Ruth Richardson's first budget in 1991, and the marketing of National's health reforms in 1993. Over $2 million was reported to have been spent on each of the latter campaigns. Political press officers, like most people working in the burgeoning field of public relations, have backgrounds in journalism or in advertising (Atkinson, 1989: 102). They have an intimate knowledge of how the media operate and have many personal contacts among the gallery journalists and other media professionals (Browne, 1996). Indeed, they are often more experienced in political journalism than the journalists they are catering to. Press officers are skilled in presenting the media with material that will match their particular requirements, carefully preparing news statements with a strong story line for the newspapers, and short quotable quotes or 'sound bites' for television and radio. By controlling the timing of announcements they can often outflank their opponents. For instance, they can release items of news just in time for the television evening news, the prime target of all political media attention, but too late for opposition parties to mount an effective reply.

However, in spite of a government's clear advantage in getting its version of events relayed through the media, no government is able to manage the news just as it would wish. For instance, while news items themselves may be presented very much in the government's own terms, there are other media occasions, such as the *Holmes* show on TV1 or National Radio's *Morning Report*, when ministers can expect to face critical questioning. They may also be required to debate an issue with their critics. In order to achieve balance between opposing points of view, the media regularly offer equal space or air-time to the government's opponents, either the opposition parties or some disgruntled interest group. On such occasions, ministers will have to answer for themselves and any weaknesses in the case they are making or in their own general abilities may be ruthlessly exposed. Such programmes, like parliamentary questions and debates, can provide genuine opportunities for public scrutiny of government performance. Indeed, given the much wider audience that television commands, it can be argued that a programme such as *Holmes* has replaced question time in Parliament as the major forum of public scrutiny and accountability.

The government's critics also have their own direct access to the media, apart from formally structured media debates. The major opposition parties have their own press officers who issue their own press statements and create photo opportunities for their leaders. They may have less easy access to media coverage than the government, being seen by the media as intrinsically less newsworthy, but they will not be totally neglected, particularly as a potential source of controversy. Opposition evidence of scandalous behaviour by government members or of divisions within the government ranks will be particularly interesting to journalists and their editors. For this reason, the media will also usually give prominence to news items from disaffected members of the government who disagree with their own party's policies or express lack of confidence in the leadership.

A notable example is the former National MP, and later leader of the New Zealand First party, Winston Peters, who skilfully exploited the media's interest in government disunity to gain publicity for himself and achieve high rankings in public opinion polls. The polls themselves also provide regular opportunities for independent assessment of the government's performance. Each month, various news media publish the results of the latest opinion polls which they have commissioned. The polls ask a random sample of voters how they would have voted if an election had been held at that time and which politician they would prefer to see as prime minister. When reporting the poll results, journalists can comment on how the electorate is viewing the government and the opposition parties and on the prime minister's and other leaders' personal standing with the public.

Governments face potential opposition in the media not only from their political opponents in Parliament but also from other interested groups in the community. Most of the major interest groups employ public relations staff who aim to attract favourable media attention. When government policies threaten their interests, they issue their own press statements which they hope the media will report. The more powerful 'insider' groups, such as Federated Farmers or the Business Roundtable (Chapter 9: 218–19), can usually expect to be reported. Others may have to resort to more dramatic photo opportunities, such as public demonstrations, in order to attract the attention of the news cameras and reporters. But they can still cause political embarrassment for a government and cast ministers in an unfavourable light. Perhaps the most successful media influence, because the least obvious, comes from financial interests, particularly banks. Economists employed by banks are regularly used by the media to provide expert comment on the government's economic performance. Their remarks are presented as if they were independent commentary, but they tend, not surprisingly, to be in the general interest of banks and their shareholders.

A government's attempt to manage the news faces possible criticism and even hostility from members of the media themselves. Press gallery journalists will often inject a note of cynical criticism into their reports of stage-managed news. Governments can expect to be taken to task in newspaper editorials. They will also be the target of comic and often hurtful lampooning by cartoonists and satirical television shows. Much of this criticism is even-handed, aimed at the government of the day, whichever party is in power. The press has a tradition of critical scrutiny towards politicians, a tradition which reflects a healthy democratic scepticism towards people in authority.

On occasion, however, sections of the media will take a more clearly partisan approach, in favour of one party and against another. For instance, most newspapers and their proprietors have been opposed to trade unionism and therefore to Labour governments, at least until the Fourth Labour government. This bias was shown not just in editorials but also in the way news reporting was slanted. In the 1980s, the media were largely in favour of Labour's economic reforms and many journalists joined in uncritical adulation of Roger Douglas and his ideas. When the split appeared between Lange and Douglas, newspapers such as the *New Zealand Herald* and the *National Business Review* clearly supported Douglas against the prime minister. Indeed, from the resignation of Douglas until the eventual defeat of Labour in 1990, the media were on the whole negative towards Labour's leaders (Lange, Palmer and Moore). Since then they have returned to a less obviously partisan approach, though they remain generally sympathetic to the restructuring policies of first Labour and then National and critical of the economic policies of the Alliance, Greens and New Zealand First parties in so far as they depart from the general direction established during the 1980s and 1990s.

Media bias

How much influence do the media actually exercise? The general issue of the political power of the media, especially television, is a matter of considerable controversy and academic debate (Rudd, 1993). Does media bias in favour of a particular party or interest increase the actual political power of that party or interest? Do people take their political values from television and the other media? Or do their own values, independently gained from other sources such as family and friends, determine how they perceive the media and therefore neutralise any potential media effects? The same arguments that surround the issue of censorship – for instance, whether media depiction of socially undesirable activities such as violence encourages people to act violently – also occur in debates about the political effects of the media.

Research suggests that the answer is complex. The media are neither all-powerful nor totally powerless. Certainly, as far as general political values and attitudes are concerned, other social institutions, such as the family and the workplace, have an important determining role. Though the media may have what theorists of structural dominance describe as a 'hegemonic' role in reinforcing dominant ideologies of class, gender and ethnicity, the influence of such social factors is likely to be conveyed as much through immediate personal contacts as through the mass media. Research on voting behaviour suggests that the main effect of the media is to confirm and reinforce people's party partisanship rather than to change it. Those who pay most attention to news programmes are people with already strongly formed political convictions which are unlikely to be changed by what they read, see or hear (Leitch, 1992: 50–52). Recent evidence of the limits of media influence in New Zealand can be drawn from the relative failure of some expensive media advertising campaigns. The National Government's attempt to sell its controversial health reforms appears to have done little to encourage public confidence in the policies. (Atkinson, 1994a: 212). The anti-MMP organisation, the Campaign for Better Government, though it greatly outspent the pro-MMP Coalition for Electoral Reform (Jackson & McRobie, 1998: 190-2; Levine & Roberts, 1994: 14; Vowles, 1995: 106), was unsuccessful in preventing the change to MMP.

On the other hand, the theory that the media audience engages with media messages without being affected by them is undoubtedly overstated (Atkinson, 1994). The declining political influence of class and decreasing levels of political partisanship (Chapter 11) may leave greater room for the media to affect the substance as well as the strength of people's political opinions. This effect may be especially evident in election campaigns (Banducci & Vowles, 2002: Chapter 3). The media's undoubted power to set the agenda of political debate may itself have an effect on political outcomes, just as the range of political alternatives presented in the media may affect the policy options considered by decision makers. The extent of political bias in the media is therefore an issue of considerable significance in assessing the distribution of power.

The positive aspects of the New Zealand media's performance should not be underestimated. Governments do not exercise overt censorship of the press, as they do in many other countries. Indeed, radio and television are much less subject to direct political control than they were previously, particularly when public broadcasting was administered like a normal government department responsible to a minister of broadcasting. Many journalists do a conscientious job, reporting what they see and hear accurately and fairly (Tully, 1992). New Zealand has not yet witnessed the excesses of tabloid 'cheque-book' journalism, with rival newspapers vying for the most sensational news stories. Indeed, most newspapers use their monopoly position in their market to provide a reasonable standard of journalism, without descending to the lowest common denominator of prejudice and tastelessness. On television and radio, a few interviewers are capable of asking pertinent and penetrating questions of politicians. Newspapers and radio offer useful opportunities for members of the public to express their political opinions. In general, most media professionals can honestly claim to be serving the public's interest in providing impartial information and keeping authorities under scrutiny.

None the less, a number of weaknesses and inequalities must be recognised. The power of governments to manage the news in their own interests has already been noted, as has the similar power of other economically powerful sectors which have the capacity to purchase media expertise. Indeed, the systematic political advantage exercised by wealthy and well-established interest groups (Chapter 9) is closely connected with their ability to obtain favourable media coverage. The advantage available to those who can produce their own professional news statements and media events is facilitated by the relatively restricted resources available to the New Zealand media. The small size of New Zealand's population and of its media market cannot readily sustain the number and quality of journalists necessary for the media to perform a sufficiently independent and critical role. 'Investigative' journalism, where a journalist is allowed to concentrate on one story for weeks, even months, is a luxury that few, if any, New Zealand newspapers can afford, or are prepared to afford. Harried journalists, required to cover a wide range of policy areas and to satisfy their editors with a constant flow of stories, will gratefully and uncritically accept press statements prepared for them by public relations professionals (Dyer, 1994: 178).

Media criticism of governments may also be muted as a result of informal pressure brought to bear either on individual journalists or on their employers. Public broadcasters, being subject to ultimate legislative control and public funding through ministerial directive, are vulnerable to government pressure. Robert Muldoon was a notorious intimidator of journalists, refusing access to those he considered particularly critical. In 1993, the minister responsible for TVNZ and Radio NZ summoned the chief executive of Radio NZ and complained about supposed anti-government bias on the influential *Morning Report*. One of the presenters was subsequently replaced.

New Zealand's defamation laws, which are aimed at protecting the reputation of individual citizens against false and damaging accusations, work overwhelmingly to the advantage of the wealthy. Court proceedings are extremely expensive and only those with considerable wealth behind them can afford to instigate them. From the media's point of view, even a successful defence against a charge of defamation can be very costly. Not surprisingly, therefore, most editors and media managers play safe, avoiding the risk of offending the wealthy, even when an important issue of public interest is at stake (Booth, 1992). Caution among newspaper proprietors about publishing potentially defamatory material is also reinforced by general habits of conservative deference to established authorities and institutions (Butterworth, 1989).

The media bias in favour of the economically powerful is not just a matter of the superior resources and expertise available to wealthy groups and individuals. It is also a result of the economic and social environment within which the media operate. The need to make a profit, by maximising returns from advertising and sponsorship while minimising production costs, permeates all sectors of the media (Wood & Maharey, 1994). With the exception of public radio, all media outlets are required to return a profit for their owners, either private corporate owners, in the case of newspapers, TV3 and private radio, or the government, in the case of TVNZ. Even the non-commercial public radio stations, the National Programme and the Concert Programme, have been subject to regular cost cutting and cannot afford to ignore their audience ratings if they wish to maintain government support via New Zealand on Air.

The need to keep costs as low as possible helps to prevent the news media from adopting a sufficiently independent and critical stance. Particularly in television, where production costs are so high, it is usually cheaper to rely on imported programmes or simply respond uncritically to media initiatives from government or other established institutions. At the same time, the need to expand market share, in the sense of maximising the number of consumers, also influences the style and content of news reporting. The journalists' sense of what is newsworthy, for instance, their preference for news about crises, conflicts and personalities, depends on judgements about what the public will find interesting. The effects of commercialism and of pursuing the maximum possible audience are particularly evident in television news and current affairs. Television, as a primarily visual medium, lends itself particularly to the conveying of dramatic, immediate images rather than general or abstract ideas. 'Good' television tends to concentrate on non-verbal messages, making its impact through visually striking events and personalities rather than through discussion of issues. Spectacular disasters and violent crimes are more newsworthy than new economic or social policies (Atkinson, 1989: 95–100). Attracting the maximum audience for early evening news programmes is pivotal to commercial success for television companies. Viewers prefer a style of presentation which emphasises the personalities of the individual newsreaders. The most popular presenters take on the characteristics of comfortable family friends, offering their own reassuring gloss to the day's events – the 'cootchie-coo news' (Edwards, 1992).

The atmosphere of uncritical self-congratulation is increased by the use of sponsorship in connection with televised sports. Repeated advertisements or 'promos' for the sponsored events celebrate the sponsor's logo and products in a context of jingoistic fervour. They infect the news programmes which report the events with the same spirit of complacent boosterism. Even where prime-time television attempts critical discussion and debate, as for instance on *Holmes*, the demands of entertainment often impair the satisfactory treatment of complex issues. The premium is on dogmatic opinion and confrontation, compressed between commercial breaks.

Television's trivialisation of news, it should be noted, is not universally welcomed by the politicians or other decision-makers, many of whom complain about the medium's obsession with images, personalities and crime and bemoan the difficulty of discussing serious issues of policy (Moore, 1992; Palmer, 1992: 217–18; Palmer, 1996). None the less, the effect of such trivialisation and commercialisation works generally in their favour, or at least in favour of the more powerfully entrenched interests in society. By distracting the mass of voters from the serious political issues of the day, television helps to ensure that the underlying distribution of economic and political power is relatively unquestioned and that many important political issues are not subject to the degree of public debate and scrutiny that they deserve.

Television, as a medium forced to pursue a mass audience, also contributes to the continuing marginalisation of minority interests. Particularly significant in this respect is television's poor record in relation to Maori broadcasting in comparison with the relative success of Maori radio stations (Fox, 1992). Maori viewers are too small a section of the population to sustain a commercially viable audience for Maori-focused programmes, including Maori language programmes. If New Zealand is serious about biculturalism, Maori language and culture need to be recognised as a vital part of the nation's life. TVNZ, with the support of subsidies from New Zealand On Air, makes some gestures in this direction, with Maori news and magazine programmes. But these are inadequate in their scope and timing, usually being rele-gated to off-peak hours. There is a strong case for having at least one television channel devoted wholly to Maori and Maori interests and publicly funded like the various Maori radio stations. The Labour–Alliance coalition moved in this direction in 2000, announcing the establishment of a Maori Television Service. The proposal ran into a range of difficulties of personnel, delays in going to air and considerable public scepticism, all of which demonstrated the political as well as the financial costs of achieving the objective.

Media bias in favour of some groups and against others is a result not just of commercial pressures, but of pervasive social values and assumptions which the media reflect and reinforce. For instance, spokespersons from well-established interests are considered to have a legitimate claim to speak and be heard. Those speaking on behalf of financial institutions are treated as neutral and authoritative commentators. In contrast, those from exploited and marginalised sections of society, for instance the more radical trade unionists, the unemployed, beneficiaries, Maori and Pacific Island activists, are less likely to have their opinions regularly sought out or listened to seriously. True, they may gain attention through spectacular acts of protest, by taking to the streets or disrupting public occasions. But such actions, though they may eventually bring important issues on to the political agenda (Chapter 9), are also damaging in that they reinforce the stereotypical view of these groups as illegitimate and disruptive (Leitch, 1992a: 158).

It has been argued that the whole ethos of impartial, balanced news is itself a conservative ethos which works to protect the position of established groups, while excluding others. The pursuit of balance, it is claimed, encourages journalists to seek the views of legitimised spokespersons, giving them equal time in relation to each other, while taking for granted the exclusion of other interests and the more radical values they represent. That is, the concepts of objectivity and impartiality operate within a set of assumptions which support the existing distribution of political power. This insight, that there is no totally value-free or objective journalism, has been used to justify the so-called 'new journalism', which makes no pretence to be balanced and is openly partisan. On the whole, however, most journalists reject such blurring of fact and opinion as even more distorting than so-called objective journalism (Harvey, 1992; Tully 1992). They see the public interest as being served by reporting which attempts to describe events accurately and unemotively, while also presenting a range of possible opinions on these events.

Attempts to safeguard such standards are made by various scrutinising bodies. The New Zealand Press Council hears complaints from the public about unsatisfactory conduct by newspapers such as biased or inaccurate reporting. The Council, established by the industry itself, consists of six members representing the public, including an independent chairperson who is usually a retired judge, and five media representatives, including two representatives of the newspaper publishers, two representatives of the journalists' union and one member representing magazines. The Council issues decisions on complaints and requires the newspaper concerned to publish them, but, beyond the adverse publicity which attends a successful complaint, has no power to enforce sanctions against offending publishers. Television and radio are covered by the Broadcasting Standards Authority, established as a result of the restructuring of broadcasting in 1988, which is concerned with matters such as the accuracy of reporting, the protection of children, the portrayal of violence and the advertising of liquor. It hears complaints from the public and can make recommendations and impose penalties on broadcasters. The Advertising Standards Authority hears complaints about misleading advertisements.

The standards implicit in the concepts of objectivity, accuracy, impartiality and balance, are not lightly to be abandoned. Indeed, the watchdog bodies may be justly criticised for not doing more to uphold them. At the same time, these standards do not deal with all aspects of bias in the media. The journalists' views of how the news should be presented, whose opinions are worth soliciting and generally what counts as being 'newsworthy', operate as an important set of filters controlling the content of the news media. For the most part, news which survives such filters tends to echo, and therefore maintain, the existing political structure and distribution of power.

In general, then, New Zealand's mass media, while displaying certain undoubted strengths, fail to give fair and accurate coverage to all values and interests in the community and do not adequately perform the informing and critical functions implicit in their claim to be the 'fourth estate' of a modern democracy. Critical commentators on the media, seeking explanations for these deficiencies, often point to trends in the ownership of the media, for instance increasing private ownership of radio and television, increasing concentration of ownership of newspapers and increasing overseas ownership of both newspapers and television (Leitch, 1992; McGregor, 1992). But ownership itself, whether public or private, local or foreign, dispersed or concentrated, may not be the main factor. There are privately owned newspapers and magazines which perform an excellent public service while returning a profit to their owners. Conversely, public ownership is no guarantee of a fearlessly critical or unbiased stance, as was clear when New Zealand radio was under direct ministerial control. There is no obvious evidence that television companies or newspapers under substantial foreign ownership (e.g. TV3 or the *Dominion-Post)* are less locally oriented in their news and other programming than their locally owned counterparts (e.g. TVNZ and the *Otago Daily Times).*

More significant than specific ownership of the media is the context within which the media must operate. The incentives provided for the New Zealand media are not conducive to the satisfactory performance of their public democratic functions. While the print media and radio (through public radio) may provide information and critical analysis for the politically active and educated elites, they do little to inform and empower the average voter. The only medium of truly mass political communication which covers the bulk of the voting public is television. Television news and current affairs are as central to our democratic system as Parliament itself. However, commercial imperatives have clearly induced television to fail in its broader public role of helping to educate the public and encouraging them to play a greater role in calling their governments to account. Thus, by catering for elites and distracting the average voter, the media as a whole contribute significantly to structures of political inequality.

Further reading

History of the New Zealand media
Butterworth (1989); Cocker (1994); Cocker (2003); Henderson & Bellamy (2002): 93–8.
Information technology and public relations
Atkinson (1989).
Political role of the New Zealand media
Atkinson (1994); Atkinson (1997); Atkinson (2003); Atkinson (2004); Hayward & Rudd (2000); Hayward & Rudd (2002); Hope (2003); Leitch (1992; 1992a); Palmer & Palmer (1997): 194–8; Wood and Maharey (1994).

Websites
New Zealand On Air: www.nzonair.govt.nz
Television NZ: www.tvnz.co.nz
Radio New Zealand: www.radionz.co.nz

13

Pluralist Democracy under Strain

The complexity of political power

This chapter draws together a number of general themes which have arisen during the more detailed analysis of the different aspects of the political system. One such theme is the complexity of the political process and the variety of influences brought to bear on decision-makers. The central focus of decision-making, in New Zealand's system of parliamentary government, is the Cabinet and Parliament, though, it is to be remembered, the courts have an occasional part to play on certain significant issues and local government routinely decides a whole range of socially important, if politically uncontroversial matters.

When the ministers of the Cabinet meet to decide a major issue, they do not do so in isolation but rather at the centre of an array of pressures, many of which have been described in previous chapters. Policy options for the Cabinet will have been drafted by public servants and will contain some input from one or more government departments. In considering the options before them, the ministers will have to be aware that their decision must run the gamut of parliamentary questioning and debate. If the policy requires legislation for its enactment, this almost certainly means scrutiny not just before the full House of Representatives, but also in a select committee, a stage which will allow all the various organised groups with an interest in the issue to make submissions and mount opposition. If the issue has economic repercussions its likely effect on the economy and business confidence will need to be assessed.

The issue may also arouse the interest of the ministers' party supporters, both in caucus and in the country at large, and may even be of sufficient consequence to have a foreseeable effect on the party's electoral fortunes. Personal factors may also be at stake if individual politicians, keen to advance their own careers or thwart those of their rivals, invest their personal ambition in an issue. At every stage the media can be expected to show an interest in aspects of the decision which they think their audiences will find particularly newsworthy.

Each of these participants in the political process interacts not only with the decision-makers at the centre but also with one another. Thus interest groups liaise constantly with relevant sections of the public service and with members of political parties, for instance with appropriate caucus committees (Chapter 9: 225). Senior members of the public service, though necessarily cautious about showing disloyalty to their ministers and thus breaching the principles of political neutrality and ministerial responsibility (Chapter 6: 148–58), keep in regular informal contact with politicians of all parties as well as with influential representatives of the private sector. Journalists, who are trying to find the news, and public relations consultants, who are trying to shape it (Chapter 12: 299), facilitate the exchange of information and the communication of influence.

Though Cabinet may be conveniently seen as the apex of this decision-making process, as the final point at which most major decisions are ultimately taken, the process itself does not have a starting-point or end-point but is best visualised as an interlocking system of continuous interaction both between the state and the wider society and within the state itself. Not only is New Zealand society a plural society but the state itself is also a plural state with many different sections each with its own distinctive clientele and agenda. Within the political system, no single group or institution is in control and few groups or institutions are without some degree of influence on some issues. This does not mean that some groups or interests are not more powerful than others or that there are no systematic biases within the system. But no group or section has all the influence.

This is the fundamental assumption of the pluralist theory of the state (Chapter 1: 9–10). To seek for the ultimate source of political control, for instance in some particular class or some elite network, is an illusory quest. Whichever group is selected as a potential candidate for such ultimate control, whether the Cabinet itself, or the capitalist class identified by marxists or the big business cabal singled out by anti-elitist populists such as Winston Peters, such a group will always turn out itself to be subject to pressures and constraints from elsewhere in society as well as having its own internal conflicts and differences of political opinion.

For a pluralist, the key to analysing political power is to recognise that there is no single key. Each aspect of policy-making needs to be studied independently in the expectation that different types of policy issue affect different sectors of state and society and give rise to different patterns of political interest. A general study of politically relevant institutions, such as that given in this book needs to be supplemented by case studies examining particular issues or policy sectors. However, by way of conclusion to this introductory overview of the New Zealand political system, a few cross-sectoral generalisations may be made, illustrating the different facets of influence and power at work in a pluralist democracy (Chapter 1: 14–16).

Many matters in politics are relatively uncontroversial and will require little discussion or consultation. For instance routine administrative matters within a government department, such as how to collect a particular tax or how to reimburse school boards of trustees for school running expenses, may be settled within the government department concerned without even getting as far as the minister. Again, when governments are called to make political appointments to statutory authorities, discussion will normally be kept within the confines of government MPs, with caucus making the final decision. Such issues may well be the subject of disagreement and debate but the argument will not extend beyond a relatively restricted circle of people. Some issues, however, might appear to be routine but become politically controversial, issues such as the subsidising of rural postal services or the bulk funding of teachers' salaries, which were the subject of political conflict under the Bolger National Government. Major interest groups become involved with attendant media publicity and caucus pressure.

The same occurs in those areas where there are well-defined 'policy communities' consisting of the relevant politicians, bureaucrats and interest groups in a particular sector, for instance agriculture, health or transport (Chapter 9: 222). Many issues will be dealt with as part of the normal steady flow of business discussed between the minister, senior public servants in the minister's department and leaders of well-established interest groups. On the other hand, occasional issues will become more politically contentious and require wider discussion.

But even when discussion is confined to a relatively few political actors within one clearly defined sector of the state, political power and influence are not so limited. Always present, at least potentially, is the power of 'anticipated reactions' (Chapter 1: 15), whereby decision-makers act in ways designed to avoid adverse reactions from others. In departments of the public service, for example, individual public servants will prefer certain options and rule out others in order to avoid controversy and political difficulty with superiors. This applies not only to junior public servants in relation to their section managers but also to chief executives in relation to their ministers and to ministers in relation to the prime minister and Cabinet colleagues. Some participants in the policy process may occasionally wish to provoke conflict in order to advance either themselves or their point of view. But, for the most part, people working in large organisations have an interest in maintaining smooth and uncomplicated relations with those with whom they must work, particularly with their immediate superiors on whom their personal advancement depends. These indirect influences from above can be particularly effective in the bureaucratic organisations of the public service, where they are linked to a professional ethic that it is the duty of public servants to carry out the policies of an elected government (Chapter 6: 161).

Thus the fact that open political controversy and conflict may be avoided does not rule out the possibility that interests may have clashed and that the policy preferences of one group may have prevailed over others. The power of anticipated reactions is found at all points in the political process, from the decisions taken by minor public servants or in a caucus committee to those taken round the Cabinet table itself. Indeed, at the level of Cabinet, anticipated reactions are the major constraining forces which severely restrict what would otherwise be almost unlimited executive power. For instance, one pressure which dominates much ministerial decision-making derives from the electoral motive (Chapter 11: 267), the desire of members of the elected government to enhance their popularity and improve their chances at the next election. The power of this motive varies with different issues, some having more likely electoral impact than others. The proximity to the next election may make a difference, as politicians are more likely to risk short-term unpopularity if the election is still some time away. The indirect pressure which the prospect of facing elections place on politicians is the single most important type of influence which the voters exert on elected governments, more influential than the simple act of voting every three years might suggest.

Another potent source of the power of anticipated reactions is the response of the business sector to government economic decisions. Those who make the key decisions relating to business investment have the power, collectively, to make or break a government. The government's popularity depends heavily on the performance of the national economy, which in turn depends on the level of economic activity in the private sector. A buoyant private sector requires that investors have confidence that they will receive a good return on investments. The level of this confidence depends on many factors, including the trends in the world economy which are beyond the control of New Zealand and its government. But one critical factor is whether business leaders and investors consider that the government is taking the right decisions in terms of its management of the economy, for instance in the levels of government expenditure and taxation. Any government which wishes to maintain a prosperous economy must therefore give especial weight to the likely reactions of business investors to its decisions (e.g. Richardson, 1995: 115, 141).

Some of these indirect influences on decision-makers may count as 'structural constraints' (Chapter 1: 15), in the sense that they depend less on the conscious intentions to exercise power on the part of any of the people involved and more on the structure of the institutions themselves and on the values of those that operate within them. Thus bureaucratic decisions which anticipate the minister's policy preferences may be analysed as resulting from the hierarchical structure common in most large-scale organisations and from the professional ethos that public servants owe a constitutional duty to elected ministers and their government.

Similarly, a Cabinet decision in favour of decisions which enhance the government's electoral chances may not be taken consciously for that reason but may simply be due to the structure of the party in Parliament which requires ministers to consult with their caucuses. Caucuses have acted as an institutional constraint on Cabinets forcing them to take more notice of the electoral effect of decisions than they might otherwise have done (Chapter 5: 115–7). Again, the extent to which economic policy favours the interests of investors is heavily influenced by structural factors, such as the decreasing capacity of governments to control national economies dependent on international financial investment and the privileged position of Treasury in relation to other departments in the public service (Chapter 6: 142). Indeed, the power of investors and markets generally, pervasive though it may be, is hard to locate precisely in any one group of people. Much of the money invested on the stock market, for instance, belongs to pension and other endowment funds which are managed on behalf of millions of small investors seeking a competitive return on their regular contributions. In such circumstances it is easier to identify the political effects of markets, seen as impersonal structures, rather than the power of groups of individual investors or capitalists.

Indirect political influences such as anticipated reactions and structural constraints are not only important factors in explaining why certain issues are decided one way rather than another. They also help to explain why other issues never even reach the point of decision because they never get on to the political agenda in the first place. Whole ranges of possible options are excluded because they are seen as politically impossible. For example, more extreme market liberals may wish to remove the unemployment benefit entirely as a means of further reducing government expenditure and exerting downward pressure on wage rates. However, this would be ruled out by politicians as electoral suicide and would therefore never be put forward as a serious option. Similarly, while many social democrats may wish to see public expenditure on health and education greatly increased, major growth in the overall level of government expenditure is kept off the agenda by the fear of adverse market reaction. Increased expenditure means either higher taxation or a greater budget deficit, both of which threaten the value of investments held in New Zealand. They are likely to prompt a flight of capital from New Zealand, a fall in the value of the dollar and loss of business confidence. Thus, investors able to move their funds in and out of New Zealand, like the New Zealand voters themselves, also set limits to the economic policy options which governments can begin to consider seriously.

Economic and political power

Issues of political power, both direct and indirect, and the structural constraints on decision-making raise the question of the inequality of power in New Zealand's pluralist democracy. Democratic values would require that all sections of the plural society should have their interests met equally by the political system (Chapter 1: 17). This does not mean that every group would have the same degree of influence regardless of size. Democratic principle requires that each person should count equally. For instance, few New Zealanders would seriously maintain that South Islanders should have as much political influence as North Islanders, given the much larger population of the

North Island. As different groups in the plural society are of different sizes and have a different stake in different issues, pluralist democracy should be taken to imply that each group should have power in proportion to its size and the extent to which its members are affected by the issue in question (Mulgan, 1989: 23–34).

How well does New Zealand's pluralist democracy measure up to these standards? One theme which has recurred throughout this study has been the persistently privileged position of business interests, or more precisely, the interests of business investors and of those who manage their investments. This power appears most obviously in those aspects of the political system where the ability to wield influence depends on the capacity to purchase the means of influence. Interest groups representing the more wealthy sections of society can sustain larger permanent secretariats providing a superior quality of research and more effective public relations (Chapter 9: 230). The wealthy are more able to avail themselves of the protection of the courts (Chapter 7: 168), including defence against possible defamation (Chapter 12: 303). Individual businesses and business leaders contribute disproportionately to political parties and thus buy access to leading politicians (Chapter 10: 255). One millionaire, Robert Jones, was even able to found and fund his own political party, the New Zealand Party. This party had a decisive effect on the 1984 election and the defeat of Robert Muldoon. It also heralded the introduction of market liberal ideas into the mainstream of New Zealand politics. Another wealthy businessman, Peter Shirtcliffe, Chairman of Telecom New Zealand, was able to use his own money to found the anti-MMP Campaign for Better Government (Chapter 12: 302). Members of the Business Roundtable and other wealthy individuals gave generously to ACT (the Association of Consumers and Taxpayers), allowing it to make a particularly effective electoral impact.

But the political power of wealth does not rely simply, or even largely, on the direct purchase of political influence. Local government, for instance, is biased in favour of the interests of the wealthier sections of local communities because of the type of person attracted to elected office, the low level of political controversy surrounding its decisions and its critical dependence on property values and property taxes ('rates') for its finances (Chapter 8). At the level of central government, the priority given to business interests depends more on their critical role in the national economy, which gives great political leverage to those who claim to represent the interests of investors.

The superior power of major economic sectors is nothing new. Farmers, for instance, who have for so long contributed greatly to New Zealand's prosperity, have always exercised political influence out of proportion to their numbers. But the extent of economic influence has increased as a result of the process of financial deregulation and state restructuring undertaken since the mid 1980s. This led to a shift in the balance between political and economic power, with governments being able to exercise less control over the economy and economic interests having greater power to influence the state.

One aspect of this change is the shrinking role of the state itself, the extent to which the state has been 'decoupled' from previously important areas of economic activity. The process of corporatising government departments and then privatising the corporations had the effect of removing political control over many major areas of the economy (Chapter 6: 142). Politicians could no longer hope to exercise influence over services such as post-office banking and telephones, or public transport by rail, sea and air as well as by local bus services (Chapter 6: 162; Chapter 8: 197). In health, the abolition of locally elected hospital boards and the creation of independent Regional Health Authorities had the effect of reducing the political accountability of public hospitals (Chapter 6: 165), a trend which the subsequent Labour–Alliance government sought to reverse with the creation of elected District Health Boards.

While management by public service bureaucrats responsible to elected politicians may not have encouraged the economically efficient provision of services to the public, political control did allow state enterprises to pursue broader social objectives, such as providing employment, maintaining a common level of service in sparsely populated rural areas and sustaining otherwise economically depressed regions. In so far as these enterprises are now wholly in the private sector and free from government direction, this has lessened the political influence of those sectors of society who were previously able to pressure politicians to direct these publicly owned services to non-commercial purposes. Moreover, the reduction of direct ministerial responsibility has deprived members of the public of an effective means of redress when public officials or agencies behave unacceptably. The capacity of governments to control the economy has also been reduced by the removal of import quotas and foreign exchange controls as part of economic deregulation.

These moves, as their advocates claimed, may have reduced the capacity for powerful economic sectors to lobby governments in pursuit of special favours. At the same time, however, they lessened the state's capacity to redistribute wealth in favour of those economically disadvantaged by the free play of market forces. Weaker interests are less able to use the government as a means of 'countervailing power' to counter-balance the already economically privileged (Chapter 9: 231–2). Governments have also deliberately limited their own power to respond to economic interests opposed to those represented by investors in financial markets. The Reserve Bank Act 1989 separated the Bank from political influence and made it concerned solely with price stability and the control of inflation. The Fiscal Responsibility Act 1994 establishes certain principles of 'responsible' fiscal (budgetary) management, for instance maintaining a 'prudent' level of public debt and, if necessary, operating budget surpluses to achieve such a level (Boston *et al.*, 1996: 284–6). Though the Act allows a government to depart temporarily from such principles, provided that it gives a justification for doing so, the intention is that governments will be kept in line by fear of the adverse market reactions which would follow any open breach of fiscal 'responsibility'.

A major factor in the increasing political power of financial interests is the greater mobility of capital. Investments held in the form of transferable funds can now be moved in and out of the country much more readily on a daily, even, hourly, basis. Such movement critically affects the value of the New Zealand dollar and also interest rates, both of which are key components of any government's economic strategy. Those who control such investment have a much more immediate and effective sanction than others whose investment is more permanently rooted in the country. Farmers, for instance, are normally committed to their land and their whole way of life as New Zealand farmers. If they do not like a government's policies, they can threaten the government with loss of export income and even the occasional boycott. But they cannot realistically threaten to transfer their farms to another country. Even if they wished to sell up and take their capital overseas, such a move would take time and would be very costly. Governments can thus afford to risk alienating farmers, at least in the short term, a factor which reduces farmers' political bargaining power in comparison with that of international financiers.

Similar considerations apply to manufacturing companies, particularly those owned by New Zealanders, who are more likely to wish to keep their investment in New Zealand. By comparison, overseas-owned manufacturing companies are more likely to move to another country. Indeed, multi-national manufacturers routinely seek to locate their factories in countries with the most economically favourable conditions in terms of wage rates, skills levels, proximity to markets, political stability, and so on. Multi-national companies can therefore exert more political leverage on domestic governments than can local manufacturers. But even they face considerable transaction costs in moving their investment from one country to another compared with financial investors who can leave one day and return the next.

The financial markets, particularly the foreign exchange market, have thus become a central participant in government decision-making. They also affect the political options available to the voting public. For instance, during 1993–6, because the Alliance and New Zealand First parties were in favour of reversing some of the policies of economic restructuring and were prospective coalition partners in a post-1996 government, increases in public support for these parties and for their leaders, Jim Anderton and Winston Peters, often led to falls in the value of the New Zealand dollar. As the election drew nearer, both parties were forced to modify their policies in order to placate investor confidence. The power of the markets is by no means even-handedly directed at the interests of all the people. Some of their concerns, such as aggregate economic growth, may be generally supported by many sections of society. But other goals are more restricted in their benefits. In particular, the financial markets, as representative of those who wish to receive a good return on their investments in New Zealand, naturally emphasise the value of controlling government expenditure and thus limiting taxation, especially direct taxation on profits from investments. The quality of public services or the social effects of unemployment are of much less concern than the rate of taxation and levels of productivity. Such preferences therefore favour those New Zealanders who themselves benefit from reduced government services, for instance those who are happy to purchase private health and education and have little need to rely on the public social welfare system.

The influence of the markets has greatly increased the political influence of those who act as their advocates (Chapter 9: 230). Within the bureaucracy, Treasury's ascendancy has been enhanced by its role as the department which reports to government on market responses. In the media, economic commentators regularly speculate about the market's likely reactions to the government's economic management as reflected, for instance, in the latest indicators of economic perform- ance, such as the balance of payments or rate of inflation. Before the annual announcement of the budget there are frequent statements about what the markets will be looking for. Though the media often treat such commentary as independent and objective (Chapter 12: 306), its purpose is not just to comment on government policy but also to in- fluence it in favoured directions by indicating the likely adverse mar- ket effects of doing otherwise. Such predictions of market reaction can sometimes be self-fulfilling. They may persuade investors in the mar- ket to react in the ways being predicted, thus confirming the accuracy of the prediction.

As fear of adverse market reaction is such a potent motive on gov- ernments, there is a strong incentive for interest groups to use predic- tions of market reaction for partisan purposes. Groups such as the Business Roundtable often exaggerate the extent to which policy op- tions they oppose will lead to falls in market confidence. They claim that a particular policy direction will lead to massive selling of the New Zealand dollar or to the downgrading of New Zealand's credit rating by one of the influential overseas credit-rating agencies. Such claims, though attempts to influence the markets in a self-fulfilling direction, are sometimes falsified by events. Exaggerated predictions of adverse market reactions were particularly frequent during the 1993 debate over electoral reform. Business leaders opposed to MMP feared that proportional representation would deflect the government from making the decisions which suited them but which were unpopular with the voters. A coalition government would be forced into greater delay and compromise through the need for inter-party consultation and negotiation and would avoid the necessary tough decisions. The Campaign for Better Government and the Business Roundtable pre- dicted the market reaction if New Zealand changed its electoral sys- tem to one which encouraged coalition governments. In the event, market reaction to the vote in favour of MMP was much less unfa- vourable than predicted. Many overseas investors have been accus- tomed to investing in economically successful countries with proportional representation and coalition governments.

All these instances of the growing political influence of financial markets and of business groups that support them lends support to a marxist-style analysis of New Zealand politics in terms of the increas- ing structural dominance of international capital (e.g. Kelsey, 1993: Parts 1–2; Kelsey, 1995). Indeed, in so far as any single theoretical analysis could explain current politics in New Zealand it would have to be one which stressed the power of financial interests and the relative impotence of domestic political forces.

However, such an analysis, if unqualified, is too simplistic and one-sided. For instance, economic interests are not monolithic. The various economic sectors which constitute the main productive elements in the New Zealand economy are not necessarily united in their economic and political objectives. Though a degree of unity has been evident in opposition to the former, more highly regulated economy, for instance through the 'top tier' grouping (Chapter 9: 222–3), there are also longstanding conflicts of interest. For instance, manufacturers and farmers have different views about the value of tariff protection, while importers and exporters disagree over the desirable exchange rate for the New Zealand dollar (Chapter 2: 38). The market liberal orthodoxy espoused by the Business Roundtable and the Treasury may be endorsed by bankers and investors who have benefited from the freeing up of financial markets and from the process of privatising state assets. But it is not fully supported by the productive sectors of the economy.

Farmers remain an important and independent political force. Though they have clearly supported some elements of deregulation, for instance access to cheaper imported manufactured goods, they have maintained their former pragmatic attitude towards the role of the state, continuing to support their 'corporatist' links with the government (Chapter 9: 224). Using their powerful political contacts, not least through the National party, they have ensured that the state-guaranteed producer boards, in spite of strong attacks from market liberal critics, have remained relatively unscathed. Not only farmers, but manufacturers too remain sceptical about some of the more dogmatic aspects of the market liberal programme and fought a determined and partially successful campaigns on issues such as the rate of tariff reduction. Some leading manufacturing executives remain conspicuously absent from the Business Roundtable's membership.

Nor should the countervailing political power of interests which oppose the economically powerful be underestimated. Within the various policy communities, considerable influence is still wielded by the many different groups even though they may have been criticised by market liberals as 'vested' interests. For instance, while the state sector professional groups such as teachers, members of the armed forces, welfare workers, hospital doctors and nurses, may have been deliberately excluded from some of the discussions surrounding the restructuring of their areas, none the less their ministers still depend on their daily cooperation and they continue to be listened to in a wide range of regular official contacts.

Other groups have been successful in at least severely restricting the market-driven exploitation of natural resources, for instance environmental groups in relation to logging and mining, and Maori interests over the transfer of state lands to SOEs. Indeed, the general resurgence of Maori interests since the mid 1970s provides a good example of the avenues of countervailing power open to apparently marginalised groups. Maori claims for greater economic and political independence were conveniently in tune with the market liberal emphasis on economic self-reliance from the state. Devolution of government control allowed some independent Maori initiatives in health and education (Kelsey, 1995: Chapter 9). The judicial system was a key element in restoring Maori resources (Chapter 7: 180–9), as was the power of public opinion both nationally and internationally. New Zealand governments have been very sensitive to the possible loss of the country's reputation for good race relations (Chapter 9: 229).

Agents for financial interests are thus not the only advocates who use international opinion as a political weapon. Not only Maori but human rights activists generally have used New Zealand's commitment to United Nations standards (Chapter 7: 172–3) as a political weapon in defence of groups such as ethnic minorities, women and refugees. No New Zealand politician wants to appear as a public defender of actions which are widely considered to be inhumane or unjust. Similarly, New Zealand's reputation for having a relatively clean and unspoilt environment gives leverage to environmental groups, such as Greenpeace, in their attempts to force governments to adopt environmental values in opposition to economic interests.

In addition, electoral power, the power that derives from the government's wish to retain power at the next election, has also helped to set limits to the extent to which governments follow advice from the markets and their market liberal spokespeople. For instance, market liberal sources, such as the Business Roundtable, have pressed for a much greater reliance on market competition and direct consumer funding ('user pays') in health and education than governments are prepared to endorse, largely because they fear adverse electoral consequences. The result of the 1993 election and the electoral referendum heralded a resurgence of electoral power. The narrowness of the second Bolger government's initial majority, followed by the loss of that majority (Chapter 4: 76), forced the government to take greater heed of public opinion. The advent of MMP means that no single party has any longer sufficient command of a parliamentary majority to be able to govern with open disregard for the voting public's opinions.

These political pressures which moderate and sometimes restrict the extent of market influence indicate, once again, the variety of political influences at work in a pluralist democracy such as New Zealand's. They confirm the analytical value of the pluralist theory of the state which recognises the fallacy of trying to locate political control in any one particular interest or group. At the same time, the strength of countervailing interests is not sufficient to refute the claim that the political system is fundamentally unequal and systematically biased in favour of the interests of wealthy investors. New Zealand's democracy falls well short of the ideal standards set by the principles of pluralist democracy and, arguably, became even less equal and less democratic in the decade of restructuring.

A New Politics of Consensus?

Since 1984, New Zealand has undergone a profound restructuring of its economy, its state-owned agencies and, finally, its electoral system and method of choosing a government. The change to the electoral system was a direct consequence of the political methods adopted in the restructuring process. New Zealand's version of the Westminster parliamentary system gave great constitutional power to the majority party in government and especially to the executive Cabinet drawn from that party (Chapter 3: 62). The democratic justification for conceding this great power to the executive was that the Cabinet was elected by the voters and accountable to them through the party system. Before an election each of the major parties put forward a set of general principles and specific election policies. They thus offered the voters a choice between alternative party governments which could be counted on to use their parliamentary majority to govern along broadly predictable lines. Accountability was reinforced by a general expectation that the elected government would remain responsive to the people through various channels of communication such as the back-bench members of the caucus and the party at large, as well through constant interaction and consultation with interest groups.

In the decade after 1984, these conventions of accountability and consultation were seriously eroded and the degree of public trust in the legitimacy of the parliamentary system correspondingly reduced. The party structure no longer provided a reliable mechanism for holding elected governments responsible to the electors. The most obvious and potent symbol of this collapse was in the willingness of governments to break clear promises to the electorate (Chapter 10: 260). It was also reflected in the diminished role of caucus as the government's sounding board for public opinion (Chapter 5: 115). The main directions of government policy were set not by the governing party but more by the government's advisers in the bureaucracy and among business leaders. The main indirect pressure came from the markets rather than the electorate.

Government repudiation of its party support was most marked under the Lange Labour government, when the policies espoused by Roger Douglas and his followers were particularly at odds with the Labour Party's principles and policies (Chapter 5: 117; Chapter 10: 246). But it continued under the Bolger National government, particularly in its initial period when the Minister of Finance's agenda was dominant and the government appeared convinced of the need to impose radical reforms in the teeth of opposition, including opposition from within its own party. The effect on the Labour and National party organisations was demoralising, as indicated by the dramatic decline in subscribing members and by the political success of splinter parties protesting at the betrayal of party principle, first the NewLabour Party and then the New Zealand First party (Chapter 10). The growing ineffectiveness of two-party politics was reinforced by declining numbers of voters who identified with either of the major parties (Chapter 11: 280) and, more generally, by a significant reduction in the levels of voter turnout and the development of a political underclass drawn mainly from the young, the unemployed and Maori and Pacific Islanders (Chapter 11: 271–2).

Restructuring also involved an attack on established mechanisms of interest group consultation and particularly on the right of representatives of economic sectors to be formally incorporated into government decision-making (Chapter 9: 224–5). Though the political influence of interest groups was not reduced altogether, certain sectional interests were weakened, for instance trade unions, which were no longer seen as legitimate partners of governments. State sector professions, though still not without influence, were often looked on as part of the problem to be solved rather than as legitimate contributors to government policy. In general, interested sections of the public could no longer assume that ministers would accept that aggrieved community groups had a right to be heard and listened to.

The changing approach of governments to the communities which had elected them was sustained by the ideology of market liberalism and, in particular, by the public choice analysis of democratic politics as being contrary to the public interest. Elections, it was held, encouraged politicians seeking office to outbid each other in making rash promises to the voters, promises which it was the duty of responsible governments, once elected, to ignore (Chapter 1: 18). Interest groups were the representatives of vested interests seeking illegitimate privileges which were contrary to the general interest. The main function of government was therefore to stick tenaciously to the market liberal agenda of reducing the role of the state, resisting all expressions of opposition on the grounds that they were contrary to the public interest. The main architect of the restructuring process, Roger Douglas, developed a set of political tactics ('Rogerpolitics' (Mulgan, 1992a)) which included the principle that 'speed is essential: it is impossible to go too fast' (Douglas, 1990).If the people were to be consulted it was as members of a disorganised and passive mass, through opinion polling (Chapter 9: 231) or through media advertising (Chapter 12: 298).

This approach to politics involved an attack not only on the democratic conventions of the Westminster system but also on deeply held values within New Zealand's political culture. New Zealanders had always taken a pragmatic, non-doctrinaire attitude to the role of the state (Chapter 2: 47–48), an attitude which sat well with the expectation that government policy would be worked out through negotiation and compromise with conflicting groups and interests. Few, apart from those who directly benefited from it, were attracted to a theory such as market liberalism which derived its view of the state from basic principles and placed a high value on logical coherence and consistency. New Zealanders, like other ex-colonial peoples, had always had a suspicion of leaders with aristocratic or other elitist pretensions. They expected their politicians to keep close to the grass roots, to be men and women of the people who would share the values and aspirations of their constituents. Many New Zealanders reacted antagonistically to governments which seemed to be closer and more sympathetic to a wealthy and privileged few, such as the high-profile members of the Business Roundtable, than to the mass of ordinary voters whom they represented.

These trends provided the background for the referendums on electoral reform in 1992 and 1993 (Vowles *et al.*, 1995: chapter 11). A majority of voters were so alienated from politics and politicians that they were prepared to risk the uncertainty of a radically new electoral system. While many members of the public knew that they disliked the existing regime, they were less clear about what they sought from a change to MMP. Much of their concern centred on a hope for greater 'consensus' which was a prime value adopted by the reform movement (Nagel, 1994) and has been a focus of academic speculation about the effects of MMP (e.g. Vowles *et al.*, 1995: Chapters 1, 11; Boston *et al.*, 1996a: Chapter 10). Yet 'consensus', like most political values, is a term of vague and uncertain meaning. Political consensus is sometimes taken to mean a level of general agreement over political values and policy directions in society as whole. For instance, it is sometimes argued that most sections of New Zealand society in the post-war period till the mid-1970s shared a consensus over the role of the state and the broad direction of economic policy ('the consensus years' (Vowles *et al.*, 1995: 3–5)). This consensus is now greatly weakened, as indicated by the rise of new social movements and the 'new politics' (Chapter 10: 247–8) as well as by continuing conflict over the value of market liberalism and the extent of state responsibility for social welfare. In general terms, New Zealand is now, and is likely to remain, a much less homogeneous, and more plural, society than it was. In this sense, political consensus must be seen as a diminishing feature of New Zealand politics, regardless of the characteristics of the country's electoral system or the conduct of its politicians.

On the other hand, political consensus, or 'consensus politics' may refer not so much to the absence of political conflict in society as to a method by which such conflict is handled by political elites. Consensus politics implies that political opponents, particularly politicians from rival political parties, seek to reach agreement by accommodating each others' differences. It is a politics of compromise and conciliation in which opponents share ultimate responsibility for decisions reached through negotiation. It may be contrasted with 'adversarial' politics' in which politicians from opposing parties emphasise their differences and avoid joint responsibility for decisions. 'Adversarial' politics is a feature of two-party systems where the majority party forms the government and the other party, as the opposition, seeks to discredit it (Debnam, 1990). Multi-party systems, on the other hand, encourage compromise and consensus because no one party usually controls a majority. In the influential typology of Arendt Lijphart (Lijphart, 1999: Chapter 3), 'consensual' democracies are associated with a number of characteristics, including proportional representation and a multi-party system, while 'majoritarian' democracies typically have two-party systems and first-past-the-post electoral systems (Boston *et al.*, 1996a: 179–82). Moreover, the institutions of consensual democracy are more suited to societies which display a wider range of social divisions other than the basic left/right socio-economic divide.

In this sense, the introduction of MMP and the breaking down of the two-party system can be said to represent a change to a more consensual style of politics in which politicians are required to negotiate and compromise across party lines, as happened with the formation of coalition and minority governments since 1996. Indeed, such a change was already apparent during the transitional Parliament, 1994–6. Arguably, the move to a more complex party system and a multi-party Parliament is more appropriate for New Zealand's increasingly plural and divided society. In this case, it may be noted, consensus politics is a remedy for the lack of consensus in society.Conversely, the former system, with its adversarial, conflictual style of two-party politics, was tolerable only on the assumption of widespread agreement about social values and political goals.

The extent of the change should not be exaggerated. Negotiation and the search for consensus were not uncommon under the previous system. Parties which aspired to win a majority were compelled to appeal to a diverse range of voters. Though the parties aimed to present a united front to the public, their policies were often the result of consultation and compromise between different sections of the party representing different interests in the community. At the same time, adversarial politics continues under the present system, with certain parties refusing to work with others and the government facing hostile opponents in Parliament. New Zealand still retains many of the features identified by Lijphart with 'majoritarian' systems, such as the fusion of executive and legislature power in the Cabinet, a single-chamber Parliament, a 'unitary' system of government and the absence of a written constitution with judicial review.

Nor should political consensus be over-valued. Agreement between political parties may be used to keep certain issues off the political agenda and thus exclude certain interests from consideration. If all politicians work cosily together there may be less chance of exposing political incompetence or corruption. Adversarial politics, the exposure of governments to unceasing hostility from political opponents in Parliament and the media, helps to keep governments responsive to public scrutiny. Indeed, it was not the adversarialism of two-party politics which turned so many New Zealanders against the former system. The cause of public anger was more the capacity of single-party majority governments to enact unpopular reforms in breach of their electoral commitments. The consensus which many supporters of reform were seeking was not so much an agreement between politicians or political parties as a relationship of trust between politicians and voters.

In so far as governments must now depend on the parliamentary support of more than one party, the chances of unpopular radical reform have been diminished. The new system is thus likely to be conservative in its impact and offers little hope of a far-reaching realignment of political power. However, there should be distinct advantages in terms of more open discussion of policy-making and a greater readiness to consult potential opponents. Such changes in process should, in turn, bring policy more into line with the preferences of voters.

A change from confrontation to conciliation should also mark a change in fundamental assumptions about the nature of good political decision-making in a democratic society. The restructuring process was underpinned by a theory of politics which assumes that there is one clearly correct view of the public interest and that all alternative views are expressions of mistaken vested interests. This theory is both philosophically naive and politically dangerous. It ignores the fact that the concept of the public interest is necessarily controversial because it involves notions of what is good for the community as whole. In a plural society there will inevitably be serious differences about political values, including about what is best for the society as a whole. These differences can never be finally resolved. The extreme market liberal approach of advocating one view of the public interest and valuing logical consistency of principle ahead of pragmatic compromise implies a preference for the values and interests of one section of society at the expense of others. Conflict over the public interest should be accepted, indeed welcomed, as an inevitable part of a free plural society. In such a society, political decision-making must be based on the principle of genuine consultation, the need to engage in discussion among different points of view, and on pragmatism, the practice of reaching compromises among conflicting goals and values.

In so far as the new constitutional arrangements will impose a greater degree of consultation and compromise, they may be seen as a victory for the principles of democratic pluralism. Admittedly they will leave much of the structure of political inequality unchanged. As already pointed out (Chapter 1: 17), pluralists accept the inevitability of some social and political inequality in a capitalist society, a concession which leaves them open to the charge of condoning injustice. However, it is incumbent on radical critics not only to point out the injustice in present-day politics but also to justify their faith that radical or revolutionary reform is both possible and desirable. While the ideal of freedom and equality for all individuals and interests cannot be met in a liberal democracy, pluralists can have little confidence that any other type of system currently on offer will do a better, or even as good, a job of achieving these principles.

Which point of view is more congenial is for the reader to decide. Some may find the pluralist's scepticism about achieving a truly just society to be unduly pessimistic or complacent. Such scepticism, however, does not imply acceptance of the status quo or refusal to work for any change. Pluralists certainly see little prospect of revolutionary change, or at least of revolutionary change for the better. But they do not look on the existing system as perfect (though some may have given the impression of so thinking). They believe that the main political effort should be directed to ameliorating the most glaring deficiencies of the present system rather than that all hope should be placed in an unlikely total transformation. True equality and freedom may be unattainable but existing practices and institutions may certainly be improved. There are degrees of inequality and lack of freedom which are worth struggling over and it is these issues which provide the key items on the political agenda for a society such as New Zealand's. Those who think that radical transformation provides the only hope of improvement, not those who work for modest and incremental reforms, are in effect the strongest ideological allies of the rich and powerful. By concentrating on the impossible they help to impede the possible.

Bibliography

A Bill of Rights for New Zealand, A White Paper (1985), Wellington, Government Printer.

Aimer, P. (1992), 'The changing party system' in Gold (ed.), *New Zealand Politics in Perspective*, 3rd ed.: 326–41.

Aimer, P. (1993), 'Was there a gender gap in New Zealand in 1990?', *Political Science*, 45: 112–21.

Aimer, P. (2001), 'The Changing Party System' in R. Miller (ed.), *New Zealand Government and Politics*: 271–82.

Aimer, P. (2003), 'United Future' in R. Miller (ed.), *New Zealand Government and Politics,* 3rd ed.: 293–302.

Aimer, P. & McAllister, I. (1992), 'Electoral behaviour in New Zealand: progress, problems, and prospects' in Holland (ed.), *Electoral Behaviour in New Zealand:* 169–93.

Alley, R. M. (1992), 'The powers of the Prime Minister' in Gold (ed.), *New Zealand Politics in Perspective*, 3rd ed.: 174–93.

Anagnoson, J. T. (1983), 'Home style in New Zealand', *Legislative Studies Quarterly*, 8: 157–75.

Anagnoson, J. T. (1987), 'Does constituency work have an electoral impact? The case of New Zealand MPs', *Political Science*, 39: 105–18.

Atkinson, J. (1989), 'Mass communication, economic liberalisation and the new mediators', *Political Science*, 41: 85–108.

Atkinson, J. (1994), 'The state, the media and thin democracy', in Sharp, A. (ed.), *Leap Into the Dark*, Auckland, Auckland University Press: 146–77.

Atkinson, J. (1994a), 'Health reform and 'thin' democracy', *Political Science*, 46: 193–214.

Atkinson, J. (1997), 'The Media and MMP' in R. Miller (ed.), *New Zealand Politics in Transition*: 234–44.

Atkinson, J. (2003) 'Tabloid Democracy' in R. Miller (ed.), *New Zealand Government and Politics,* 3rd ed.: 305–19.

Atkinson, J. (2004), 'The Campaign on Television' in J. Vowles *et al.*, *Voters' Veto. The 2002 Election in New Zealand and the Consolidation of Minority Government*: Chapter 4.

Awatere, D. (1984), *Maori Sovereignty*, Auckland, Broadsheet.

Bagehot, W. (1963), *The English Constitution;* with an Introduction by R. H. S. Crossman, London, Collins.

Bale, T. (2003), 'The Greens' in Miller, R. (ed.), *New Zealand Government and Politics*, 3rd ed.: 283–92.

Bean, C. (1988), 'Class and party in the anglo-american democracies: the case of New Zealand in perspective', *British Journal of Political Science*, 18: 303–21.

Bean, C. (1992), 'New Zealand', in M. N. Franklin, T. T. Mackie, H. Valen *et al.*, *Electoral Change: Responses to Evolving Social and Attitudinal Structures in Western Countries*, Cambridge, Cambridge University Press: 284–306.

Bean, C. (1992a), 'Party leaders and local candidates', in Holland (ed.), *Electoral Behaviour in New Zealand*: 141–68.

Bedggood, D. (1980), *Rich and Poor in New Zealand*, Auckland, Allen & Unwin.

Belich, J. (1986), *The New Zealand Wars*, Auckland, Auckland University Press.

Booth, P. (1992), 'Investigative journalism, the New Zealand experience', in M. Comrie & J. McGregor (eds), *Whose News?*, Palmerston North, Dunmore Press: 161–9.

Boston, J. (1989), 'The case for a Department of Prime Minister and Cabinet', *Public Sector*, 12: 7–11.

Boston, J. (1991), 'Reorganising the machinery of government, objectives and outcomes' in J. Boston *et al.* (eds), *Reshaping the State: New Zealand's Bureaucratic Revolution*, Auckland, Oxford University Press: 285–307.

Boston, J. (1992), 'The Treasury: its role, philosophy and influence' in Gold (ed.), *New Zealand Politics in Perspective*, 3rd ed.: 194–215.

Boston, J. (1994), 'On the sharp edge of the State Sector Act: the resignation of Perry Cameron', *Public Sector*, 17 (4): 2–14.

Boston, J. (1996), 'Origins and destinations. New Zealand's model of public management and the international transfer of ideas' in P. Weller and G. Davis (eds), *New Ideas, Better Government*, Sydney, Allen and Unwin: 107–31.

Boston, J. (2003), 'Forming a Government' in R. Miller (ed.), *New Zealand Government and Politics*, 3rd ed.: 117–34.

Boston, J. & Cooper, F. (1989), ' The Treasury: advice, coordination and control' in Gold (ed.), *New Zealand Politics in Perspective*, 2nd ed.: 123–44.

Boston, J., Martin, J., Pallot, J. & Walsh, P. (1996), *Public Management: the New Zealand Model*, Auckland, Oxford University Press.

Boston, J., Levine S., McLeay, E. & Roberts, N. S. (1996a), *New Zealand Under MMP: A New Politics?*, Auckland, Auckland University Press with Bridget Williams Books.

Boston, J., Levine S., McLeay, E. & Roberts, N. S. (1997), *From Campaign to Coalition. The 1996 MMP Election*, Palmerston North, Dunmore Press.

Boston, J., Church, S., Levine S., McLeay, E., & Roberts, N. S. (eds) (2000), *Left Turn. The New Zealand General Election of 1999*, Wellington, Victoria University Press.

Bremer, R. (1993), 'Federated Farmers and the state' in B. Roper & C. Rudd (eds), *State and Economy in New Zealand*, Auckland, Oxford University Press: 108–27.

Brookfield, F. M. (1989), 'The New Zealand Constitution, the search for legitimacy' in Kawharu (ed.), *Waitangi*: 1–24.

Brookfield, F. M. (1992), 'The Governor-General and the Constitution' in Gold (ed.), *New Zealand Politics in Perspective*, 3rd ed.: 77–85.

Browne, A. (1996), 'Reporting the politicians: feasting in the gallery' in J. McGregor (ed.), *Dangerous Democracy?*, Palmerston North, Dunmore Press: 64–74.

Buhrs, T. & Bartlett, R. V. (1993), *Environmental Policy in New Zealand*, Auckland, Oxford University Press.

Bunkle, P., Irwin, K., Laurie, A., & Middleton, S. (eds) (1992), *Feminist Voices*, Auckland, Oxford University Press.

Burrows, J. F. & Joseph, P. A. (1990), 'Parliamentary law making', *New Zealand Law Journal*, September: 306–8.

Bush, G. (1990), 'The historic reorganization of local government' in M. Holland & J. Boston (eds), *The Fourth Labour Government*, 2nd ed.: 251–69.

Bush, G. (1995), *Local Government and Politics in New Zealand*, 2nd ed., Auckland, Auckland University Press.

Bush, G. (2003), 'Local Government' in R. Miller (ed.), *New Zealand Government and Politics*, 3rd ed.: 161–70.

Butterworth, R. (1989), 'The media' in D. Novitz & B. Willmott (eds), *Culture and Identity in New Zealand*, Wellington, GP Books: 142–59.

Cabinet Office (1996), *Cabinet Office Manual*, Wellington, Cabinet Office.

Carter, I. (1994), 'Rural' in P. Spoonley, D. Pearson, & I. Shirley (eds), *New Zealand*

Society: A Sociological Introduction, 2nd ed., Palmerston North, Dunmore Press: 55–65.

Catt, H. (1996), 'The other democratic experiment: New Zealand's experience with citizens' initiated referendum', *Political Science*, 48: 29–47.

Catt, H. (2003), 'Citizens' Initiated Referenda' in R. Miller (ed.), *New Zealand Government and Politics*, 3rd ed.: 400–9.

Chapman, G. B. (1985), 'A bill of wrongs, the argument against the proposed Bill of Rights', *New Zealand Law Journal*, July: 22–31.

Chapman, R. (1989), 'Political culture: the purposes of party and the current challenge' in Gold (ed.), *New Zealand Politics in Perspective*, 2nd ed.: 1–32.

Chapman, R. (1992), 'A political culture under pressure: the struggle to preserve a progressive tax base for welfare and the positive state', *Political Science*, 44: 1–27.

Cocker, A. (1994), 'Broadcasting myths and political realities: New Zealand's experience in comparative perspectives', *Political Science*, 46: 234–44.

Cocker, A. (2003), 'Media Institutions' in R. Miller (ed.), *New Zealand Government and Politics*, 3rd ed.: 320–29.

Crothers, C. & Vowles, J. (1993), 'The material conditions of voting' in Vowles & Aimer, *Voters' Vengeance*: 95–109.

Cox, N., & Miller, R. (2003), 'Monarchy', in R. Miller (ed.), *New Zealand Government and Politics*, 3rd ed.: 50–62.

Dahl, R. A. (1961), *Who Governs?*, New Haven, Yale University Press.

Dann, C. (2003), 'The Environmental Movement' in R. Miller (ed.), *New Zealand Government and Politics*, 3rd ed.: 368–77.

Dalziel, R. (1992), 'The politics of settlement' in G. W. Rice (ed.), *The Oxford History of New Zealand*, 2nd ed., Auckland, Oxford University Press: 87–111.

Debnam, G. (1990), 'Adversary politics in New Zealand: climate of stress and policy aggressors', *Journal of Commonwealth and Comparative Politics*, 28: 1–24.

Deeks, J. (1992), 'Introduction: business, government and interest group politics' in J. Deeks & N. Perry (eds), *Controlling Interests: Business, the State and Society in New Zealand*, Auckland, Auckland University Press: 1–15.

Deeks, J. (1997), 'Business and Politics' in Miller (ed.), *New Zealand Politics in Transition*: 428–36.

Devere, H., & Scott, J. (2003), 'The Women's Movement' in R. Miller (ed.), *New Zealand Government and Politics,* 3rd ed.: 388–99.

Dixon, C., (1997), 'Marxism' in Miller (ed.), *New Zealand Politics in Transition*: 350–8.

Douglas, R. (1990), 'The politics of successful economic reform', *Policy*, Autumn: 2–6.

Douglas, R. & Callan, L. (1987), *Toward Prosperity*, Auckland, Bateman.

Downs, A. (1957), *An Economic Theory of Democracy*, New York, Harper & Row.

Drage, J. (ed.) (1999), 'Local Government in New Zealand', Special Issue, *Political Science*, vol. 50, no. 2.

Drage, J. (ed.) (2002), *Empowering Communities? Representation and Participation in New Zealand's Local Government*, Wellington, Victoria University Press.

Drage, J. (2003), 'The Impact of New Local Government Legislation on Political Representation', *Public Sector*, 26, 2: 11–15.

Dunleavy, P. & O'Leary, B. (1987), *Theories of the State, The Politics of Liberal Democracy*, London, Macmillan.

Du Plessis, R., & Higgins, J. (1997), 'Feminism' in Miller (ed.), *New Zealand Politics in Transition*, Auckland, Oxford University Press: 328–40.

Durie, M. H. (2003), 'Mana Maori Motuhake. The State of the Maori Nation' in R. Miller (ed.), *New Zealand Government and Politics,* 3rd ed.: 488–502.

Durie, E. T. & Orr, G. S. (1990), 'The role of the Waitangi Tribunal and the development of a bicultural jurisprudence', *New Zealand Universities Law Review*, 14: 62–81.

Duverger, M. (1964), *Political Parties: Their Organization and Activity in the Modern State*, London, Methuen.

Dyer, S. C. (1994), 'A news flow analysis of the sale of a public asset', *Australian Journal of Political Science*, 29: 172–8.

Eaddy, R. (1992), 'The structure and operations of the executive' in Gold (ed.), *New Zealand Politics in Perspective*, 3rd ed.: 162–73.

Easton, B. (1994), 'How did the health blitzkreig fail?', *Political Science*, 46: 215–34.

Easton, B. (1997), *The Commercialisation of New Zealand*, Auckland, Auckland University Press.

Edwards, B. (1992), 'The "cootchie coo" news', in Comrie & McGregor (eds), *Whose News?*: 15–25.

Electoral Commission (1996), *Everything You Need to Know about Voting Under MMP: New Zealand's Electoral System*, Wellington, GP Publications.

Electoral Commission (2002), *The New Zealand Electoral Compendium*, 3rd ed., Wellington, Electoral Commission.

Fitzgerald, P. (1992), 'Section 7 of the New Zealand Bill of Rights Act 1990: a very practical power or a well intentioned nonsense?', *Victoria University of Wellington Law Review*, 2: 135–58.

Fleras, A. (1986), 'The politics of Maori lobbying: the case of the New Zealand Maori Council', *Political Science*, 38: 27–43.

Fox, D. (1992), 'The Maori perspective of news' in Comrie & McGregor (eds), *Whose News?*: 170–80.

Galvin, B. V. (1985), 'Some reflections on the operation of the executive' in Gold (ed.), *New Zealand Politics in Perspective*: 66–83.

Gidlow, B., Perkins, H., Cushman, G. & Simpson, C. (1994), 'Leisure' in Spoonley, Pearson & Shirley (eds), *New Zealand Society*, 2nd ed.: 253–70.

Gold, H. (1992), 'The social and economic setting' in Gold (ed.), *New Zealand Politics in Perspective*, 3rd ed.: 2–13.

Gold, H. (1992a), 'Political culture: contemporary patterns' in Gold (ed.), *New Zealand Politics in Perspective*, 3rd ed.: Auckland, Longman Paul: 14–39.

Gold, H. (1992b), 'Society and party in 1990' in Gold (ed.), *New Zealand Politics in Perspective*, 3rd ed.: 471–92.

Gold, H., & Webster, A. (1990), *New Zealand Values Today*, Palmerston North, Alpha.

Goldfinch, S. (1997). 'Treasury and Public Policy Formation' in C. Rudd and B. Roper (eds.), *New Zealand Political Economy*, Auckland, Oxford University Press.

Goldfinch, S. (2003), 'The State' in R. Miller (ed.), *New Zealand Government and Politics,* 3rd ed.: 547–56.

Gregory, R. (1987), 'The reorganisation of the public sector: the quest for efficiency' in Boston & Holland (eds), *The Fourth Labour Government*: 111–33.

Gregory, R. (1995), 'Post-reform activities of New Zealand's senior public servants: a follow up study', *Political Science*, 47: 161–90.

Gustafson, B. (1986), *The First Fifty Years: A History of the New Zealand National Party*, Auckland, Reed Methuen.

Gustafson, B. (1992), 'The Labour Party' in Gold (ed.), *New Zealand Politics in Perspective*, 3rd ed.: 263–88.

Gustafson, B. (1993), 'Regeneration, rejection or realignment: New Zealand political parties in the 1990s' in G. Hawke (ed.), *Changing Politics?*: 68–102.

Harris, B. V. (1992), 'The constitutional base' in Gold (ed.), *New Zealand Politics in Perspective*, 3rd ed.: 56–76.

Bibliography

Harris, P. (1989), 'Pressure groups and protest' in Gold (ed.), *New Zealand Politics in Perspective*, 2nd ed.: 295–311.

Harris, P. (1992), 'Democracy and referendums' in A. Simpson (ed.), *Referendums: Constitutional and Political Perspectives*, Wellington, Department of Politics, Victoria University of Wellington: 47–67.

Harris, P. & Levine, S. (eds) (1992), *The New Zealand Politics Source Book*, Palmerston North, Dunmore.

Harris, P. & McLeay, E. (1993), 'The Legislature' in Hawke (ed.), *Changing Politics?*: 103–30.

Harrison, R. (1995), 'Domestic enforcement of international human rights in courts of law: some recent developments', *New Zealand Law Journal*, August: 256–65.

Harvey, B. (1992), 'Inventing the truth' in Comrie & McGregor (eds), *Whose News?*: 101–10.

Hayward, J. (2003), 'The Waitangi Tribunal in the Treaty Settlement process' in R. Miller (ed.), *New Zealand Government and Politics*, 3rd ed.: 514–21.

Hayward, J., & Rudd, C. (2000), 'Metropolitan Newspapers and the Election' in J. Boston *et al.*, (eds) *Left Turn. The New Zealand General Election of 1999*: 89–104.

Hayward, J., & Rudd, C. (2002), 'The Coverage of Post-War Election Campaigns: The *Otago Daily Times*', *Political Science*, 54, 2: 3–20.

Held, D. (1989), *Political Theory and the State*, Cambridge, Polity.

Henderson, J. (2003), The Prime Minster: Powers and Personality' in R. Miller (ed.), *New Zealand Government and Politics*, 3rd ed.: 106–16.

Henderson, J., and Bellamy, P. (2002), *Democracy in New Zealand*, Christchurch, Macmillan Brown Centre for Pacific Studies, and International Institute for Democracy and Electoral Assistance.

Hill, M. (1994), 'Religion' in Spoonley, Pearson & Shirley (eds), *New Zealand Society*, 2nd ed.: 292–307.

Hodder, J. (1992), 'Judges: their political role' in Gold (ed.), *New Zealand Politics in Perspective*, 3rd ed.: 410–26.

Holland, M. (ed.) (1992), *Electoral Behaviour*, Auckland, Oxford University Press.

Hope, W. (2003), 'Media and Political Process' in R. Miller (ed.), *New Zealand Government and Politics*, 3rd ed.: 330–41.

Ingle, S. (1995), 'Electoral reform in New Zealand: the implications for Westminster systems', *Journal of Legislative Studies*: 76–92.

Jackson, K. (1987), *The Dilemma of Parliament*, Wellington, Allen & Unwin/Port Nicholson Press.

Jackson, K. (1992), 'Caucus: the anti-parliamentary system?' in Gold (ed.), *New Zealand Politics in Perspective*, 3rd ed.: 233–46.

Jackson, K. (2003), 'Parliament' in R. Miller (ed.), *New Zealand Government and Politics*, 3rd ed.: 77–88.

Jackson, K., & McRobie, A. (1998), *New Zealand Adopts Proportional Representation. Accident? Design? Evolution?*, Aldershot, Ashgate.

James, B. & Saville-Smith, K. (1989), *Gender, Culture and Power: Challenging New Zealand's Gendered Culture*, Auckland, Oxford University Press.

Jesson, B. (1992), 'Lobbying and protest: patterns of political change at the informal level' in Gold (ed.), *New Zealand Politics in Perspective*, 3rd ed.: 365–78.

Jesson, B. (1997), 'The Alliance' in R. Miller, (ed.) *New Zealand Politics in Transition*: 156–64.

Jordan, G. (1990), 'The pluralism of pluralisms: an anti-theory?', *Political Studies*, 38: 286–301.

Joseph, P. A. (1993), *Constitutional and Administrative Law in New Zealand*, Sydney,

Law Book Co.

Joseph, P. A. (1996), 'Constitutional Law', *New Zealand Law Review*, 1996: 1–14.

Julian, R. (1992), 'Women: how significant a force?' in Gold (ed.), *New Zealand Politics in Perspective*, 3rd ed.: 401–9.

Kawharu, I. H. (ed.) (1989), *Waitangi: Maori and Pakeha Perspectives of the Treaty of Waitangi*, Auckland, Oxford University Press.

Keith, K. J. (1985), 'The courts and the constitution', *Victoria University of Wellington Law Review*, 15: 29–45

Keith, K. J. (1990), 'The Treaty of Waitangi in the courts', *New Zealand Universities Law Review*, 14: 37–61.

Keith, K. J. (1992), 'On the constitution of New Zealand', *Political Science*, 44: 28–34.

Kellow, A. J. (1989), 'Politicians versus bureaucrats: who makes public policy?' in Gold (ed.), *New Zealand Politics in Perspective*, 2nd ed.: 145–53.

Kelsey, J. (1990), A *Question of Honour? Labour and the Treaty, 1984–1989*, Wellington, Allen & Unwin.

Kelsey, J. (1993), *Rolling Back the State*, Wellington, Bridget Williams Books.

Kelsey, J. (1995), *The New Zealand Experiment: A World Model for Structural Adjustment?*, Auckland, Auckland University Press with Bridget Williams Books.

King, M. (1992), 'Between two worlds' in *The Oxford History of New Zealand*, 2nd ed.: 285–307.

Ladley, a. (1997), 'The Head of State: The Crown, the Queen and the Governor-General', in R. Miller (ed.) *New Zealand Politics in Transition*: 51–61.

Lamare, J. (1984), 'Party identification and voting behaviour in New Zealand', *Political Science*, 36: 1–9.

Lamare, J. (1992), 'Party identification' in Holland (ed.), *Electoral Behaviour in New Zealand*: 51–70.

Leitch, S. (1992), 'The media and politics' in Gold (ed), *New Zealand Politics in Perspective*, 3rd ed.: 40–54.

Leitch, S. (1992a), 'Sources of discontent' in Comrie & McGregor (eds), *Whose News?*: 153–60.

Levine, H. & Henare, M. (1994), 'Mana Motuhake – Maori self-determination', *Pacific Viewpoint*, 35: 193–209.

Levine, S. & Roberts, N. S. (1992), 'Policies and political perspectives: the importance of issues and problems in New Zealand electoral behaviour' in Holland (ed.), *Electoral Behaviour*: 71–90.

Levine, S. & Roberts, N. S. (1994), 'The New Zealand electoral referendum and general election of 1993', *Electoral Studies*, 13: 240–53.

Levine, S., & Harris, P. (eds) (1999), *New Zealand Politics Source Book*, 3rd ed., Palmerston North, Dunmore.

Levine, S., & McRobie, A. (2002), *From Muldoon to Lange. New Zealand Elections in the 1980s*, Rangiora, MC Enterprises.

Levine, S., & Roberts, N. S. (2003), 'The 2002 General Election' in R. Miller, (ed.), *New Zealand Government and Politics*, 3rd ed.: 219–32.

Lijphart, A. (1984), *Democracies*, New Haven, Yale University Press.

Lijphart, A. (1999), *Patterns of Democracy. Government Forms and Performance in Thirty-Six Countries*, New Haven & London, Yale University Press.

Lindblom, C. E. (1977), *Politics and Markets*, New York, Basic Books.

Maharey, S. (1996), 'Politicians as news sources' in McGregor (ed.), *Dangerous Democracy*: 94–111.

Marshall, G. (1984), *Constitutional Conventions*, Oxford, Oxford University Press.

Martin, J. (1988), *A Profession of Statecraft?*, Wellington, Victoria University Press.

Bibliography

Martin, J. (1994), 'The role of the state in administration' in A. Sharp (ed.), *Leap into the Dark*, Auckland, Auckland University Press: 41–67.

Martin, J. (2003), 'The Public Service' in R. Miller (ed.), *New Zealand Government and Politics*, 3rd ed.: 135–47.

Mascarenhas, R. C. (1991), 'State-owned enterprises' in Boston *et al.* (eds), *Reshaping the State*: 27–51.

McCraw, D. (1979), 'Social Credit's role in the New Zealand party system', *Political Science*, 31: 54–60.

McGee, D. (1992), 'The House of Representatives' in Gold (ed.), *New Zealand Politics in Perspective*, 3rd ed.: 86–101.

McGregor, J. (1992), 'Who owns the press in New Zealand?' in Comrie & McGregor (eds), *Whose News?*: 26–38.

McGregor, J. (1996), 'Talkback and the art of "yackety yack" in politics' in McGregor (ed.), *Dangerous Democracy?*: 75–93.

McLeay, E. M. (1991), 'Two steps forward, two steps back: Maori devolution, Maori advisory committees and Maori representation', *Political Science*, 43: 30–46.

McLeay, E. M. (1992), 'The state in New Zealand' in Gold (ed.), *New Zealand Politics in Perspective*, 3rd ed.: 427–49.

McLeay, E. M. (1993), 'Women's parliamentary representation: a comparative perspective', *Political Science*, 45: 40–62.

McLeay, E. M. (1995), *The Cabinet and Political Power in New Zealand*, Auckland, Oxford University Press.

McLeay, E.M. (1996), 'Responsibility as accountability', unpublished conference paper.

McLeay, E. M. (2000), 'The New Parliament' in J. Boston *et al.*, *Left Turn. The New Zealand General Election of 1999*, Wellington, Victoria University Press: 203–16.

McLeay, E.M. (2003), 'Cabinet' in R. Miller (ed.), *New Zealand Government and Politics*, 3rd ed.: 89–105.

McRobie, A. (2003), 'Elections and the Electoral System' in R. Miller (ed.), *New Zealand Government and Politics*, 3rd ed.: 175–87.

Metge, J. (1976), *The Maoris of New Zealand*, revised ed., London, Routledge & Kegan Paul.

Miller, R. (1992), 'The minor parties' in Gold (ed.), *New Zealand Politics in Perspective*, 3rd ed.: 310–25.

Miller, R. (ed.) (1997) *New Zealand Politics in Transition*, Auckland, Oxford University Press.

Miller, R. (1997a), 'The New Zealand First Party' in R. Miller, (ed.) *New Zealand Politics in Transition*: 165–76.

Miller, R. (ed.) (2001), *New Zealand Government and Politics*, Auckland, Oxford University Press.

Miller, R. (ed.) (2003), *New Zealand Government and Politics*, 3rd ed., Melbourne, Oxford University Press.

Miller R. (2003a), 'Labour', 'New Zealand First' in R. Miller, (ed.), *New Zealand Government and Politics*, 3rd ed.: 235–50, 261–73.

Mintrom, M. (2003), 'Policy Entrepreneurs, Thinktanks and Trusts' in R. Miller (ed.), *New Zealand Government and Politics,* 3rd ed.: 357–67.

Mitchell, C. (2003), 'The New Local Government Legislation', *Public Sector*, 26, 2: 2–5.

Molineaux, J. (1995), 'The concentration of ownership in the New Zealand daily newspaper industry', *New Zealand Journal of Media Studies*, 2: 3–11.

Moloney, P., (1997), 'Pluralist Theories of the State' in R. Miller (ed), *New Zealand*

Politics in Transition, Auckland, Oxford University Press: 317–27.

Moloney, P., (2003), 'Neo-liberalism: A Pluralist Critique' in R. Miller (ed.), *New Zealand Government and Politics*, 3rd ed.: 568–77.

Moore, M. (1992), 'The reporting of New Zealand politics' in Comrie & McGregor (eds), *Whose News?*: 81–89.

Morrow, J., (2003) 'Neo-liberalism' in Miller (ed.), *New Zealand Government and Politics*, 3rd ed.: 557–67.

Mulgan, R. (1989), *Democracy and Power in New Zealand*, 2nd ed., Auckland, Oxford University Press.

Mulgan, R. (1989a), *Maori, Pakeha and Democracy*, Auckland, Oxford University Press.

Mulgan, R. (1990), 'The changing electoral mandate' in Holland & Boston (eds), *The Fourth Labour Government*, 2nd ed.: 11–21.

Mulgan, R. (1992), 'The elective dictatorship in New Zealand' in Gold (ed.), *New Zealand Politics in Perspective*, 3rd ed.: 513–32.

Mulgan, R. (1992a), 'The Principles of Rogerpolitics', *Public Sector*, 15: 16–17.

Mulgan, R. (1993), 'A pluralist analysis of the New Zealand state' in Roper & Rudd (eds), *State and Economy in New Zealand*: 128–46.

Mulgan, R. (1993a), 'Political culture' in Hawke (ed.), *Changing Politics?*: 43–67.

Mulgan, R. (1993b), 'Multiculturalism: a New Zealand perspective' in C. Kukathas (ed.), *Multicultural Citizens*, Sydney, Centre for Independent Studies: 75–90.

Mulgan, R. (1995), 'The democratic failure of single-party government: the New Zealand experience', *Australian Journal of Political Science*, 30: 82–96.

Mulgan, R. (1996), 'A race relations lesson from across the Tasman', *Australian Quarterly*, 68 (2): 77–87.

Nagel, J. H. (1994) 'What political scientists can learn from 1993 electoral reform in New Zealand', *PS: Political Science and Politics*, 27: 525–9.

NZES (2002), New Zealand Electoral Study Programme.

Olson, M. (1965), *The Logic of Collective Action*, Cambridge, Harvard University Press.

Olson, M. (1982), *The Rise and Decline of Nations: Economic Growth, Stagflation, and Social Rigidities*, New Haven, Yale University Press.

Orange, C. (1987), *The Treaty of Waitangi*, Wellington, Allen & Unwin.

Palmer, G. (1987), *Unbridled Power? An Interpretation of New Zealand's Constitution and Government*, 2nd ed., Auckland, Oxford University Press.

Palmer, G. (1992), *New Zealand's Constitution in Crisis—Reforming our Political System*, Dunedin, John McIndoe.

Palmer, G. (1996), 'Towards a constitutional theory for the media in the MMP era' in McGregor (ed.), *Dangerous Democracy?*: 17–29.

Palmer, G., and Palmer, M. (1997), *Bridled Power. New Zealand Government under MMP*, Auckland, Oxford University Press.

Pearson, D. (1989), 'Pakeha ethnicity: concept or conundrum?', *Sites*, 18: 61–72.

Pearson, D. (1990), 'Community', in Spoonley, Pearson & Shirley (eds), *New Zealand Society*: 25–38.

Pearson, D. (1990a), *A Dream Deferred*, Wellington, Allen & Unwin.

Pearson, D. (1991), 'Biculturalism and multiculturalism in comparative perspective' in P. Spoonley, D. Pearson, & D. G. Thorns, (1983), *Eclipse of Equality—Social Stratification in New Zealand*, Sydney, Allen & Unwin.

Pearson, D. & Macpherson, C. (eds) (1991), *Nga Take: Ethnic Relations and Racism in Aotearoa/New Zealand*, Palmerston North, Dunmore Press: 194–214.

Perry, P., and Webster, A. (1999), *New Zealand Politics at the Turn of the Millennium.*

Bibliography

Attitudes and Values about Politics and Government, Auckland, Alpha Publications.

Phillips, J. (1987), *A Man's Country? The Image of the Pakeha Male, a History*, Auckland, Penguin.

Reid, N. (2003), 'ACT' in Miller, R. (ed.), *New Zealand Government and Politics*, 3rd ed.: 274–82.

Richardson, I. L. M. (1985), 'The role of judges as policy makers', *Victoria University of Wellington Law Review*, 15: 46–52.

Richardson, R. (1995), *Making a Difference*, Christchurch, Shoal Bay Press.

Ringer, J. B. (1991), *An Introduction to New Zealand Government*, Christchurch, Hazard Press.

Rishworth, P. (1992), 'Civil liberties' in Gold (ed.), *New Zealand Politics in Perspective*, 3rd ed.: 143–59.

Roberts, J. (1987), *Politicians, Public Servants and Public Enterprise*, Wellington, Institute of Policy Studies.

Roberts, J. (1987a), 'Ministers, the Cabinet and public servants' in Boston & Holland (eds), *The Fourth Labour Government*: 89–110.

Roper, B. (1992), 'Business political activism and the emergence of the New Right in New Zealand, 1975–87', *Political Science*, 44: 1–23.

Roper, B. (1993), ' A level playing field? Business political activism and state policy formulation' in Roper & Rudd (eds), *State and Economy in New Zealand*: 147–71.

Roper B. (2003), 'Neo-liberalism: A Radical Critique' in R. Miller (ed.), *New Zealand Government and Politics*, 3rd ed.: 578–89.

Royal Commission on the Electoral System (1986), *Report of the Royal Commission on the Electoral System: Towards a Better Democracy*, Wellington, Government Print.

Rudd, C. (1991), 'The changing structure of public expenditure' in Boston *et al.* (eds), *Reshaping the State*: 140–65.

Rudd, C. (1993), 'Elections and the media' in Roper & Rudd (eds), *State and Economy in New Zealand*: 119–40.

Sartori, G. (1976), *Parties and Party Systems*, Cambridge, Cambridge University Press.

Scott, K. J. (1962), *The New Zealand Constitution*, Oxford, Clarendon Press.

Sharp, A. (1990), *Justice and the Maori: Maori Claims in New Zealand Political Argument in the 1980s*, Auckland, Oxford University Press.

Sharp, A. (1992), 'The Treaty, the Tribunal and the law: recognising Maori rights in New Zealand' in Gold (ed.), *New Zealand Politics in Perspective*: 123–42.

Sharp, A. (1995), 'Why be bicultural?' in M. Wilson & A. Yeatman (eds), *Justice and Identity: Antipodean Practices*, Wellington, Bridget Williams Books: 16–33.

Sharp, A. (2003), 'Constitution' in R. Miller (ed.), *New Zealand Government and Politics*, 3rd ed.: 39–49.

Shaw, R. (2003), 'Advisers and Consultants' in R. Miller (ed.), *New Zealand Government and Politics*, 3rd ed.: 148–60.

Skene, G. (1992), 'Parliament: reassessing its role' in Gold (ed.), *New Zealand Politics in Perspective*, 3rd ed.: 247–62.

Smith, M. J. (1990), 'Pluralism, reformed pluralism and neo-pluralism: the role of pressure groups in policy making', *Political Studies*, 38: 302–22.

Sorrenson, M. P. K. (1986), 'A history of Maori representation in Parliament', Appendix B to Royal Commission on the Electoral System.

Sorrenson, M. P. K. (1991), 'Treaties in British colonial policy; precedents for Waitangi' in W. Renwick (ed.), *Sovereignty and Indigenous Rights: The Treaty of Waitangi in International Contexts*, Wellington, Victoria University Press: 15–29.

Spoonley, P. (1991), 'Pakeha ethnicity: a response to Maori sovereignty' in Spoonley, Pearson & Macpherson (eds), *Nga Take*: 154–70.

Spoonley, P. (1993), *Racism and Ethnicity*, 2nd ed., Auckland, Oxford University Press.
Spoonley, P. (1994), 'Racism and ethnicity' in Spoonley, Pearson & Shirley (eds), *New Zealand Society*, 2nd ed.: 81–97.
Statistics New Zealand (2002), *New Zealand Official Yearbook 2002*, Wellington, Statistics New Zealand.
Stockley, A. P. (1996), 'Becoming a republic? Issues of law' in L. Trainor (ed.), *Republicanism in New Zealand*, Palmerston North, Dunmore Press: 81–112.
Stockley, A. P. (1999), 'Constitutional Law' in *New Zealand Law Review*: 185–6.
Stockley, A. P. (2003), 'Judiciary and Courts' in R. Miller (ed.), *New Zealand Government and Politics*, 3rd ed.: 63–76.
Street, M. (2003), 'Trade Unions' in R. Miller (ed.), *New Zealand Government and Politics*, 3rd ed.: 378–87.
Swain, D. (1990), 'Family' in Spoonley, Pearson & Shirley (eds), *New Zealand Society*: 10–24.
Tenbensel, T. (2003), 'Interest Groups' in R. Miller (ed.), *New Zealand Government and Politics*, 3rd ed.: 345–56.
Trotter, C. (2001), 'Alliance' in R. Miller (ed.), *New Zealand Government and Politics*: 252–61.
Truman, D. B. (1951), *The Governmental Process*, New York, Knopf.
Tully, J. (1992), 'Media ethics . . . holding on to the high ground' in Comrie & McGregor (eds), *Whose News?*: 143–52.
Venables, D. (1988), 'Our old boy network', *NZ Listener*, 16 April.
Vowles, J. (1987), 'Liberal democracy: pakeha political ideology', *New Zealand Journal of History*, 21: 215–27.
Vowles, J. (1989), 'Playing games with electorates: New Zealand's political ecology in 1987', *Political Science*, 41: 18–34.
Vowles, J. (1992), 'Business, unions and the state: organising economic interests in New Zealand' in Gold (ed.), *New Zealand Politics in Perspective*, 3rd ed.: 342–64.
Vowles, J. (1992a), 'Social groups and electoral behaviour' in Holland (ed), *Electoral Behaviour*: 91–118.
Vowles, J. (1993), 'Capturing the state' in C. S. Thomas (ed.), *First World Interest Groups: A Comparative Perspective*, Westport, Greenwood Press: 97–110.
Vowles, J. (1993a), 'Gender and electoral behaviour in New Zealand: findings from the present and the past', *Political Science*, 45: 122–38.
Vowles, J. (1994), 'Politics' in Spoonley, Pearson and Shirley (eds), *New Zealand Society*: 177–92.
Vowles, J. (1995), 'The politics of electoral reform in New Zealand', *International Political Science Review*, 16: 95–115.
Vowles, J. (2003), 'Voting Behaviour' in R. Miller (ed.), *New Zealand Government and Politics*, 3rd ed.: 188–200.
Vowles, J. & Aimer, P. (1993), *Voters' Vengeance: The 1990 Election in New Zealand and the Fate of the Fourth Labour Government*, Auckland, Auckland University Press.
Vowles, J. & Aimer, P. (eds) (1994), *Double Decision: The 1993 Election and Referendum in New Zealand*, Wellington, Department of Politics, Victoria University of Wellington.
Vowles, J., Aimer, P., Catt, H., Lamare, J., & Miller, R. (1995), *Towards Consensus? The 1993 Election in New Zealand and the Transition to Proportional Representation*, Auckland, Auckland University Press.
Vowles, J., Aimer, P., Banducci, S., & Karp, J. (eds) (1998), *Voters' Victory? New Zealand's First Election Under Proportional Representation*, Auckland, Auckland

Bibliography

University Press.

Vowles, J., Aimer, P., Karp, J., Banducci, S., Miller, R., & Sullivan, A. (2002), *Proportional Representation on Trial. The 1999 New Zealand General Election and the Fate of MMP*, Auckland, Auckland University Press.

Vowles, J., Aimer, P., Banducci, S., Karp, J., & Miller, R. (eds) (2004), *Voters' Veto. The 2002 Election in New Zealand and the Consolidation of Minority Government*, Auckland, Auckland University Press.

Walker, R. (1987), *Nga Tau Tohetoh —Years of Anger*, Auckland, Penguin.

Walker, R. (1990), *Ka Whawhai Tonu Matou —Struggle Without End*, Auckland, Penguin.

Walker, R. (1992), 'The Maori people: their political development' in Gold (ed.), *New Zealand Politics in Perspective*, 3rd ed.: 379–400.

Walker, R. (2001), *He Tipua. The Life and Times of Sir Apirana Ngata*, Auckland, Viking.

Walsh, P. (1991), 'The State Sector Act 1988' in Boston *et al.* (eds), *Reshaping the State:* 52–80.

Ward, A. (1999), *An Unsettled History: Treaty Claims in New Zealand Today*, Wellington, Bridget Williams Books.

Waring, M. (1988), *Counting for Nothing: What Men Value and what Women are Worth*, Wellington, Allen & Unwin.

Whitcombe, J. (1992), 'The changing face of the New Zealand public service' in Gold (ed.), *New Zealand Politics in Perspective*, 3rd ed.: 21–32.

Wilkes, C. (1994), 'Class' in Spoonley, Pearson & Shirley (eds), *New Zealand Society*, 2nd ed.: 66–80.

Williams, D. V. (1990), 'The constitutional status of the Treaty of Waitangi: an historical perspective', *New Zealand Universities Law Review*, 14: 9–36.

Wilson, M. (1992), 'Employment Equity Act 1990: a case study in women's political influence 1984–90' in Deeks & Perry (eds), *Controlling Interests*: 113–31.

Wilson, N., Russell, D., & Paulin, J. *et al.* (1990), *Life in New Zealand—Summary Report*, Wellington, Hillary Commission for Recreation & Sport.

Wood, B. & Maharey, S. (1994), 'Mass media' in Spoonley, Pearson & Shirley (eds), *New Zealand Society*: 193–212.

Wood, G. A. (1986), 'New Zealand's patriated Governor-General', *Political Science*, 38: 113–32.

Wood, G. A. (1988), *Governing New Zealand*, Auckland, Longman Paul.

Wood, G. A. (1991), 'Political studies in New Zealand', *APSA Newsletter*, 52: 2–28.

Wood, G. A. (1992), 'The National Party' in Gold (ed.), *New Zealand Politics in Perspective*, 3rd ed.: 289–309.

Wood, G. A. (2003), 'National' in R. Miller (ed.), *New Zealand Government and Politics*, 3rd ed.: 251–60.

Index